Rights

This pioneering new book suggests how different traditions of sociological thought can contribute to an understanding of the theory and practice of rights. A substantial opening chapter reviews the emerging field of sociology and rights, and therefater the volume is divided into four parts, each with a brief introduction:

Part I considers a political economy approach to the questions of rights, taking a holistic and systems-based view;

Part II focuses on status, norms and institutions in the allocation and functioning of rights;

Part III has a broadly interpretive approach towards the issue of rights, in which context and meanings are paramount;

Part IV contemplates how an apparent clash of rights has been dealt with in a variety of contexts.

A final chapter refers back to issues raised in the opening chapter, and draws out some general conclusions on the basis of the volume as a whole.

Insodoing, this book provides a sociological treatment of a wide range of substantive issues, but without losing sight of key theoretical questions. It considers some varied cases of public intervention, including welfare, caring, mental health provisions, pensions, justice and free speech, alongside the rights issues they raise. Similarly, it examines the question of rights from the point of view of distinctive population groups, such as prisoners and victims, women, ethnic minorities, indigenous peoples and lesbians and gays.

Rights offers a diverse and detailed exploration of the contribution sociological thought can make to this increasingly important aspect of social life and will be an invaluable aid to students.

Lydia Morris is a Professor in the Sociology Department at the University of Essex. Her recent research interest has been in the politics of migration in the EU, looking at citizenship, rights and inequality. Her recent publications include *Managing Migration: Civic Stratification and Migrants' Rights* (2002); *Social Divisions* (1995); *Dangerous Classes* (1994) and *The Workings of the Household* (1990).

Rights
Sociological perspectives

Edited by
Lydia Morris

Routledge
Taylor & Francis Group

LONDON AND NEW YORK

First published 2006
by Routledge
2 Park Square, Milton Park, Abingdon, Oxon OX14 4RN

Simultaneously published in the USA and Canada
by Routledge
270 Madison Ave, New York, NY 10016

Routledge is an imprint of the Taylor & Francis Group

© 2006 Lydia Morris for selection and editorial matter; the
contributors for individual chapters

Typeset in Sabon by
RefineCatch Limited, Bungay, Suffolk
Printed and bound in Great Britain by
TJ International Ltd, Padstow, Cornwall

British Library Cataloguing in Publication Data
A catalogue record for this book is available from the British Library

Library of Congress Cataloging in Publication Data
A catalog record for this book has been requested

ISBN10: 0–415–35522–2 (pbk)
ISBN10: 0–415–35521–4 (hbk)

ISBN13: 9–78–0–415–35522–3 (pbk)
ISBN13: 9–78–0–415–35521–6 (hbk)

Contents

Contributors

Ted Benton is a Professor of Sociology at the University of Essex. His interests are in environmental issues and modern social theory, especially in links between socialist and 'green' perspectives, and he also works on philosophical assumptions of social science. His publications include *Philosophical Foundations of the Three Sociologies* (1977), ' "Objective" Interests and the Sociology of Power', *Sociology* (1981), *The Rise and Fall of Structural Marxism* (1984), *Natural Relations: Ecology, Animal Rights and Social Justice* (1993), (with M. Redclift, ed.) *Social Theory and the Global Environment* (1994), and (ed.) *The Greening of Marxism* (1996).

Robin Blackburn is a Professor of Sociology at the University of Essex. One strand of his work analyses the dynamics of slavery, slave resistance and anti-slavery, embodied in two books, *The Making of New World Slavery: from the Baroque to the Modern, 1492–1800* (1997) and *The Overthrow of Colonial Slavery, 1776–1848* (1988). These works look at the formation of racial ideologies and national identities in a world beset by rivalry and in transition to modernity. The other strand concerns the workings of today's financial institutions, and especially pension funds, an interest pursued in *Banking on Death* (2002).

Joan Busfield is a Professor of Sociology at the University of Essex. She trained initially as a clinical psychologist at the Tavistock Clinic. She then worked on a study of the social influences on family size, published (with M. Paddon) as *Thinking About Children: Sociology and Fertility in Post-War England* (1977). Her subsequent research has focused on psychiatry, gender and mental disorder and the health services. Main publications include *Managing Madness: Changing Ideas and Practice* (1986), *Men, Women and Madness* (1996) and *Health and Health Care in Modern Britain* (2000).

Eamonn Carrabine is a Senior Lecturer in the Department of Sociology at the University of Essex. He has published in three broad areas. The first draws on his research in the sociology of imprisonment and he has published articles in *The Howard Journal of Criminal Justice* (1998), *Theoretical Criminology* (2000) and *Punishment and Society* (2002). His book *Power, Discourse and Resistance: A Geneology of the Strangeways Prison Riot* (2004), has been published by Ashgate in their Advances in Criminology series. The second area is his joint research with Prof. Brian Longhurst on youth culture, and together they have published articles in *New Formations* (1999), *Journal of Popular Music Studies* (2000), and *Sociological Review* (2002). The third area lies in criminology generally and includes, with Essex colleagues, *Crime in Modern Britain* (2002) and *Criminology: A Sociological Introduction* (2004).

Diane Elson is a Professor of Sociology at the University of Essex. Her current research and teaching interests are in global social change and the realisation of human rights, with a particular focus on gender inequality. Recent publications include (co-ed.) Special Issue of *World Development* on Growth, Trade, Finance and Gender Inequality (July 2000), UNIFEM Reports on *Progress of the World's Women* (2000 and 2002), 'Socializing Markets, Not Market Socialism', *Socialist Register* (1999/2000), 'Gender Justice, Human Rights and Neo-Liberal Economic Policies' in M. Molyneux and S. Razavi (eds) *Gender Justice, Development and Rights* (Oxford University Press, 2002).

Miriam Glucksmann is a Professor of Sociology at the University of Essex. Her research interests cover gender; work and employment; social divisions and their intersection, including ethnic divisions in women's work. She was awarded a three-year ESRC Professorial Fellowship, which runs from 2004 to 2006, to undertake a programme of research on 'Transformations of work: new frontiers, shifting boundaries, changing temporalities'. Her publications include *Structuralist Analysis in Contemporary Social Thought* (1974), *Women on the Line* (1982) published under the pseudonym of Ruth Cavendish, *Women Assemble: Women Workers and the New Industries in Inter-War Britain* (1990) and *Cotton and Casuals: The Gendered Organisation of Labour in Time and Space* (2000).

Paul Iganski is a Lecturer in Sociology at the University of Essex. Before becoming an academic he worked as a psychiatric nurse, and later as a Research Officer at the Home Office Research and Planning Unit. His main areas of research are 'hate', violence, 'rights', racial stratification and equal opportunities. His most recent publications include *Hate Crimes Against London's Jews* (2005), with Vicky Kielinger and Susan Paterson, *A New Antisemitism? Debating Judeophobia in 21st Century Britain* (2003), co-edited with Barry Kosmin, *The Hate Debate* (2002), an edited collection of essays on hate crime laws, and *Ethnicity, Equality of Opportunity and the British National Health Service* (2002), co-authored with David Mason.

Lydia Morris is a Professor of Sociology at the University of Essex. For many years her main intellectual concerns revolved around aspects of labour market change, gender relations, social rights and the underclass, based on research in South Wales (University of Swansea) and the North East of England (University of Durham). Though some of these interests continue, her most recent work has been on the politics of immigration and asylum in the EU, and the sociology of rights more generally. Her publications include *The Workings of the Household* (1991), *Dangerous Classes* (1994), *Social Divisions* (1995), and *Managing Migration* (2002).

Ken Plummer is a Professor of Sociology at the University of Essex. He has researched and written widely on sexuality (especially lesbian and gay studies), and is interested in the development of a humanistic method and theory (especially through narrative, life story and the postmodern turn). He is the author/editor of *Sexual Stigma* (1975), *The Making of the Modern Homosexual* (1981), *Documents of Life* (1983), *Symbolic Interactionism* Vols 1 and 2 (1991), *Modern Homosexualities: Fragments of Lesbian and Gay Experience* (1992), *Telling Sexual Stories* (1995), *Chicago Sociology: Critical Assessments* (1997: 4 volumes), *Documents of Life-2: An Invitation to a Critical Humanism* (2001), *Sexualities* (2002: 4 volumes) and, with John Macionis, *Sociology: A Global Introduction* (2nd edn, 2002). He is the editor of the journal *Sexualities* and his most recent book is *Intimate Citizenship* (2003).

Carlo Ruzza is an Associate Professor of Sociology at the University of Trento, and a Visiting Fellow in the Department of Sociology at the University of Essex. His research interests include the role of organised civil society in transnational arenas, with particular reference to the normative and policy implications of the inclusion of public interest associations in decision making and deliberative fora. Recent publications include *Europe and Civil Society: Movement Coalitions and European Governance* (2004), 'The Northern League: Winning Arguments, Losing Influence' in *Movements of Exclusion: Radical Right-Wing Populism in Western Europe*, edited by J. Rydgren (2004).

Colin Samson is a Senior Lecturer in the Department of Sociology at the University of Essex. He has been working with the Innu peoples of the Labrador-Quebec peninsula since 1994. Some of his work has been linked to a human rights campaign on behalf of the Innu with *Survival International*. This resulted in the publication of the widely cited report *Canada's Tibet: The Killing of the Innu* in 1999. This report won the Italian Pio Manzo peace prize in 2000. His book on the effects of forced assimilation of the Innu, *A Way of Life that Does Not Exist: Canada and the Extinguishment of the Innu*, was published by ISER Press in Canada and Verso Press in the UK and US in 2003. He is currently working on a project to document the physical and mental health benefits of cultural continuity among indigenous peoples in different parts of the world.

Damien Short is a Lecturer in Human Rights at the Roehampton Institute. He completed his PhD, on Australian Aboriginal rights, in the Department of Sociology at the University of Essex, where he later held an ESRC post-doctoral Fellowship. He is the author of 'Australian "Aboriginal" Reconciliation: The Latest Phase in the Colonial Project', *Citizenship Studies* (2003), 'Reconciliation, Assimilation and the Indigenous Peoples of Australia', *International Political Science Review* (2003), and 'Reconciliation and the Problem of Internal Colonialism', *Journal of Intercultural Studies* (2005).

Rob Stones is a Senior Lecturer in the Department of Sociology at the University of Essex. His research interests include social theory in general and structuration theory in particular; the critical analysis of documentary and fiction films, and of their contribution to the public sphere; the relevance of sociology to debates between liberals, communitarians and multiculturalists; the nature of experience in late modernity; and the relationship between abstract social theory and substantive case studies. Publications include *Sociological Reasoning: Towards a Post-Modern Sociology* (1996), *Key Sociological Thinkers* (ed.) (1998), and *Structuration Theory* (2005). He is the editor of Palgrave Macmillan's book series *Traditions in Social Theory*.

Acknowledgements

All contributors to this book are, or have been, members of the Sociology Department at the University of Essex. I wish to acknowledge here the debt that many of us owe to our one-time colleague Bryan Turner, and his enduring interest in the study of rights, a topic he viewed as ripe for socio-logical intervention. We also owe much to the Human Rights Centre here at Essex for stimulating and coordinating intellectual interest and activities in the area of rights. My own work for this book was completed during sabbati-cal leave, first at the Center for European Studies at Harvard University (September to December 2004), and then at the Centre for the Study of Human Rights at the London School of Economics (February to June 2005). I greatly appreciate the stimulation and support I received in both places and hope that this end product repays their interest.

Lydia Morris
Essex

Sociology and rights – an emergent field

Lydia Morris

A number of factors have conspired to place the concept of 'rights' high on the social, political and intellectual agenda. Among such factors are the consolidation of human rights principles in the post-war era, an associated and expanding framework of international conventions, the emergence of various regional systems of protection and some notable cases of the strengthening of remedies at domestic level.[1] Some have seen in human rights a potential transnational platform from which to contest the unpalatable aspects of capitalist globalisation, raising questions about the social obligations of international corporations (Freeman, 2002). Others have argued that with the end of Cold War politics, and disillusionment with the socialist regimes attempted in the Eastern bloc, universal principles furnish us with new ideals of equity and justice (Wilson, 1997). To these views we can add the conviction – in the face of a growing diversity of culture and belief – that human rights may offer the means to bind and cement an otherwise fragmentary society; a solution to the problem of 'values for a godless age' (Klug, 2003). The promise of universalism has also been used as a basis for claims to recognition for neglected particularities (e.g. Taylor, 1994), and as a means of superseding citizenship as the dominant status for rights claims (e.g. Soysal, 1994). It would therefore seem that the late twentieth century may reasonably be described as the 'age of rights' (Bobbio, 1995), yet as Turner (1993) has argued, sociology as a discipline has no obvious foundation for a contemporary theory of rights.

It was prescient of Turner to identify this gap, at a time when few other sociologists had recognised the area of rights as central to social structures, processes and identities, and his writing on the topic is a necessary starting point for all others wishing to focus on these issues. Part of Turner's explanation for the absence lies in what he deems a limitation of classical sociology: its failure to provide an ontological grounding for a theory of rights. In his account, Durkheim's (1895) insistence on the analysis of social facts as things ruled out a consideration of normative concerns, and evaded truth claims by treating moral and legal norms simply as external constraints on individual behaviours. The result, argues Turner, is a positivistic account of law and values that, despite best efforts, cannot fully expunge the question of social justice from causal explanation. A similar point could be made about Weber's (1948) insistence on value-free social science. Furthermore, in Turner's view, Weber's argument on the increasing rationality of law meant that he emphasised the decline of its 'metaphysical dignity' (Weber, 1978: 875), and focused instead on relations of authority, legitimacy and the struggle for resources. Turner's (1975: 146–74) account of Marx's work in relation to rights also emphasises power relations, viewing the law as an instrument of class rule and human rights as a façade to mask economic and social inequality.

We return to these issues below, and a variety of classical and other frameworks are explored in the chapters to follow. For Turner, however, the absence of a normative basis for the study of rights in the work of these early sociologists has left a heritage of scepticism, and no means of responding to a relativist position on rights and values. A resolution to this problem, he feels, would require an ontological foundation for claims to universality, and he seeks such a foundation through the common condition of bodily frailty and social precariousness (ibid.: 184–5). Such a move provides the basis for claims to a universal need for protection, while also prompting the feelings of sympathy for others that might give emotive force to such a system. His argument thus offers simultaneously a perspective on the conditions that make a universal system of protection possible, and a recognition of the limits of human sympathy that make it necessary, ideas that are explored in Chapter 5.

However, there is scope for a considerable gap between recognition of the need for protection and its achievement in practice, and this is arguably a gap that sociology as a discipline is well placed to address. We do not yet have a fully operative, globally enforceable system of universal rights, and the strengths and weaknesses of both national and transnational systems of entitlement and protection are themselves topics worthy of study. So too are the social processes by which groups accrue rights, and correspondingly the ways in which already established rights can be eroded, while the active delivery of rights and impediments to their realisation would also repay close study. These and related issues produce an agenda for the sociological study of rights that is in some respects less ambitious than Turner's quest for a foundational grounding, but more in tune with the traditional interests and strengths of the discipline. It is also an agenda that might profit from a return to the classics, and other works, for guidance as to how to pursue the sociological analysis of rights in practice.

The sociological classics

It is beyond the scope of this introduction to give a fully developed account of how classical works might inform a sociology of rights, but with the help of secondary texts, a few steps can be taken in this direction. As we have seen, Durkheim (1938: 27) was famously wedded to the study of social facts as things, and was interested in the way social life can generate a collective consciousness that is constituted by individual social agents but also exerts a reciprocal influence on their actions. Thus, in his study of religious belief (Durkheim, 1961; Lukes, 1973: 465–72; Pickering, 1975) he sees worship as the means by which society celebrates its own identity and in doing so strengthens its social bonds. In fact, for Durkheim, a fully human existence was dependent for its meaning on some connection with a wider social world, a view that was supported by his interpretation of suicide statistics (Durkheim, 1951; see Chapter 1). He was preoccupied with the problem of anomie in modern society, and the perceived need for a new moral consensus, feeling that with growing individualism 'there remains nothing that men may love and honour in common, apart from man himself' (Durkheim, 1975: 67). Some writers (Cladis, 1992; Parkin, 1992; Pickering and Watts Miller, 1993) have interpreted this position as an incipient doctrine of human rights, which implicitly views rights as a possible source of social cohesion.

Pickering and Watts Miller have written explicitly on the topic, seeing in Durkheim's work a view of human rights as social facts, not inherent in man but bestowed on individuals by society. He is thus argued to offer a relativist understanding of rights, as developed in a particular place and subject to change over time; a view of rights that therefore lies in the realm of practice, not theory, for 'It is the state that creates, organises and makes a reality of these rights.'[2] Pickering (in Pickering and Watts Miller, 1993) identifies related ideas in *Suicide*, which discusses a 'cult of human personality on which all our morality rests' (Durkheim, 1951: 334), and sees in this the basis for a secular moral authority that makes man sacred in the eyes of man. Durkheim (1975: 62) seems to rely heavily on the state for the promotion of his incipient notion of rights, and is commonly criticised for rather too naive an assumption of this possibility. However, as Parkin (1992: 76; cf. Lukes, 1973: 271–4) observes, he also notes the need for strong intermediary organisations, and has a vision of society in which the state and civil society are mutually balancing, each having a malign and benign potential.

Durkheim has also been criticised for his failure to deal adequately with diversity. His work prefigures many aspects of contemporary debate between liberals and communitarians, the former position emphasising individual autonomy and the latter the collective foundations of identity. These ideas are explored in Chapters 1, 7 and 10, and have been discussed extensively by Cladis (1992), who sees in Durkheim (1887)[3] an attempt to overcome the impasse between the two positions. Durkheim saw both advantages and disadvantages in liberalism, believing in a free-spirited and civic-minded individual but troubled by the threat of anomie in the absence of shared beliefs and values that might bind the individual to society. According to Cladis, Durkheim (1975: 62) finds a unifying position in the assertion of a moral individualism: 'a religion in which man is, at the same time, the believer and the god', such that the individual is neither a totally discrete unit nor simply a social product but a being of 'situated freedom' (Taylor, 1979; cf. Lukes, 1973: 23). Thus, argues Durkheim, 'Very far from there being the antagonism between the individual and society which is often claimed, moral individualism, the cult of the individual, is in fact the product of society itself. It is society that instituted it and made of man the god whose servant it is.'[4] This position is apparently accepting of both diversity and autonomy (Cladis, 1992: 115), though only within the commonality of a shared moral position.

Even if persuaded by Turner's reading of Durkheim, we can still find in the latter's work an agenda for the study of rights and a theoretical position within which to locate such a study. Certainly, his arguments seem to support a relativist, or more correctly a 'social constructionist', view of rights, but one that is grounded in the collective consciousness (though for him the rights of *man* meant exactly that; Parkin, 1992: 81; see also Lehmann, 1994). His approach immediately provokes questions about rights as a route to social cohesion, the implicit nature of public support for a system of fundamental rights, the role of the state in either securing and protecting or undermining such rights, the capacity of civil society groups to act as a check or balance on the state and their role in both generating and defending rights. His work begs questions about not only the depth of public support for fundamental guarantees but also how far such support is fully accepting of diversity, and able to incorporate groups that appear to hold contrasting beliefs; whether liberal freedoms can really coexist with other traditions of thought and practice. This raises broad and difficult issues, some of which are pursued in Chapter 7, but Durkheim was posing such questions and addressing a related body of research more than 100 years ago. It is as instructive to take up and work with the direction of his argument as it is to identify its limitations and failings.

One predominant theme in Weber's writing is the exclusion of value judgements from social scientific work. For him: 'evaluative ideas are ... empirically discoverable and analysable elements of human conduct, but their validity cannot be deduced from empirical data' (Weber, 1949: 111). Similarly, in 'Science as a vocation' (Gerth and Mills, 1948: 145), he argues that the historical and cultural sciences teach an understanding of social and political phenomena but give no answer to the question of how to judge activity in these realms. This position seems consistent with his rejection of natural rights (see Strauss, 1953), not just because human thought is held to be historical, but because an unchangeable variety of principles of right or good conflict with each other, and none can be proved superior. Thus, as Turner (1978: 875) notes, he rejects the idea of a universalistic and normative foundation for law, and hence rights, and sees the relativisation of legal norms under juridical rationalism as leaving the law 'unmasked ... as the product or technical means of a compromise between conflicting interests'. A central theme in Weber's work is the drive towards rationality in modern society, one element of which is argued to be the growing use and significance of bureaucracy. The capitalist market economy demands precise, continuous and speedy administration, and so too do the administrative tasks associated with the great state and the mass party. As a tool for the large-scale organisation of political and economic activity, bureaucracy provides a means of management and administration that is argued to operate the more perfectly the more it is dehumanised (Gerth and Mills, 1948: 216).

Weber's work in this area implies a relationship between bureaucracy and rights, as he sees the rise of the former inevitably to accompany the rise of mass democracy (and to signify an increase in public expenditure). Bureaucracy in this context is held to guarantee the sharp separation between an objective legal order and the subjective rights of the individual. Public law therefore regulates the interrelationship between public authorities and their subjects, and the rights between governed individuals (Gerth and Mills, 1948: 239). Weber also argues (Rheinstein, 1954) that the demand for legal equality and guarantees against arbitrary judgement requires formal rational objectivity in administration, though this detached, rule-bound nature of bureaucracy comes into conflict with the democratic ethos. Thus, 'The propertyless classes in particular are not served, in the way in which [the] bourgeois are, by formal "legal equality" and "calculable" adjudication and administration' (ibid.: 355). Weber has been criticised for highlighting the positive functions of bureaucracy and ignoring its disfunctions (Parkin, 2002: 36), but here he comes close to recognising that it does not deal well with broader questions of social justice, an idea pursued further in Chapters 4 and 6.

While Weber notes the role of state bureaucracy in the administration of social welfare (Gerth and Mills, 1948: 213), he does not expand more generally on state involvement in the construction and administration of the rights of citizens, though his work on social closure is directly relevant. This process is bound up in the struggle for power and resources, with the number of strata and sub-strata increasing as each tries to secure its position against other groups (Parkin, 1992: 100). Weber's discussion of 'Class status and party' (Gerth and Mills, 1948: 180) also throws some light on this competition, as outlined in Chapter 4, though Parkin notes that Weber's neglect of the role of the state in processes of social closure is a serious flaw in his account. However, Parkin suggests some ways in which the idea could be linked to racial and ethnic closure following colonial conquest or the creation of second-class citizens by forced migrations, while Marshall (1950) explores the promise of equal status implicit in the idea of citizenship. Lockwood (1996) takes these connections further through an analysis of the mutually reinforcing nature of market, bureaucracy and citizenship, which yields a structure of 'civic stratification', or a system of legitimate inequality overseen through the administration of rights by state bureaucracy. Thus, while Weber rejects the idea of 'natural rights', his work is rich with concepts and arguments that are suggestive of a very challenging agenda for the development of a sociological approach to the practice of rights.

Unlike Durkheim and Weber, Marx does not espouse a value-free model of the social sciences. Though he may see dominant moral concepts as an expression of the interests of the ruling powers in a society, Benton (1993) notes a commitment in Marx's work to an alternative morality of emancipation. Turner argues that Marx's critique of rights is part of a more general critique of bourgeois ideology, bound up with a rejection of human and citizenship rights as manifestations of a partial liberation that leaves intact the fundamental relations of capitalist exploitation. This view has been detailed by Lukes (1991: 173–88), who notes that Marx and Engels always wrote disparagingly about the language of rights and justice, seeing the moral claims of *recht* (rights) as a mask for the protection of bourgeois interests. Marx's critical comment on the civil rights embraced by the constitutional declarations of France and North America is undisputed, and expressed in specific opposition to their underlying (and undesirable) view of human nature. This is one source of the argument that Marx sees human rights as a façade, with the key practical application of liberty being a right to property – to enjoy and dispose of it freely, 'without regard to other men' (Marx, 1975: 163). The right to equality and security are also argued to rest on a view of self-sufficient and egoistic individuals, meeting their needs through the ownership and exchange of property.

This understanding of rights offers a view of a society held together by need and private interest, such that 'None of the so-called rights of man, therefore, go beyond egoistic man, beyond man as a member of civil society, that is, an individual withdrawn into himself, into the confines of his private interests and private caprice, and separated from the community' (ibid.: 164). Furthermore, argues Benton (1993), civil society is seen as a counterpart to the modern democratic state, logically entailed in its civil rights; an autonomous sphere of alienated, egoistic individuals. Hence, both political and civil rights are limited in the way that bourgeois civil society, built on the primacy of the individual and on private property ownership, is limited. Nevertheless, Benton (ibid.: 108) challenges common readings of Marx's position in 'On the Jewish question', to argue that, at the very least, Marx fully recognised the importance of the bourgeois right to freedom of expression and association, stating that 'Political emancipation is, of course, a big step forward' (Marx, 1975: 155). Though falling short of the 'final form' of human emancipation, these rights went as far as the existing order permitted and could be the basis for protest against established relations of oppression. Thus, argues Benton (1993: 109), Marx's position is 'a critique of the theory and practice of rights, not of rights as such', which leads on to the question of whether human emancipation promises 'some richer, socially content-full realisation of human rights, or whether it entails the transcendence of rights' (ibid.: 110).

For Lukes (1991: 198), 'despite its rich view of freedom and compelling vision of human liberation', Marxism offers no assurances in the realm of individual freedom and leaves an unclear vision of what the morality of emancipation promises in terms of the future organisation of society. For Benton, however, bourgeois rights in themselves are viewed not as unacceptable distortions that inhibit emancipation, but as limited by their context and falling short of recognising full human potential. So Marx leaves us with the implied questions of how rights might function towards the achievement of human emancipation; whether (as in Lukes's reading) such emancipation should render rights unnecessary, or (alternatively) whether human emancipation will usher in truly universal moral rights whose content has yet to be determined. These questions themselves contain an agenda for future research in the realm of rights; an agenda extended by Benton's own work (1993; Chapter 1 in this volume), which embraces a naturalist view of human beings, and explores social belonging, embodiment and environmental integrity as the foundation for rights to protection. This position goes beyond Turner's view of bodily frailty and social precariousness as an ontological grounding for human rights, to raise questions that permeate the nature of all social relations and institutions. It seeks to explore human autonomy and commonality, our relations with non-human beings and the environment, and the realisation of our 'species being'.

Marx, Durkheim and Weber, though differing among themselves, from Marx's utopianism, through Durkheim's pragmatism, to Weber's pessimism (cf. Parkin, 1992), have much to say, not so much about the ontological grounding of rights, but about the searching questions that may be asked of how rights come into social being and operate in social practice, whose purpose they serve and what interests they protect, and whether they are guaranteed or constrained by the letter and practice of the law. While Turner's (1993: 175–6) argument may still stand – i.e. that 'Sociology finds it difficult to accept the notion of human rights without acknowledging a universalistic ontology', and in its absence 'recognises "rights" merely as claims for services or privileges by social groups involved in competitive struggles' – there is still much to study here, including whether the struggle must necessarily be competitive. Even with the growing interest in and emphasis on universal human rights in contemporary society, very few rights are absolute and most are in some way limited or conditional. It is therefore precisely these kinds of questions that provide the most fertile ground for sociological analysis.

T. H. Marshall and his critics

The sociological work that has most directly engaged with the area of rights as an interesting and legitimate subject matter is, of course, Marshall's (1950) essay on citizenship and social class, which Turner (1993: 187) argues has served in the place of a sociology of rights. A key feature of Marshall's classic work is its implicitly evolutionary account of the development of civil, political and social rights in Britain from the eighteenth to the twentieth centuries. These respectively represent the right of individual freedom, the right to participate in the exercise of political power and the right to what would now be termed social inclusion, encompassing a range of guarantees from 'the right to a modicum of welfare and security to the right to share to the full in the social heritage and to live the life of a civilised being according to the standards prevailing in the society' (Marshall 1950: 8). Marshall's main interest, however, is in the role of social rights in accommodating the tension between capital and citizenship, and the possibility that equality of status (via citizenship) may override the material inequalities of social class. Duties as a necessary counterpart to rights receive a brief mention, including notably the duty to work, though it was Marshall's belief that the general direction of change had been away from duties and towards rights. However, he recognised that the ideals of citizenship had been only imperfectly achieved, and that, indeed, 'there is no universal principle that determines what those rights and duties shall be'. He also conceded that the associated rights themselves functioned as a basis for inequality of various kinds, with readily identifiable gaps between policy and delivery with respect to a number of rights, stemming from both class prejudice and the unequal distribution of wealth. Among the interesting questions he posed was whether there are 'limits beyond which the modern drive towards equality cannot pass' (ibid.: 7). Some of these issues are pursued further in Chapters 1, 4 and 11.

For Turner, the concept of citizenship has succeeded in a limited way, as a middle-range theory of the evolution of social welfare, which permits the evasion of questions about a universal ontology, Turner's key requirement for an adequate theory of human rights. Furthermore, the debate about citizenship is argued to be covertly normative – though there is nothing covert about Marshall's probing treatment of the relationship between the needs of market capitalism and the promises of a system of social rights. Indeed, his treatment of this tension, as we saw above, raises very interesting questions about the functioning of a system of rights in practice, and the formal and informal inequalities that may be entailed. In fact, in Marshall's essay we find echoes of some of the issues emerging from the treatment of rights in the three classical traditions touched on above: Marshall's account of the idealised promise of citizenship is close to Durkheim's notion of a society worshipping itself, and his awareness of the stratified nature of some rights and failures of delivery are firmly in the tradition of Weber's concern with the formal and informal dimensions of a status order. His interest in the (limited) role of welfare in addressing the tension between capital and citizenship underlines Marx's critique of liberalism, though the structures of institutional and economic inequality represented by market capitalism are not seriously called into question.

In addition to his considerable insight into the functioning of rights, a major contribution to flow from Marshall's work is the richness and variety of critical responses to his essay, which have opened up an extremely interesting and demanding agenda for the study of rights (whether universal or otherwise). Marshall's work has, of course, been widely criticised on a variety of now familiar points, most notably the peculiarly British nature of his account of citizenship, and the implied evolutionary logic in his view of the development of rights (Mann, 1987; Turner, 1990). It is not clear whether Marshall's intention was to offer a particularistic account of British citizenship, or to set up this account as a universal model – there is no explicit claim for the latter. While an evolutionary premise is dominant, there is some recognition of 'rights' as a terrain of struggle, and he notes the importance of civil rights in workers' battle for social rights. The 'intensely individual' nature of civil rights was thus turned to address collective interests (Marshall, 1950: 26) in the development of economic and social rights. A growing awareness of rights as a contested terrain is thus prefigured in Marshall's work, has been recognised and developed by subsequent writers (e.g. Giddens, 1985) and is further explored in a number of the chapters to follow (see Chapters 5 and 8). There is also an incipient awareness in Marshall of the interdependence of different rights: that the right to property means little to those who have none, as the right to freedom of expression may mean little to the uneducated, and equality before the law may in practice depend on access to legal aid. Furthermore, he sees the substance of citizenship itself as a possible source of legitimate inequality.

We have noted that Marshall's theory takes market capitalism as its setting, but Chapter 1 sets up a framework for thinking about rights in the broader context of structured inequality, and Benton provides a critique of liberal rights in these terms, without departing from some acceptance of the need for protections against harms from a variety of sources. Chapter 2 gives a specific example of the way different investment and taxation decisions can radically affect the substance, content and equity of 'rights' in relation to pensions. In other respects, perhaps the most apparent limitation of Marshall's perspective is its failure to address the position of non-citizens, revealing for some a gulf between universal human rights and citizenship rights. Viewed from the inside, citizenship rights may represent the fullest attempt to deliver on the promise of universally recognised human rights, but viewed from the outside they can function as a tool of exclusion and closure (Brubaker, 1989). Turner gives the example of aboriginal peoples, for whom the operation of national citizenship can be oppressive in a variety of ways, as explored in Chapter 9. A similar point may be made about the position of non-citizen immigrants and asylum seekers, who must be somehow integrated into a system of rights outside of the operation of citizenship (see Chapter 4). These instances relate to a broader argument (Turner, 1993: 15) that citizenship needs to develop in such a way as to take account of the globalisation of social relations and the increasing differentiation of the social system, which is in some respects related to this trend. Thus eliding analysis and prescription, Turner argues that the national citizenship model of rights needs simultaneously to be more universal and more particular, and so must be extracted from its location in the nation state. This argument is increasingly common, but in seeing 'human rights solidarity as a historical stage beyond citizenship solidarity', Turner (1993: 498) comes perilously close to the much criticised evolutionary perspective.

In fact, a number of writers have attempted to address the limitations of Marshall's perspective by reaching for the universal, in Turner's case by seeking a universal ontology for the grounding of rights. However, interest in and optimism about the 'universal' aspect of rights have also been linked to broader institutional developments that have been argued to transcend the level of the nation state. Thus Giddens (1990) identifies a new phase in modernity, centred on 'the extreme dynamism and globalising scope of modern institutions' and linked to a 'stretching process' whereby different social contexts and regions become networked across the globe. Meyer *et al.* (1997) have addressed a similar set of issues by emphasising the force of 'world culture' in shaping the form and actions of nation states, which operate not as independent rational actors, but as culturally embedded occupants of a role. Nation states are argued to show strong consensus for principles such as citizenship, development, justice and human rights, for which they claim universal applicability and which have come to form the basis of a constraining institutional framework. States are thus depicted less as autonomous agents who are collective authors of their own history and more as enactors of 'conventionalised scripts'. In similar vein, Soysal (1994) has argued that national citizenship has been superseded by post-national membership on the basis of universal personhood, such that the rights of non-citizens have been built into national regimes of rights. Some of these ideas are discussed in Chapter 6, which considers the diffusion of universalist ideals to localised settings, in the context of EU anti-discrimination policy.

There have, of course, been a number of concrete developments since Marshall's essay, which to some extent reflect the criticisms of his work, notably the entry into force of the European Convention on Human Rights (ECHR) in 1950, and the two key International Covenants on Civil and Political Rights and on Economic, Social and Cultural Rights (both in 1966), along with a wealth of other transnational conventions. However, the nation state remains the principal instrument for the delivery of rights, whether grounded in international conventions or in national rules of citizenship. Indeed Meyer *et al.* (1997: 154–5) note that the principles of world culture may not mesh with practical experience, such that the 'broad and diffuse goals' of nation states lead to a 'decoupling' of purpose and structure, intention and result. In other words, one likely outcome is a clash of national interests with global culture, or at least an eclectic mix of conflicting principles. Such a view is not inconsistent with the social-constructionist position sketched out by Waters (1996), which emphasises the cultural and historical character of 'universal' human rights, and the variable role of rights in consolidating political support and control at national level (cf. Giddens, 1985; Mann, 1987). The way in which different levels of interest and entitlement interact is, to some extent, an empirical question, which among other issues raises the question of the degree of national autonomy in the granting of rights to non-citizens, discussed in Chapter 4. However, a comparative approach to rights regimes can also be valuable in showing how systems of provision, and their correlative sets of rights, can vary radically according to different national traditions and cultures, and that legal entitlement is not the only basis for a claim to rights, as we see in Chapter 3.

The problem of particularity

In addition to the recognition and delivery of entitlements according to different rights regimes, there is a related question about the capacity of any such regimes to deal with particularity. This issue engages with two other points sometimes raised in relation to Marshall's original essay. One is the theoretical argument associated with postmodernism, which views national citizenship as part of a broader process of 'modernisation', with its evolutionary assumptions and veiled ethnocentrism (Turner, 1993: 14), addressed in Chapters 9 and 10. The other point focuses on process, to note that social struggles over rights tend to be overlooked (though not completely ignored) in Marshall's broad evolutionary perspective. Indeed, the struggles of different groups for recognition and resources have proved a rich vein of inquiry for writers interested in the granting and delivery of rights, and are strongly represented in the chapters to follow (e.g. Chapters 5, 6 and 8). Such struggles have sometimes been construed in terms of 'status politics' (Turner, 1988), which build on the way the ideals of citizenship have introduced a principle of equality into the terrain of rights. Hence, particular groups increasingly seek to challenge what are perceived as *de facto* disadvantages and to mobilise around claims to particular needs for recognition and/or resources. This argument is indirectly supported by the view that even the construction and practice of rights that profess universality are in fact particularist in content; that is to say, they have been constructed around a set of assumptions about the content of social life, the model for which – at least implicitly – has been the white heterosexual male (Phillips, 1992; Chapter 5 in this volume).

As a result, a further important development within the literature on citizenship has been a focus on the embodiment of rights; that is, the way in which rights translate into lived experience with respect to diversity. Notable examples are differences of gender and sexuality (see Bhabha, 1996; Richardson, 1998) and their role in shaping access to rights, though such analysis may be readily extended to race (Anthias and Yuval-Davis, 1992), disability, age, etc., and their mutual interconnections. An exploration of these issues invites attention to the way in which formal status equality and its associated rights are shaped by normative prescriptions and expectations that implicitly deny particularist needs – recent examples have been the failure to accommodate women's reproductive role in conceptions of the occupational career, the absence of recognition for the cultural expression of minority citizens and denial of the validity of same-sex unions. The process of access to rights, or the machinery for their delivery, may furthermore incorporate informal systems of social esteem related to such particularisms, as with judgements that seek to identify the deserving and undeserving.

Processes of stereotyping, prescription and devaluation have been argued to function in close interaction with class-based disadvantage in shaping or constraining access to rights, and this position is captured by Fraser (1995) in her analysis of redistribution and recognition. The former concept relates principally to material distinctions of class and/or welfare divisions, and the latter to cultural or normative distinctions that generate differing degrees of social esteem or status. A similar configuration of influences may be found in Turner's (1988) model of three dimensions of stratification – class, entitlement and culture – and is illustrated by some of the debate surrounding the concept of the underclass and the classical distinction between the deserving and the undeserving (see Chapter 4). However, these insights also apply to a number of other areas, and Chapter 8 documents aspects of the gay and lesbian movement as a struggle for both recognition and rights, the two being inextricably related, while Chapter 11 looks at shifting perceptions and treatments of mental disorder. The literature on gender and rights has challenged the construction of rights by virtue of their confinement to the public sphere (e.g. Lister, 1997), arguing that both formal entitlement and the active realisation of public rights may be shaped by constraints that derive from the private sphere (Pateman, 1989). In this respect, gender functions as a status in two ways: in the ascription of features that dictate the distribution of private obligations of caring (see Chapter 3), and by the associated allocation of esteem, which devalues the private sphere (Fraser, 1995). Both of these aspects of a gendered status regime limit access to the public sphere and therefore to certain rights (see Chapter 5).

There has been some reaction against such arguments, one view being that generalised structures of disadvantage (as in the case of gender difference) cannot be addressed by a focus on individual rights (see Cook, 1993: 233), while other criticisms go further, and wish to challenge any unitary category of 'woman' (Butler, 1990; Nash, 2002; see for discussion Chapters 5 and 10). This complicates, rather than invalidates, a gender focus, however, and certainly cannot undermine the claim that some such generalised view of 'woman' has to date structured access to a variety of rights. Certainly a historical account of gender and citizenship (Lister, 1997) reveals that perceptions of women held by legislators and interpreters have been impediments to equal treatment. We also find that where formal equality has been established, informal assumptions and expectations can produce a deficit in its active attainment. Yet a gender-blind approach can also produce discrimination through a failure to take account of the circumstances most common to women's lives, thus generating the equality versus difference dilemma, and the challenge of combining both claims, ideas explored in

Chapter 5 (see also Scott, 1988). The claims generated by particularisms of all kinds have led to the quest for an approach to 'differentiated universalism' (Lister, 2003) that can accommodate sameness and difference, to be arrived at through a process of deliberative toleration, though how this might be achieved is by no means self-evident (Chambers, 1996; Norval, 2004).

Race has in common with gender the fact of being a basis for social differentiation whose markers are borne on the body. Though the idea of race as a biological category that can directly account for social difference has long been discredited, it nevertheless has a continuing (though often indirect) significance as a system for the 'assignments of rights to individuals' (Rex, 1986: 19). This significance also extends to ethnic differences based on a claim to common origins or a shared culture, whose manifestations may be in the form of cultural signals as much as literal physical characteristics. There are also distinctions of nationality, which may coincide with or be cross-cut by racial or ethnic difference (Smith, 1995) – and in the latter case such classifications can underpin processes of ethnic cleansing in which the 'international community' has sometimes seemed powerless to intervene. Like gender, the issues of race and ethnicity can be linked to demands to be treated as both 'same' and 'different' in relation to rights. Chapter 6 notes the way in which these ideals can sometimes collide in differing approaches to anti-racism. Claims to sameness can occur when informal judgements of esteem or desert impede access to formally held rights, as with suspicion of any 'foreign-seeming' client seeking access to public provisions. The argument can also carry over to formalised inequalities in entitlement that consolidate (ex-)colonial relationships and may be apparent in aspects of immigration law[5] (see Chapter 4), while Chapter 12 problematises the ideal of equal treatment before the law in the case of racially aggravated offences.

The claim to difference, however, has opened up a larger, more complex debate about whether protections for racial and/or ethnic minorities can be achieved within the liberal, individualistic framework that has traditionally underpinned guarantees of universal human rights. While anti-discrimination legislation classically addresses the issue of minority rights within such a framework, the communitarian argument of a collective basis for rights is at its strongest in relation to cultural rights. Thus Taylor (1994), for example, has argued that individual identity is by its nature relational, and that cultural rights in particular cannot be pursued on an individual basis. He therefore supports not simply the provision of facilities to enable collective expressions of cultural identity, but a positive valuing of other cultures in the form of 'recognition'. However, anthropologists have increasingly come to view culture as a site of contestation (Gupta and Ferguson, 1997; Wilson, 1997), which points to the risks of reifying a culture such that it is artificially maintained against change, and Taylor recognises this difficulty. Such reification is particularly at issue where beliefs and practices place constraints on individual autonomy, as discussed in Chapter 7, bringing the liberal and communitarian orientations into potential conflict (Kymlicka, 1989). It is also salutary to ask what 'culture' really stands for in such debates, and in some cases the claim is not so much for the passive valuing of recognition, but for the active allocation of resources (see Fraser, 1995; Chapters 5 and 6 in this volume). In extreme cases, the very legal framework conferring sovereignty, citizenship and land rights may be at stake, as we see in the case of aboriginal rights, discussed in Chapter 9. This is but one example of the problems emerging from the arrangement whereby the nation state is at once the guarantor and transgressor of human rights.

Potentially competing value frames are explicitly discussed in Chapter 7, which advocates a context-sensitive approach to rights, weighing questions of individual autonomy against the background of culturally specific inter-pretations of social duties and obligations to others. At the extreme, it may be argued that every individual is particular, 'the only one of his kind' (Levinas, 1993), and this hints at the possible oppressions exerted by any general (including universal) rule or law. It is in this sense that Derrida (1992) counterposes universality and justice, with justice calling attention to the uniqueness of every situation (see Chapter 10). He writes of the undecid-able tension that lies between the generalising nature of law and the particu-larity of its application in any individual case. Hence, 'Justice as law [*droit*] seems always to suppose the generality of a rule, a norm or a universal imperative. How are we to reconcile the act of justice that must always concern singularity, individuals, irreplaceable groups and lives . . . with rule, norm, value or the imperative of justice which necessarily has a general form' (ibid.: 17). Huge significance thus attaches to the interpretation and application of a rule or law, though sensitive interpretation can never over-ride the rendering of a judgement over one who does not share the language in which the law is inscribed (ibid.: 18) (see, for example, Chapter 9).

Levinas highlights other limitations in the application of justice, and writes of 'a possible war between multiple freedoms, or a conflict between reasonable wills', noting that a resolution through 'justice' will ultimately represent 'a certain limitation of rights and free will'. From this perspective, a clash of rights is almost inevitable, and one example is explored in Chapter 12, which considers the case of hate speech, whereby the right of minorities to be protected from the public expression of hostile sentiments can be said to collide with the right to free speech. The conventional solution to such a clash is a utilitarian reference to the 'general good' of the com-munity, though even the conception of this general good requires an act of interpretation. Other cases of particularity can also involve a clash of rights, and certainly raise questions about the protections owed to groups who are constrained or contained for the supposed better good of society and (some-times) themselves – prisoners and mental health patients. These two groups, alongside the sexually 'deviant', have been a focus of interest in the work of Michel Foucault. His concern is with the triangle of power, right and truth

(Foucault, 1977; Burchell *et al.*, 1991), and in particular the discursive power that lies outside of sovereignty. His work has emphasised the manifold relations of power that permeate the social body, and the disciplinary function of discourse that operates through the institutionalisation and professionalisation of truth, and extends to the very constitution of the individual, as outlined in Chapter 11. Foucault's work therefore draws attention to the controlling aspect of rights, which offer not simply a means of provision, but also a mechanism of surveillance and control, apparent in different ways in Chapters 4, 10 and 11. However, against such a disciplinary exercise of professional expertise, he recognises the centrality of subjugated knowledges, in some respects called into being by the disciplinary exercise itself, but which may none the less provide a basis for its subversion. These ideas have proved a source of insight for the gay and lesbian movement, and for those interested in the rights of prisoners and mental health patients (see Chapters 8, 10 and 11).

Purpose of the book

We began this introduction with a reference to Turner's argument that sociology is uncomfortable with the concept of rights, and especially universal human rights, in the absence of any clear ontological foundations for their existence. Lukes (1991) concedes some difficulty in establishing a clear theoretical source, but observes that a belief in such rights is widespread among politicians, statesmen, lawyers and activists. He adopts a working definition from Feinberg[6] that sees human rights as 'generically moral rights of a fundamentally important kind held equally by all human beings, unconditionally and unalterably'. Lukes recognises that these rights may be sometimes understood as 'ideal' in the sense that they are not necessarily fully recognised in practice, and that few are absolute. Indeed, an insistence on including only those rights that are absolute would have the effect, he argues, of ruling out most of the rights specified in the UN Universal Declaration of Human Rights and its associated instruments. His sketch leaves us with a vision of human rights that has not been fully actualised, and a system of rights that is in some degree open to qualifications or conditions. This is especially the case for those rights that operate outside of the framework of universal human rights, and are more properly held to be in the gift of the state, as with some of the rights that may be granted to non-citizens. This is a picture rather in conflict with Dworkin's (1978: xi) conception of rights as 'trumps' that individuals hold against the state, though in practice very few rights function in this categorical manner. In fact, Dworkin himself recognises the need for distinctions between different types of rights, contrasting 'background' rights, which function in an abstract way against community or society as a whole, with 'institutional rights', which are much more concrete and context-bound.

I am therefore drawn to the conclusion that it is the very indeterminacy of rights that is sociologically interesting, and that among the questions that might be posed are at what level particular rights operate, which rights may be placed under the umbrella of universal human rights, how particular social groups lay a claim to such rights, what are the acts of interpretation by which social actors are required to legislate on such claims, and how claims to rights are affected by the social, political and economic context in which they operate. For all of these reasons we refer to 'rights' rather than 'human rights' in the title of this volume, and in doing so accept the prevailing consensus (Donnelly, 2003) that universal human rights are historically and socially contingent, the product of a particular time, place and set of circumstances, and a work in permanent progress, ideas I return to in the conclusion.

The intention of the present volume is to explore the sociological resources that can be brought to bear on an understanding of rights in practice. It is of necessity an eclectic collection, intended to demonstrate a variety of approaches rather than to cover exhaustively all possible areas of provision and protection. The chapters to follow are therefore organised, as far as possible, on the basis of theoretical orientation rather than substantive focus, though in practice most draw on more than one perspective. The first grouping of chapters shares a political economy approach to the questions of rights, taking a holistic and systems-based view; the next grouping shares a focus on status, norms and institutions in the allocation and functioning of rights; the third grouping shares a broadly interpretive approach, in which context and meanings are paramount. The last grouping slightly departs from this logic, and looks at how an apparent clash of rights has been dealt with in a variety of contexts. Each part is prefaced by a brief introduction.

Notes

1 Such as the British Human Rights Act (1998).
2 Quoted in Pickering and Watts Miller (1993: 56), from *Leçons de Sociologie* (1950: 74).
3 Quoted in Cladis (1992: 1), from *La science positive de la morale en Allemagne* (1887).
4 Quoted in Cladis (1992: 115), from 'The determination of moral facts' (in Durkheim, 1974: 59).
5 An example was the notorious primary purpose rule, abolished in 1997, which required applicants for family unification to demonstrate that the primary purpose of the marriage did not have an economic motivation.
6 Quoted in Lukes (1991: 176).

Part I

Political economy
and rights

The opening part of the book contains three chapters that fall roughly into the tradition of political-economy analysis, in which an emphasis is placed on the holistic understanding of a social formation, through a focus on the political and economic relationships that underpin social life. The first of these chapters considers a radical critique of the liberal tradition of rights, though from a position generally accepting of the priority placed on individual well-being, and on equal worth. The argument of the chapter, however, challenges the broader assumptions that have prevailed in rights discourse, notably a view of the individual as divorced from both benign and malign dependencies. Neglect of the former underestimates the extent to which individual identity is located in interpersonal relations, while neglect of the latter underestimates the effect of socio-economic inequality on access to, and the value of, individual freedoms. Instead of questioning this framework, it is argued that existing human rights guarantees seem to operate from within and to offer forms of amelioration that contain rather than challenge inherent tensions. A similar argument was advanced by Marshall (1950), but Benton goes further, in advocating an approach that places rights in a much wider context, and asks, for example, why restraint on the actions of others should be so central to well-being, and what the implied sources of harm might be.

When viewed in truly universal terms, the answer to this question extends to the system of trade regulation disadvantaging the poorer countries of the world, tied to export-led growth, a high reliance on imports, low public spending and gross indebtedness; a package that siphons off a large proportion of their available revenue. The broader context of rights and possible harms would also take in the 'organised non-liability' endemic in the 'risk society' (Beck, 1992), linked to damaging occupational histories and environmental hazards, both of which are most likely to characterise life at the lower end of the class hierarchy. These harms are not readily addressed by an individualised regime of rights, and even assuming that they were, the liberal model carries the implied assumption that if secured from such harms all individuals have the capacity to construct for themselves a fulfilling life. Benton argues that this view neglects both the impact that unequal access to material, cultural and educational resources can have on such a capacity, and the interpersonal relations and community bonds that for many are the source of meaning in life. His argument closely connects with attempts to develop a more enabling approach to rights by a focus on capabilities (Sen, 1999; Nussbaum, 2000), and leads to Benton's alternative vision for a regime of rights that recognises the underpinnings of effective presence and agency in society, and the interpersonal relationships on which it builds.

The second chapter to adopt the political economy approach also evokes questions about the nature of interpersonal and community dependencies in the context of pension rights. It is, in addition, concerned with larger-scale issues shaping the generation and commitment of resources to address the pressing problem of provision for old age. If we accept Turner's bodily frailty and social precariousness as a basis for claims to rights, none could seem as unquestionable as a right to support in old age, yet the basis and substance of pension rights has become a pressing problem in contemporary capitalist society. Truly universal state pensions tend to take the form of minimal, residual provision, though ageing populations in the developed world mean this still poses a huge challenge to national exchequers. Occupational pensions have become less and less viable, and in private schemes, while there is a right to be fairly and honestly treated, the market risk of investing is borne by the contributor, and there is no guarantee of a pension. The variable mix of public and private provision in operation can be construed more readily as a system of civic stratification (as outlined in Chapter 4) than as a viable system of universal entitlement, especially when tax relief on private schemes, which favours wealthier savers, is taken into account.

At the heart of the pensions problem lies the question of the relationship across generations and the nature and degree of responsibility that the current taxable population carries for the contemporary elderly. In a tax-based system, each contributor pays not for their own needs in old age, but for the needs of the prior generation. When the age cohorts are dramatically out of balance this relationship either imposes a huge responsibility on a small cohort or undermines the entitlements of the larger cohort. So what does a system of cross-generational justice look like in these circumstances, and who bears the cost of a socially responsible approach to old age? When pensions are considered in this light, the language of rights seems rather distant, and the approach serves instead to highlight the difficult configuration of rights, resources and the location of responsibility. The temptation for states to privatise all provision, thereby opting for a system of self-responsibility, is immense, but as Blackburn points out, an expensive solution given the marketing and salary costs of private providers. It would also be a classic example of the desocialised, atomised individual represented by the classical liberal model of rights discussed in Chapter 1, and is of course grossly inequitable.

The third example of a political economy approach to rights also grapples with the problem of ageing, but in relation to the right to physical care. The issue of a right to care is in some respects more complex than that of the right to a pension, requiring the recognition of caring as fundamentally relational, but separable from other aspects of a social relationship, and identifiable as a form of work. As in the case of pensions, making the philosophical case for a right to care is rather less challenging than the implementation of such a right in practice. This requires not only the acceptance of a universal principle, as in the 'frailty' theory of rights, but also the delivery of particularised provision, according to differing dependencies and vulnerabilities. Again like pensions, the place of each individual in the underpinning roles and relationships will shift as they move through the life course. As Chapter 3 makes clear, the ensuing nexus of rights, relationships and responsibilities will be historically and culturally variable, and care is therefore to be analysed as an embedded feature of contrasting systems of exchange, reciprocity and obligation premised on very varied socio-economic arrangements.

Of course, the recognition of a right to care also entails a more difficult decision to identify cases in which the resource investment may be too great when weighed against the diminishing benefits. In this sense, the right to care requires judgements of relative desert, which are partially resource driven, and which will be resolved differently according to the social, economic and cultural context. The comparative approach advocated in Chapter 3 is particularly revealing in this respect, and demonstrates how the concept of rights need not be confined to legally based claims and calls on the state. It may equally operate in the context of culture and tradition, based, for example, on kinship obligations and expectations, often gendered, that operate to varying degrees in different societies. We might also find that several systems of provision operate simultaneously in any given society, embodying different types of exchange relations and yielding multiple and possibly conflicting expectations and obligations. Different systems will also raise their own problems with respect to equity, standards, monitoring and respect for the rights of both givers and receivers of care.

1 Do we need rights?

If so, what sort?

Ted Benton

In what follows I want to consider the implications of a long tradition of radical scepticism about rights. The arguments of the sceptics have a number of rather different sources and targets, some turning on the effects, intended or not, of the institutions through which rights are allocated, some calling into question the conceptual foundations of rights discourse. Here I try to bring together the main lines of argument against rights – specifically 'human rights' – to see how effectively they address current social and political realities. I conclude by considering what alternative normative framework or institutional order might achieve what the prevailing discourses and practices of 'rights' arguably fail to do.

Liberal rights: the classical view

The classical (i.e. seventeenth- and eighteenth-century) advocacies of 'natural' rights, or 'rights of man', have well-rehearsed limitations in terms of their implicit exclusions, but these are not central to the arguments I want to develop here. For our purposes there are two main moral intuitions in the classical discourse of rights: (a) the moral priority accorded to the well-being of the individual person; and (b) the notion that all individuals have equal value, are equally worthy of respectful treatment. In the classic statements there is some diversity in the ways individual well-being is characterised. These often appear as differences of emphasis, but the emphasis does have implications. Sometimes the emphasis is on the vulnerability of individuals, so that the moral requirement is to protect them from abuse. Sometimes the emphasis is on individuals as agents, capable of autonomously devising a life-plan and living it. Here the moral requirement is to remove obstacles in the way of their autonomous action.

Irrespective of diversity in conceptions of the good for individuals, the twin moral intuitions of classical liberal political philosophy imply advocacy of an authoritative normative framework, with the concept of rights at its core. The well-being of each citizen is to be assured by a legal order that restrains both sovereign and citizen with regard to those acts that might impinge on it: citizens are defended in their freedom of action in so far as their exercise of it is consistent with an equal freedom on the part of others. To be thus protected in their circumscribed sphere of autonomy is the right of each citizen:

> Liberty consists in being able to do anything that does not harm another person. Thus the exercise of the natural rights of each has no limits except those which assure to other members of society the enjoyment of these same rights; these limits can be determined only by law.
> (Article 4 of the *French Declaration of the Rights of Man and Citizen,* 1789)

Depending on how the well-being of the individual is conceptualised, I speak of 'passive rights' (with the focus on protecting individuals from abuse), and 'active rights' (with the focus on their pursuit of a self-chosen life-plan).

For the arguments that follow, it will be helpful to draw attention to some of the further underlying assumptions of this classical liberal discourse of rights. The first is that self-identity is a 'given' property of individuals independently of their social participation, as, in the case of the requirement for active rights, is the capacity to devise and live out a life-plan. A second, closely related, assumption is that, given protection from interference by others, each individual can achieve their own well-being independently of those others: that is to say, 'well-being' is a non-relational property of individual persons. A third assumption – otherwise why do we need an authoritative apparatus to restrain it? – is that citizens and the sovereign are disposed to abuse or obstruct one another in the exercise of their basic freedoms. A fourth is that a clear distinction can be made between those acts ('self-regarding') that do not risk infringing the well-being of others, and those ('other-regarding') that do carry such a risk, and so can be legitimately restrained. The fifth, and, for our purposes, final, assumption is that the harms from which individuals need to be protected, or the obstacles in the way of their fulfilment of their life-plans, arise from the intentional acts of other individuals, or the sovereign power (usually thought of as a 'super-subject', or leviathan).

Radical scepticism about liberal rights

Now to the arguments of the radical sceptics about rights. Most of these (at least, those whose arguments I want to explore here) share with the liberal tradition at least two normative intuitions. These are: a recognition of individual persons as bearers of intrinsic value; and a commitment to the equal value of each person. However, there are differences in the way individual persons are conceptualised, and, especially, in the way these critical traditions think about individual well-being. As we shall see, the significance of individual vulnerability, as well as the moral importance of the autonomous pursuit of one's own good, may be endorsed, but with rather different outcomes.

The antagonism of interests

The first step in the sceptical critique is to ask why securing the well-being of each individual should require the allocation of basic rights, conceived as restraints on the actions of citizens with regard to each other, and of the sovereign power with respect to the citizens. This can only be because it is assumed that either the sovereign or other citizens, or both, would otherwise be liable to abuse or invade the sphere of autonomy of each individual. It is, in other words, assumed that there is an endemic conflict of interests between individual citizens and between them and the sovereign power. But these assumptions can be seen as appropriate only to a specific historical period or form of social order. Alternative forms of social coexistence can be imagined in which individual citizens were not disposed to abuse one another, or to interfere with one another's pursuit of their chosen life-plans, and in which there was no public power set over and against the citizens. Some socialist, ecological and anarchist utopias postulate such a way of social living. Such a mode of life, if it were possible, would be one in which the well-being of each would be secured spontaneously, without need of the discipline of an apparatus of rights and justice. It was the philosopher David Hume who famously specified two key conditions for such a state of affairs: unlimited abundance and mutual benevolence.

Personal identity – given or achieved

Below I consider in more depth the feasibility of this most radical version of the sceptical argument. First, however, it is necessary to consider some more specific conceptual and empirical issues surrounding the liberal view of rights. First is the conception of personal identity as a 'given', as a property of individuals prior to social participation. This is implicit in classical notions of a 'state of nature' prior to the establishment of a social contract that underpins the authority of the public power and its laws. It is also present in the work of more recent political philosophy, most influentially in the Rawlsian notion of an 'original position' behind an imagined 'veil of ignorance' (Rawls, 1971). By contrast, sociologically informed thinking about personal identity understands it not as a 'given', but as an achievement. It is an achievement won in the course of participation in social practice and through reflection upon it. Personal autonomy, then, is an achievement made possible only where the developing individual has the interpersonal, emotional-relational, cultural-linguistic, social structural and material-ecological conditions of life that sustain and favour it.

Life-plans and how to live them

Connectedly, the ontology of the liberal view of active rights supposes that each individual is able to devise and to live out a life-plan, as long as she or he is not interfered with by others. But there are several respects in which this view is too sociologically thin, or 'minimalist' (respects that parallel those in which the neo-liberal view of the minimal state is too 'thin'). First, to devise a life-plan that is in the required sense one's own life-plan presupposes the achievement of autonomous self-identity. This, as I have just suggested, has complex cultural, social and ecological conditions, failure or neglect of any of which may lead to failure to acquire the capacity even to devise a coherent plan of life. Second, for a life-plan to be devised as a meaningful expression of the will or identity of its agent (and this is surely required if it is to bear the moral weight attached to it in liberal thought) it must be one chosen or constructed within a cultural world that includes a variety of such visions and the materials for comparing and evaluating them, together with access to the personal skills and competences for appreciating and choosing: in short, a rich and diverse public culture and access of individuals to it (at the very least, a broadly based education, accessible to all).

The third consideration has its classic expression in the work of Durkheim. No fully human life is possible without some connection with the life of society. Even the hermit or religious recluse can make sense of their self-exclusion from society in terms drawn from the wider stock of cultural resources, and the monastic life is itself a form of society. So the life-plan I devise will of necessity be one that includes a certain vision of my relationships with others – with a sexual partner, parents, offspring, siblings, friends, acquaintances – and with a range of favoured experiences – artistic creation, a certain sort of work or career, inhabiting a certain chosen physical or cultural environment, playing or watching a certain sport or game, living according to a chosen set of moral beliefs and so on. Others, when we start to give concrete form to the idea of a life-plan, figure not just as potential obstacles to our project, but, instead (or also) as indispensable partners, associates and conditions for it. We cannot, in other words, have a life-plan that is not inseparably intertwined in its very constitution with the living out by others of their life-plans.

This suggests that autonomous living presupposes a deeper commonality of shared understandings and purposes. Durkheim (1951) used statistical variations in suicide rates to argue a closely related point. A society that promotes individual egoism at the expense of such deeper commonalities risks becoming one in which individuals are incapable of linking their own private purposes with wider social meanings. Durkheim's claim is not just that this is dangerous for the society, but that it is dangerous for the individual: that what sustains our ability to make sense of our own lives and their purposes is their connection with the life of the wider society. Lacking this sense of the place of our own life-plan in the communities to which we belong, we are vulnerable to a loss of meaning in our own life even to the point of finding that life not worth living. Of course, there are hazards for the society, too, in the shape of a drift towards instrumentalism, fragmentation and the corruption of public life, on the one hand, and increased vulnerability to the appeal of demagogic and totalitarian versions of community, on the other. Even as early as the latter part of the eighteenth century, Smith and Ferguson, luminaries of the Scottish Enlightenment, viewed the emergence and spread of the egoistic 'commercial society' with some foreboding for just these reasons.

Inequality, dependency, property and rights

The fourth reason why we need more than just non-interference to be able to devise and live out our life-plans is the best known. The classic location for this argument is Marx's (1975) 'On the Jewish question', but it is widely diffused in subaltern culture in such sayings as 'property is nine points of the law'. Marx's dictum that all rights resolve into property rights is a polemical exaggeration – and probably was even in Marx's day – but there is an important kernel of truth in it. There are two interconnected aspects. First, to be able to implement a life-plan requires cultural and material resources. In a society characterised by massive inequalities in the distribution of resources of all types, there can be no such thing as equality in the ability to live out our life-plans. My life-plan might be to sample the cultures and cuisines of the world in a life of perpetual tourist extravagance, without the distractions of work and social obligation. An unemployed and demoralised miner or steel worker might aspire to have secure and meaningful work to be able to provide for his family and regain self-respect. A single mother of pre-school children might have a life-plan that includes going to university, having a richer social life, having time to read or to see friends. The life-plans we are able to devise are constrained and shaped both by our cultural horizons and by our actual placing in society, with its current pattern of fulfilments and frustrations. But in each case our ability to live out whatever plan we might devise will be conditioned by our access or lack of access to resources.

This is true however we think of well-being. If the emphasis is less on the active aspect of living out an autonomous life-plan than on the recognition of individual vulnerability, then here, too, distributive inequality radically qualifies the role of rights. If sound and secure living conditions, clean drinking water, effective waste disposal systems, unpolluted air to breathe, nourishing food, daily exercise and access to aesthetically uplifting environments play a significant part in sustaining health (and there is plenty of evidence that they do), then most of the world's population lacks some, and some of the world's population lacks all, of these basic requirements. The aspiration to health equality remains a goal of the World Health Organization and of many national governments, but we rarely hear the demand for provision of the necessary conditions for health articulated as a human right. Here, too, the conceptual assumption is that health can be taken as a given 'normal' state. Sickness and disease are hazards to be met by provision of public health services that aim at treatment to restore us to 'normal' health. Equal access to health care in this sense is the aspiration sustained by the more thoroughgoing liberal rights discourse. It is, of course, immensely valuable, but it fails to address the deeper social inequalities in vulnerability to poor health and premature death. I return below to a fuller discussion of the issues posed by this.

Marx's argument about rights and property is certainly about inequality, but it is about inequality in a more profound sense than simply inequality of access to material and socio-cultural goods. It is also about the workings of the particular inequalities of power that characterise a capitalist society. Marx enthusiastically endorsed the rights that accompanied the emergence of distinctively modern political systems: freedom of expression and association, freedom of conscience and the positive rights slowly won over generations of struggle to vote, to play a part in the process of democratic decision-making. But Marx also drew attention to the gap between this (limited) political emancipation and full human emancipation. We are familiar with the extent to which wealthy and powerful interests are able to shape the agenda of public debate as well as intervene in the processes of policy formation and legislation. Even where the right to vote is universal, some votes count more than others.

More than this, Marx emphasises the contrast between the political realm of free expression and equal rights and the realm of capitalist employment relations in which workers are subject to the dictatorial authority of the employer. This is no mere contingency, but is implicit in the employment relation itself. In selling their labour time to their employers, workers hand over, as a commodity, to its new owner the power of disposition over their mental and bodily activity. The wage relation thus differs from slavery in that loss of self-ownership is limited to working hours. The market in labour also means that the worker may have some choice of employer, but not, in general, the choice not to sell her or his labour time to someone. To the extent that those who do not own productive resources are materially unable to meet their subsistence needs other than by entering the labour market, they live under the sway of one or other members of the employing class. Their autonomy is constrained, and, during working hours, given wholly over to the employer. This is a form of economic inequality that implies not just differential access to resources of various kinds, but also relations of structured domination and subordination. The life-plan of the employer has at its disposal the life-activity of many fellow citizens, who, in turn, lose to him the power of autonomous pursuit of their own well-being for at least that part of their lives that has been sold.

Of course, this is not the only form of dependency relationship. In Marx's day domestic service was more widespread than today (it was, of course, a feature of Marx's own household) and in many respects it entailed an even deeper form of dependency than wage labour. Women, too, where excluded from the labour market by customary expectations, by a gendered division of domestic labour and child-care, by legal restrictions on their employment or by discrimination in employment, have suffered a double dependency: directly on their husband or partner as well as indirectly on his employer. Interestingly, all these forms of socio-economic dependency relations were seized upon by the opponents of the extension of political rights to women, servants and the propertyless on the grounds of the loss of the capacity of autonomous judgement entailed by these relations. The Marxian or feminist argument is a simple inversion: if we desire real, as distinct from merely formal, equality of political rights, then these relations of dependency and subservience must be abolished.

The general outcome of this line of thought is to emphasise the difference between the juridical allocation and recognition of universal rights, and the very unequal *de facto* ability of individuals to exercise the rights they are formally allocated. Equality under the law is compromised by unequal ability to pay for legal advice and representation, and by the deep cultural gulf between a specialised legal profession and many of those who might otherwise benefit from the protection of the law. The law protects the property of the poor no less than that of the wealthy, but in protecting the property of the wealthy, it maintains the division between the poor and the wealthy. So, to the extent that the discourse of universal rights is proclaimed and legally enforced in a society characterised by endemic social inequality, it functions as a means of both legitimating and reproducing those inequalities. It is in this sense and under these conditions that rights do resolve into the rights of property.

What harms can rights protect us from?

So far I have explored some of the arguments of the radical critique of liberal rights as they bear upon the way individuals and their well-being are conceptualised. Essentially the case for the prosecution is that the classical liberal view takes too little account of the social conditions under which individuals develop and pursue their life-purposes, and too little account of the interdependence of individual life-plans and their necessary connection with the wider society. At its strongest, the case against liberal rights makes it out to be a form of legitimation of inequality and injustice. This is because its failure to theorise the ways in which social and economic relations affect the ability of individuals to envisage and realise the good for themselves renders the human cost of inequality and dependence near unthinkable. Of course, there are responses to these harsh criticisms from within the liberal traditions, and I will return to consider them at a later stage in the argument. For now, it is enough to repeat that the argument so far calls into question a certain way of thinking about individuals and their well-being. It is not an argument against the moral priority liberalism accords to individual well-being.

The next step in the argument is to consider the classical liberal view of the harms from which individuals are at risk. The liberal discourse of rights seeks to restrain both citizens and the public power with regard to those acts that might harm other individuals, or infringe their autonomous pursuit of a life-plan. The protections it offers to individuals cover such abuses as might result from the (other-regarding) intentional acts of other individuals or the sovereign power. This focus on abuses resulting from intentional acts eclipses and so renders at best marginal several sorts of avoidable harm to which individuals are susceptible.

First, both public bodies and private companies that provide goods or services may do damage to consumers, employees or others, such as near neighbours. This category may include industrial diseases and injuries, food poisoning, long-term ill-health (e.g. as a result of tobacco smoking) and death and injury resulting from traffic accidents (ferry, coach and air disasters in the tourist industry) and from specific sources of environmental pollution (factory discharges, release of hazardous materials, such as at Bhopal, Seveso and Chernobyl). In a legal order devoted to identifying individual responsibility, the introduction of a robust regime for assigning corporate responsibility faces considerable difficulty. This is to some extent connected to the disproportionate power of the corporate sector and public bodies themselves to shape legislation. It may also be in part linked to a prevailing set of (liberal) cultural assumptions about the nature of crime and criminals: political discourse on crime and media representations focus on individual acts of theft and violence, crimes of the mad, the powerless, the homeless and the stigmatised, not those of the rich and the powerful. No doubt the difficulty of establishing the requisite causal connections between an identifiable institutional practice and the harms alleged against it is also an obstacle. But except in the case of strict liability offences, there is also a requirement to establish corporate knowledge and consequent culpable negligence. This has been a particular difficulty faced by attempts to pursue legal claims on behalf of smokers. The tendency has been for courts to seek some individual office-holder to whom the relevant responsibility has been assigned, and whose negligence can then be attributed to the corporation. This has produced the paradoxical outcome that in some cases firms without clearly defined allocations of responsibility for safety or environmental health have escaped conviction.

Natural disasters, so-called 'acts of God', constitute a second category of harms to which we might be vulnerable. Flash floods, landslides, climatic anomalies, epidemics and pandemics of infectious disease, earthquakes and so on take a heavy toll of human life. The tsunami of December 2004 is a terrifying example, claiming at least 300,000 lives directly, but leaving in its wake emotional distress and economic hardship on an unimaginable scale. Hazards of these kinds are often seen as 'external' risks by sociologists as well as the wider public. In the work of Beck (1992) and Giddens (1994), for example, these risks and hazards are represented as characteristic of earlier 'traditional' societies, displaced by the 'manufactured' risks of industrial modernity. Of course, such disasters continue to threaten industrial societies, too, but to characterise many of them as 'external' is also open to question. Floods, landslides, epidemics and climate change may be at least partly caused by human social and economic activities. Even where this is clearly not the case, as with the tsunami, the impact on human communities may vary very considerably, depending on the geographical location of settlements, the existence of warning and evacuation procedures and the state of readiness of emergency services. Whether these take into account known hazards or are effectively resourced will often depend not only on the priorities and resources of government, but also on the socio-economic status of the communities at risk. In the case of the tsunami, an effective warning system had been in place to cover the Pacific, so the provision of a parallel system to cover the areas hit by the tsunami was presumably quite technically feasible.

A third sort of harm or hazard not easily acknowledged in the terms of classical liberal political philosophy arises from participation in 'given' or taken-for-granted modes of life. These are not chosen, but flow as a matter of course from the prevailing economic and social power relations within which people live out their lives. These harms and hazards are continuous with those of the first category, but are roughly distinguished by their less specific or identifiable sources. They can be thought of as general consequences of what Beck calls 'organised non-liability'.

There is empirical evidence connecting the incidence of a range of injuries, diseases and mortality rates with occupational life-histories, though these may not be attributable to a specific period of employment with an identifiable employer. More generally, there are very robust disparities in morbidity and premature death between the social classes. Environmental social movements in many countries have provided evidence of the ways in which poor living environments also correlate with class and ethnic divisions. Working-class residential estates are sited downwind of polluting factories or close to incineration plants, are more likely than are upmarket developments to be built on potentially toxic landfill sites, are likely to have less secure and effective pest control, waste disposal and fresh water supplies. Engels documented much of this in the big industrial cities of the 1830s and early 1840s, but the US environmental justice movement, the Silicon Valley Toxics Coalition and countless other organisations across the globe testify to the continuing validity of the analysis.

There are other examples. The prevailing system of food production, processing and distribution entails a class-skewed pattern of dietary imbalances and associated health risks. The design of modern towns and cities premised on general access to the private car as the dominant mode of transport not only contributes significantly to air pollution, but favours lifestyles in which physical exercise is effectively squeezed out of daily life, and the convivial sociability of public open spaces is replaced by a threatening arena of real or imagined criminality.

Yet another source of harm derives from the intentional acts of public powers. The harms belonging to this category are the unintended and usually unwanted, but often foreseen, consequences of state policies. One currently topical example is that of war, and the fate of its victims characterised in the official discourse as 'collateral damage'. The offensive launched against Iraq in the spring of 2003 began with a bombing raid on Baghdad proudly boasted to inspire 'shock and awe'. In the subsequent land invasion and occupation many thousands of civilians have been killed, and countless others dreadfully maimed. Cluster bombs, known to cause widespread death and injury, especially to children, were extensively used by the UK military. One city, Falluja, was effectively razed to the ground by the use of massive firepower and chemical weapons, on the excuse that it was a stronghold of 'insurgents'. Despite repeated claims that every effort had been taken to avoid civilian casualties, independent estimates give figures ranging from 10,000 to more than 100,000 deaths by the time of writing. The occupying forces have not deemed it worthwhile even to count these deaths and other casualties.

During the period of occupation photographic evidence came into the public domain evidencing instances of inhumane and degrading treatment amounting to torture of Iraqi captives in Abu Graibe prison. Evidence later emerged of similar treatment meted out to captives by UK personnel. These images were immediately relayed through the world media, and induced moral outrage and expressions of deep regret and condemnation by the political leaderships of the occupying forces. Individual perpetrators were quickly brought to well-publicised trial and conviction. The abuses of captive hostages committed by some groups of insurgents were also given high-profile media coverage and intensive moral vilification.

The contrast between the moral outrage rightly evoked by inhumane treatment of prisoners and hostages, on the one hand, and the sanguine expressions of regret at civilian casualties on such a vast scale (outnumbering the 9/11 casualties many times over), on the other, is stark. This no doubt reflects to some extent widely held cultural presumptions and also, perhaps, the way the images connected with particular media framings of events. But the central concern of liberal political philosophy, and the legal order linked to it, with harms directly resulting from intentional acts of individuals, is strikingly at work. The deliberate infliction of suffering and humiliation on a captive subject is evil and must be punished by law. The killing and dreadful maiming of many tens of thousands of non-combatant men, women and children as a by-product of an invasion by a coalition of liberal democratic states is regrettable, but not even sufficiently significant to merit recording it.

Another example is more contentious but also perhaps more pervasive. The global system of trade regulation, investment and development aid – symbolised by the trio of World Trade Organization (WTO), World Bank and International Monetary Fund (IMF) – enforces a neo-liberal model of economic policy across the world. Institutional dominance of the richest countries is widely thought to shape the policies of these organisations in favour of the interests of those countries and the transnational corporations that remain linked to them. The IMF's prescriptions of export-led growth combined with cuts in public spending have arguably had massively negative effects on the poorest groups in the countries affected by them, depriving people of desperately needed public services, and driving small-scale subsistence agriculturalists off the land. In the case of the World Bank, its record of funding large-scale prestige projects, often at deep cost to indigenous populations and local environments, is well documented. There is also a well-developed critical literature on the way the GATT agreements and practice of the WTO sustain global trading relations that disadvantage poorer countries, and undermine attempts of nation states to maintain environmental standards and raise working conditions. A currently topical case is the pressure exerted by the USA and WTO to globalise environmentally hazardous genetically modified crop technologies against democratically expressed popular sentiment in many countries.

The radicalisation of liberalism: from negative to positive rights

At least some of these elements in the radical case against the classical rights discourse have evoked a response, stimulated by the rise of mass labour movement agitation from the mid-nineteenth century onwards, from within the liberal tradition. Liberal social and political theorists of this period have generally recognised the implications of social and economic inequality for the enjoyment of rights. This was already clear in the later work of J. S. Mill, and, after him, of Hobhouse (1922). The struggles that eventually brought extensions of democratic political rights to male workers and finally to women led at the same time in the countries of Western Europe to a extension of publicly provided education. From the political right this was seen as a necessity if the workers were to be persuaded to give their allegiance to the existing property order, but in any event literacy was an increasingly valuable asset in realising the aspirations of organised workers and women suffragists. But the Second World War provided the most effective stimulus, as mass mobilisation for the war effort required assurances that there would be no going back to the mass unemployment and insecurity of the pre-war period. Practically, the post-war extension and consolidation of welfare states in the main combatant nations, with universal provision for social security, health and education, gave institutional form to the aspirations of a liberalism now radicalised and revitalised by democratic socialist thinking, and challenged by increasingly powerful communist mobilisation in those Western countries that had experienced Nazi occupation.

Perhaps the most fully developed and influential intellectual statement of the new liberalism was the work of T. H. Marshall (1963). In his classic essay of 1949 he proposed an extension of citizenship to include positive economic and social rights, indirectly vindicating Marx's insight that full emancipation would necessitate a transcendence of the division between state and civil society. However, Marshall stops short of a thoroughgoing egalitarianism in the social and economic spheres. Instead, liberal democratic welfare capitalism is for him an institutional framework within which continuing tensions between class-divided wealth creation and compensatory citizenship rights could be contained. The near-simultaneous UN Declaration of Human Rights works within a closely similar frame. In addition to reiteration of the classic liberal rights of man and citizen it asserts:

> Everyone has the right to a standard of living adequate for the health and well-being of himself and his family, including food, clothing, housing and medical care and necessary social services, and the right to security in the event of unemployment, sickness, disability, widowhood, old age or other lack of livelihood in circumstances beyond his control.
>
> (Article 25)

The universal right to education, at least at the elementary stage, is also asserted, as is the right to participate in the cultural life of the community, enjoy the arts and share in scientific advancements and their benefits. In a further significant shift beyond the generally 'negative' character of the protections offered in the classic liberal proclamations, there is a clear recognition that enabling members of society to enjoy the exercise of their rights involves the positive allocation of resources:

> Everyone, as a member of society, has the right to social security and is entitled to realization, through national effort and international co-operation and in accordance with the organization and resources of each state, of the economic, social and cultural rights indispensable for his dignity and the free development of his personality.
>
> (Article 22)

Significantly, as in Marshall's thought, the institutional order of liberal democratic capitalism is clearly discernible despite the normative universalism of the text: the health and well-being of 'himself and his family', the assertion of trade union rights, paid holidays, equal pay, limitation of working hours and so on. Wage labour, the nuclear family and gender division of labour, it seems, will not be challenged, but they will be regulated and the disadvantages attaching to them ameliorated or compensated by the public power.

In those Western societies where social democratic parties have sustained large-scale popular support the ameliorations and compensations have been very significant:

- free, universal public education;

- state-sponsored health care, provided universally and often free of charge at the point of need;
- state-sponsored public service broadcasting, often with a legal requirement for unbiased reporting of current affairs, and independent of government control;
- legislation outlawing discrimination on grounds of gender, race and ethnicity, disablement, sexual orientation and religious or other beliefs;
- legal immunities for official trade union disputes, and general rights for trade union membership and activity;
- a minimum wage and, in some countries, entitlement to consultation by management on a range of company policies affecting workers;
- health and safety standards set and enforced by government-sponsored bodies;
- general environmental standards and planning regulations;
- social security benefits offering an economic safety net in the cases listed in Article 25 of the Universal Declaration;
- access to legal aid.

Limitations of the liberal response

The problem of inequality

Does this mean that the radical critique of liberal rights no longer has purchase? The answer here must be 'no', for two main reasons. The first takes us back to the key point that the basic structural inequalities and relations of power and property that characterised earlier phases of capitalist development remain in place and are in important respects more intractable than they ever were. At their best, the compensations and ameliorations provided by welfare capitalism were only partially successful. Public education has provided room for significant social mobility, but has still been predominantly a means of reproducing class relations in each successive generation. In general, discriminatory practices in employment have been difficult to monitor and eliminate, and minimum wage rates have generally been set at levels acceptable to employers' organisations and have often led to a lowering of wages to the minimum standard. Health and safety standards are perpetually under pressure in strongly competitive environments. Despite generalised rights to trade union membership, many employers are able to resist union organisation effectively, and research persistently reveals very high levels of bullying and intimidation at work. The increasing recourse to more individualised assertion of employment rights through industrial tribunals provides some recompense, but often at the cost of subsequent employment discrimination.

If the reach of social democratic liberalism is limited even in the countries where it has been most fully implemented, this is still more so in most of the rest of the world, where social democracy has had limited impact, or where patterns of clientalism, corruption, authoritarian rule or economic and political dependency have given little space for easing the social, human and ecological costs of capitalism in the raw. Given this very limited geographical scope of social democratic liberalism in practice, the radicalised liberalism of the Universal Declaration and subsequent documents stands as a continuing indictment of current practice across the world, rather than, as with the classic liberal declarations, an ideological mystification of it. This is, arguably, a situation reinforced and intensified by the increasing role of transnational economic institutions and flows of goods, services and capital. As economic and political power shifts to the transnational corporations, capital markets, the WTO, IMF and World Bank, the capacity of progressive social movements to influence policy at nation state level is diminished, along with the room for manoeuvre of national governments themselves.

The vulnerability of progressive liberalism

This leads us to the second main reason why the critique of liberal rights still has purchase. This is that in leaving largely untouched the prevailing concentrations of economic and political power, social democratic welfare states have remained vulnerable to elite pressures to roll back gains made by generations of progressive reform. Since the 1970s this pressure has become more intense and effective in the heartlands of social democracy. A full analysis of this would be far beyond the limitations of this chapter, but a combination of increasing power on the part of organised workers and the slowing down of the post-war boom put profits under pressure, leading to fiscal crises. Tensions between more marginal, unorganised workers and those outside the labour market, on the one hand, and organised workers able to maintain incomes through industrial power, on the other, provided a popular base available for mobilisation by a resurgent 'new right', committed to a return to the free-market economics and minimal state of the classical liberal tradition. At the level of ideology, the classical tradition's association of freedom with property rights was deployed in a persuasive attack on the burden of taxation as an authoritarian imposition by the state, restricting the right of individuals to spend their own money as they chose. As far as the corporate sector was concerned, the key requirements have been the weakening of trade union power and removal of state 'interference' and 'red tape'. The collapse and discrediting of the state centralist regimes of Eastern and Central Europe, together with the increasing internationalisation of capitalist economic dominance, have consolidated the rule of the neo-liberal revival, demolishing what little had been achieved in the direction of reform outside the social democratic heartland, and putting under severe pressure the framework of welfare and social security within it.

Another world is possible

The rule of neo-liberalism is not without its critics and opponents. As a century or more of reforms are dismantled, the purchase of the radical critique of liberal rights and the society whose inequalities and abuses it legitimated becomes ever more apparent. New, more diverse, broadly based and open-textured forms of resistance are emerging in the shape of coalitions of social movement organisations, non-governmental organisations, social forums, international peace and environmental activism, and important developments in popular participation in some of the countries of Latin America. Even at the level of international economic governance, the hegemony of the richest nations is under challenge.

So the question of alternatives seems, at last, to be back on the agenda of international politics. What sort of alternative can be envisaged? Must it be one in which social relationships are regulated by the discourses and apparatuses of rights? The argument thus far has been premised on two moral intuitions shared by both liberalism and the radical critique in the form in which I defend it. These are the moral priority accorded to human individuals and their well-being, and the commitment to equality of respect for all individuals. For reasons not presented here, I think that the first of these intuitions needs to be reconciled with an extension of the scope of moral concern to include non-human beings, but still the centrality of the concern with individuals is retained. The argument so far has been to the effect that these shared moral intuitions can only be made real if a range of interpersonal, social structural, cultural and ecological conditions are met. The prominence of the discourse and apparatus of rights is explained by its emergence within a society in which those conditions are generally not met spontaneously. Hence the conceptual impoverishment of the classical tradition, and the minimal, 'negative' character of the protections it offers. The key limitations and vulnerabilities of the progressive radicalisation of the tradition of liberal rights are, I have suggested, a result of the persistence and internationalisation of the concentrations of economic and political power that both generated the requirement for rights and denied the conditions for them to give the protections they promise.

This takes us back to a fundamental ambiguity in the radical critique. Marx has been widely read as advocating a future society in which the conditions for spontaneous mutual respect would be met, and the need for rights transcended. But what might those conditions be? Hume, as we saw, mentioned two: benevolence and abundance. Steven Lukes (1985), in an influential critique of Marx's moral thinking, adds two more: value consensus and perfect knowledge of the effects of our actions on the well-being of others. Even given benevolent intentions, we might harm others through ignorance.

A society in which all four prerequisites for spontaneous mutual respect and harmony were actualised seems somewhat unlikely, and might not be desirable even if possible. A society of abundance would be one in which some of the causes of competitive antagonism might be eliminated, but we denizens of contemporary consumer society know that, as Adam Smith (1891) once put it, 'the desire of the conveniencies of building, dress, equipage, and household furniture, seems to have no limit or certain boundary'. Only if deeper socio-economic, cultural and psychological roots of escalating consumer demand were addressed might abundance bring some amelioration of mutual antagonism. But abundance itself, certainly a feature of Marx's vision of the future society, now looks distinctly problematic in view of the ecological unsustainability of even current levels of material production and consumption. As for benevolence, the optimistic view that our dispositions to mutual antagonism and aggression can be explained in terms of the frustrations and deprivations of an economic and social system premised on an individualistic struggle for existence is increasingly hard to sustain. In any case, it would be a rather risky assumption on which to base a vision of the future. It is better to play safe with the deeply pessimistic view of the later Freud, that the suffering we endure at the hands of our fellow humans is as 'fatefully inevitable' as that meted out by the forces of nature and the frailty of our own bodies. Value consensus, too, seems a deeply improbable and probably undesirable prospect – though it is equally difficult to see how any functioning and convivial society could do without consensus on some very basic norms.

Perhaps, then, the vision of a future society in which we could live happily without need for rights is a utopia of the unfeasible kind. In any case, the real world we now confront is one in which economic, political and military power is arguably more unequally distributed than ever before. It is also one in which, even in the most liberal societies, there are severe and persistent threats to such civil rights as centuries of struggle have secured.

Nevertheless, the defence of our liberties need not be a merely negative act of resistance – it can be, and increasingly is – enlivened by a more sober and practical utopianism. To work for a more egalitarian distribution of wealth and power, a more collabrorative and convivial institutionalism of our public and private lives, the discovery of alternative sources of pleasure and fulfilment and a more respectful engagement with the rest of nature might take us in the direction of ways of living together in which the requirements of rights and justice were more in accord with the prevailing culture and moral sentiments of its citizens. Such a society would be one in which rights might need to be enforced less, but might achieve their purposes more successfully.

Note

This chapter presents a condensed and reworked version of the argument given in more detail in Chapter 4 of Benton (1993).

2   Return of the proletariat?

Pension rights and pension finance in the ageing society

Robin Blackburn

Many approaches to understanding social stratification, whether they focus on class or status, ethnicity or gender, assume a continuous present. They seek to identify who gains and who loses, who is included and who excluded, by core social practices at a given moment in time. Age cohorts can be isolated and identified in this way too. Their relative size, situation, cultural resources and historical experience lay the basis for generational identities and projects. Thomas Jefferson observed that each generation was a new country. As individuals bid for self-expression, recognition, responsibility and rewards they will appeal to, or help to constitute, a generational character and project. On the other hand, each generation is bound to its predecessors and successors by the life course, and locked into a cycle of inter-generational dependence applying to the young and the old alike.

Generations are trapped in a one-way flow of time, posing a challenge to the market's rules of simultaneous exchange. However, the life course still offers scope for a cycle of delayed reciprocity, whereby the debt to parents is repaid when they are supported in old age. In pre-industrial societies kinship systems furnished a mechanism for meeting the needs of dependent young and old, while charity dealt with those without kin or in poverty. National 'cradle to grave' welfare regimes sought to end poverty and to use risk-pooling both within and between generations, to promote modern aspirations to equality, liberty and solidarity.

Pensions, by their very nature, are devices for conferring rights to future streams of income. It is interesting that capitalism is also such a device. The rights of the capitalist stem from ownership of means of production, conferred by inheritance, saving ('abstinence'), arbitrage, and entrepreneurialism, comprising both the extraction and the realisation of surplus. However, capital itself is the discounted present value of the future stream of earnings to be anticipated from an asset. There is thus a continual flattening of perspectives as the future value of an asset is, as the financial jargon has it, 'marked to market'.

The pensioner's rights have traditionally been built up through public or private service, or financial contributions. Usually they take many years, or even decades, to acquire. The power to confer a pension exercised by a sovereign or government, or by a private institution or wealthy individual, is a reflection and confirmation of their power and their recognition of service. Pensions can thus best be understood by a kind of longitudinal political economy that roots them in today's social arrangements, while understanding that the final shape of the rights that have been granted – whether it be by the sovereign to the subject, the government to the citizen, the employer to the worker, the master to the servant, the financial supplier to the customer or the husband to the wife – will only be known when the last payment is made due under the pension agreement.

In an essay that anticipated some later debates on the 'ageing society' Bryan Turner saw pensioners and the elderly as stigmatised by their lack of function and their economic reliance on today's worker (Turner, 1989). Turner was later to argue that rights can be seen as a device for meeting human frailty, and pensions seem to qualify under this rubric (Turner, 1993). But the construction of rights to pensions has been about much more than the duty of care to the frail elderly. It is about the opportunity to enjoy life after retirement, to have more free time and to be able to command a modicum of respect from friends and relations. Those who are frail have a claim on the public that is sometimes achieved at the cost of a dependent, supplicant status. The right to a pension in retirement has been seen precisely as a far preferable alternative to being in receipt of poor relief.

In the UK and USA there was widespread pensioner poverty in the 1960s, a poverty that could prompt guilt, pity or contempt, or a mixture of these. The improvement in the relative position of many pensioners in recent decades changed attitudes towards the growing number of more affluent and assertive retirees. With more children than pensioners in poverty the plight of the elderly receded and they could even be represented as an excessively privileged group, notwithstanding the persistence of poverty among elderly women.

Turner believed that the stigmatisation of the aged stemmed from the fact that they were simply recipients within the welfare schema. However, Sarah Irwin challenged this view by pointing to opinion poll evidence that the aged were seen as deserving recipients of public funds, in contrast to the unemployed and 'welfare scroungers' (Irwin, 1996). She argued that intergenerational dependence could generate solidarity rather than conflict. However, the corrosive effect of market-based perceptions can indeed erode a sense of reciprocal obligation between young and old. Modernity itself requires the young to throw off the tutelage of the old. It nourishes a cult of youth that associates ageing with negative traits (Gullette, 2004). Yet there remains an awareness that personal and social identity develops in and through essentially transgenerational relationships. Human beings are distinguished from other animals not only by neotony – lengthy childhood – but also by the greater relative importance to them of culture, hence the past and the future, their predecessors and successors.

Historical patterns

The first pensions were conferred as privileges rather than rights, the recipients being soldiers or public servants who had rendered conspicuous service. The English Poor Law allowed that aged paupers should be given some relief, but local gentry and municipalities had great discretion in awarding it. Each parish was responsible only for its own and relief could be refused, or administered only in the most humiliating way, to those deemed to be bad characters. Nevertheless, by the eighteenth century most parishes did pay modest old age pensions to those deemed past work, and it was not until the 1830s that residence in a poor house became a common condition of receiving this stipend. From the late seventeenth century the wealthy could purchase annuities for their spouses or favoured retainers. Advances in the calculation of life tables and risk enabled suppliers of life insurance like the Equitable Life Society, founded in 1762, to offer annuity products that enabled their clients to pool risk (Jones, 2004).

It is possible to distinguish between a 'Puritan' and a 'baroque' approach to pension provision. The Puritan approach was individualistic and stressed the rewards of thrift, prudence and hard work. Not a few of today's large pension providers, whether in London, Edinburgh, Boston or New York, stress their roots in Protestant self-help. The baroque tradition reflected the claim of good monarchs to relieve the problems of deserving subjects. The Elizabethan Poor Law had elements of both approaches. In France there were several proposals in the last years of the Ancien Régime to develop a universal system of old age pensions. Condorcet argued that risk-pooling on a national scale would enable the scourge of old age poverty to be banished. In April 1794 the Revolutionary National Convention enacted a decree to this effect, also setting up old people's homes in every department, with a special day set aside every year to honour aged citizens and to invite them to impart to the young a hatred for tyranny (Blackburn, 2002). But the overthrow of the Jacobin republic doomed this attempt and it was left to Bismarck, the German Chancellor, to introduce the first national old age pension in 1889. He believed that the legitimacy of the monarchy, challenged in different ways by the Social Democrats and the Catholic Church, would be strengthened by the monarch's ability to raise the aged out of poverty, and prevent them from becoming a burden on their relatives. In Britain social reformers and trade unionists pressed for a similar programme, leading, in 1908, to Lloyd George's Old Age Pension Act. These pension systems embodied a weak notion of pension rights – weak because the pensions were not that generous and were conditional on means testing to prove poverty.

Increases in longevity, industrialisation and urbanisation, and the rising numbers of the population without a claim on small property, helped to encourage the idea that the public authorities should furnish an element of social insurance to risks like old age and disability. There were campaigns for old age pensions, and governments saw pension provision as a way of boosting their legitimacy and weakening opponents. The pension systems not only alleviated poverty but also tended to confirm patriarchy and the social hierarchy – there was an echo of the baroque here, which could be seen in differential contribution/pay-out conditions and in special regimes for the military and key civil servants. Esping-Andersen (1990) sees a legacy from absolutist monarchy in such arrangements.

The pressure for universal provision developed slowly and in the meantime many of the aged worked till they dropped, or congratulated themselves on the fact that they had a paternalist employer, or a profession, or just enough property (a farm or small business) to keep them going in old age and to ensure the help of their heirs. In the United States it was not until the Social Security Act of 1935 that a national retirement pension scheme was introduced and not until 1950 that it became truly universal in scope. Puritan resistance to a public pension was greatly weakened when the Great Crash of the 1930s wiped out the savings of millions of hard-working Americans. Nevertheless, President Roosevelt insisted that, in order to safeguard the programme from future attacks, it should be financed by specific contributions rather than from general taxation. Thus it was the contribution record that established the right to the pension, not the mere fact of being a citizen or resident of the United States. By 1950 nearly all US citizens would be covered, since all employees had a payroll tax deducted from their wages – their spouses and dependants were covered too. Indeed, the Social Security card and number itself became the most often used badge of civic identity.

The construction of the first public universal pension systems and the wider process of the 'invention of retirement' created a new status but were themselves products of a type of class struggle. Trade unions and social democrats accused employers and governments of either working older employees to death or throwing them on the scrap heap. While willing to accept company schemes, they still usually insisted that governments alone had the scope to establish universal measures of social insurance. The political leaders who sponsored the first public old age pensions – Bismarck, Lloyd George, Franklin Roosevelt – were bidding for support at times of great social questioning and unrest. They saw themselves as heading off class conflict and showing how a more enlightened policy could boost the authority of the established order. President Truman was responding to a showdown between unions and employers when he approved the vital Social Security amendments in 1950.

Many of those who pressed for the introduction of old age pensions saw them as a way of rescuing the aged from poverty – but also of extending free time. In the UK in 1931 over a half of workers over 65 were in work; by 1961 this had dropped to a quarter and by 1981 to only one in ten. In his influential analysis of welfare regimes, Gosta Esping-Andersen (1990) describes pensions as a powerful instrument for the incremental 'decommodification' of life and labour in a capitalist society. Precisely because public pensions have been a mechanism of decommodification they have also become the target of 'reforms' that might revise or cancel the gains and concessions they embody. The same is true of pension rights conceded by public or private employers who can try to revoke agreements made decades ago. As argued above, it is only across considerable stretches of time that it becomes clear who has gained from a protracted tug-of-war. It is also necessary to grasp the operational logic of rather complex rules and structures in a context of scarce fiscal resources. Pension provision requires such huge resources – great chunks of GDP – that its ability to promote 'social integration' can place great strain on 'system integration' if appropriate fiscal means are not found (Lockwood, 1996: 535).

The logic of public provision

Universal public pension systems in the industrialised countries stem from the period immediately following the Second World War, with its heightened social expectations, and the immediately following period of the post-war boom and Cold War. The tremendous boost that war gave to the taxing capacity of the state played a key role in showing that it was possible to pay for something as expensive as a universal retirement system.

As the new pension systems were established or extended, the contribution requirement was only loosely applied. Older male workers were usually credited with contributions that they had not made, or that they had made to a system that had been destroyed by hyper-inflation and economic collapse. This 'blanketing in' was possible because these systems all make great use of the pay-as-you-go financing system. Over time benefits were increased, contributions were raised and the contribution record came to determine the precise entitlement. Wives derived rights to a pension according to their own or their husband's contribution record, conditions that left many older women with a weaker entitlement. The 'pay-as-you-go' system of pension finance enabled fairly good pensions to be paid out quite quickly and was generally adopted. The stream of income to the system was used to pay current pensions, with any surplus going to a trust fund, which was invested not in the stock market but in low-interest public bonds.

The pay-as-you-go system can only be used by a public authority, since only the government can count on revenue from future generations to discharge the entitlements of today's workers – whose contributions pay current pensioners. This system, as Paul Samuelson (1958) pointed out in a classic article, only balances its books by counting on a draft from the unborn. Commercial organisations cannot do this and are obliged to prefund, namely to use contributions to set up a fund that will eventually be able to pay a pension. The language of pension rights applies in somewhat different ways to public pension schemes and personal pension plans, and, since both are linked to contributions in some way, neither is an unqualified 'right'. It is true that public pensions go to everyone who has had a job or been married. But women's coverage is weaker, if they didn't marry, or their husband failed to make contributions, or their formal employment was limited or broken. Above all, women's unpaid labour in the home was given no direct recognition by these contribution systems, but was weakly reflected in spousal rights. Likewise, members of immigrant communities often do not have the prescribed length of contribution record – say 39 years for a full pension. There are currently proposals in several European countries to introduce 'citizens' pensions' paid regardless of contribution, but these require naturalisation, or are graded according to length of residence.

From the mid-1970s welfare regimes came under strong pressure to cut the value of pension benefits and to extend commercial coverage and subsidies. The parties of the left failed to consolidate and extend welfare gains, or to come up with effective answers to the 'stagflation' that brought an end to the post-war boom in the 1970s. Trade unions were greatly weakened by these developments and by a large expansion of the available labour force, as the baby-boom generation came of age, as women entered the workforce in larger numbers and as jobs were outsourced to newly industrialising lands.

Nevertheless, public pension regimes in most countries other than the UK proved quite resilient. The public French, German and Italian pension systems have delivered, and to some extent still deliver, a more generous pension than do those of the USA or the UK. The US Social Security system delivers a better pension than the UK's basic state pension (BSP) and has so far withstood successive attempts to weaken it under Presidents Reagan, Clinton and George W. Bush. These pension systems – the US one included – are based on the principle that all those who contribute receive a benefit, as of right. In Britain too everyone who has the appropriate contribution record receives the BSP, but a means test limits the right to the more generous Pension Credit.

Private pensions and 'implicit privatisation'

In countries with a strong stock market – Britain, the USA, Switzerland and the Netherlands – the leading finance houses continued to offer pension products, such as annuities, to the better off. They successfully argued for valuable tax breaks for private saving. The result was what Jasper Hacker (2002) has called the 'divided welfare state', in which both public and private contribution entitlements create 'path dependence', or a vested interest in the scheme's continuance.

The 'defined contribution' pension scheme or product has the logic of a commercial transaction. Those who contribute to a personal plan have the right to be fairly and honestly treated but no specific pension promise is being made. In this type of plan or scheme – they include the 401(k) plans in the USA and the 'Stakeholder' plans in the UK – market risk is borne entirely by the contributor. If the market slides then the pension will follow it. Governments in a growing list of countries now give tax relief to such schemes and employers have increasingly switched to offering them over the past two decades.

On the other hand, there are still many so-called 'defined benefit' occupational pension schemes – though many are now closed to new members – which appear to offer something quite close to the specific entitlement of a public pension. In the case of schemes for public sector workers the parallel is even closer, since it is the state that stands to guarantee the promise. When a private company sponsors a defined benefit scheme it is pledging its own resources to fulfilling the promise – though, as we will see, this is a promise that companies may vow never to repeat, and may try to wriggle out of.

Contrary to what is sometimes claimed, governments find it difficult, at least in the short run, openly to renege on pension promises. However, they can sometimes get away with apparently small changes to the rules – for example, indexing future pensions to prices, not earnings – and over a long period this can greatly diminish the value of the promise. This is what Margaret Thatcher did in 1980 and in consequence the basic UK state pension slipped from being 20 per cent of average earnings in 1980 to being 15 per cent of average earnings in 2003. But few pension 'reformers' have been as effective as Margaret Thatcher. Such varied political figures as Ronald Reagan, Alain Juppé, the French centre-right premier, Silvio Berlusconi in Italy in the 1990s and Helmut Kohl in Germany were all forced to back down because of broad hostility to their attempts to make deep cuts in public pension entitlements. Moreover, even in Britain, from about 2000 onwards, the government has been under increasing pressure from the large number of older voters to raise the pension in line with earnings and to come up with sundry pension supplements.

The pressure to reduce public provision has not abated and the first decade of the twenty-first century witnessed new attempts to cut back public provision in the USA, Europe and Japan. It was argued that the public systems were far too generous, embodying promises that – with population ageing – would ruin the national accounts if not drastically curtailed. It was also claimed that they inhibit private saving (the evidence does not bear this out) or that payroll taxes raise the cost of labour and hence increase unemployment (there is a *prima facie* case here). The logic of this type of reform represents either explicit or – more often – 'implicit' privatisation (Pierson, 1997). The latter downgrades public coverage with the effect of obliging those affected to resort to commercial fund managers if they wish to avoid poverty. Finance houses in search of more custom and employers anxious to shed pension commitments help to constitute a powerful lobby group in favour of pension reform no matter how reluctant voters are to endorse the approach.

Governments find the attempt to cancel pension entitlements a delicate and explosive undertaking. The past decade has seen huge public battles over these issues in the core states of the European Union. However, governments can simply close public sector schemes to new entrants and in that way curtail the growth of new entitlements.

Corporate managers offered 'defined benefit' pensions as a method of labour retention, and as a seemingly cheap concession, at a time when employment was tight. The future cost of these schemes did not, until quite recently, even figure in the annual accounts. But with maturation of the schemes, liabilities mount. The trustees of the scheme are meant to build up a fund that will pay a pension based on final salary and the number of years spent in the scheme. When stock markets were buoyant British and US companies were allowed to take quite protracted 'contribution holidays', only to be forced to make extra contributions when the stock market shrank and inflation subsided. If there is a shortfall in the pension fund it is the sponsoring corporation that is obliged to make it up. In 2004, US companies had pension deficits of over $300 billion and UK corporations had pension deficits of £85 billion. The payments required to mend these deficits reduce the resources available for investment. Sometimes workers would be sacked en masse in order to save the pension fund. In other cases elaborate restructuring – involving receivership, spin-offs, mergers or takeovers – enabled the pension fund to be deprived of the sponsor's assets. Public outcries against defaulting companies led to the setting up of insurance agencies, the Pension Benefits Guaranty Corporation (PBGC) in the USA and the Pension Protection Fund (PPF) in the UK. If the sponsor goes bust then supposedly the quango-like insurance body will guarantee some scaled-down benefit. However, companies that are in difficulties often skip their contributions and can inveigle their employees to sacrifice their pension rights in order to keep their jobs. The PBGC, which had a deficit of $23 billion in 2004, has often condoned the devaluation of entitlements as well as the non-payment of contributions by sponsoring corporations. The British PPF has very modest resources and, in the event of a large company going bust, could not rescue its pension scheme (Blackburn, 2004b).

The public systems have generally survived for more than half a century, while famous finance houses (Equitable Life) and famous corporations (Enron) have collapsed, or simply languish like so many once-powerful concerns – a half of the blue chips of the US or UK stock markets in the 1970s are now gone or mere shadows of their former selves. Public systems are not as exposed to market squalls and consumer fads. They gain because we know a government will be there in fifty years' time. Not only can they count on future taxes, they are also cheap to administer, the contributions being automatically deducted as a part of the payroll in most cases. By contrast, commercial suppliers have to market their wares and customise their collection and delivery. Because pension plans are a long-term commitment it makes sense for suppliers to invest huge resources in signing up customers who will pay over a stream of contributions for decades to come. The resulting intense competition is very expensive; salaries in the financial sector are also high. Another factor leading to exorbitant fees is the fact that pension plans are complex and providers are much better informed concerning their workings than their customers. It is common for fees and charges to amount to between 1.5 and 2.0 per cent of the fund each year; at this rate the pension 'pot' suffers a reduction in yield of 30–40 per cent over thirty or forty years (Blackburn, 2002; Pensions Commission, 2004).

From the standpoint of the individual customer the impact of high charges is somewhat softened by tax relief. In the UK tax relief on pension contributions costs the Treasury about £13 billion a year, the equivalent 'tax spend' in the USA being $100 billion. The lion's share of this tax relief goes to wealthier savers, with the richest tenth receiving over a half of all tax relief in the UK. In the USA and the UK about a half of all adults lack any significant private pension entitlement (Hughes and Sinfield, 2004).

Tax-favoured private and occupational pension funding has led to the growing importance of pension funds on the stock exchanges and in the boardrooms. This has led to a species of 'grey capitalism' in which the influence of pension money is wielded not by policy-holders but by corporate-nominated trustees and by the fund managers of the leading bankers and brokers. This regime is marked by an accountability deficit, by over-mighty chief executive officers and by scandal (Useem, 1995; Blackburn, 2002; Prins, 2004). Just occasionally the managers of public sector worker funds, such as the California Public Employee Retirement System (CalPERS), the largest pension fund in the world, do consult with their members and throw their weight behind better corporate governance or socially responsible investment (SRI).

The 'generational contract' versus 'generational accounting'?

Philosophically the publicly sponsored pay-as-you-go systems have been claimed to embody a contract between the generations. Each generation makes a contribution and each receives a benefit. Where there is economic growth pensions can grow with national prosperity as long as there is a broad balance between age cohorts. A problem arises when generational cohorts are of very unequal size, because of increased longevity and/or 'baby booms', followed by declining fertility. Rapid growth of productivity can absorb the strain, but if growth slows generational imbalance will make for awkward choices. There are options: (a) members of the smaller cohort have to pay much more than did members of its larger predecessor in order to cover the latter's pensions; (b) the pension received by the members of the larger cohort is scaled back so that contribution rates don't have to rise; (c) contribution rates are raised, and pensions are cut, until a fit is found based on shared sacrifice; or (d) resources are found elsewhere in the system so that the shared burden is somewhat reduced.

These are not easy choices to make, yet they are unavoidable. There are many in the USA and Europe today whose past contributions entitle them to pensions they may not receive. As noted above, there has been great opposition to those politicians who try to downsize public pensions and encourage people to make their own arrangements instead. But though wholesale reform is often rejected, entitlements are nevertheless often gradually and sneakily whittled down, with the real reductions not coming into force for a few decades. Some opponents of pension privatisation claim that there is really no problem. But in most parts of the developed and developing world the demographic shock of ageing is large enough to be a major problem unless new sources of revenue are brought into play.

The Puritan/baroque contrast now yields to a conflict between 'generational solidarity' and so-called 'generational accounting'. The generational solidarity approach, in its most radical form, insists that the qualitative bond between parents and children makes any precise calculation of who gains and who loses unseemly and inappropriate. Supporters of loading all pension needs on to the pay-as-you-go systems incline to this approach and regard talk of a crisis of the 'ageing society' as needless alarmism. A very different assumption is made by the partisans of the generational accounting approach, which emerged among economists in the USA in the 1980s and 1990s (Kotlikoff and Burns, 2004). Just as the Puritan approach stressed individual self-reliance, so advocates of generational accounting argue that each generation should pay its own way, relying on no help from parents or children. Risk-pooling within a generation is OK, but not between generations. The supporters of generational accounting argue that if modern states only came clean with their implicit pension debt – that is, the present value of their future pension liabilities, minus the present value of future payroll taxes – they would find that they are all staring bankruptcy in the face. They regard the attempt to impose this burden on today's children and those not even born as the height of injustice; to do so will halve the incomes of rising generations and cause untold social strife.

The methodology of generational accounting is very questionable. The choice of discount rates with which to establish a 'present value' for liabilities and future revenue is difficult and arbitrary. There may be deficits but we don't really know how big they are going to be because we don't know what future wage growth, interest rates or inflation will be and differences of a single percentage point, or less, can make a huge difference to the final number. In isolating every generation, enthusiasts of generational accounting and privatisers (an overlapping but not identical category), like to argue that today's workers, paying their payroll tax (social security contribution), are making a bad investment since they are not likely to get a good rate of return. But if they considered their payroll tax as a way of paying the pensions of their parents and those Peter Laslett calls their 'predecessors at large', then there would be no reason to expect a rate of return (Laslett, 1996; Baker and Weisbrot, 2000).

The reasoning of the partisans of generational solidarity is to be preferred to that of the supporters of generational accounting, but is flawed none the less. Each generation has a right and duty to revise the social arrangements it finds in place. While they have obligations to their parents' generation, these are not limitless. Talk of a literal generational compact would be wrong, since the newborn find many choices already made on their behalf. The debate on John Rawls's philosophy of justice provoked Brian Barry to bring out the inter-generational dimension this should acquire. He writes: 'the key here is a willingness to claim and be claimed upon in virtue of a given principle. Justice must be fair from both sides. . . . The point here is that we should think not of a choice made by a particular generation at a single point in time but of a collaboration over many generations in a common scheme of justice' (Barry, 1989).

I think that such conclusions invite us to come up with formulas for the equal sharing of the burdens of an ageing society – and, given the probability that these might be considerable, to find appropriate fiscal innovations to meet them. The fair sharing of burdens requires that overall pension provision should be adjusted so that the ratio of pensioner incomes to average incomes is held broadly constant (Myles, 2002). At the present time in Europe and North America the overall income of the average pensioner is a little over 70 per cent of average income. These averages do not, of course, tell us about inequality between pensioners, or in society at large. But they do indicate a generational ratio, with the retired having lesser outgoings than those with the responsibility of growing families. To maintain something like this overall ratio, while improving intra-generational distribution, could be seen as a scheme of inter-generational justice. To do so would require a raising of future contribution rates but also, perhaps, a greater effort to pre-fund tomorrow's pensions by raising savings rates and obliging employers to contribute more effectively – the employers' contribution has plummeted with the switch from 'defined benefit' to 'defined contribution' schemes.

The past three decades have seen a sharp rise in inequality in most of the leading capitalist states, especially in the UK and USA. It is quite possible to address the issue of generational equity and also tackle the issue of a more equal distribution within pensioner incomes and average incomes. Traditionally all public pension schemes have involved an element of redistribution from rich to poor, even if many still allowed those who had contributed more to receive a somewhat higher entitlement. Commercial pre-funded schemes obviously make no attempt at such redistribution, though they do incorporate some risk-pooling. When some proponents of 'generational solidarity' claim that all pre-funding is inimical to redistribution they are wrong. For example, restoration of the employers' contribution could help to build a pension reserve pledged to supplying secondary pensions to all. The famous baby-boomers also still have some time to build up a reserve so that all the costs of their future pensions will not have to be met from payroll taxes alone. Should the baby-boomers bear some of the consequences for having fewer children? It would be unfair to see the plunging birth rate in the 1970s as simply a preference for consumption over child-rearing, since it also reflected the squeeze on earners and women's greater participation in the labour force. However, the baby-boomers have great political clout and they would be wise to anticipate the costs of ageing.

The costs of the ageing society

Ageing will mean that a quarter of the population will be over 65 in all the large European Union states within 25 years and some way should be found of ensuring that their retirement income gives them an appropriate share of gross domestic product (GDP) – if their incomes are to be 70 per cent of average income then this would amount to something in the range of 13–16 per cent of GDP. The onset of ageing is likely to be somewhat slower in the USA than in Europe because the US birth rate is higher, immigration is higher and life expectancy among the black and Hispanic minorities is still considerably below that of the white population. Nevertheless, the number of those aged 65 or over is set to rise from 36 million in 2003 to 70 million in 2032, or from 12 to 20 per cent of the total population. The trustees of the social security system warn that it will be unable to pay promised pensions by 2042 and that it faces a cumulative deficit of $3.5 trillion by the latter part of the century. The Medicare programme, which supplies medical care to the elderly, faces a projected deficit that is about three times as large.

The ageing of the population is a feature of both developed and developing countries. The UN mid-range projection tells us that the over-60s, who comprised 30.7 persons per 100 adults of working age in 1998 in the developed countries, will comprise 62.3 persons per 100 adults of working age in those countries in 2050. The great success story of the past quarter-century has been the dynamic growth of the Chinese economy, but this has been based in part on a reduction in the birth rate, which will lead to a rapid ageing of the population in coming decades. In Asia, including China and India, the anticipated proportion of those over 60 rises from 14.1 per 100 adults in 1998 to 40.8 by 2050 (UN Population Division, 2000).

The proportion of the British population that is over 65 is set to rise from 15 per cent today to 24 per cent by 2031. The UK Pensions Commission has warned that there will be a pension shortfall of 4–5 per cent of GDP by 2050. Britain has a very mean state pension, so, at current levels of entitlement, it will absorb little future national income – only about 4.4 per cent of GDP by 2050. Private provision looks unlikely to supply more than about 4 per cent of GDP, and a raising of the effective age at which workers retire could add, at most, two percentage points. The Pensions Commission has estimated that to maintain pensioners' current relative income in 2050 would require 13.9 per cent of GDP, assuming that women work as long as men, an ambitious goal (Pensions Commission, 2004). If one is optimistic about raising the number of 60–70-year-olds in work then they might earn as much as 2 per cent of GDP to add to their other entitlements. But there is still a gap of over 4 per cent of GDP – a very large sum – between what they are likely to receive and what they need if their relative position is not to decline sharply. The consequent pensioner poverty will also be exacerbated by the fact that pension entitlements and savings will be very unequally distributed among those of pensionable age. Many – the majority – will suffer a drastic drop in living standards unless something is done (about which more below).

Of course, the foregoing projections make assumptions about continued ageing of the population that reflect current trends. Europe's well-established ageing trend is rooted in low fertility as much as increased life expectancy. In both old and new member states women are having fewer than two children each. In Italy, Poland, Germany and Spain average life-time fertility in 2000 was only 1.2 to 1.3 children per woman. In Scandinavia and France, where governments have made an effort to frame child-friendly policies, it was a little above 1.7 (UN Population Studies, 2002; Therborn, 2005). While some of this decline represents women's desire to escape from the burden of multiple child-rearing, most women would still like to have at least two children. If good child care was widely available and cheap, and if there was generous maternity and paternity leave, it could encourage women to have more children. Even with child-friendly policies, it will remain the case that having children is expensive and that many women will wish to delay childbirth, both considerations tending to smaller families.

It is a delusion to suppose that there are 'free lunch' solutions to the problems of the ageing society. Compulsory retirement should end and employers' prejudices against older employees should be challenged. But the extra time at work in later life is likely simply to offset later entry to the workforce and increasing numbers of career breaks, occasioned by retraining and parenthood, while education and training to ensure a productive 'third age' will require new social investments (Laslett, 1996).

Existing population projections already assume the maintenance of immigration at current rates. Further increasing the numbers of immigrants is desirable in itself, helping to foster a more multicultural society and enshrining a right to freedom of movement that we all cherish. But it will not have much impact on the ageing trend, since immigrant populations swiftly adopt the demographic profile of the host populations, with greater longevity and lower fertility, meaning ever larger numbers are required. So to maintain Europe's 1995 age profile in 2050 would mean a rise in population to more than a billion (UN Population Division, 2001). Furthermore, the source countries will not wish to lose all their expensively educated and trained workforce, especially as most of these countries have ageing populations themselves, as we have seen. At the very least, much greater provision should be made for the remittance of immigrant earnings to their countries of origin, which have borne the costs of their upbringing and education.

Policy implications

Europe will have to pay for proper old age and health protection – and must do this at the same time as paying for child-friendly policies and more expenditure on education and research. The Anglo-American path of individualisation and commercialisation generates heavy costs of its own and leads to 2–3 per cent of GDP being absorbed by intense marketing and the exorbitant salaries of the financial sector. There is a need to find other ways to finance needed social programmes. Following earlier setbacks to the 'reform' project, which saw defeats for Juppé, Berlusconi and Kohl, more limited measures were enacted by Dini in Italy, Raffarin in Italy and Schroeder in Germany. These measures slashed entitlements that were located decades in the future while preserving those of workers over 40. So these cutbacks will hit those who retire in 2025 and after. Often those who will lose out continue to pay heavily into a social insurance system that will give them pensions that will replace less than a half of their previous salary instead of the 70 per cent or more that current retirees in much of Europe still receive (Math, 2004). Because they leave large entitlements in place for a decade or two further instalments of reform are still being negotiated.

We have seen that in the UK likely pension provision from all sources in 2050 will still fall short by 4 per cent of GDP of what would be needed simply to maintain pensioner incomes at about 70 per cent of average incomes. The cumulative impact of pension reform over several decades will be to open up a similar gap in European provision, with the state pension still a little more generous than in the UK but with private coverage in most countries (apart from the Netherlands) being more modest. Early indications from the new member states of the EU who have adopted commercial fund management suggests that there will be disappointments here too. In Hungary and Poland heavy charges prevented any accumulation in the first three years of the new pension funds (Feltz, 2004). It is also difficult to ensure universal coverage for private-funded pensions where there are wide disparities in wage and salary levels. Compulsory contributions are usually not appropriate for those in debt because they will be paying much greater interest on the debt than they earn on their savings. In the UK overall indebtedness is now running at 130 per cent of disposable income.

Pension rights are rooted in the arrangements to be found in specific territories, whether nation states or federations like the European Union. Notwithstanding globalisation, states still furnish the essential framework for trade, capital flows, taxation and welfare (Wood, 2003). Corporations that need access to specific resources and markets – especially important ones such as the USA, the EU, Japan or China – can be obliged to pay for this, or to conform to rules established by the relevant authority. But governments have let large corporations off lightly, as they contribute less and less, whether in taxes or contributions, to employee welfare.

The best way to restore faith in the future and to mend pension deficits is to find ways of obliging all corporations to contribute but in a manner that does not tie the employee to the fluctuating fortunes of their own particular employer or subtract from the resources they need for investment. Disproportions between age cohorts, whether caused by baby booms or rising longevity, do pose a problem, as we have seen. Existing pay-as-you-go pension regimes certainly still have a vital role to play in pension provision, because they are highly cost-effective and because they have considerable public understanding and acceptance. But placing the whole burden on payroll taxes is unwise and potentially undermines other aspects of a well-functioning economic order.

For the past two decades the core states of the EU have unsuccessfully grappled with abnormally high unemployment. The deliberately deflationary policies adopted at Maastricht in 1992 and by the European Central Bank are certainly to blame for this. But pay-as-you-go systems have also weakened demand and raised labour costs. Payroll taxes are generally not 'progressive'. They fall heavily on workers earning only average or low salaries. Laying a 'tax wedge' of 40 per cent on average incomes, they consequently weaken demand and discourage high rates of employment. With officially recognised unemployment running at 10 per cent, and many of the unemployed not even getting on the register, certain categories of the population – above all the under-25s and the over-50s – have been condemned to poverty and idleness. Not surprisingly, the demagogues of the far right have often flourished in these conditions.

If we compare the USA and UK with mainland Europe we find that the different socio-economic regimes generate different types of unemployment. The company-specific formula of corporate welfare provision that flourishes in the Anglo-Saxon countries has destroyed good jobs in manufacturing and exposed employees to 'sponsor risk' (if their employer goes bankrupt they suffer benefit loss too). Europe's high 'payroll taxes' have been consistent with manufacturing strength and the protection of good jobs. But overall they weaken demand and deter the creation of formal jobs in the service sector, helping to explain why employment rates among those aged 18–65 are ten to fifteen percentage points lower than in the USA or UK (Directorate General of the EU, 2002). In practice unemployment has been concentrated among younger workers and older workers, but eventually almost everyone falls into these categories and they find their contribution record impaired. Europe faces a severe ageing shock and is not prepared for it. The problem is no longer that the pension burden will be too heavy and has instead become that there is likely to be a return to widespread old age poverty in a decade or two as pay-as-you-go systems buckle under the strain. What is needed is the establishment of social funds that could help to meet pension needs.

The share levy: a new way to finance future pensions?

It is now some time since governments dared to ask the owners of the large corporations to contribute more to the wider society, without which their own profits would be impossible. The most far-seeing attempt to think through the types of new finance that would be needed to guarantee generous social provision was the advocacy of 'wage-earner funds' in the 1970s and 1980s by Rudolf Meidner, chief economist of the main Swedish trade union federation (LO) and co-architect – with Gosta Rehn – of the Swedish welfare system.

Of all the EU states the one that has most persistently sought to ensure good benefits with low unemployment is Sweden. A distinguishing feature of the Rehn/Meidner model was that it embraced pre-funding for supplementary pensions on top of the basic state pension. Sweden enacted a funded supplementary state pension in 1959. It also incorporated a wage-bargaining round that helped to protect high employment levels. Corporate taxation also strove to be 'counter-cyclical'; that is, to moderate the impact of economic fluctuations and the trade cycle. Whereas Anglo-Saxon companies are encouraged to take 'contribution holidays' during upswings of the trade cycle, Swedish corporations were, and are, encouraged to stow operating profits in special tax-exempt reserves.

Anticipating the new social expenditures that would be entailed by an ageing and learning society, Meidner came to believe in the need to set up strategic social funds – 'wage-earner funds' – to be financed by a share levy. This did not work like traditional corporate taxation, which subtracts from cash flow and, potentially, investment. Instead Meidner's levy falls on wealthy shareholders, the value of whose holdings is diluted, not on the resources of the corporation as a productive concern. According to the original plan every company with more than 50 employees was obliged to issue new shares every year equivalent to 20 per cent of its profits. The newly issued shares – which could not be sold for several years – were to be given to a network of 'wage earner funds', representing trade unions and local authorities. The latter would hold the shares, and reinvest the income they yielded from dividends, in order to finance future social expenditure. As the wage earner funds grew they would be able to play an increasing part in directing policy in the corporations they owned (Meidner, 1978; Pontusson, 1994).

Meidner's visionary scheme was very attractive to many trade unionists and members of the Social Democratic Party but strongly opposed by the privately owned media, and by the '20 families' who dominated the country's large corporations. The family cartels quickly grasped that the levy would threaten their control. Attacks on the scheme claimed that it would aggrandise the trade unions leaders who would dominate the 'wage-earner funds'. It was also alleged that the scheme unfairly favoured employees in the private sector, since they were to be the first to receive shares from the levy. After a scare campaign the Social Democratic government eventually diluted the proposed share levy but set up social funds financed by a more modest profits-related tax. These came to own 7 per cent of the Swedish stock market but, to prevent them getting any larger, were wound up by the incoming Conservatives in 1992. The already accumulated assets were used to finance a string of scientific research institutes. So Meidner's plan has yet to be properly tried, though even in its dilute form it helped to propel Sweden to the forefront of the knowledge-based economy.

David Lockwood has pointed out that the fiscal regimes that prevail in modern capitalist states are often highly complex and that they create winners and losers in opaque ways that appear to cut across the lines of class conflict, as classically conceived. The majority of voters are cautious about proposals for higher taxes, even if these are supposedly progressive in character, fearing that they will in the end catch many on middling incomes and that the rich will know how to evade them. While there is at least a keen awareness of tax issues, there is much less understanding of how tax relief works. In the UK in 2002–3 net tax relief on pension savings cost the public purse £13 billion, or more than 1 per cent of GDP. While more than half the workforce gain something from this relief, 51 per cent of the total sum accrued to the top 10 per cent of earners and 67 per cent to the top 20 per cent (Hughes, 2004). Although the majority of adults now own some shares, especially via pension funds, there is still a very great concentration of share-holding wealth among the richest tenth and richest 1 per cent. Any proposal to tax shares, or dilute their value, would lead the wealthy to pose as the champions of a broad coalition. I have drawn attention to pension deficits, yet here too Lockwood's caveat would apply: 'Fiscal deficits are neither socially transparent nor class specific' (Lockwood, 1996: 545).

Yet the prospect of pension deficits has inspired huge social movements and has toppled governments in Europe over the past decade. These movements brought together members of several generations, with groups of workers often playing a key role. In the USA, the American Association of Retired Persons (AARP) has joined in defending the social security old age pension – but those aged between 30 and 55 have been just as hostile to privatisation. The 'grey vote' is a growing factor – 42 per cent of those who voted in the British general election of 2005 were aged 55 or over – but 'grey' parties have not appeared. Implicitly or explicitly these movements in defence of pension rights appeal to an ideal of the nation and its citizens as a sort of extended family that demands decent treatment of all those whose past effort and sacrifice have built and defended the national 'home' (to use a Swedish locution). These movements are thus civic, national and in a sense 'proletarian'. The proletarians in Ancient Rome were those who produced sons and daughters – it was their labours, in their widest sense, that reproduced the Republic. Certainly pensions will not survive the time when there are no longer any children and, as Samuelson forecast, the members of the last generation will die a lonely and comfortless death (Samuelson, 1958).

The movements to defend pension rights have had a purely defensive character. This has been a strength and a weakness. But generational solidarity is likely to be unsustainable – or to be worn down by disappointment – unless it finds a way to tax the greatest concentrations of wealth in present-day capitalist society, as Meidner proposed. It is noteworthy that citizens of today's capitalist democracies pay tax on the houses they live in but large-scale owners of shares pay nothing for the power this gives them. If existing taxes are required to cover all the escalating costs of the ageing society then this will compete with other claims on the public purse (education, health, child care) and it will raise tax rates in a way that is counterproductive, actually lowering the eventual yield.

I have elsewhere shown that in both the USA and the UK a Meidner-style share levy calculated at 10 per cent of profits would, over 26 years, raise a total fund worth $10 trillion in the USA and £1 trillion in the UK, and that in both cases such a fund could augment resources needed for pension provision by 2 per cent of GDP (Blackburn, 2004a, b).

With the coming retirement of the baby-boomers, the cost of pension and health care will grow steeply. Politicians fear the electoral consequences if they raise taxes just as much as they fear the backlash if they cut pension entitlements. Some might see the advantage of a share levy. But many will hesitate because it would target a supremely influential group – the capitalist class – and might presage the advent of a new type of collective ownership. A share levy remains a rather good match for looming pension deficits but as a forecaster one would have to be cautious and say that it will not be tried until all else has failed.

3 Developing an economic sociology of care and rights

Miriam Glucksmann

Care is high on the public and political agenda, not only in Western welfare states, but increasingly on a global scale with recognition of the care 'deficit', work/life balance and international chains of care (e.g. Ehrenreich and Hochschild, 2003) as shared international issues. Fundamental normative and practical questions are raised about the principles and provision of care, with implications for rights as well as for claims, including potential expansion of both the terrain of rights and the groups on whose behalf they are claimed.

Perhaps the simplest way to understand this emergent crisis is as a consequence of the disruption of earlier modes of looking after those unable to care for themselves. Multiple changes have impacted on ways of caring that were previously taken for granted or integrated with other activities, so disembedding them from their cultural, social and economic underpinnings. The shift in welfare states from a male breadwinner to a dual earner model, heightened emphasis on individual worth and dignity, the effects of urbanisation and economic development for traditional kin-based structures and responsibilities, life course alterations arising from increased longevity and time spent in education and retirement, are just some of the changes. At the same time as provoking new problems of care, this disordering also provides a stimulus to new ways of thinking about how care is conducted, acknowledging historical and cross-cultural variety, and the different groundings for rights implicit in differing modes of provision.

Such concerns are at the heart of this chapter, which explores the different kinds, bases and understandings of rights associated with different social organisations of care. The approach is informed by a number of core premises. First, groups conceived as dependent and in need of care are constructed socio-historically. There is nothing universal or fixed about care needs. On the contrary, they are emergent, changing, specific to time and place and immensely variable. Second, needs may be met by care provisioning systems that also differ considerably across cultures, nations and history, both in how they are organised and in the extent to which they are differentiated from other social relations. Third, varied systems of provisioning have their own correlative sets of 'rights'. Again these may take many forms:

informal or formal, prescribed by tradition and convention or by laws enforced through criminal justice systems. They may be understood as a 'private' matter between individuals and families or publicly recognised and articulated. This framework for care rights conceives of systems of care as overall processes that include provision as well as entitlement. An economic sociology perspective will be evident in the focus on exchange, reciprocity and obligation, the work and cost of care and the conditions shaping its demand, delivery and consumption. However, since socio-economic relations may be understood only in relation to the culture and history with which they are bound, elaboration of the argument draws on a wide disciplinary range of evidence and analysis.

A brief review of approaches to care, drawing out some its social particularities, precedes a discussion of issues raised in applying a rights perspective to this field, notably those of provision and correlative duties. The central parts of the chapter elaborate the argument that differing modes of care in different times and circumstances give rise to contrasting kinds of rights, a proposition that is then explored in greater detail and cross-culturally with respect to elder care.

Concepts and landscape of care

Care is both a slippery and a complex concept (Thomas, 1993; Leira and Saraceno, 2002), associated with a variety of meanings, activities and practices, as exemplified in the extensive literature resulting from feminist scholarship, welfare state research and public and social policy. Even the word has different connotations in different languages: the English 'care' combines the emotional feeling of 'caring about' with the activity of 'caring for' in the sense of 'looking after' or 'taking responsibility for', but this is not the case even for some other European languages (Ostner, 1999; Ewijk *et al.*, 2002).

Pioneering feminist work in the 1970s and 1980s drew attention to care as a form of female domestic labour, based on unquestioned naturalisation of caring as a feminine attribute and activity, undertaken often as a 'labour of love' within the family (Finch and Groves, 1983; Graham, 1991) or on a very low paid basis. Political demands were made for both its recognition and remuneration. The focus later shifted towards care receivers and the potential for patronising and oppressive care. Disability rights groups highlighted the power of professional carers, and relations of dependency that could divest recipients of dignity and control. While some have stressed the emotional character of care, others foreground it as a 'work' activity (Waerness, 1984; Ungerson, 1990; Thomas, 1993; Harrington Meyer, 2000). In recent work, scholars challenge any strong distinction between cared and cared for (Williams, 2001; Fink, 2004), since, through reciprocity and interdependence, we all experience the giving and receiving of care at one time or another. This recognition of the vulnerability of the human condition is complemented by a universalist paradigm proposed by some feminist moral and political philosophers to undermine the gendered connotations of care and replace it with care as a normative orientation. Rather than treating care as inherently female, thus reinforcing its devaluation and exclusion from public life and political concern, the alternative 'ethic of care' would establish a 'general habit of mind' (Tronto, 1994: 127) characterised by attentiveness to the needs of others, responsibility, competence and responsiveness. Pursuing this ethical turn, Sevenhuijsen (1998) critiques the individualism and self-sufficiency she sees in rights discourse and argues for notions of care to be brought centrally into citizenship, justice and morality.

Welfare state research echoes all these developments. Daly and Lewis (1999, 2000), for example, develop a three-dimensional conception of social care as labour involving costs, inhabiting a normative framework of responsibilities and obligations, which straddles public and private boundaries. Gender-inflected revisions of Esping-Andersen's (1990) regime typology (notably Lewis, 1992, 1999; Orloff, 1993, 1996; O'Connor, 1993; O'Connor *et al.*, 1999; Sainsbury, 1999; Boje and Leira, 2000; Daly, 2002) throw much light on the configurations of paid and unpaid care, and the respective responsibilities of family versus state and market in different welfare regimes and in varied conditions of welfare state restructuring. Focusing on the nation state or European Union level, they introduce the issue of citizenship to the debate and raise the question of rights to receive, and indeed give,[1] care as integral elements of a putative inclusive citizenship (e.g. Knijn and Kremer, 1997).

The approach to care/rights developed here is rooted in this broad literature. In particular, I would emphasise the significance of gender as a structuring principle in the organisation of care. Although challenged by the rights issue, gender has been so deeply implicated in care relations that it would be tedious to draw attention to it repeatedly. Even when unstated, gender is none the less central to the discussion. A second key point is that care, however it is arranged, involves labour and work.[2] This remains the case whether or not the work is recognised as such, paid, physical or emotional. Although care becomes more obviously visible as work when undertaken as paid employment outside informal and familial settings, the activity of caring always presupposes an allocation of labour, and hence economic resources, even if this is obscured by taken-for-granted gender divisions of labour.

Another social particularity of care, less evident from the literature but important for the discussion below, is that it is not usually differentiated out as a self-standing field but overlaps and intersects with the state, family, education and health systems, but in different ways in different countries. What is understood as distinctively 'care' activity varies considerably because of this even in European welfare states. For example, in Nordic countries where child care is increasingly defined as pedagogy, aimed at educational and personal development of the child, it is subsumed in the education system, with a requirement for professionally skilled staff. In the UK and Netherlands, however, the prime purpose of child care has been to enable mothers to enter waged work or to combine employment with family responsibilities. In this scenario there is less emphasis on child development and the training of nursery staff, and rather more on 'flexible' working time in the guise of 'family friendly' or work/life balance policies initiated by ministries of employment. Elder care, by contrast, differs in the extent to which it is separated from care of the sick or disabled. Where the overlap is especially strong, as in Sweden, it tends to be medicalised, and occupational statistics so aggregated that it becomes difficult to distinguish numerically between nurses and carers for the dependent elderly, while in the UK (with the exception of Scotland) a strict distinction remains between the social and health care needs of the elderly. In Italy, however, where migrant maids are often employed to undertake household tasks, including care of family members, it becomes problematic to distinguish elder care from domestic labour (Lyon, 2005). Appreciating such comparative variation has direct relevance for a discussion of rights. Moreover, the fact that care provision occurs within national systems that organise it in different ways inevitably shapes how claims and entitlements are articulated, to whom and on what scale. The potential for trans- or supranational rights would also assume a distinctive and problematic character.

Established or human rights: theory or practice

At first sight asserting that the frail, vulnerable or sick, dependent infants and children have the 'right' to care might seem uncontentious, an imperative ethically incumbent on any society with pretensions to be enlightened, civilised or humane, let alone those claiming to be democratic, progressive or inclusive. Strong moral and philosophical arguments may be mobilised in defence of the proposition that care be recognised as a human right. Indeed, a convincing case has been made (Turner, 1993) for 'the frailty theory' (ibid.: 508) in which the sociological analysis of human rights is grounded (ibid.: 489) in the very concepts of 'human frailty, especially the vulnerability of the body' and 'in a theory of moral sympathy' (ibid.). Existing human rights conventions do already contain broad principles. Article 3 of the Universal Charter of Human Rights states 'Everyone has the right to life, liberty and security of the person', echoed in Article 5(i) of the European Convention on Human Rights. Article 5 of the UN Declaration and Article 3 of the ECHR declare 'No one shall be subjected to torture or to inhuman or degrading treatment'. The 'degrading treatment' clause would be especially relevant in claiming rights for the elderly and disabled, while the catch-all 'right to life and security of the person' could be deployed in claiming rights to care for all in need of it.

However, while the claim for universal human rights to care may be theoretically or philosophically unproblematic, claiming such rights in practice is a completely different matter and far from straightforward. Claims for rights are predicated on the prior recognition of need. But in order for care to be articulated as a need in the first place presupposes that it has been differentiated from other dimensions of interpersonal relations and established as a specific concern and distinct practice. In reality this may often not be the case. Suppose, however, that it is. Then, for the right to care to be effective, rather than a wish or intention, it has to be provided. Otherwise the right has very little meaning. The right to receive care thus implies a correlative duty or obligation on the part of others to provide it. Someone or some institutional body must assume the responsibility of delivery. And as care provision rests on resources being allocated to it, the costs of labour, money and time have to be met. In any claim for rights the question of who assumes responsibility for, financially resources and undertakes the actual work of care has to be addressed. In this way, a right to care also implies a political economy of care, a point implicit in this chapter, if not fully elaborated.

The distinction between formal and substantive rights, or putative and established rights, is paramount in the case of care. There cannot be the right without the duty. Care, in common with education, welfare and other social rights, differs in kind from political and civil rights that safeguard the freedom to vote, free speech and freedom from religious persecution and discrimination. Guaranteeing a right to care requires active intervention. Moreover, as with other 'second generation' rights (Bobbio, 1995), establishing a right to care involves moving beyond the abstract individual, since protection is sought for people of different statuses whose rights are based on age, health and varying kinds of dependency or vulnerability.

That claims for care are historically emergent and culturally specific complicates the question of universal rights. Even though it could be conceivable nowadays to claim care as a universal right, the articulation of actual claims varies immensely, as I shall argue, between countries and cultural and social traditions, over time and space, and according to the basis of the need (infancy, frailty, mental impairment and so on). However, attention to cultural and historical difference is not an argument in favour of relativism. Understanding that care provision and its attendant rights are cross-culturally variable and often limited underscores that they are a historical achievement. A view of rights as emergent is entirely consistent with the proposition that care of those in need is incumbent on all societies with sufficient resources. Further, a concept of rights as emergent signals the possibility of their continuing expansion or ratcheting up. That physical disciplining of children is now denounced as abuse of children's rights is one example. Similarly, rights to comfort and longevity for the elderly are implied in the UK winter fuel allowance, which is premised on the notion that it is intolerable for people to die of hypothermia. Debates about health care rationing are more explicitly about rights to medical care. As wealth increases we may anticipate a ratcheting up and expanding political economy of rights, rather than minimum floors and safety nets.

If care giving and receiving are interdependent and formed in relation to each other, any rights approach involves recognising their fundamentally relational character. As the right to receive is predicated on a duty to provide, the care relation rests on there being a 'couplet' of receivers and givers. Care may be understood as interdependent in a second way, as highlighted by recent commentators (e.g. Williams, 2001). At differing points in the life course people may be either recipients or givers of care. All are cared for in infancy, some in old age, and many care for others during long periods of their lives. Given that dependency takes many forms and varies over time, it would be misleading to conceive either of mutually exclusive groups of givers and receivers, or of society as comprised of a class of always-dependents and always-carers. Turner's arguments about both frailty and sympathy are given added force by the relational and interdependent nature of care.

Many sociological perspectives qualify as candidates for thinking about rights to care. Building on the writings of Lockwood (1996) and Morris (2002), a Marshallian-derived conception of social rights of citizenship could be developed in terms of civic stratification. In citizen-based rights to care, citizenship would evidently be central. However, conditions of residence, nationality, migrant, marital and family status, level of income and wealth could all be used by national governments to rule in or out eligibility to entitlement to care, thereby creating access stratified according to citizenship criteria. A more hermeneutic approach to actors' understandings of rights, on the other hand, would help to unpack discourses of care rights and interpret frames and regimes of justification, throwing light on subjectivity in the care relation. If common-sense expectations about rights and entitlements are historically sedimented in particular national cultures and their respective welfare regimes, then a comparative interpretive framework would have much to offer. Alternatively, a Foucauldian inflected analysis could examine rights against a view of care as power/knowledge based around the emergence of expert systems. The very construal of groups 'in need of care' resonates with Foucault's (1967) analysis of the 'ship of fools'. The more that care recipients are conceived as dependants and professional carers as possessing knowledge as to their best interests, the more relevant a power/knowledge perspective with its focus on technologies of care and professional occupations. Finally, debates about social capital, individualisation, risk and 'bowling alone' (Giddens, 1998; Putnam, 2000; Beck, 2002) also provide potentially fruitful approaches to care rights, especially when placed against recent empirical evidence about the reshaping of personal communities and patterns of friendship (Pahl, 2000; Pahl and Spencer, 2004; Williams, 2004). All these raise important questions about historically changing communal and personal obligations and practices relating to care needs.

The approach outlined below is not intended as an exclusive approach. It could be deployed in combination with these or other sociological perspectives.

Modalities of care provision: relationality and exchange

The framework that I want to develop for exploring rights rests on prior acknowledgement of diversity – historical, cross-cultural and national – in systems of care or processes of entitlement and provision. Of the wide variety of systems, some are formalised and legal, while others are so rooted in traditional social relations that they are hardly recognised. Such diversity has obvious implications for rights to care since these will inevitably be shaped according to the provisioning system that is their context.

In many societies care activities are undertaken without being appreciated as such or formulated in terms of entitlement. But, even in contemporary Western democracies or welfare states, where rights to care are more likely to be explicitly articulated, care is also provided in large measure on the basis of taken-for-granted, usually gendered, familial obligation, or religious or charitable commitment. The historical construction of those deemed to be dependent or in need of care is thus a basic precondition even of the call for rights, let alone the establishment of citizen- or employee-based entitlements. Four broad groupings of dependants are the most widely 'recognised' today: children, the elderly, the sick and the physically or mentally disabled, each with its own history of emergence, construction and specificity in different societies. Anthropological evidence suggests that in many subsistence societies there are no disabled, and few in ill-health, as babies with deformities are left to die, and serious illness or impairment in adults leads rapidly to death. In Europe it was only in the seventeenth and eighteenth centuries that the child was created and childhood conceived as a status and life-phase distinct from adulthood (Aries, 1979). Similarly, Foucault documented the creation of insanity and its confinement.

Such considerations underscore the importance of a cross-cultural and historical approach towards care and care/rights. Appreciating variability in why, when, how and under what circumstances the 'right to care' is likely to emerge as a demand, or not emerge, is fundamental to a sociological approach. To conceive of rights as attaching only to citizens and states would impose an arbitrary and quite unnecessary restriction of the field. Consequently, I adopt a broad comparative perspective towards care/rights in general and with respect to the elderly. The prime reason for so doing is to avoid erecting an artificial boundary around the analysis that would exclude non-legally based claims and duties from the terrain of 'rights'. At the same time, such a perspective implicitly endorses the critique (e.g. Nussbaum, 2000; and elaborated in other contributions to this volume) that human rights discourse reflects Western philosophical conceptions of the abstract individual. On the other hand, understanding that rights are linked to the circumstances in which they emerge does not imply a relativistic position that would judge them all as equally good or bad.

In order to attract 'rights' in the first place, then, care has to be differentiated from other social relations, thereby creating the potential need. Additionally, as suggested earlier, care inherently involves at least two parties, receivers and givers, connected by relations of interdependency in a process of care. A third general feature of systems of care provision and rights is that many are characterised by relations of exchange, resulting in distinct economies of care. Exchanges may be equal or unequal, and direct or indirect. They may occur simultaneously or be deferred, be serial or intergenerational, and may be structured in various ways by gender and age and other implicit or explicit criteria. Diverse modes of care provision are likely, moreover, to be associated with different kinds and qualities of relationship between care givers and receivers, giving rise to particular understandings on the part of recipients as to their 'rights'.

Premised on a conception of care as a differentiated and relational activity involving differing kinds of exchange and expectation, it becomes possible to distinguish schematically between distinct modes or systems of care provision. In pre-industrial, traditional or kin-based societies, reciprocal rights, obligations and duties between different generations within a family are to the fore, while rights in welfare states revolve around 'entitlement' (whether universal, means tested or selective). Quite other considerations arise when care services are directly purchased from care providers (individuals or the market) by or on behalf of individuals in need of care. Each of these modes entails a distinctive set of exchange relations between receivers and givers and institutional providers: mediated by taxation and social insurance in welfare systems; social reciprocity of labour when kin undertake caring; and monetary exchange in the case of the market or private purchase. To these a fourth care-system could be added, based on unpaid labour, voluntary finance, or charitable activity. Here relationships more closely resemble those of a 'gift economy' outlined by Cheal (1988) and implied in Titmuss's (1970) study of blood donorship than those of exchange.

In the real world, of course, different systems of provision operate at the same time. The increasing tendency of European welfare states to rely on the voluntary sector to provide social care, while simultaneously encouraging delivery by the market, produces an ever more hybrid and variegated 'mixed economy' of care, where private and public, market and state, paid and unpaid, formal and informal become inextricably intertwined. Different countries are characterised by differing combinations of these basic modes of delivery provided formally by the state, market and voluntary organisations, and informally by the family, neighbours or volunteers. The resultant national patterns of provision will shape not only the demands that are made of the state but also the rights that are established, given that the construction of a division of social responsibility for care will also be constitutive of different kinds of rights.

National configurations of care/rights systems link loosely with gendered typologies of the welfare state (Lewis, 1992; Esping-Andersen, 1999; Sainsbury, 1999), and with patterns of women's paid employment. Thus the USA, where reliance on the market for individual purchase of care services is strong, displays high levels of women's full-time employment and a smaller welfare state than Western Europe. However, there is no simple one-to-one association. Women's employment is also high in the Nordic countries but here the 'social' state is far more comprehensive, with publicly funded care services. In Britain, Germany and the Netherlands, with their varying levels of women's paid employment and pronounced pattern of part-time working, state and market modes of care provision are more closely integrated, though in differing ways, and informal and voluntary activity also make a major contribution. In Italy, the (market) employment of migrant workers as carers represents an important component of 'private', 'informal' household and family provision.

Struggles over the proportionate contribution of the state *vis-à-vis* other care providers are high on the political agenda of these and many other economically developed countries in the world. The debate is frequently couched in terms of 'choice', a discourse that individualises the issue as one of enabling care recipients to choose between multiple providers. The danger of such rhetoric, according to its critics, is to draw attention away from state responsibility for public provision, which would need to be already available in the first case in order for individuals to make an effective choice between alternatives.

That differing systems of provision operate alongside each other, in combination, complementing each other or filling the gaps, does not imply that they are well integrated. They may result in multiple and perhaps conflicting expectations and obligations on the part of givers and receivers. The onus usually falls to those seeking care to create their own 'package' (Knijn *et al.*, 2003), for instance, when a working mother goes part-time and relies on her own parents as well as pre-school facilities to meet child care needs. At this practical individual level, people juggle between what is available to produce their own jigsaw of services. At a societal or systemic level too, combining the various systems of care provision is far from a simple matter of addition, especially in ideological terms. The problem is exacerbated by the diverse logics underlying principles of provision, which may rest on differing priorities that oppose rather than reinforce each other. In the Netherlands, for example, the dominant forms of care provision (bureaucratic, professional, familial and market) are associated with distinct logics and vocabularies (Knijn, 2000: 234–7), promoting incompatible conceptions of care recipients and providers, construals of the basis of care and system of control.

Contrasting systems of rights

What implications for rights may be drawn from the variety of systems of care provision? It seems almost self-evident that different systems, with their diverse underlying logics, will be associated not simply with different kinds of effective rights, but also with different conceptions and understandings of rights on the part of both care receivers and givers. Some possible contrasts are schematically sketched out below as ideal types in the abstract, rather than rooted in time or place. In practice, of course, there are no pure systems, only instituted ones, which combine in different ways.

Where there is state or public provision, rights to receive care are likely to be citizen-based. In this case citizens or qualifying residents are entitled to receive care on the basis of legally instituted criteria. These might specify conditions for receiving care (such as only to those who have no other sources of care or who have contributed to a national insurance scheme, or they might be means tested) but they are intended to apply according to a set of impartial rules. Citizens have a legal right to receive provision, in terms of cash or services, as long as they fulfil the qualifying criteria. Agencies of the state with duties to deliver care become legally liable for instances of abuse or failures in their 'duty to care'. Several 'scandals' of this kind have been well publicised in Britain in recent years, for example, when sexual abuse in residential homes came to light decades after the event or when failure to spot cruelty to an 'at risk' child in the care of social services culminated in her death. Public enquiries and legal proceedings often follow the discovery of such 'derelictions of duty' in the attempt to attribute blame and rectify loopholes in provisions and practices.

Rights to care by family and relatives have a quite different character. They are informal, rather than legally instituted, and dependent on goodwill, duty or traditions of reciprocity. Innate gender characteristics are often assumed, placing the responsibility for care squarely on female relatives. There are few sanctions against particular people not providing care, although strong social and moral conventions may operate. Parents expect and are expected to care for their children, as indicated by social disapproval, potential legal charges and media exposures that accompany cases of 'home alone' children left behind by parents who go away on holiday. Societies assume general responsibilities in relation to the next generation. But the question of whether children universally enjoy the 'right' to be cared for by their parent(s) is not as clear-cut. Similarly, do the sick, disabled, elderly and others unable to care for themselves have the right to be cared for by relatives? Cultures of honour and shame play a dominant role in many countries in enforcing family care, as do gossip and other mechanisms of social control and local convention. Nevertheless, 'familial' rights with respect to care cannot easily be legally enforced, despite legal liability in instances of abuse or neglect, especially where children are concerned.[3] But this is a different matter from a legal requirement that familial care be undertaken.

In many countries care services, particularly for pre-school children and the elderly, are increasingly provided on a commercial basis by private companies. Different kinds of rights are associated with the market and with state and family. A simplistic view would be that the duty of firms is to make a return on investment for their owners and that rights are restricted to those of financial exchange. However, in reality markets have their own socially instituted rules and norms that govern the behaviour of firms and business practice, including trading rights (Boyer, 1997; Fligstein, 2001; Nelson, 2002). The rights to care that are purchased are more akin to consumer than to citizen rights, in the sense that care agencies are legally responsible in terms of trades descriptions or consumer protection. If providers undertake to supply care of particular kinds or quality, then consumers are entitled to sue if these are not fulfilled. Where publicly funded care is contracted out to the private sector, standards are often state imposed, with market providers subject to regulation and inspection. How high the standards and how rigorous the inspection regime are of course key issues for public policy and effective enforcement. Moreover, consumers in this area are vulnerable to manifold abuses arising from contracts that are by the nature of the case 'incomplete', given the impossibility of *ex ante* specification of care requirements. Depending on particular national regulatory regimes, private care agencies will be more or less open to public scrutiny and the requirement to reach minimum criteria. Individual purchasers would have resort to public regulations in claims against businesses that fail to provide or to meet prescribed standards. Care 'consumers' may also have a right to 'value for money' (a concept that now permeates quasi-market/state provision), and in the best-case scenario to quality established through market standards, reputation, even branding and norms of corporate social responsibility.

In the final ideal-type, voluntary care, issues of rights and obligations are more amorphous, especially at the individual level. By definition no one is obliged to volunteer care. Voluntary care organisations, however, were established precisely for the purpose, and often contract with the state or private persons to provide it. But this formal obligation does not require any particular individual to give their services for free. It is therefore important to distinguish clearly between individuals and organisations providing voluntary care, and their complex relationship. The latter are increasingly run on bureaucratic lines, employ paid staff and are subject to government regulations relating to financial arrangements and governance as well as service provision. In terms of rights, there can be no question of receivers having formal entitlements to care from volunteers. People may wish for the services of volunteers or voluntary organisations but have no right to expect them. The actions of voluntary care givers, on the other hand, may rest on altruism or an ethic of generalised reciprocity, in the hope that giving now implies a right to receive later on. Where unpaid volunteer care activity is widespread it could reflect a more widespread societal conception of rights and obligations, as, for example, in the Netherlands. Here the high level of volunteering, though religious in origin, is now secularised into an almost national ethical imperative and form of citizenship (Burger and Dekker, 2001).

In practice, actual systems of provision, and the rights pertaining to them, are considerably more complex than these schematic ideal-types. As state welfare policy in many European countries relies increasingly on delivery of care services by the private and voluntary sectors, as part of public provision as well as supplementing it, it becomes hard to disentangle state, market and voluntary modes from each other. The resultant public–private–voluntary hybrids impact not only on standards and regulations but also on rights. The UK Labour Government, for example, has expanded financial support to the voluntary sector, which assumes ever greater responsibility for supplying front-line services, and it also stimulates massive growth of the private care business by contracting out services. The introduction of voucher schemes enabling those entitled to 'public' care to receive it from the private sector effectively extends to designated categories of people the 'right' to receive market care without paying for it themselves. But even if market, public and voluntary modes of provision are structurally intertwined, a question mark remains over what happens to principles of rights in such hybrid forms. Do the logically distinct conceptions associated with each component mode merge or in some way alter in accordance with the new realities?

Moreover, the relation between modes of care and the 'rights' attached to them is always mediated by everyday understandings. People will have specific expectations of their 'rights' and duties depending on the particular relation between care receiver and provider. National variations in common-sense conceptions of rights are likely to accompany different modalities and mixes of provision. While understandings of citizen-based rights may be widely spread throughout the population to which they apply, familial obligations and rights may be shared on a smaller scale, varying on ethnic, income, regional or religious lines, and subject to historical change.

In terms of familial rights, there is little expectation in Britain nowadays that an unmarried daughter will live at home to care for elderly parents, although this was common until the mid-twentieth century. And in the case of public provision, it would be fair to assert that most UK citizens feel they are entitled to free health care. The National Health Service, publicly funded through taxation, provides health care free at the point of delivery. 'I've paid in all my life, and so am entitled to receive treatment' is a frequently rehearsed refrain. Strong views prevail with respect to NHS entitlement, extending beyond narrow exchange: not simply that those who contribute are entitled to receive an equivalent value of care but that socialisation of the fund for health care entitles all to provision, and that people should not be excluded by the severity of their illness, cost of treatment, poverty or other factors. Similar attitudes probably apply to disability: that the disabled should be cared for and not penalised for their vulnerability. However, the same UK population do not assume an equivalent or automatic right to public elder care. In Sweden and other Nordic countries, by contrast, where higher rates of taxation fund forms of elder care which are not publicly provided in the UK, people express views about elder care rights similar to those of UK citizens about health.

Through this schematic exploration of the rights putatively attaching to differing modalities of care, I hope to have demonstrated the importance for sociological analysis of care rights of encompassing not only socially instituted systems of provisioning and their respective logics of rights, but also everyday understandings of entitlements and obligations.

The example of elder care

Elder care is used in this section to elaborate several themes of the approach being proposed. Again the value of comparative perspective is stressed, and a wide range of empirical examples is selected to bring out points of contrast.[4] As will be clear, some of these hardly qualify as 'processes' or 'rights', prompting the question of the appropriateness of a rights discourse. Although 'rights' may be too formal a term, social conventions and cultural norms nevertheless exist about whether care is provided, to and by whom, resulting in definite expectations and duties. They may have no legal force, but to view them merely as informal customs would underestimate their quasi-compulsory significance in societies very different from our own. Cross-cultural evidence indicates that particular kinds of right to elder care are operative in many societies other than advanced industrial countries, even if they are less differentiated, and differently instituted and understood. The expectation of inheriting wealth, or living as an extended family, for instance, will have implications for rights as well as for care. An examination of elder care reinforces the argument that exclusive focus on places and times possessing formal systems of rights would be both ethnocentric and anachronistic.

Two initial considerations merit emphasis. Like other care groups, the 'elderly' are socio-historically constructed rather than a universal or distinct grouping found in all societies. For elder care to be an issue presupposes in addition that 'care' and 'needs' are differentiated from other personal relations, and disembedded from other social activities.

Anthropological evidence from North and South America amply demonstrates both points, suggesting that in near subsistence or scarce conditions those who cannot support themselves are often not supported by the rest of society. Among the Athapaskan-speaking Arctic peoples, for instance, many did not live to see old age (Vanstone, 1974: 82–3) while those who survived suffered loss of prestige and power as soon as they could no longer bear children or work. When the time came to migrate to new hunting grounds, the normal practice for some indigenous peoples was to leave behind, effectively to die, those unable to fend for themselves. For others, respect for elders as bearers of traditional shamanic wisdom led to different treatment, conceptions of death, the afterlife and spiritual cosmos interplaying with material conditions in significant cross-cultural variation. Further south, Aymaran speakers of the Andes have no term that directly translates as 'care', as distinct from rearing or looking out for. When people are old in Pocobaya their descendants give them cooked food but in return they are expected to herd animals, and in practice are often left alone for extended periods with little food or the ability to cook it. No issue of care arises if those who cannot feed themselves die. Being old and infirm seems pretty miserable, with death coming quickly and few surviving to great age. Among these different peoples living in harsh conditions, the elderly clearly form a distinct grouping, whether involving inclusion or exclusion. But in neither case does this lead to what could strictly be understood as 'care'.

In many other societies, historically and across the globe, where norms of care are associated with old age, familial obligations dominate. When kin or family are basic institutions for protection and support, the duty of care for elderly parents usually falls to their children. In Britain until well into the twentieth century, this role fell traditionally to the youngest daughter, as mentioned above. She was expected to stay 'at home' caring for parents until their death rather than marry and form her own family. This practice produced a population of 'spinsters', a social grouping that has now all but disappeared, but that was a frequent object of derision and pity (Glucksmann, 2000; Holden, 2001, 2004). Further afield, in the Indian subcontinent, obligations extend to the larger kinship group rather than the immediate family, and Hindu culture places the onus for elder support primarily on the eldest son. Across Southeast Asia, traditions of filial piety survive and children are strongly socialised into the duty of paying back to parents what they have been given. Failing this obligation still entails shame. In China and Taiwan, the oldest son is again charged with looking after elderly parents. But the gendering of responsibility, shaped also by patriliny, patrilocality and the marrying out of daughters, does not absolve women from elder care. On the contrary, daughters-in-law traditionally undertake the actual physical and emotional work of caring (Lin, 2003) while sons' responsibilities revolve around financial support.

Despite rapid urbanisation and economic development, the elderly still rely heavily on married sons and daughters (Lee *et al.*, 1994; Lillard and Willis, 1997), a dependence exacerbated by the lack of social provision across the region. However, the continuing viability of these traditional care relations is increasingly compromised by demographic transformation, mass participation of women in paid employment and the demise of the daughter-in-law role. Although strong demands are voiced in some countries for public provision to meet the new care needs, solving the problem still falls primarily to the family and to individual private solutions – such as Thai daughters sending 'home' as remittances part of the wages from their work in towns or abroad, or the widespread employment of migrant maids in Taiwan and Hong Kong (Lin, 1999; Lan, 2003). In these new circumstances, traditional expectations and rights with regard to care also undergo change and can no longer be taken for granted. Physical care may be separated out from financial support and purchased on a market basis, thus shifting provision across economic domains, while claims for social rights emerge for the first time on a public terrain.

Unlike East Asia, protection and care of the elderly is broadly articulated and accepted as a socio-political right and (to a lesser extent) responsibility in Western welfare states. But here too it has become a hot topic, as welfare state retrenchment coincides with an expansion of the elderly population potentially in need of care.

The current 'crisis' of care, and consequently of 'rights' to care, has many roots. Increased longevity and time spent in education, combined with low birth rates, produce an ageing population and altered balance between those who are working and dependent. Such is the extension of life expectancy that the life course is now commonly treated as quadri- rather than tripartite. The 'Third Age' of post-employment, previously the final stage of retirement, decline and death, is seen now as a time of personal fulfilment (Laslett, 1989: 4), while the fourth age of infirmity and dependency is chronologically delayed to the late seventies or eighties. Concurrently, notions of dignity and independence in old age raise expectations of quality of life for the elderly. The extension of women's paid employment and the shift from a male breadwinner to a dual earner model, loosening of familial responsibilities and increasing spatial mobility effectively disrupt traditional systems of elder care, including established settlements between familial and state provision. Rather than simply extending the demand for care, such change also impacts on the shape and content of demand. Given the strength of welfare state traditions in Western countries, claims for rights to care in these new circumstances are expressed largely in political terms through debate over public responsibility and the continuing obligations of the state.

However, significant variations exist between welfare states in the proportionate responsibility assumed by the state, family, market and voluntary sector. And particular national divisions of social responsibility between these modes have consequences for claims to rights, not only the kind and extent of claims that are made and from whom, but also common-sense understandings of those rights. For example, in Britain, Germany or the Netherlands it is fairly common for women to undertake paid work on a part-time basis in order to look after elderly parents. The residential care home alternative is not only very costly, but also attracts a certain social disdain or disapproval. But in Sweden, by contrast, there is a widely shared notion that it is not right, or even shameful, for family members to undertake elder care. A woman would be discouraged from giving up work to care for parents, and warned of the loss of earnings and pension rights that could in turn jeopardise her own old age. Here the elderly expect and prefer care to be publicly provided rather than depending on families (Stark and Regner,

2002). Receiving services from unpaid volunteers is also considered demeaning, like charity or the workhouse.

In the Nordic, unlike other European or North American, welfare models, a mutual contract between the state and individual citizen underlies social provision, with public responsibility taking priority over intrafamilial duty and voluntary activity. In return for long-term full-time employment, and high levels of taxation and social insurance, extensive state funding of care, including elder care, is provided, a form of exchange that is reflected in the taken-for-granted expectations about social care.

A broad brush comparison of elder care provisioning in subsistence and traditional societies, rapidly developing countries and established welfare regimes highlights some central propositions of this chapter. Elder care depends, in the first instance, on the emergence of a group in need of care, and of specific kinds of need and care. For there to be an extended period of retirement or even dependency that minimises misery and maximises fulfilment is a massive historical achievement. Varying cultures, structures and political economies of elder care give rise to different kinds of 'rights', many of which are informal or conventional, enforced by normative and social sanctions even though they are not legally enacted. Needs, modalities of care and the 'rights' associated with them are best analysed together as an integral package. This does not imply harmoniously functioning or fixed unchanging systems. On the contrary, demands, provisions and rights are to be understood as changing dynamically in relation to each other. Especially in times of socio-economic transformation, systems of provisions and rights may be characterised by tension, contradiction and imbalance, becoming the subject of both political and personal struggle to achieve more acceptable solutions.

Conclusion

The analytical framework outlined in this chapter is rooted in an understanding of the practice and activity of care as a relational process between receivers and givers, usually involving exchange. This supports a substantive concern with historical, cultural and national variation between different overall systems of care provision and the rights that attach to them. Approached this way, the many different possible groundings and kinds of rights come into sharp focus. Informal, taken-for-granted expectations and personal or traditional obligations are equally to be considered under the heading of rights as formalised entitlements or state-enforceable laws prescribing citizen- or employment-based rights or putative human or universal rights with their international sanctions. I have concentrated on the right to receive care, but other additional rights, which there is not space to discuss, would be directly implicated in this. The right to give care is the most obvious, but the rights of care workers (paid and unpaid) would also be significant, especially with respect to employment and working conditions. In the case of migrants, whose contribution to care work is so crucial in many parts of the world, entry and residence rights come to the fore.

To develop the analytical perspective I distinguished schematically between state, familial, market and voluntary modalities of care and the rights associated with them, drawing attention also to the diverse everyday understandings that may accompany them. Exploring the particular case of elder care across a range of times and places reveals considerable variability in provision, rights and expectations, confirming the argument that rights are shaped according to the socio-economic, political and cultural circumstances in which they are found. However, relativity does not imply relativism. A concept of rights as emergent and expanding is entirely consonant with the view that rights are particular to the context of which they are a part. This too raises horizons beyond the scope of the chapter towards political questions about the most effective ways of establishing a strong footing for rights to care on the political agenda. This could be approached by redefining citizenship to include care or through campaigns in support of an ethic of care and degendered moral philosophy. An alternative or additional strategy would be to direct greater scrutiny at the governance of systems of care with the aim of entrenching norms of best practice and collective social responsibility. This could arguably side-step the problem that rights can only be demanded of others, the state or employers. The capabilities paradigm of Nussbaum and Sen might provide another potential route to the same objectives. But whatever means are deployed, rights are a historical achievement rather than natural or automatic. They change and expand in scope or terrain, but only as the result of concerted human action.

Notes

1 Although the right to give care is a dominant theme in current policy discussion, this chapter focuses on the right to receive, given that this is the more basic right and would need to be established before the right to give could become an effective question.
2 My prime research interest in care is as work. The material for this chapter is drawn from comparative research currently being undertaken collaboratively with Dawn Lyon on modes of paid and unpaid care work and employment in Europe. This is part of a larger research programme on 'Transformations of work: new frontiers, shifting boundaries, changing temporalities' funded by the ESRC (Award RES-051-27–0015), for whose support I am extremely grateful.
3 There are exceptions where familial responsibility is a legal requirement. For example, in Germany until recently, adults in need of long-term care were obliged to turn first to their children for some financial support even if they fell below the social assistance threshold (Ostner, 1999: 112).
4 The material for this section is drawn from interviews with care experts in Europe and other respondents from East Asian countries, in addition to published sources. I am grateful to Andrew Canessa, Colin Samson and Rob and Ja Stones for ethnographic information about conditions for the elderly in the Andes, sub-Arctic and Thailand.

Part II

Status, norms and institutions

The second part of this volume groups together three chapters that, in different ways, illustrate the significance of normative ideals and status difference for an understanding of entitlement and implementation with respect to rights. An emphasis on status is most explicit in Chapter 4, which considers the Marshallian heritage in the light of Weber's (1948) writings on status, and Lockwood's (1996) subsequent work on civic integration and class formation. Though Marshall was interested in the effect an equal status of citizenship could have on ameliorating the inequalities of the market, he was aware of the possible influence that class prejudice and inequalities of wealth could have on the implementation of rights. He also saw that citizenship rights themselves could function as a basis for inequality, and Lockwood expands these insights through his concept of civic stratification; a system of inequality generated by the rights that can be claimed from the state. This inequality functions on two dimensions: the formal designations of inclusion and exclusion with respect to rights, and the informal processes of gain and deficit. He notes, but does not develop, the idea that particular groups or particular areas of rights can undergo periods of expansion with respect to entitlement, such that the map of rights is never fixed but subject to contestation and change.

Chapter 4 explores the application of these ideas to the analysis of welfare and work in the context of debate both on 'the underclass' and on immigration and asylum. The chapter considers the dominant arguments of the 'underclass' debate and the emergence of an increasingly contractual welfare policy, setting out the status issues associated with these developments. These operate through both the differing conditions of benefit imposed on different claimant groups and the degrees of stigma that may be attached to dependence. Most vulnerable are the long-term unemployed and single parents, and Morris notes the possibility that negative perceptions of these groups are fuelled by policy rhetoric emphasising responsibilities over rights. The chapter then moves on to consider the varying circumstances of migrants and asylum seekers with respect to work and welfare rights, arguing that 'universal personhood' with respect to rights has yet to be fully established. The emphasis is instead on the role that a differentiated system of rights can play in the process of management and control, though such systems do not go unchallenged. Instead, work and welfare rights operate within a contested terrain of both expansions and contractions, and rather than guaranteed certainties we find a negotiated pragmatism.

Chapter 5 presents the claim that 'women's rights are human rights' as a claim to equal status, though the status dimension of the analysis goes further and deeper than this assertion. The chapter begins with a juxtaposition of Turner's search for ontological foundations and Waters's social constructionist position *vis-à-vis* rights, and finds a parallel in feminist debates, through Nash's normative commitment to equality and Walby's focus on structural changes in a gender regime as possible bases for rights claims. In presenting her account of the platform and achievements of feminist organisations in the struggle for rights, Elson draws on both positions. She highlights how a change in gender regimes from a domestic to a more public form can mean enhanced public status for women, and how an engagement with the language of human rights rather than women's rights is a status issue. The Human Rights Sub-Commission on the Status of Women had to fight to make the claim to equal status a reality, even in terms of the allocation of recognition and resources within the UN. Similarly, the international response to the Convention for the Elimination of Discrimination against Women was to view it as in some sense secondary, and this is reflected in the number of reservations registered by signatory states.

To make their claims tell, women had to establish themselves not just as women but as 'half of humanity'. The argument that systematic abuses arising out of gender-specific issues are human rights abuses is both an endictment of androcentrism in perceptions and definitions of human rights, and a challenge to the underpinning status order. Similarly, 'the personal is political' is a claim for status recognition of relations in the personal and private domain, which has traditionally played a poor second to the public sphere. This questioning of the established status order does not stop there, however, as the issue of recognition erupts again when feminist post-colonial theorists shine the light of equality on ethnocentric conceptions of women's rights and human rights. The chapter moves on to consider the danger of reifying and essentialising difference through recognition, and considers the arguments for both revaluing and degendering 'female' qualities; the former recognising and the latter challenging difference. Finally, in acknowledging the constraints of legal discourse, Elson argues for an appeal to moral legitimacy in attempts to transform practices, perceptions and understanding.

Chapter 6 focuses on the implementation of established norms through the example of anti-racist policy in the EU, which legitimises EU-level action to combat discrimination. The chapter distinguishes two related processes: the importation of new ideas and ideals, in which social movements play a prominent role; and their translation into policy, which involves the mediation of differences and competition for resources. The former is rooted in a cultural dynamic and the latter in an institutional dynamic – and the move from one to the other is seen to be critical for the translation of norms into rights. One problematic aspect of this 'translation' can be the way that different actors seek to represent norms in terms of their own pre-established interests and orientations, which can highlight the existence of contrasting perspectives on the ultimate goal of anti-racism. Thus, status and struggle can still be an issue, and as a relatively recent area for active intervention, anti-racist norms have encountered certain difficulties in moving from broad principles to concrete interventions. Some of these difficulties have been related to both recognition and resource issues, as competing policy frames and embedded interests come together in a complex coalition of activists and bureaucrats.

The growing primacy of anti-racist policy on the EU agenda has thus been conducive to broad alliances, but less so to the cohesive framing of policy, and a clear direction for anti-racist policy has yet to emerge. Interaction with other aspects of social inclusion is also revealing, as the advocacy groups – who play a significant role in the EU policy world – confront the need to coordinate their complementary but at times competing interests. This same tension also exists within the key institutions of the EU – the European Parliament and the Commission – alongside an implicit contradiction between member states which embrace differing varieties of assimilation and multiculturalism. In practice, the question of 'fit' with the established EU project has meant that economic rights tend to take precedence and translate into an emphasis on integration through the labour market. However, the chapter argues that broad normative agreement is in itself a significant achievement, and that even where the details of implementation remain unclear or contested, such agreement serves to secure a significant value position outside the realm of individual choice.

4 Social rights, trans-national rights and civic stratification

Lydia Morris

We saw in the introduction to this volume that 'rights' have recently risen to prominence as a focus for social, political and intellectual debate, yet as Turner (1993) has argued, sociology as a discipline has no obvious foundation for a contemporary theory of rights. While a sociology of citizenship has to some extent served as a substitute, a number of critiques (e.g. Brubaker, 1989; Bottomore, 1992; Soysal, 1994) have argued that available frameworks (usually based on Marshall's (1950) classic work) are inadequate to address a set of pressing contemporary issues. These include the growth of transnational migration, the alleged expansion of 'post-national membership', and the proliferation of positions of partial membership, to which we can add the erosion of the social rights of full citizens. The analytical tools to do justice to such phenomena are, however, underdeveloped and although there have been various attempts to address this gap, there is as yet no satisfactory comprehensive framework.

The introduction notes that one response to the question of how to think sociologically about rights has been to move beyond nationally bounded citizenship and to invoke the universal. However, while there has been growing interest and speculation about the scope and potential of universalism (Turner, 1993; Soysal, 1994; Meyer *et al.*, 1997), there has also been an awareness of the limitations imposed by definitions of the national interest, and a variety of recent contractions with respect to entitlement. In this context, a focus on the power of universalism has only rarely engaged with a number of common limitations and even erosions in the delivery of universal human rights to non-citizens, much less with the constraints that are increasingly imposed on full citizens. A growing emphasis on duties alongside rights has been the site of some instances of contraction in contested areas of provision, most notably in the area of welfare support, whose status as a universal human right is far from clear. By addressing the specific issue of welfare rights in the broader context of both the classical and emergent literature on citizenship rights and migrant rights, this chapter seeks to point the way to one possible foundation for a sociological approach to the field that could yield a more nuanced analysis of rights than has yet been available.

Class, status and power

One foundation for a fuller sociological approach to the issue of rights may be found in Weber's (1948) classic essay on class status and party, which addresses the distinction between the social order or distribution of honour, and the economic order of class situations determined by market position. The key to class situation is the disposal of property through exchange in the market, which functions to the great disadvantage of the propertyless, with only their services to sell. Weber continues: 'Those men whose fate is not determined by the chance of using goods or services for themselves on the market, e.g. slaves, are not, however, a class in the technical sense of the term. They are rather a status group' (ibid.: 183). A status situation is then defined as: 'every typical component of the life fate of men that is determined by a specific positive or negative social estimation of honour'. For contemporary society Weber's comments yield two dimensions of status, which may be related: first, a fate determined outside the market; second, a position defined by the values governing conferment (or otherwise) of social honour. He also notes that status groups will tend to constitute communities, and that 'stratification by status goes hand in hand with a monopolisation of *ideal* and *material* goods and opportunities' (ibid.: 190, emphasis added).

Status, as Weber defines it, is argued to be a hindrance to the operation of the free market, and once a status order has established stability, its translation into legal privilege can easily follow. The relevance of this notion of status for the study of rights lies in the conception of a formal position outside the market, which in contemporary society is likely to be state supported,[1] the less formalised dynamic attributing social honour to different social groups, and the interesting possibility that these two dimensions may coincide. One other aspect of Weber's essay should be noted before we move on, and that is the distinction between communal action, related to feelings of mutual belonging, and societal action, based on a rational means – ends orientation. The relevance of this distinction will become clear later in the chapter, and potentially engages with two different possible bases for rights: mutuality and contract. For the present, is takes only a short step to see the relevance of Weber's observations on status for a sociological understanding of rights, in both their conception and operation.

Citizenship and social class

There are echoes of Weber's position in Marshall's (1950) work *Citizenship and Social Class*, the first explicit approach to a sociology of citizenship. Marshall sets out to examine the possibility that a basic equality associated with the status of citizenship may not be inconsistent with economic inequality. He begins with a brief account of what he describes as 'the modern drive towards equality' (ibid.: 7), noting its evolutionary development over a period of 250 years, and observing a continuing urge in this direction. His account covers the chronological unfolding of civil rights associated with personal liberty, political rights associated with participation and social rights associated with a share 'in the full social heritage and to live the life of a civilised being'.

Marshall takes civil and political rights as formally established at the time of writing, civil rights being essential to the functioning of a free market, though he does note some impediments to their full realisation, which hinge on class prejudice or on economic inequality. Thus, like Weber, he invokes two dimensions of status: one based on a formalised position with respect to the rights of citizenship, and the other based on the largely informal role of wealth and prestige, hence underlining a potential fissure between entitlement and delivery in the functioning of rights. However, the field of social rights is the true focus of Marshall's essay; the 'invasion of contract by status', which subordinates the market to social justice, replacing bargaining with rights, and 'creating a universal right to real income which is not proportionate to the market value of the claimant' (ibid.: 28). While early forms of relief commonly required a withholding of civil rights, Marshall observes that this dynamic had been reversed in 'modern' society, such that social and economic rights had often been achieved through the exercise of civil and political rights. In relation to social rights, the role of status equality is deemed paramount, hence: 'Equalisation is not so much between classes as between individuals within a population which is now treated for this purpose as if it were one class. Equality of status is more important than equality of income' (ibid.: 33). The same point is made of citizenship itself, in that 'all who possess the status are equal with respect to the rights and duties with which the status is endowed' (ibid.: 18). It is possible to interpret status here as both a formal legal standing in society and an informal evaluation of worth.

The broad shape and substance of his position are well known, and there have been a number of commentaries that point to the inadequacies of his argument for contemporary analysis (see Bottomore, 1992), notably the taken-for-granted standing of the nation state as his 'community' of reference. There are, however, a number of points to be derived from Marshall's essay, which still have a powerful bearing on the form and scope of a developing sociology of rights. The first is that in idealised form, the possession of citizenship offers an equality of status whose effectiveness may be measured against the standard of 'full participation' in society, though part of its potential is to make the inequalities of the class system more acceptable, and hence less vulnerable to attack. He also recognises that the full scope of citizenship has not yet been realised, and that civil and political rights can play a vital role in the expansion of other areas of entitlement. Conversely, he argues that citizenship may itself be 'the architect of legitimate social inequality', and that status inequality (in the sense of prestige or prejudice), and economic inequality can both create impediments to the realisation of formally held rights. Furthermore, he emphasises the state's role in balancing the collective interests of society and individual social rights, though at the time of writing (1949) he detected a shift in emphasis away from duties towards rights. He notes, however, that the relevant duties of citizenship had as yet been only vaguely addressed, and that one must clearly be the duty to work.

Each of these insights has implications for how we might build a sociology of rights, and they recur in various forms in the discussion that follows.

Civic stratification

David Lockwood's (1996) work on civic integration and class formation systematically addresses a number of the issues sketched out or only hinted at in the pieces by Weber and Marshall. His focus is on the way in which the 'institutional unity' of citizenship, market and bureaucracy mediates the impact of social class in structuring life chances and identity. In capitalist welfare state democracies, the common legal status of citizenship is argued to have reduced institutionalised status difference but enhanced the institutionalisation of power (embodied in state bureaucracies), such as to limit incongruities in both fields. In terms of hierarchical status, this leaves only what he terms the weaker forms of social inclusion and exclusion, and deference and derogation. However, like Marshall, Lockwood wishes to pose the question of how far the central institutions of society function efficiently in 'delivering the goods', and what contribution they make to securing social integration. In doing so, he throws light on a number of the key points of interest listed above.

He notes, for example, that much of the legitimising effect of an equal status of citizenship stems from the role of bureaucracies that oversee the inequalities and rewards attaching both to occupational positions and to the delivery of citizenship rights, by the application of impersonal rules (as through the tax and welfare systems). Furthermore, like Marshall he sees civil and political rights as a basic requirement for the functioning of capital, leaving only the 'fine-tuning' of social rights to mediate the potential conflict between status and contract. This means that governments have only limited room for manoeuvre, which must rest on some form of selectivity based on merit or demerit; in other words, the designation of deserving and undeserving claimants. Lockwood (1996: 536) also agrees with Marshall that 'citizenship remains an ideal whose actualisation is always less than complete' and that its operations will therefore provide a potential focus for the structuring of group interests, conflict and discontent.

This possibility is then explored with reference to two axes of inequality; the presence or absence of rights, and the possession of moral or material resources. The distinction captures the two different dimensions of status referred to earlier, which are implicit in Weber's essay, the one derived from a formalised position,[2] and the other principally from prestige factors of either honour or wealth, which will often operate informally. On the basis of these two axes of inequality, Lockwood derives what he terms four types of civic stratification – civic exclusion, civic gain, civic deficit and civic expansion – which are in fact two sets of paired oppositions. Civic gain and deficit refer to the enhanced or impaired implementation of rights,[3] civic exclusion refers to the formal denial of rights, while expansion may refer to either the expanding claims of particular groups, or the expanding terrain of rights more generally – and universal human rights are given as an example. Bechhofer (1996) has already argued that civic exclusion and expansion sit uneasily together, and here I suggest a slight amendment, pairing exclusion with inclusion to denote formal access to rights, and introducing a third opposition, civic expansion and contraction, to refer to the shifting character of a regime of rights or of a specific area within its ambit.

Social rights and the underclass debate

A particular focus in this chapter is the dynamic of social rights, a form of entitlement that departs from the passive freedoms of protection from, to require the active provision of facilities and services by the state (see for discussion Steiner and Alston, 1996). As both Marshall and Lockwood observe, they represent the least consolidated aspect of citizenship rights and offer governments most scope for negotiation. Certainly, the degree of commitment contained in the UN Covenant on Economic Social and Cultural Rights is rather limited. Although it espouses a set of minimum expectations (Dent, 1998), states' obligations are confined to what is feasible in resource terms, with a commitment simply to develop provision over time. In practice, the availability of social rights has been very variable, and even in well-developed welfare states there are impediments to their full achievement.

We have already noted Marshall's comments on the tension between status and contract, which subordinates the market to social justice, but in doing so makes the setting of benefit levels rather contentious. The level must inevitably be set with an eye to the income of the lowest-paid workers, and has usually been associated with concerns about the erosion of a 'work ethic' (see Morris, 1994). Further judgements are required about the legitimacy of claims in terms of both need and 'membership', and Freeman (1986: 52) addresses the balancing act required of governments as follows: 'The welfare state requires boundaries because it establishes a principle of distributive justice that departs from the distributive principles of the free market.' In other words, the group of people protected by welfare must somehow be delimited. Freeman poses this question in the context of expanding immigration, and one mechanism for limiting rights is the narrowing of legal entitlement, or civic exclusion in Lockwood's terms, as conventionally applied to migrants in the early stages of their stay or those defined as 'guest-workers' (see below). However, even for full citizens, welfare support will usually rest on decisions about both material need and moral desert, invoking Lockwood's reference to merit and demerit. As a result, social rights under the modern welfare state involve both the 'rational' administration of national resources and the moral identification of a 'legitimate' claim.

The 1990s debate about an emergent British 'underclass' illustrates a number of problems concerning how social justice and the market combine in practice, and we immediately find examples of both formal exclusions and informal deficits. The 'underclass' debate was transferred from America to Britain, at a time when the tension inherent in welfare was heightened by various social changes: notably the decline of the sole male breadwinner and of the nuclear family household. Throughout the 1980s and 1990s attention therefore focused on male unemployment and rising single motherhood, both argued to be linked to aspects of welfare provision, and each thought to raise questions about the acceptability of guaranteed social rights. One position has argued that the 'underclass' is a group excluded from the increased affluence of the majority population (Field, 1989), supported by evidence on the inadequacy of benefit payments (Morris, 1996), the soul-destroying nature of unemployment and the despair of many living in poverty (Jordan *et al.*, 1992). However, the dominant view was that the welfare state has been over-generous, is abused by many and has created a culture of dependency. This is thought to have undermined the work ethic and been damaging to the stability of the nuclear family (Murray, 1990), such that welfare rights have contributed to eroding the moral fabric of society.

Such arguments strike an odd contrast with Marshall's idealised model of social rights as the guarantee of social inclusion through social citizenship, which he defined as full membership of the community. In practice, a *right* to social inclusion is, for some groups, held to be questionable, and linked to the condemnation of a culture of dependency we find the growth of policies stressing social obligations above social rights, a theme that has persisted and strengthened in the UK, despite a change of government.[4] The major obligation is now to work for a living (Green, 1999), and associated with this growing emphasis we have seen increasing conditionality with respect to welfare claims, which does little more than gesture towards the very unequal regional and class distribution of opportunity. This conditionality operates differently for different claimant groups, with the young unemployed subject to the most stringent controls and the retired elderly to the least, while the mature unemployed, single parents and long-term sick and disabled claimants occupy intermediate positions.

Of course, much rests on the manner in which the duties of welfare claimants are imposed, but even throughout the high unemployment of the 1980s and early 1990s, the field has been dominated by a scepticism about the motivation of the benefit-dependent and a view that social rights had become a destabilising force. In the case of long-term unemployment there have traditionally been a number of means through which claimants must demonstrate that they are deserving of benefit, one being submission to a means test to prove need. Other conditions may include the demoralising proof of job search, and the question of whether the claimant is genuinely available for work. The failure of such a test and denial of benefit would amount to an instance of civic exclusion, but the test itself is regarded as stigmatising, as is the receipt of the benefit. Thus Barbalet (1988: 66), for example, argues that 'It is likely that those most in need of social services are least likely to receive them as rights properly understood.' In other words, the administration of the system detracts from the value of the right, introducing a form of civic deficit to the realisation of social support.

There is clearly a tension between the right to welfare and the obligation to be self-supporting where possible, and while Marshall noted the need for some work requirement in relation to welfare, he also saw the consolidation of citizenship as part of a movement away from duties towards rights. Recent developments in the debate about citizenship have reversed this dynamic, moving the emphasis away from rights and towards duties, and supporting the assumption that the state-dependent must be *compelled* to give something back to society. Though control is almost inevitably pervasive in systems of welfare, Van Reenan (2001) documents a shift away from the late 1960s view of the unemployed as victims, who serve society by accepting their fate, to an increasingly punitive approach as their numbers rose in the 1980s. In more recent policy this approach is ameliorated by official statements (Cm 3805) in ostensibly enabling terms, which recognise *state* responsibility for the provision of opportunity. However, the location of responsibility often shifts with political rhetoric, hence 'Opportunity to all, responsibility from all. . . . I don't think you can make the case for spending tax-payer money . . . without this covenant of opportunity and responsibilities together' (Blair, 2000).

The history and background of both individual and community is surely important here, and some account should be taken of the fate of previous generations for whom the inheritance of a lifetime's work in the coal pits, steel works and shipyards has been damaged health, invalidity and/or redundancy. Responsibility is only convincing as an argument where the background distribution of assets and opportunities is reasonably equal. Thus, while White (2000) supports some degree of conditionality, he nevertheless argues that disadvantaged individuals in non-egalitarian societies have no moral obligation to cooperate in their own exploitation. On the basis of the reciprocity principle implied by the 'rights and responsibilities' rhetoric, we should instead expect to see fair choice and opportunity, as well as a decent share of the social product.

In fact, the New Deal for moving the young unemployed into work goes further in imposing conditions on benefit than at any time since the launching of the post-war welfare state, withdrawing benefits from those who do not accept an offer of subsidised employment, training or community work. Some research, however, has questioned the quality of these 'opportunities', which yield near poverty wages and a repeated experience of unemployment (Dickens, 2001; Macdowell, 2002; Morrison, 2004). Nevertheless, the scheme has been extended to the long-term unemployed (Lister, 2000) and to a lesser extent to single parents, while the 'economically inactive' have been made the object of recent attention (*Guardian*, 2005). This group includes the disabled and long-term sick, who are now to be the latest focus in a redrawing of the boundaries of rights and duties. While a denial of opportunity to these groups would clearly be discriminatory, again much rests upon the quality of opportunity offered and the degree of coercion involved in its acceptance. But as Daly (2003) has argued, a small change at one moment can pave the way for more substantial change through effects on – among other things – normative expectations.

Gender and the underclass debate

Single mothers have always been a particular focus for concern in the underclass debate, but while gender differentiation permeates the substance of discussion, it is rarely made explicit in analysis. The dominant view in the literature derives from Murray's (1984, 1990) argument that the absence of a male role model in the family unit is the key to explaining the alleged growth of an underclass. This view firmly locates the task of socialisation in the family, with the underlying assumption that a subculture of the underclass is generated because the single mother is inadequate to the task of socialisation. There have been two responses to this argument. One is based on the assertion of rights, and cites the feminisation of poverty argument (e.g. Bane, 1988), suggesting that women are being made to carry the burden of society's poverty, and that better provision should be made for them. The other more dominant view is that some work requirement should be placed on single mothers (e.g. Mead, 1986), both as a deterrent to welfare dependency and presumably to foster the work ethic in their children.

While the latter position illustrates the social control dimension of welfare rights, it seems not to address the real concern expressed in the underclass debate, which centres on the alleged withdrawal of young men from the labour force. Applying these arguments to the British situation, we find a solution that brings women's work role and family role into conflict and raises questions about the basis for women's social inclusion. Taken together, poor employment options in part-time or low-paid work, alongside the demands of motherhood, mean that many women require some other source of support – the state in the case of single mothers, and for married mothers a husband. Thus the gender-related issues that arise from the debate about the underclass partly stem from unresolved questions about the sexual division of labour in society, and the structuring and restructuring of employment. Where constraints on welfare spending impose tighter conditions on receipt of benefit, challenging the genuine availability of single mothers for employment, these women may face a form of civic exclusion (from benefit). In so far as their position of dependence on the state evokes a negative moral judgement, they experience a deficit in the enjoyment of their social rights, while the absence of affordable child care can also constitute a further deficit in relation to their right to work.

There has been considerable debate as to whether the 'underclass' constitutes a social class, and if so whether it may be construed as such in its own right, or is better viewed in terms of the labour market position of the majority of its members. The answer to this depends in part on which aspect of the debate one wishes to engage. For example, it is the labour market position, or 'class' vulnerability of manual workers, particularly unskilled, that leads to their concentration in long-term unemployment. But it is their 'status' position as state dependants that causes their stigmatisation and thereby constitutes them as a group with common interests and potential for a collective identity.[5] The position of single mothers is more complex. They are also likely to share a class position by virtue of their labour market vulnerability and concentration in low-skilled, part-time work. However, it is their 'status' as women that leaves them primarily responsible for child care, and exposed to exploitation in this way (cf. Fraser, 2003), while their relationship to the state confers a stigmatised dependency status should they claim welfare support.

Status and contract in British welfare

In exploring the role of citizenship rights in relation to social cohesion, Lockwood raised a number of questions about the integrative function of citizenship. Earlier in this chapter, reference was made to Weber's distinction between communal action which he relates to a feeling of mutual belonging, and societal action which applies to the rationally motivated adjustment of interests. A similar opposition is to be found (by implication at least) in Marshall's distinction between citizenship as a status indicating full membership of a community and the contractual relations that dominate exchange in the market. This same distinction now features in political debate on the foundations for a claim to welfare, and indeed for rights more generally.

In the British case, Sarah Hale (2004) has noted the rhetoric of community at the heart of the New Labour image, but identifies an inconsistency in so far as the basis of community is commonly expressed through the language of contract, whereby rights or opportunities are offered in exchange for the fulfilment of responsibilities. This element was of course present in Marshall's essay, by virtue of his reference to both the rights and duties of citizenship, notwithstanding his view that the duties of citizenship were somewhat vague and that the overall direction of change was away from duties towards rights. The reversal of this dynamic has been noted with respect to debate about the underclass (e.g. Mead, 1986) and Hale's argument is that the logic of contract has come to dominate New Labour thinking on welfare provision and entitlement, as for example expressed in 'A New Contract for Welfare' (1998). In her view, the effect is to supplant the classical view of rights as inherent in individuals and to place them in the gift of the state, which potentially sets up an embattled relationship. Even Etzioni (2000: 29–30), one source of inspiration for the contractual approach, cautions against the denial of rights for non-fulfilment of 'responsibilities'.

The more rights become conditional on particular requirements, the more closely they are linked to enhanced control, as we saw in the above discussion of the underclass debate. The implication of such a shift in emphasis is to undermine the mutuality built into the welfare system, though Hale calls into question the genuinely *contractual* basis of provision that is strongly conditional and in some sense coercive. The element of choice in such an agreement and the possibility of bargaining are argued to be the true foundation for a contract, and these Hale finds to be missing if the alternative is destitution. Her position interestingly echoes Marshall's observation that the recognition of the right to collective bargaining in late nineteenth-century Britain meant that the strengthening of civil rights provided a possible route to social rights. He goes on to state, however, that this position was transitional and that rights in their true sense should supersede the need for negotiation of this kind; that 'rights are not a proper matter for bargaining' (Marshall, 1950: 40).

There is perhaps a danger of polarising or even caricaturing debate, such that the rights and duties linkage represents a zero-sum relationship. A more realistic position is to recognise that rights are rarely absolute, and that a judgement about reasonable balance is required. In the case of welfare rights the concept of civic stratification alerts attention both to differential conditions of access for different groups, and to the justifications that might support such difference. However, there is research which suggests that coercion is only effective for those who are easy to help (and for whom it is arguably inappropriate), and is ineffective for more difficult cases (Dean, 1998). It could, in fact, have a negative impact, and we can begin to examine the relationship between what have been described here as the formal and informal aspects of status, and whether a tightening of formal conditions of entitlement can negatively effect the informal standing of certain groups in society. Hills (2001), for example, cites evidence to suggest that ministerial rhetoric about welfare spending and levels of fraud can negatively affect public sympathy for the plight of the unemployed, which has traditionally been weaker than for other state-dependent groups (e.g. the elderly and disabled). Finally, we might consider whether the conditions attached to social support can impede the exercise of other rights.

The introduction to this chapter noted the growing significance of international conventions as 'universal' reference points for policy and debate about rights, and as a source of adjudication. Thus, another approach to this issue might be to look beyond the nation state and consider the standards embraced in relevant conventions. As we saw above, the Covenant on Economic Social and Cultural Rights offers little purchase, calling simply for the progressive development of social rights, in line with available resources. While it might be possible to pursue the issue of resource availability, as a basis for the assertion of unconditional rights the covenant's hold on signatory states remains rather weak. Another convention that might be relevant is the International Labour Organisation (ILO) Employment Policy Convention (no. 122), which entered into force on 15 July 1966. However, this is similarly exhortative rather than a strictly defined conferment of rights. It requires signatory states to pursue policy designed to promote full, productive and freely chosen employment, placing particular emphasis on choice and opportunity. As such, it provides a statement of ideals against which policy may be judged, and at least raises the question of how far the more coercive dimensions of recent policy comply.

Civic stratification and migrant rights

Immigration is an issue for which claims to transnational conventions and universal human rights are even more salient, as these rights purportedly transcend the boundaries of the nation state. However, as with systems of national welfare, the area of immigration engages a rather complex set of interests and influence, in which the boundary drawing referred to by Freeman (1995) is even more to the fore. Control of borders is the essence of sovereignty and most liberal states in practice seek to regulate immigration and prevent competition between citizen and alien workers, while also protecting national resources. Like welfare support for the unemployed, immigration creates a tension between rights and markets, and a key question is how states can manage the economic and humanitarian imperatives that respectively underpin immigration and migrants' rights.

Hollifield (1992) maintains that the liberal position that has prevailed in both the USA and Europe provides a market-based incentive for labour immigration, which is reinforced by rights-based politics, though he notes a tension between these two aspects of liberalism (his 'liberal paradox'). A number of writers have emphasised the expansion of rights, and Soysal (1994), for example, argues that citizenship has been superseded by the rights of long-term residents, based on claims to 'universal personhood'. Meyer *et al.* (1997) also see states as firmly embedded in a world culture of universalist values, which shapes their policy and actions, while Freeman (1995) has identified an 'expansionary bias' in the immigration policies of liberal democracies. The force of universalistic rights is central to his argument, and in particular family unification, under the right to family life, though he notes a counter-tendency towards deterrence in dealing with asylum claims, and an intensification of control.

Since Hollifield made his argument the field has become more complex – as he predicted, rights-based immigration has facilitated considerable family unification, and has also been associated with the arrival of asylum seekers on an unprecedented scale, so much so that the nature of states' commitments to transnational rights has at times been called into question. In fact, although most authors addressing the issue of transnational forces with respect to rights concede some degree of complexity or contradiction (Freeman, 1995: 889, 894; Meyer *et al.*, 1997: 154; Sassen, 1998: 20), this is rarely given detailed attention. The result is an overstatement of the impact of transnational instruments or principles, despite the fact that closer examination of the transnational dimension of rights immediately introduces a number of limitations to the argument.

A full understanding of state responses to immigration cannot be readily construed in terms of either national closure or transnational expansion, but must be approached in terms of the management of contradictory forces (cf. Hollifield, 1992). To do justice to both the force and the limitations of transnational dynamics we must therefore examine the principles that govern the granting and withholding of rights, the qualifying conditions of access and the nature of the interplay between domestic, transnational and supranational law. An emphasis on the growing significance of universal, or at least transnational, rights has some foundation, but renders an incomplete understanding. Indeed, while Brubaker (1989) emphasises the continuing significance of national citizenship, he has also noted the absence of a theory of partial or limited state membership (ibid.: 5), and his observations on the *ad hoc* proliferation of lesser statuses open up the possibility of a broader perspective. This undertheorised phenomenon arguably holds the key to a more nuanced understanding of migration and migrant rights, which may be viewed as the outcome of a set of contradictory or conflictual dynamics.

A means of advancing this view may be found in the civic stratification framework described above, which can be extended beyond its initial focus on the rights of citizenship to consider the position of non-citizens, while remaining cautious with respect to what is claimed for universal, transnational rights. All advanced capitalist welfare states employ an elaborate hierarchy of formal statuses for the designation of rights, with different rights attaching to different statuses. An idealised notion of full citizenship can be used as a yardstick against which to assess the impact of transnational rights for non-citizens, though we should not lose sight of the possibilities of contraction even for full citizens. Marshall and Lockwood both view civil and political rights as having been secured for full citizens, while non-citizens are routinely denied full political rights, and we find their civil rights can be selectively restricted, as in the case of detention for asylum seekers.[6] It is in the area of work and welfare rights, however, that we find the most elaborate differentiation, and again we see the impact of two types of status distinction: those operating primarily through the formal designation of immigration status, and those operating through the informal effects of gain or (more probably) deficit.

Welfare, work and immigration

Despite recent optimism about the post-national expansion of rights (Soysal, 1994; Sassen, 1998), international conventions have only limited power over security of residence and social rights, and are constrained by the recognition of state control over entry and stay. So, for example, while the International Convenant on Social and Economic Rights has a minimal core of expectations whereby individuals should not be deprived of essential foodstuffs and basic care (Dent, 1998: 7), this does not imply a right to residence or protection from removal. Under the European Convention on Human Rights (ECHR) the right to life and freedom from inhuman and degrading treatment (articles 2 and 3) can be a basis for protection and support, but only for those with no feasible alternative; for example, in cases of failing health.[7]

Other conventions secure more substantive rights for specific groups; for example, the European Convention on Social and Medical Assistance grants equal treatment in social security for contracting parties (only) and prohibits repatriation on the sole ground of need for assistance. This prohibition only applies, however, after five years of continuous residence (Plender, 1999: 269). Thus with respect to social rights, those granted on the basis of 'universal personhood' are strictly limited, and the discourse of universality applies more to aspirational effort than to established entitlements. Though immigrants who have achieved full residence status will be accorded the same social rights as citizens, formal distinctions by immigration status still retain considerable force in relation to both work and welfare rights.

While one of the duties attached to the status of citizenship is the obligation to work, for non-citizens this is a closely guarded privilege to which they do not necessarily have ready access. An exception to this rule comes with the creation a single market in the EU, such that all citizens of European Economic Area (EEA) states have the right to work and reside across Europe.[8] This arrangement aside, on the basis of their entry status, transnational migrants may have the right to work completely denied or restricted in a variety of ways – to a particular area of employment, or by giving priority to citizens, or by limitations on the duration of their stay. It is also common for entry to be conditional on 'no recourse to public funds' for a specified period (up to five years in Britain), and even where access is in principle permitted (as, for example, in Germany), receipt of social support can be an impediment to achieving a renewal of residence and hence security of stay. This connection between public funds and security of residence again opens up the possibility that delivery of social rights can be harnessed as a vehicle of control, and as a means of monitoring legal status.

The expansion of formal exclusions from aspects of social support, as in Britain in the course of the 1990s (Bolderson and Roberts, 1995), created a climate of suspicion surrounding any foreign-seeming claimant (NACAB, 1996). This can act as a deterrent to claiming even where a legitimate right exists, and has also led to uncertainty about the boundary of entitlement, again constituting a deficit. A similar dynamic operates with respect to the difficulties incoming spouses and even black British citizens may experience in realising the right to take employment (NACAB, 2000). The right exists simply as the absence of a prohibition, which is difficult to demonstrate, and the problem is heightened by sanctions imposed on employers who recruit unauthorised workers. While these sanctions in theory serve to protect the terms and conditions of employment for legitimate workers, they can have the indirect effect of impeding some in the realisation of their right to take work, hence creating a deficit.

Welfare as related to transnational rights

Given the weakness of welfare support as a universally acknowledged entitlement, the 'no public funds' constraint can have an impact on claims to other ostensibly universal rights, such as the right to family life (as in article 8 of the ECHR). This right is commonly cited as a principal source of continuing immigration, and one over which nation states have little control (e.g. Hollifield, 1992; Soysal, 1994: 121; Freeman, 1995: 889). However, there is an inherent ambiguity in the European Convention itself, which accepts interference with family life (only) 'in the interests of national security, public safety or the economic well-being of the country' (ECHR, article 8(2)), and distinctions are to be found between national citizens, EEA citizens and others (third country nationals, TCNs).

While some countries (not including Britain) grant their own nationals unconditional unification rights,[9] for TCNs the 'right' is usually subject to a test of the original migrant's ability to house and maintain additional family members. This in effect excludes them from social rights for a transitional period – the duration of which may be nationally variable. Family unification is not, therefore, established as a direct right, but may be made subject to qualifying criteria that can themselves be open to interpretation, and may change with national circumstances.[10] Furthermore, there are common deficits in realising the right and meeting the associated conditions. Reliance on informal sector employment can be an impediment to demonstrating self-maintenance, especially since anticipated earnings for the incoming spouse are not included in the calculation, and generally low income may interfere with access to adequate housing in a competitive market. Where the conditions for family unification involve an exclusion from public funds for a specified period, this also has the effect of cutting families off from the supports available to others, and even creating a hesitation to claim support to which they are in fact entitled. Thus, the (qualified) right to family life is formally stratified with respect to the conditions of entitlement (inclusion and exclusion), and informally stratified with respect to its delivery in practice (gain and deficit).

Key examples of absolute rights are international obligations with respect to recognised refugees and a variety of other statuses of protection. Under the Geneva Convention the central obligation of receiving states is that of '*non-refoulement*' – a commitment not to return the asylum seeker to a situation that threatens life and freedom. There is an implied guarantee of access to status determination procedures, but no obligation to facilitate the arrival of asylum seekers at national borders. Indeed, the use of visas (JCWI, 1987) in combination with carrier sanctions (Cruz, 1995) has served to create a deficit in accessing the right to seek asylum. The same may be said of the EU practice that denies the choice of host country to the asylum seeker, and permits one application only, usually in the member state of first arrival. We should also note that the forms of protection available themselves constitute a sub-system of civic stratification, ranging from full recognition, through humanitarian protection, to discretionary leave or temporary protection, each with different associated rights.

Welfare is significant in the treatment of asylum seekers as a further example of the close interconnection between rights and controls, and through the introduction of an element of stratification into systems of social support. Asylum seekers in Britain are no longer granted the possibility of employment, and 'late-claimers' may be denied support, though the provision of maintenance has been endorsed by British courts as necessary for the pursuit of their claim.[11] However, several countries have developed systems of provision that are explicitly linked to deterrence, variously using reception centres and/or largely cashless maintenance to discourage any who might (it is believed) be drawn by the availability of direct payments through the welfare system.[12] The administration of such systems can provide a means of keeping track of claimants that all but ties them to a particular locality, especially where there is a compulsory system of dispersal (as in Britain and Germany), linked in the German case with an overt denial of freedom of movement outside of the local district. Should systems of support become too severe, however, there is a danger that this will provoke withdrawal and subsequent loss of control. Though the legal status of asylum seekers is secure until they receive a negative decision, they may still become part of a floating population living on the margins of society, outside of any formal system of support. Furthermore, the continuing presence of rejected asylum seekers is one source of an apparently expanding underground population, who have difficulty asserting any contractual (employment) rights they may have, and receive social rights only *in extremis*.

Testing the boundaries of rights

The material presented here has provided ample evidence of the way in which formal and informal status differences are a central factor shaping entitlement and delivery of work and welfare rights – for both citizens and non-citizens. We have yet to address the third dimension of civic stratification: the scope for expansion or contraction of either a whole regime of rights or a specific area within its ambit. This issue is in all probability closely associated with some interplay between entitlement and estimations of social honour, and there are a number of different potential linkages: a granting of entitlement may lead to enhanced social standing; a contraction in entitlement may encourage stigma; enhanced social recognition may prompt entitlement; and a deterioration in such recognition may prompt a contraction of rights. This is an area that awaits full empirical investigation, but in separating out contraction and expansion from the analysis of formal and informal status distinctions, we are encouraged to focus on the issue of change, on the principal agents in distributional struggles over rights, and on the different possible interactions between the formal and informal aspects of status.

Judicial rulings have been one important factor, and Woodhouse (1998) argues that in Britain the 1990s were characterised by a more interventionist stance on the part of the judiciary, noting a relaxation of the rule that requires applicants for Judicial Review to be personally affected by the decision. This opens up the possibility for various civil society groups (such as Joint Council for the Welfare of Immigrants (JCWI), Child Poverty Action Group and the Refugee Council) to be actively involved in bringing cases before the courts. Woodhouse also cites a number of cases in which a negative right (such as the right to life, or the right to seek asylum) is deemed to require the provision of positive rights of social support for its realisation, and predicts an increase in judicial intervention to defend the rights historically associated with the welfare state. 'Claims making' has certainly become a key issue in negotiating the dynamic expansion and contraction of rights as civil society groups embrace an expansionary discourse on rights, often testing its effectiveness in the courts. The unprecedented scale of asylum and immigration legislation in Britain from 1993 onwards[13] furnishes a number of examples, and has been shadowed by a series of prominent cases that have challenged government policy (for accounts, see Morris, 2002a; Webber, 2004) with varying degrees of success.

This chapter has reviewed some contentious aspects of work and welfare rights, as related to citizens, immigrants and asylum seekers. Each group displays a differing combination of the formal and informal dimensions of civic stratification, and each highlights some significant shifts in British policy. In the case of the welfare rights of citizens, we have noted a move away from mutuality and towards contract in entitlement and delivery, and Flynn (2004) has argued that a similar dynamic is at work in relation to immigration and asylum. He notes the expansion of opportunities for migrants in possession of desirable skills, but the much more limited opportunities available to lower-skilled migrants, which sit alongside harsh restrictions of rights in the treatment of asylum seekers. Though differing in detail, these tendencies are echoed elsewhere in Europe, and Flynn goes on to argue that the apparently conflictual influences of the market and of rights have been united in a set of utilitarian principles related to growth and modernisation.

For him, the concept of absolute rights has become all but obsolete, while the *privilege* of rights is increasingly reserved for those who can show their usefulness in the growing, dynamic world economy.

This chapter has focused on rights to work and welfare, an area in which international conventions have only limited purchase, and where provisions commonly rest on varied qualifying criteria and behavioural conditions. It has been argued that the concept of civic stratification is helpful in analysing both the differing statuses of formal entitlement and their relationship to informal aspects of gain and deficit. Above all else, what the material reveals is the dynamic nature of rights, and their close association with aspects of control. Marshall offered us an evolutionary account of the progressive unfolding of the rights of citizenship, and observed a forward urge in this expanding field. Similarly, Lockwood noted the push for ever fuller citizenship, captured by his reference to 'civic expansion'. The debates and developments recorded above, however, show the terrain of rights as a shifting one, where we can find contractions as well as (and even alongside) expansions. This calls attention to the role of government policy interests, political rhetoric, the involvement of the judiciary and the impact of civil society groups in negotiating the profile of rights that are rarely demonstrably 'self-evident'.

Notes

1 For example, single mothers, the disabled, the long-term unemployed, the elderly.
2 For example, location *vis-à-vis* the market, or immigration status.
3 Lockwood (1996: 537) makes a further division into the three sub-areas of power, stigmatisation and fiscal deficits.
4 A New Labour Government came to power in 1997 and has continued the trend to tighter conditions on welfare benefits, especially, but not exclusively, for the unemployed.
5 See Lockwood (1996) for an argument that the potential for collective identity and action is unlikely to be realised.
6 Detention facilities for asylum seekers in Britain rose from 900 in 1997 to 1750 in 2004 (*Guardian Weekly*, 24 September 2004). Their use is not confined to rejected applicants.
7 See European Court of Human Rights case *D* v. *UK*, application number 30240/96.
8 Council Directive L 16/44 will extend this right to long-term resident TCNs.
9 Usually limited to the immediate nuclear family (as in Germany), but possibly including dependent parents (as in Italy).
10 A European Court of Human Rights ruling in 1985 found gender discrimination in Britain's rules on family unification, which disadvantaged women seeking unification with a spouse, as compared with men. The clear objective of the rule had been job protection, and the British response was to equalise downwards, further limiting the rights of men (Bhabha and Shutter, 1994: 76).
11 For British examples, see 1996 AII ER 385, and 1997 1 CCLR 85.
12 For a challenge to this argument, see Bloch and Schuster (2002).
13 Five acts plus the Human Rights Act (HRA), which also has a bearing.

5 'Women's rights are human rights'

Campaigns and concepts

Diane Elson

The claim that 'women's rights are human rights' has served as a focus for organizing and advocacy by large numbers of feminist organizations throughout the world since the early 1990s. However, during the same period many feminist social and political theorists have been very critical of the concept of 'universal rights', and of the deployment of the concept of 'women'. This chapter explores what lies behind this apparent discord and discusses how far feminist theory and practice can be reconciled.

To provide a framework for sociological interpretation, I draw on the interchange in *Sociology* between Bryan Turner and Malcolm Waters (Turner, 1993, 1997; Waters, 1996) and on two recent articles in *Economy and Society* by feminist theorists Kate Nash and Sylvia Walby (Nash, 2002; Walby, 2002).

Sociology of human rights

There is a large body of sociological analysis of citizenship rights, but sociological analysis of human rights is sparse and began only in the 1990s. The pioneering debate between Turner and Waters exemplifies two different approaches. Turner wants to construct an understanding of the moral appeal of human rights: on what grounds can we make sense of the moral force of a claim to have a right by virtue of being human rather than by virtue of a particular system of laws? In contrast, Waters wants to construct an explanation of the emergence and operation of human rights institutions at a specific time and place; he asks the question, whose interests do such institutions serve?

Turner argues that without some universal foundation, a recognition of some shared human experience, it is impossible to talk of justice. He founds the morality of human rights not in the capacity to reason, but in a combination of universal bodily frailty, experience of the precarious nature of the protection afforded by the law and the state, and emotional capacity for empathy. The first two of these features can be interpreted as explaining the need for rights that derive their legitimacy beyond the state; and the first and last as explaining the possibility of the recognition of the moral claims of other human beings:

Ultimately my argument has to assume that sympathy is also a consequence of, or supplement to, human frailty. Human beings will want their rights to be recognized because they see in the plight of others their own (possible) misery. The strong may have a rational evaluation of the benefits of altruistic behaviour, but the collective imperative for other-regarding actions must have a compassionate component in order to have any force. The strong can empathize with the weak, because their own ontological condition prepares them for old age and death.

(Turner, 1993: 506)

The invocation of empathy points to the importance of social connection, not just individual experience, in the moral appeal of human rights. As Turner concludes: 'In my argument, it is from a collectively held recognition of individual frailty that rights as a system of mutual protection gain their emotive force' (Turner, 1993: 507).

Waters argues that the important task for sociologists is to explain the social construction of human rights, including the historical origins of human rights institutions, and historical and cultural variation in the making of human rights claims. For this, we need to look at the interplay of specific interests rather than supposedly universal experiences of frailty, precariousness and empathy: 'the institutionalization of rights is a product of the balance of power between political interests' (Waters, 1996: 595).

Waters argues that the production (in 1948), and subsequent use, of the Universal Declaration of Human Rights can be explained in terms of four sets of interests: the interests of the victors of the Second World War in stigmatizing and penalizing those they defeated; the interests of the two sides in the 'Cold War' that followed in undermining each others' legitimacy; the interest of superpowers in legitimizing intervention in the affairs of other states; and the interests of disadvantaged groups in being able to claim human rights. The moral force of human rights derives from the collective endorsement of such rights, even though the motivations and interests underlying this endorsement vary. There is no need, in his view, for any further explanation.

In response, Turner argues that Waters's account of human rights, as merely the agreed outcome of specific political struggles, cannot account for their moral authority. To explain this, Turner argues, it is necessary to go beyond the contingent circumstances of the social construction of particular human rights institutions and practices, to identify universally shared human characteristics to which human rights respond.

A weakness in Turner's argument is the unproblematic assumption of a universal ability to empathize, to put yourself in the place of the other. In a later discussion, he links this ability to the experience of bodily frailty: 'vulnerability opens us to social interactions with and dependency on other social agents. . . . There are social processes of interaction that produce countervailing forces (emotions) of trust, sympathy and empathy' (Turner and Rojek, 2001: 123). But he has to admit that 'sympathy appears to be in short supply in places like Bosnia'.

If sympathy were always freely available in adequate quantities, it is hard to see why we would need human rights. Human rights address the limitations of sympathy with others, as well as stemming from the possibility of sympathy with others. Human rights institutions and practices address our moral frailty as well as our bodily frailty. They oblige us to extend our sympathies beyond those belonging to our group (whether it is our family, community, ethnicity, nation, gender, age group, etc.). The interplay of political interests at particular times and places helps to explain how far these obligations are recognised and met. The approaches adopted by Turner and Waters are not mutually exclusive, as Turner (1997: 566) recognizes. A sociology of human rights needs both approaches to make full sense of human rights.

Walby (2002) and Nash (2002) are both valuable pioneering contributions to a sociology of gender and human rights. Sylvia Walby's approach is similar to that of Waters. In the introduction to her article, she explains that she seeks to understand some specific constructions and appropriations of human rights by feminist groups in the 1990s:

> neither the use of the notion of equal rights nor demands on the state are entirely new within feminism, but both the extent of the use of universalist conceptions of human rights . . . and the extent of the orientation to states constitute new developments. This raises a number of questions as to how this is to be understood and why this is happening.
>
> (Walby, 2002: 533)

In providing an answer, Walby points to: structural changes in the gender regime; women's increased access to economic and organizational resources; changes in political opportunity structures; and globalization. She recognizes that the framing of feminist demands in terms of universal human rights is a challenge to much contemporary feminist theory, which has stressed the salience of differences between women, and criticized discourses of rights as androcentric, ethnocentric and too individualistic. But her main concern is not to legitimize the invocation of human rights by feminist activists, but to explain it in terms of historical developments.

Kate Nash's approach is more like that of Turner, conceptual rather than historical. She is concerned with the moral force of appeals to human rights, and with the 'normative timidity' of some contemporary feminist theory. She subscribes to the anti-essentialism of post-structural feminism; but is sensitive to the criticism that it is 'unable to elaborate universal principles that would constrain the unjust possibilities that must arise if contestation and the openness of ungrounded universalism are the only ideals to which we subscribe' (Nash, 2002: 416). She argues that a normative commitment to equality is indispensable to feminism, but seeks to ground that commitment in an ontology of the fluidity of human difference ('there is nothing about sexual difference which is fixed or necessary'; ibid.: 420), rather than the absence of difference. Though Nash does not specifically link her argument to the sociology of the body, one might perhaps see it as grounded in the universal experience of bodily change through the life course, a point also recognized by Turner.

The rest of this chapter explores in more detail the campaigns and concepts underlying the claim that 'women's rights are human rights', drawing on research that refers to activism and scholarship of women in both the 'South' and 'North' of the globe.

The emergence of a global feminist movement

Despite the promise of her introduction, Walby devotes most of her article to explaining the increased orientation of Western feminist organizations to the state in the 1990s. The articulation of feminism through a discourse of human rights is treated (briefly) as an extension of campaigns to stop violence against women. These, in Walby's account, moved from the establishment of autonomous women's projects (such as rape crisis centres and refuges for battered wives), to an engagement with state institutions to secure policies to reduce the incidence of violence and offer state support to women victims of violence, to an engagement with inter-state institutions such as the European Union, and ultimately to the United Nations:

> By the early 1990s this demand to stop men's violence against women was articulated in international forums, including those of the UN. . . . This was translated into language and concepts more appropriate for the predominantly male forum of the UN, that is the language of human rights rather than men's oppression of women.
>
> (Walby, 2002: 541)

Walby sees this as typical of a general trajectory of feminist activism in industrialized countries, from a politics of small, autonomous women's groups to attempts to mainstream gender equality and equal rights in public policy, at national, regional and international levels, through coalitions and alliances between different groups of women. She argues that this was facilitated by a change in the gender regime, from a more domestic form to a more public form, marked by greater female participation in labour markets, in civil society institutions and in the state, as more women became officials and elected representatives. This provided women with more access to economic and organizational resources and new political opportunities.

Walby suggests that globalization (which she defines as 'a process of increased density and frequency of international or global social interactions relative to local or national ones'; ibid.: 534) projected this trajectory beyond the national to the global level in two ways. First, it facilitated increased communication between feminist organizations in different parts of the world, and strengthened international feminist networks. Second, it facilitated the opening of new political spaces beyond the nation state. However, this interpretation of globalization does not foreground the diversity of global interactions. While some are benign and founded on mutuality, they take place in a context shaped by asymmetric and disruptive global interactions structured around the pursuit of profit, not mutuality. Because of this, globalization is a contradictory process.

Though Walby, referring to the 1990s, writes of a discourse of human rights being 'strategically utilized by collectively organized women' (ibid.: 549), she does not enter into discussion of how these strategies were constructed and what prompted the engagement with human rights. The history of this engagement is longer and more complex than emerges from Walby's account. Arvonne Fraser (1999: 888) points out that advocates of women's rights were active in the UN from its foundation in 1945, including women from the 'South' as well as from the 'North': 'Led by South American delegates, notably women from Brazil, Mexico, and the Dominican Republic, and with support from Indian and North American NGOs, the linkage between women's rights and human rights was effectively made in the UN Charter in its introduction and in four separate articles.' The Human Rights Commission almost immediately set up a Sub-Commission on the Status of Women. Many women in the national delegations to the UN General Assembly lobbied for this to become a free-standing Commission and this was agreed in 1946.

Women's rights advocates were active in the drafting of the Universal Declaration of Human Rights, and argued strongly for inclusive language, with Mrs Mehta from India objecting to the use of terms such as 'all men' and 'brothers'. Fraser (ibid.) argues that such interventions led to the extensive use of the term 'everyone' in the Declaration. Fraser explains the engagement of women's rights advocates with the founding of the human rights system, and their later engagement with the system in the 1990s, through factors similar to those invoked by Walby. She points to the increase in women's participation in the paid labour force in the Second World War, the success of the movement to get the vote for women in national elections, the presence of women in civil society organizations (especially the international labour movement) and women's experience in lobbying governments.

The Commission on the Status of Women (CSW) was active in securing the adoption of a number of Conventions on specific areas of women's rights in the 1950s and 1960s, including economic and social rights, as well as civil and political rights. The younger generation of women in the new autonomous feminist groups that began to be formed in the industrialized countries in the late 1960s did not engage with the CSW and the human rights system (Fraser, ibid.: 893), but 'second wave' feminism did begin an engagement with the UN system in 1975. When the first UN inter-governmental conference on women was held in Mexico in that year, a conference of non-governmental organizations (NGOs) was held, parallel to the inter-governmental conference, in which many women from autonomous feminist groups (from both 'South' and 'North') participated.

The inter-governmental conference called for the drafting and adoption of a new overarching human rights treaty, the Convention on the Elimination of All Discrimination against Women (CEDAW). This was achieved in 1979. According to Fraser, most of the new feminist groups did not pay attention to CEDAW, but this was to change with the Third UN Women's Conference in Nairobi in 1985. There were 15,000 women at the parallel NGO Forum and a number of international women's rights networks were set up. International Women's Rights Action Watch was organized to monitor and support the implementation of CEDAW (ibid.: 901), and three important regional networks were set up: the Latin American Committee for the Defense of Women's Rights; the Asia-Pacific Forum on Women, Law and Development; and Women in Law and Development in Africa (Friedman, 1995: 24). Nevertheless, Fraser acknowledges that until the issue of violence against women came to widespread prominence, the majority of women's organizations did not pay any attention to the human rights system.

Feminist organizations claim human rights for women

Fraser explains how the CEDAW Committee (the official UN body that monitors compliance with CEDAW) took up the issue of violence against women in 1989 and 1992, through General Recommendations 12 and 19, which made it clear that although CEDAW itself does not specifically mention violence against women, gender-based violence constitutes discrimination against women and thus violates the convention.

She reports that: 'The momentum around the issue [of gender-based violence] made women's human rights the most dramatic agenda item at the 1993 World Conference on Human Rights' (Fraser, 1999: 903). But Fraser, who served both as a director of International Women's Rights Action Watch and as a member of the US official delegation to the Vienna Conference, does not acknowledge the way in which feminists campaigning for women's rights and against gender-based violence had criticized the human rights system. Their aim was not just to make women's human rights a 'dramatic agenda item' but to contest existing understandings of human rights and create new ones. In contrast, Walby (2002: 541) does recognize that there was 'a call for a transformation of the existing human rights agenda and for a new interpretation that placed women's issues at the heart of the mainstream'.

A leading role in articulating the call for transformation was played by Charlotte Bunch, Director of the Center for Women's Global Leadership at Rutgers University. Bunch argued that women's rights were not generally understood to be human rights by governments, by human rights NGOs and by the UN Commission on Human Rights. She suggested that:

> In the UN system, the Human Rights Commission has more power to hear and investigate cases than the Commission on the Status of Women, more staff and more budget, and better mechanisms for implementing its findings. Thus it makes a difference what can be done if a case is deemed a violation of women's rights and not of human rights.
>
> (Bunch, 1990: 492)

Bunch noted the existence of CEDAW but doubted its capacity to address violence against women effectively, arguing that 'Within the UN, it is not generally regarded as a convention with teeth' (ibid.: 496), and that it is treated by governments and most NGOs as a document dealing with rights that are 'secondary' to real human rights. (These arguments were supported by other feminist commentators, such as Stamatopoulou, 1995). About one-third of states that have ratified CEDAW have entered substantive reservations to various articles of the treaty, meaning that they have not undertaken to implement it in full. This is more than for any other international human rights treaty. Some of the reservations in effect nullify some of the most important provisions of the treaty (Zwingel, forthcoming).

What was required, argued Bunch, was something more radical: a 're-visioning' of human rights from a feminist perspective, without waiting for 'permission from some authority to determine what is or is not a human right issue' (Bunch, 1990: 497). At the core of Bunch's 're-visioning' is a requirement to break down barriers 'between public and private, state and non-governmental responsibilities' (ibid.: 497). Only thus, she argued, would abuses that 'arise specifically out of gender such as reproductive rights, female sexual slavery, violence against women, and "family crimes" like forced marriage, compulsory heterosexuality and female mutilation' (ibid.) be addressed. Bunch thus explicitly recognizes the androcentric-ism of human rights (much criticized by feminist legal scholars, such as Charlesworth, 1995; and feminist social theorists, such as Peterson and Parisi, 1998), but believes that this is a historically determined aspect that can be changed. I would suggest that her arguments may also be seen as an extension of, rather than a break with, the claim of the autonomous femi-nist groups of the 1960s and 1970s that 'the personal is political'. They also represent a challenge to the status order of the time, whereby the position of women, and their associations with the private sphere, took a poor second place to abuses of rights (especially civil rights) in the public sphere.

Bunch envisages 're-visioning' of human rights as a possibility because she sees human rights as not only 'one of the few moral visions ascribed to internationally' (Bunch, 1990: 488) but also as a dynamic and open-ended idea, its meaning expanding 'as people reconceive of their needs and hopes' (ibid.: 487). This is an approach that fits Nash's approving description of an 'anti-foundationalist' approach as comprising:

> reflexive consideration of the ultimate grounds of truth claims or moral universals with a view to understanding how they have been contingently established in particular texts or historically specific traditions of thought. Such an understanding is supposed to contribute to the contestation of their unquestioned status as foundations and so to the democratization of thought (though not to the eliminations of foundations as such, which are indispensable to thought).
>
> (Nash, 2002: 416)

But theory is never enough: Bunch recognized that feminists could not change the meaning of human rights simply by argument; they had to work through the 'due process' of human rights institutions to secure a new consensus among governments, UN human rights institutions and human rights NGOs. This was possible because the repertoire of human rights instruments extends beyond the drafting, signing and ratifying of treaties, to include the 'General Comments and Recommendations' of treaty bodies (like the CEDAW Committee), the 'Concluding Observations' of these bodies on reports submitted by governments, the reports of 'Special Rapporteurs' on specific topics and the deliberations of the UN General Assembly, and of UN world conferences on specific topics.

UN world conferences are particularly important because accredited NGOs are allowed to attend as observers, and because the practice has grown of facilitating parallel or satellite NGO meetings, beside the intergovernmental meetings. The UN Conference on Human Rights in Vienna in 1993 provided the ideal opportunity to promote a 're-vision'; and Bunch was one of the leaders of a well-organized international movement of hundreds of thousands of women from around the world that ensured that the Vienna Declaration initiated the construction of such a new consensus (Friedman, 1995). It stated that 'the full and equal enjoyment by women of all human rights' must be a priority for national governments and the UN system. It led to the appointment of a UN Special Rapporteur on Violence against Women and the adoption of a Declaration on the Elimination of Violence against Women by the UN General Assembly. Nash (2002: 417) comments that 'The use of human rights to challenge structures and incidences of violence against women across the world has been the most successful way of extending human rights to women.'

Half of humanity: the fight for equal status

Why did so many women in so many countries agree with Bunch's diagnosis of the androcentrism of the human rights system, yet also agree with her that the human rights system could be enormously valuable in the struggle to end systemic gender-based violence against women, and in other struggles to increase women's well-being? Friedman (1995) and Stivens (2000) go some way to answering this question. Both point to the perception that the human rights system has widespread international legitimacy, even though it is reinterpreted and reworked in different ways in different places. Stivens (2000: 8) suggests that the prominence given by feminists to the human rights system in the 1990s is also linked to 'the political and intellectual decline of the left, with human rights acting as a global rallying point for intellectuals and activists stricken by its collapse worldwide'.

Friedman mentions that several of the activists she interviewed, including Bunch, also linked the rise of human rights to the decline of other forms of social internationalism. She also points to the significance of the disillusion of women activists in Latin America with the fruits of democracy. Women played a major role in the struggle to end the dictatorships, often drawing upon their roles as mothers to give their protest legitimacy. However, democratization did not fully include the realization of their rights, nor address the issue of systemic violence against women (Molyneux and Razavi, 2002). Women in Latin American quickly realized the limitations of the democratic state, and turned to human rights not as much as an extension of their engagement with the democratic national state but as a necessary corrective to reliance on the actions of democratic national states.

One of the Latin American activists interviewed by Friedman makes an important point about women's strategic use of human rights: 'they began to use the human rights framework to advance women's rights. Instead of claiming rights as *women*, they claimed the human rights of *half of humanity*' (Maria Suarez, Costa Rica; Friedman, 1995: 22).

In parts of Asia and Africa, women activists invoked a 're-visioned' human rights system strategically to counteract the deployment of falsely static and homogeneous notions of 'tradition' and 'culture' by male politicians keen to preserve the existing gender regime (Rao, 1995; Stivens, 2000). They also reminded men that women want 'social justice in accordance with internationally accepted standards' (Friedman, 1995: 23).

Globalization was a further reason to turn to human rights: not the benign globalization of social interactions described by Walby (2002: 534), but the asymmetric and disruptive globalization that wrenches people from their homes and deposits them in a strange land. Human rights provides an indispensable resource for campaigning for the rights of people who lack citizenship rights in the country in which they live, a group whose numbers, both male and female, have rapidly increased as a result of intensified migration, both documented and undocumented (Sassen, 1996; see also Chapter 4). Indeed, the human rights system, which includes economic, social and cultural rights, as well as political and civil rights, may (with some 're-visioning') provide a basis for women to contest the fundamental asymmetry of globalization, which privileges the property rights of owners of large amounts of capital above all other rights (Elson and Gideon, 2004).

Feminist activists claiming human rights are under no illusions about the efficacy of the human rights system. They understand that international implementation mechanisms are weak; and recognize that human rights treaties ultimately depend for their implementation on the actions of states (Zwingel, forthcoming). Nevertheless, the human rights system provides an additional space for political struggle in which even states that in formal terms are democratic can be 'named and shamed' for their failure to promote, protect and fulfil human rights. As Nash (2002: 417) notes, 'symbolically, rights discourse provides a powerful vocabulary for challenging wrongs. Feminist activists therefore advocate the extension of human rights, despite their limited effectiveness, because of the way they can contribute to a culture in which justice is furthered as an ideal.'

Walby (2002: 546) sees the turn to human rights as a turn away from anti-systemic politics; but the human rights system has some capacity to support anti-systemic politics, as well as to uphold the status quo (Baxi, 2002; Elson and Gideon, 2004). Much depends on how human rights are deployed and by whom. When women's human rights are invoked to justify US invasions of other countries, clearly it is imperial power that is being upheld. But demands for an end to systemic gender-based violence against women, and for the realization of women's economic, social and cultural rights, can be an important challenge to existing configurations of male and class power (Bunch, 1990; Elson, 2002; Molyneux and Razavi, 2002).

Universality, difference and equality: deconstructing and reconstructing the conceptual basis for women's human rights

Feminist social and political theorists have criticized concepts of universal rights as androcentric. They have argued that a false universalism has been promulgated, which in fact is not universal at all but based on the experience and needs of men. Rights are available primarily in the public sphere, not in the private sphere. This critique has been developed mainly in relation to citizenship rights (e.g. Phillips, 1992; Lister, 1997; Vogel, 1997) but is also applicable to human rights. Feminist postcolonial theorists have revealed the ethnocentricism of deployments of universal human rights that cast women in postcolonial societies as 'the Other', lacking any agency, requiring rescue by Western women (e.g. Lazreg, 1990; Mohanty, 1991). Post-structural feminists argue that 'women' are not an already existing constituency, but one that has to be constructed (Nash, 2002: 423).

These criticisms have not stopped feminist activists, neither in the West, nor in other regions of the world, from claiming human rights for women. But they have done so in ways that reject abstract universalism and simultaneously claim both universality and difference. In asserting that 'women's rights are human rights', they have simultaneously claimed that women are half of a universal humanity; and that this humanity is differentiated into women and men, who suffer systematically different abuses of their human rights. Both men and women suffer bodily frailty, but abuse of this frailty takes systematically different forms, and involves different kinds of power relation. Violence against women is argued to be systemic, not random, or individual or personal, and to be central to maintaining male power over women (e.g. Heise, 1989; Bunch, 1990). Nevertheless, everywhere women resist, despite their vulnerability. While the specificities of gender-based violence differ between different countries and cultures, as do the most urgent and appropriate ways to combat this violence, feminist activists have been able to construct international coalitions based on the recognition of violence against women as a systemically determined violation. Such activists have constructed a politics of 'differentiated universalism' (Lister, 1997), recognizing difference both between men and women and between different groups of women, and reworking human rights to create new meanings and practices that strive to avoid androcentrism and ethnocentrism, and to claim equal human rights for all women and men. It is a politics that appreciates diversity but does not displace a normative commitment to equality.

But there is a danger that difference, once recognized, may become essentialized, and rendered static and fixed. This is the danger that most concerns Nash, who locates herself as a post-structuralist feminist. She distinguishes two different existing visions of equality: the 'difference' vision and the 'degendering' vision (Nash, 2002: 419). The 'difference' vision sees men and women as physically, socially and psychologically different. The problem is that the qualities that women possess are given less social value than those that men possess. Equality requires that these different qualities should have equal social value. Nash rejects this vision because it may contribute to solidifying current patterns of gender difference. The 'degendering' vision sees differences between women and men as shaped by gender stereotypes, and calls for the elimination of these stereotypes, and the elimination of any gendered pattern of social valuation. This vision is linked to an ideal of androgyny, which Nash rejects because it eliminates rather than celebrates diversity. She argues for a third vision – 'deconstructive equality' – which would involve:

> the continual disruption of gendered practices and identities *without penalty or disadvantage* to any person. In other words, it would mean the transformation of social practices such that any sex, gender or sexual orientation – and poststructuralist feminists would not expect these to be binary – could be occupied by any individual, was always open to contestation and change and was not discriminated against.
>
> (Nash, 2002: 421)

Nash then examines the text of CEDAW and finds that there is within it some scope for all of these visions; including her 'deconstructive' position, for which she finds some support in article 5 (a) (the most radical article in CEDAW), which requires states 'To modify the social and cultural patterns of conduct of men and women, with a view to achieving the elimination of prejudices and customary and all other practices which are based on the idea of the inferiority or the superiority of either of the sexes or on stereotyped roles for men and women.'

This enables her to conclude that it is possible to understand human rights in a way that does not undermine the post-structuralist commitment to 'continual contestation, disruption and difference' (Nash, 2002: 416). However, she has to admit that women's movements across the world are more oriented to the 'difference' model of equality, and that a commitment to 'deconstructive' equality is rare (Nash, 2002: 427, 428). Certainly the arguments used by Bunch for understanding violence against women as a human rights violation reflect the 'difference' vision of equality. She quotes approvingly the statement by Lori Heise that 'This is not random violence . . . the risk factor is being female' (Bunch, 1990: 490). Although 'compulsory heterosexuality' is included in the list of abuses of women, the argument is for the most part constructed on the basis that there are two sexes, and the problem is to end the domination of the female sex by the male sex.

It is not surprising that the post-structuralist values of continual contestation and change do not have a widespread appeal to women. For all but the most well-off and most self-confident, disruption is frequently experienced as insecurity, not an opening up of exciting new possibilities, and asymmetrical globalization often intensifies the negative aspects of social flux. A focus on broadening and equalizing the range of capabilities enjoyed by women and men is probably a more appealing form of fluidity than an emphasis on continual contestation and complete openness. This might be called 'transformative' equality, and has to be underpinned by supportive economic, social and political structures that enable people to experiment and take risks by guaranteeing their enjoyment of the economic, social and cultural human rights (such health, education, an adequate standard of living and full participation in the public life of the community). 'Transformative' equality thus encompasses what Nancy Fraser calls 'transformative redistribution combined with transformative recognition' (Fraser, 1995: 91): 'Transformative' equality would address the concerns expressed by Nash, that we need a concept of equality that allows a woman or man to claim they are discriminated against when they experience disadvantage through choosing to do something that is more typically associated with the other sex; but it would also address the issue of the economic, social and political structures they need in order to be able to make those choices.

Fortunately, CEDAW provides a flexible framework in which a variety of different visions of equality can be accommodated; and which can be appropriated by diverse groups of women in ways that best serve their specific contexts. In the fifteen years since Bunch dismissed it as 'toothless', its implementation mechanisms have been strengthened, and more women have begun to use it as a reference point in struggles for their human rights at national level (Landsberg-Lewis, 1998; Zwingel, forthcoming). It allows for positive action measures to offset deeply embedded structural discrimination, and sets a standard of substantive, not merely formal, equality. It encompasses economic, social and cultural rights, as well as civil and political rights.

Though Nash, like Turner, is concerned with the social philosophy of human rights, she is reluctant to anchor their moral appeal in anything outside her own biography. She concludes that '[t]hus those of us for whom universal human rights *are* actually compelling can only trace the arguments, situations, and political histories through which we have come to this position; we will be able to find no ultimate justification for our belief and feelings' (Nash, 2002: 425). In this she is influenced by Rorty (1993), who argues that there is no rational, extra-community point from which judgement can be exercised. We may agree with this latter argument without concluding that, therefore, we can only fall back on our individual biographies. Turner (1993) argues for an anchor point, not in some rational extra-community space, but in shared bodily and emotional experiences that are constitutive of what it is to be human – though we find that even this is gendered.

This emphasis on human rights as rooted in what human beings share, and in mutual recognition of our neediness, is important given the undoubted priority that human rights give to individual autonomy. Nash insists on the importance of individual autonomy because it enables fixed gender identities to be continually contested; but she is concerned about the charge that this is ethnocentric (Nash, 2002: 422). She resolves this through a discussion of Uma Narayan's critique of conceptualization of culture as a unified totality, which, Narayan argues, is particularly problematic in relation to insubordinate groups within a culture (Narayan, 1997). Nash concludes that in the end it is impossible to avoid the responsibility of making judgements about what is progressive and puts forward the ideal of 'deconstructive equality' as the benchmark to guide these judgements.

Walby argues persuasively that human rights are not necessarily individualistic, in the sense of being in opposition to collective action, providing examples where individual rights are claimed through individuals presenting themselves as part of a group and taking collective action (Walby, 2002: 548). Individual autonomy does not have to imply disconnection from others, from families and communities. Instead it can imply a reworking of connection, so that instead of the connection being one of dependency it can be one of mutuality (cf. Chapter 1). Individual autonomy does not mean there are no legitimate constraints on individual behaviour. All human rights are qualified by the obligation to respect the human rights of others.

Nor are individual rights necessarily in opposition to collective rights. Collective rights always have to be exercised by persons. The questions are: who those persons are; through what process they come to have the power to exercise those rights; and how accountable they are to the other members of the collectivity. Individuals can have rights to a say in how collective rights are exercised, and can have rights to use collective property in stipulated ways. Individual rights should be distinguished from privatized rights, which consist of rights to exclude others from the enjoyment of something, and are exercised in the market through buying and selling for commercial gain.

In some parts of the world women are engaged in a complex reconstruction of the relation between individual rights and collective rights. An important example is Mexico, where indigenous women are intervening in the restructuring of rights taking place at federal, state and local level. This restructuring is taking place both through amendments to the federal and state constitutions (to some extent influenced by aspects of the human rights system, especially the ILO Convention on the Rights of Indigenous People) and through the reshaping of so-called 'traditional' customary law (*usos y costumbres*), influenced by the new *usos y costumbres* introduced in the Zapatista Autonomous Municipalities. Indigenous women have taken up issues of domestic violence, forced marriage, equal participation in a wide range of political arenas, rights to housing, education, jobs, medical care and land rights (Hernandez Castillo, 1997; Gutierrez and Palomo, 2001). Some Mexican researchers have described this as 'indigenous feminism', which attempts to protect indigenous people's rights and women's rights all at the same time, and which sees both as connected sets of individual and collective rights (Hernandez Castillo, 1997; Sierra, 2003). Indigenous women have been organizing to stake claims to use land for themselves through the notion of collective indigenous rights (Stephen, 2003). There is a national indigenous women's network dedicated to getting women's rights enforced through processes of enlarging the autonomy of indigenous communities. These women do not take their culture as static and univalent; instead they strategize to reshape it. They do not see a dichotomy between individual and collective rights. Instead they aim for a new synthesis.

The limitations of rights

There are some disadvantages to framing feminist struggles in terms of rights, whether human rights or citizenship rights, especially if this results in all gender politics being subsumed into a discourse of human rights (Stivens, 2000: 16). One disadvantage stems from the social limitations of legal discourses and processes, which everywhere tend to serve the interests of the powerful better than the interests of subordinated groups. Judges, lawyers and juries tend to interpret and apply the law in male-biased ways (Kaufman and Lindquist, 1995: 116). For instance, in cases of sexual assault and sexual harassment of women, the victim rather than the perpetrator is often the one who is judged and found 'guilty'.

But the issue goes beyond the prejudices of those involved in applying the law. Legal discourse is often premised on a false universalism. In the name of impartiality and consistency, relevant differences are ignored. Judges in the USA, for instance, for long argued that equal treatment in the workplace precluded paid maternity leave, because only women would be eligible for such benefits (Kaufman and Lindquist, 1995: 116). Moreover, rights are necessarily formulated in ways abstract from particular circumstances and the meanings attached to them. As Menon (1995: 371) points out, 'the law permitting or facilitating women's access to abortion can also permit select- ive abortion of female fetuses'. Whether this is a problem in practice depends on the social context, especially the prevalence of preference for sons.

The abstract quality of law does, however, leave space for new interpret- ations. For instance, the 1951 Geneva Convention on the right to asylum does not include among the grounds for asylum fear of persecution on grounds of gender, but it does include fear of persecution on the grounds of being a member of a particular social group. In a recent case in Britain concerning two women asylum seekers from Pakistan, the House of Lords judged that they were entitled to asylum on grounds of belonging to the social group 'women in Pakistan', because this group had well-grounded fears of persecution if they were accused of adultery (Morris, 2002: 133).

It may be argued that claims for rights are not necessarily legal claims. They can still make very good sense as moral claims, without necessarily being translated into a precisely specified legal right which is the subject of coercive legal rules. Sen (2005) argues that this was the sense in which Mary Wollstonecraft, one of the pioneers in articulating women's rights, vindicated women's claims to universal rights. However, some feminists argue strongly against formulating moral reasoning in terms of rights. Instead they argue that moral reasoning should be formulated in terms of an ethics of care (e.g. Tronto, 1993). An ethics of care implies that morality is founded in a sense of specific interpersonal connections; and an ability not just to base concern for the plight of others on what one would feel if one were in their place, but to see others as different in important ways from ourselves, yet still extend to them an understanding of their needs and interests (Robinson, 1998: 68).

This ethical foundation is in many ways similar to that invoked by Turner (1993) as the foundation for human rights, but the important difference is the compassion for those whom we see to be different from ourselves, as well as those whom we see to be similar. This is a noble ideal, but at this particular historical conjuncture there is an asymmetry of care. Social norms currently construct women as the ones who give care, who are 'naturally' good at caring, whose duty is to care; whereas men are the ones who receive care, who can legitimately demand care, who are not 'naturally' good at caring. In this context, an undifferentiated ethics of care can perpetuate women's inequality and subordination, and encourage women to be com- plicit in this perpetuation. An ethics of care has limitations, as well as an ethics of human rights. In my view we need both, in a mutually constitutive dialogue, with an emphasis at the moment on women's human rights and men's human care obligations.

A discourse that appeals to the moral legitimacy of the human rights of women does not necessarily entail an emphasis on taking cases to national courts and to UN human rights bodies. Instead it may lend the moral legitimacy of human rights to efforts to transform women's sense of themselves, and to transform cultural practices and understandings. Women in several parts of Africa have understood this well in relation to the practice of the cutting of female genitals as part of a rite of passage to adult womanhood. While recognizing this as a violation of human rights, they have strategized to reduce its prevalence through mediation and through building a new consensus in communities, including the creation of alternative rites of passage (Ibhawaoh, 1999).

Conclusions

Feminists who base their campaigns on the claim that 'women's rights are human rights' are generally well aware of the limitations of 'actually existing' human rights. They seek to transform human rights, as a concept, and as a practice, while at the same time drawing on the moral force of human rights.

There are continuities, and doubling backs, as well as breaks, in the trajectory from a politics of small-scale autonomous feminist groups, to a politics of engaging with state and inter-state institutions. Perhaps the most important continuity is an insistence on breaking down the distinction between public and private spheres of life; though there is also some continuity of transformatory, anti-systemic politics. The engagement with human rights, as distinct from citizenship rights, stems from an understanding of the limitations, as well as the possibilities, of state action to end gender inequality.

The politics of women's human rights is certainly facilitated by the more benign aspects of globalization, especially the diffusion of new communications technology. But it is also necessitated by the asymmetrical aspects of globalization, which leaves many women with no recourse to citizenship rights, and in a position whereby their access to rights is mediated by men.

Since human rights do not have a final and completely fixed meaning, they can be understood in ways that are consistent with a post-structural feminism committed to continual contestation and disruption, provided that the latter also recognizes the importance of a commitment to equality. But in the context of globalization, many women experience contestation and disruption as intensified insecurity, not expanded possibility. In this context, it is important that human rights, as well as having a capacity for openness to new meanings, are nevertheless grounded in an appreciation of the bodily and moral frailty of human beings; and the importance of stabilizing the right of all individual human beings to claim assistance from others, in a mutually constituted and egalitarian system of interconnectedness.

Note

An earlier version of this chapter was presented at the Manchester Centre for Political Theory, University of Manchester, at a conference in honour of Ursula Vogel, March 2005. Thanks are due to those present for helpful comments. Thanks are due to Kate Nash and Sylvia Walby for alerting me to their innovatory contributions to the sociology of rights; and to Lydia Morris for her editorial guidance.

6 Human rights, anti-racism and EU advocacy coalitions

Carlo Ruzza

Efforts to clarify the mechanisms that further the diffusion and institutionalization of human rights have frequently concentrated on the role of norms in the international arena. In connection to this issue, analysts have examined how human rights have emerged as new transnational norms with a binding impact on domestic regimes. However, the ways in which these norms emerge, are connected to specific policies, and come to play a role, are underspecified, as is the analysis of mechanisms operating in different types of international arenas. This chapter examines the connection between the concept of human rights as a global construct and anti-discrimination policy, and more specifically the emergence and institutionalization of anti-racist policy at the EU level. In this context, it elucidates some of the mechanisms that favour the emergence and diffusion of norms in a supranational setting: the EU.

The relevance of the EU as an expanding source of legislation in a growing number of countries and policy areas is unquestioned, and it is therefore an important setting in which to examine processes of norm diffusion. In addition, as a setting that is broader than nation states but still connected to them in clear and observable ways, the EU constitutes a good test case of several types of interaction that take place between international and domestic arenas. Examining specific forms of interaction between domestic and international contexts also helps in clarifying the mechanisms that connect the different levels of governance. Within the EU, anti-racist policy is a relatively new policy area that is often connected to human rights.

In recent years, racism has again emerged as an important issue in the political debate throughout Europe, raising a range of concerns and interpretations. A set of new policy instruments has emerged. In particular, the new article 13 of the Amsterdam Treaty legitimating EU-level action to combat various forms of discrimination, including racial discrimination, reflected the growing importance that this subject has acquired. Following the approval of article 13, several related initiatives have also emerged in recent years and were intentionally connected in legislative texts to the issue of human rights. If anti-racism is defined in terms of human rights and therefore constitutes an articulation of broad international norms, the approval of anti-racist legislation then constitutes a good test case of the mechanisms that connect broad principles and concrete policy decisions. Studying the emergence and diffusion of transnational norms offers a view of the sociological mechanisms that translate them into concrete and enforceable operating standards.

In this chapter, I explore the operating modalities of the advocacy coalition that has put anti-racism on the agenda, and also the reasons for both its successes and its weaknesses. I argue that transforming a shared norm such as the condemnation of racism into actual policy involves mediating among contrasting policy frames, defining issues in such a way that a variety of actors with contrasting interests and views can converge and focus their efforts on a process of policy change. I examine the limitations to the agenda-setting efforts of a complex coalition of Brussels-based activists and bureaucrats, which has attempted to achieve a stronger policy response. I explore its modes of operation and likely prospects, as well as examining their promotional role and their responses to the initiatives already approved. This examination allows the emerging policy process of anti-racism that article 13 and two subsequent directives have jump-started to be put into sociological context.

At the EU level anti-racism is characterised by a long history of declarations of principle in which its character as a transnational norm and definition as a human right has been enthusiastically supported and reiterated by a range of political actors – notably in the European Parliament. However, concrete policy initiatives in this area were absent for at least twenty years (Ford, 1992). This changed with the proposal and then the approval of article 13, which emerged as the outcome of pressure exerted by a composite advocacy coalition. It included a variety of institutional actors and networks of non-governmental organizations (NGOs). Several public interest lobbies and social movement organizations address the EU institutional context and had a prominent role in advocacy activities in anti-racism and related areas. They include organizations concerned with issues of anti-racism, women's issues and disability rights and movement-related groups, where a range of political parties, NGOs, movements, organizations and churches collaborate in representing the elderly, defending civil liberties, acting against homelessness, or poverty, or on behalf of refugees, migrants and asylum seekers. The role and number of these transnational organizations has grown at the EU level, paralleling a growth of similar organizations in other international arenas (Keck and Sikkink, 1998: 10).

While the support of non-state actors was important in representing issues of human rights and the value of anti-racism in institutional contexts, without the support of EU-level institutional actors they would not have been able to achieve policy change. It is therefore important to differentiate between two processes. One is the importation of new ideas in a policy environment, which in this case, and in other international contexts, is prominently affected by social movements and other conscience constituencies. A second one is the specific sociological dynamics that help to translate principles into policy proposals. The first kind of process presupposes the formation of a sufficiently coherent discursive frame. The second kind relates to the variables that facilitate the seizing of political opportunities by an advocacy coalition, which also involves acquiring needed resources, mediating among conflicting interests, action repertoires and operating procedures. The first type relates to cultural dynamics that are influenced by interactions between movements and the media and take place in an increasingly global arena. The second refers to policy events that, even when they take place in international settings, are the outcomes of complex processes of intermediation taking place within specific policy communities. As the introduction to this volume points out, the second type of process includes a variety of moderating influences on the impact of globalised conceptions of human rights emerging at the global level, such as considerations of national interest, considerations of political expediency of specific actors, etc. The relation between the two is therefore complex and has often been seen as problematic. I review these two processes separately.

Human rights, transnational principles and activist networks

The concept of human rights has received much recent scholarly attention, including the study of the use and diffusion of the term, and the study of its status in the social sciences and in social movements as embedding a new systemic utopia in the wake of other overarching utopias, particularly in the West (Woodiwiss, 2005: 79–91). Under the label of human rights, one finds a few related issues. In international settings and for mobilization purposes the language of human rights dates back to the inter-war period (Keck and Sikkink, 1998: 81) and is often utilised with reference to movements for the abolition of torture and the work of organizations such as Amnesty International, but in more general terms it is also referred to in the work of organizations focusing on race and gender issues. The debate on the role of human rights at transnational or supranational level points to the need to shift some of the analytical emphasis away from research on the nation state to issues such as the impact of transnational activist networks and their relation to global ideas circulating in international and supranational organisations (Smith *et al.*, 1997; Keck and Sikkink, 1998; Boli and Thomas, 1999; O'Brian *et al.*, 2000).

Transnational networks have been studied in a large body of literature, which has focused on the international impact of social movements (Willetts, 1982; Risse Kappen, 1995; Smith *et al.*, 1997; Keck and Sikkink, 1998; Risse *et al.*, 1999). This literature stresses the impact of activist networks that mobilise themselves to promote 'global ideas', the role of which has been depicted by scholars in various ways. Soysal (1994: 43) gives as examples the ideas of development (Ferguson, 1990), progress (Meyer, 1980) and freedom (Patterson, 1991), and adds the 'world-level organising concept' of human rights. Each of these concepts has at various times been entrenched in a social movement network.

At any point in time there exist a few distinct families of social movements reflecting ideologies with varying degrees of coherence but with a central core that characterises them as political doctrines (Freeden, 1996). Just as a language may have several local dialects, so movements take different forms in specific historical and local contexts, such as the EU and its member states. They react to different sets of problems and are shaped by different political contexts. In this respect 'human rights' come to constitute an ideology that inspires the broad family of transnational activist coalitions inspired by left-libertarian movements, but whose specific definition and relevance have varied historically on the basis of a range of variables: the viability of previously dominant ideologies, institutional considerations of political opportunity etc.

The literature on transnational activist networks is often inspired by a historical neo-institutionalist approach. Neo-institutionalists in particular, who stress path-dependent approaches, point to the role of ideas in legitimating policies and opening new policy paths, and on the time-dependent mutual adaptations of ideas and interests in particular social groups.[1] Summarising this field, and with particular reference to the international relations literature,[2] Checkel (1999) notes: 'Scholars are asking how global norms affect and constitute particular domestic agents, be they states, individuals or groups (NGOs, say). At issue, then, is how norms "out there" in the international system get "down here" to the national arena and have constitutive effects.'

The specific mechanisms that transfer ideas to the global level and then diffuse them in specific settings are still unclear, and criticism of the neo-institutionalist paradigm has focused on its inability to articulate mechanisms of diffusion (for discussions, see Risse Kappen, 1994; Finnemore and Sikkink, 1998; Checkel, 1999). This is a topical issue, as it touches upon the controversy as to the ever more flexible use of the concept of human rights to justify policies that are radically different from the ethos promoted by the left-libertarian family of movements that has emphasised the concept in international arenas – one can think, for instance, about the debate on the use of human rights to justify military interventions, and 'exporting democracy' frames. In the rest of this chapter and with reference to the EU, I seek to specify the mechanisms that constrain the range of uses that the concept can take in specific environments.

The complexity and unpredictability of institutional dynamics invites explanation at the institutional–organisational level. Applying these dynamics in fields where movements play a major role, such as social policy, a hypothesis of this chapter is that because some movements' ideas now refer to areas of generalised legitimacy, professional political actors, religious leaders and business people will subscribe to them and even take their importance for granted, while redefining them in terms consonant with their organisational/institutional cultures. In the language of sociological neo-insitutionalism, mechanisms of coercion, mimesis and normative factors will orient the adoption and redefinition of transnational norms, such as the definition of racism, as a violation of fundamental rights (DiMaggio and Powell, 1991; Peters, 2000).

The global principle of anti-racism and its political sponsors

Racism has at various times been connected to a limitation of different types of rights – in Marshallian terms racism has been seen as connected to a diminution of all kinds of rights (Marshall and Bottomore, 1992). Its connection to a diminution of legal rights have been documented in several societies. In terms of political rights (vote, organize, form unions), racism has been identified as acting as a filter in the concession of citizenship rights. And in terms of social rights (right to welfare, education and health as preconditions of political participation), it has been seen as a filter in the operation of the welfare state. Given its broad relevance, different definitions of the problem and possible solutions are feasible when facing racism as a policy issue. It is a problematic that, given its wide ambit of applicability and potential ambiguity, leads itself to a 'garbage can' model of policy approach (March and Olson, 1989). Actors match problems and solutions on the basis of preferences and their availability.

Recent geopolitical events have only marginally restricted the versatility of anti-racism – for instance, by emphasising its connection to migration issues and urban policy. In recent years, geopolitical factors, such as increased migration rates in several EU countries, regional economic recessions and the process of European integration – which makes borders more permeable – have made issues of all these kinds of rights newly relevant and salient in a growing number of European states.

The right-wing reactive social movements and parties that have emerged in several areas and the consequent attacks against racialized minorities have placed the issue of regulation of 'race' on the agenda of several countries, particularly those of new migration where there is a vacuum in this policy area. Anti-racist movements, which reject claims of a common enemy and the idealization of the nation as a cohesive community, constituted reservoirs of commitment on this issue and sources of policy proposals. They therefore have a particularly important role in politicizing issues of race, connecting them to the human rights discourse, giving them visibility in a range of social institutions and rebutting growing negative stereotypes. In addition to movements conceived as networks of people focused on organizing protest events, anti-racism also derives its impact from its character of cultural current diffused throughout society, but particularly in parties of the left, trade union movements and other left-libertarian social movements.

A bloc of anti-racists has emerged in several EU countries. It grew out of smaller migrant associations and turned into a counter-movement against attacks. It is a movement that, in addition to protesting against institutionalised racism and the mistreatment of racial minorities and migrants, promotes an ideal of tolerance and multiculturalism and is an independent voice in public discussion of the nature of the new integrated Europe. Anti-racist mobilizations exert their efforts in a variety of ways, in protest actions or within institutional domains. I will refer to them broadly as 'anti-racist movements', aware, however, that they employ widely different forms of pressure, some disruptive, some not, but with a view to stressing an empirical continuity of people and purposes.[3] The nature of this movement is difficult to define, as anti-racist protest events have occurred in a variety of contexts, within a time frame that was not unified by clear geopolitical episodes (such as the cruise missile crises or the Chernobyl incident, which unified protest activities on a continental scale). It has therefore been a movement with broad oscillations in participation.

What was new in the 1990s was that the migration-related prominence of the issue created the perception of a crisis and the need for EU-wide policy response. This spurred a search for new policy solutions. This perception of crisis and search for solutions is reflected, for instance, in several policy documents both at the EU level and in several member states. One possible source of reflection on the issue comes from the anti-racism movement conceived broadly as an advocacy coalition – a proposed solution opposite to the 'Fortress Europe' model of an equally strong reactive coalition of nationalist and ethno-nationalist movements and parties. The role of anti-racist movement activists in redefining policy areas that are perceived as in a state of crisis has been often documented in the literature (Alink et al., 2001). Their effectiveness depends on a range of variables, such as the presence of a coherent alternative set of policy proposals, and more generally of definitions of the situations, of causes of problems and possible solutions.

However, anti-racism is a movement frequently described as being in a state of crisis and self-doubt (Bonnett, 2000). At the ideological level, some have argued that anti-racism should be a set of dimensions of the multifarious and changing identity of various ethnic groups, connected to their religious and cultural identities. Others have privileged a cohesive political identity whereby the anti-racist struggle takes place in association with, or is even superordinate to, class and gender conflict. A further division has often emerged between minorities and 'white' anti-racist activists, with some arguing that anti-racists should let minorities speak for themselves and others advocating a broader and more inclusive movement; that is, a movement of people from different backgrounds who face issues of racism in their everyday working and social lives, such as educationalists and other professionals. There are also those who see education of the public at large as the main goal of anti-racism, and they are criticized for only concerning themselves with the white majority. This split is connected with a contested identification of the source of racism, with some focusing on individual dispositions and others on institutional procedures (Ben-Tovim, 1997: 219). In institutional settings, particularly in UK schools and local authorities, but also among social workers, probation officers and social security officials, there has been a difference concerning what should be at the focus of attention: racism or multiculturalism. Externally to the movement, there have been attacks by the popular press on the ideology of anti-racism, which has been associated with the traditional left and with what the press has regarded as a culture of intolerance within the movement (Gilroy, 1990).

None the less, as with other social movement frames such as 'gender equality' or 'environmental sustainability', 'anti-racism' has gained from its growing role of approved societal concern – a transnational norm – that stimulates discursive institutional compliance. Combating racism is traditionally a defining characteristic of the left and has in recent years received attention in the media and mainstream politics as a reaction to substantial advances of the extreme right in several EU countries.

Movement and political party activists working against racism are aware of this broad anti-racist ethos, and attempt to turn what they perceive as a universally approved declaration of principles into specific cultural and policy responses. However, this can result in limited and even contradictory institutional initiatives. It is therefore in a context of uncertainty that anti-racism policy had to develop at the European level. The status of approved general principle and the concern for the growing number of racist attacks made an EU proactive approach necessary, but did not clarify in which direction to intervene: whether, for instance, to focus on economic activities, on institutional domains, on dispensing resources to victims and potential victims, on educational initiatives. This is in addition to decisions on the modes of intervention. As previously mentioned, in case of interventions a decision had to be taken on which identities had to be recognised: whether to reinforce self-esteem, to promote group identities or a unified 'black' consciousness.

Anti-racism and the EU

Given a substantial uncertainty on how to approach the issue, the first important intervention in the area was clearly oriented by existing transnational norms as formulated by relevant international conventions. European anti-racism policy reiterates principles already present in the 1950 Council of Europe Convention for the Protection of Human Rights and Fundamental Freedoms and in the 1966 United Nations 'International Covenant on Economic, Social And Cultural Rights. Article 13 was approved after unanimous agreement of member states of the Amsterdam Treaty of 1997, which entered into force in 1999. Noting that the European Union 'is founded on the principles of liberty, democracy, respect for human rights and fundamental freedoms', it establishes the rights of individuals not to be discriminated against on several grounds, which include race and ethnic origin, age, disability, religion and sexual orientation. It complements measures to outlaw gender and nationality discrimination, which have long been covered by the treaties. And it is part of a concern with the principle of non-discrimination for racial and ethnic reasons, which had already frequently appeared and would then be reiterated by key EU legal texts. It is, for instance, the subject of article 37 of the Charter of Fundamental Rights, and non-discrimination on the basis of race and ethnic origin, which are listed in article 21 (European Parliament, 2000).

Following from the new legal authority conferred by article 13, two directives were passed in 2000. As directives, they had to be transposed into national legislation within a set period if no extensions were requested. The first directive, known as the Racial Equality Directive (2000/43/EC), focuses on preventing discrimination on the grounds of race and ethnic origin. The second, known as the Employment Framework Directive (2000/78/EC), focuses on religion, sexual orientation and disability.[4] The directives define the basis for ensuring a common minimum level of legal protection against discrimination. As the date for transposition was the end of 2003, infringement procedures have now been launched by the European Court of Justice against some of the states that have not complied, and a ruling was passed for countries such as Austria (Ruling of 4 May 2005, Infringement Procedure IP 05/543) and Germany (Ruling of 28 April 2005, Infringement Procedure IP 05/502). In addition, a Community Action Programme was established to combat discrimination (2001–6), which includes funds for cultural and educational initiatives and also focuses at the local level.

As can be seen from this brief review of initiatives, article 13 marked a change of direction in approaches to racism. In historical terms the approval of article 13 and subsequent developments were first made possible by a set of historical events. Article 13 was approved after there was a change of government in the UK, which had been vetoing legislation in the area for several years. The two 'racial' directives were made possible by the concerted reaction of all EU governments to the Haider presence in government in Austria (Ruzza, 2004). Observers have noted that the rapid approval of the two directives marked a need to stress the importance of human rights when they appeared threatened by the presence of a right-wing extremist in government but also came at a time when a show of European unity appeared essential in a period of declining legitimacy of the EU integration process. Some initial answers on how transnational norms are implemented can now be identified. EU-level anti-discriminatory legislation is the result of a wide set of variables, but factors that resonate with general institutional goals of legitimacy and institutional identity play a role.

In addition to the general historical factors just mentioned, one has to investigate the workings of the Brussels institutional environments, as successful legislation ultimately depends upon them. The implementation of transnational norms in specific measures can be facilitated by historical dynamics but has to pass through EU institutions. In order to understand how a general human right such as the right of non-discrimination on racial grounds comes to be translated by specific actors into strategies, and the following complex interactions in policy outcomes, one has to investigate their typical goals, operating procedures and taken-for-granted assumptions. Here only the role of the major institutions can be reviewed. With the exception of the Council, which expresses member states' positions and whose influence can be subsumed in the above mentioned historical factors, anti-racism was prominently supported by advocates in the EU Parliament and in the Commission, and by the advocacy efforts of organised civil society.

This review of the role of different actors in anti-racist policy is based on a set of over fifty in-depth interviews conducted at different times over the decade 1995–2005. Reference will also be made to a structured text analysis of policy documents produced by the different types of actors and analysed in 2003 (for a description of the methodology see Ruzza, 2006).

The EU anti-racist movement advocacy coalition

In Brussels the anti-racist advocacy coalition has strong personal and institutional contacts with a range of other movements concerned with social exclusion. There are a variety of organisations with different tasks and philosophies lobbying EU institutions for legislation and funds. There are a few large and loosely organised networks that encompass a variety of social exclusion causes, such as the Social Platform, Solidar, the Youth Forum (EYF), the European Federation for Intercultural Learning, the European Human Rights Foundation and religious organisations. Solidar, for instance, coordinates social welfare and aid activities on an EU level, and in 1997 engaged in a prominent campaign against racism. The Social Platform coordinates about 25 umbrella organisations, each of which represents a number of organisations ranging from a few to several hundreds and whose focus varies, with some interested in disability rights issues, others in ageism and still others in racism. All these organisations have good contacts with EU institutions, and at the same time support protest activities of some of their activist member organisations and the service and welfare activities of other members.

If anti-racism is embedded in other movements, it is also a distinct social movement area with a separate identity and a variety of loosely collaborating organisations directly connected, even if represented in other networks. While some organisations have stressed their anti-racist concerns, particularly at key points in time, such as in 1997, which was declared the European Year against Racism, there are organisations for whom anti-racism is the main concern or a dominant one. The most prominent are the European Migrants' Forum, Starting Line (no longer in operation), the Anti-Poverty Lobby, and then to a lesser extent the Youth Forum and the Women's Lobby. Taken together they express in EU institutions the concerns of a broad

European movement of several hundred organisations and unaffiliated individuals. Its Brussels representation, as in the case of the environmental movements, excludes the more radical, small and institutionally peripheral groups, but includes a wide variety of concerns, philosophical positions and strategic orientations. Since 1998 a specific anti-racist network (the European Network against Racism, ENAR) has been active, even if fragmentation of the field persists and worries activists. As previously mentioned with general reference to European societies, ideological fragmentation also induces self-doubts and policy uncertainty in the EU-level environment.

The pro-inclusion left-liberal organisations of organised civil society constitute a very broad movement family with only limited internal ideological cohesion. Each branch of the family can attach anti-racism to its main grievances and reinterpret it as one of its competencies, but often not the main one. Gender and class issues, poverty, migration, human rights as protection from torture, labour disputes and so on, are all seen as affected by racism, and all concerned sectors of movements spend time and energy on anti-racism. They also claim resources and would like to prioritise their field. If this is an advantage for the anti-racist movement because it makes it globally relevant, it is also a disadvantage because the specific constituency of victims of racism is often too weak to claim its own discursive space. The issue is 'tagged on' to the other movements that claim it. This is making it more difficult for anti-racists to maintain relevance.

Political and administrative environments

EU institutions have played a generalised facilitating role in the establishment of anti-racist movements in Brussels and then of anti-racist policy. There are both common and separate reasons for the involvement of the two main institutions in this field: the Parliament and the Commission. For both bodies, the role of social movements is important as a consequence of the perceived need for democratic legitimacy of the 'European Project'. This point emerges clearly from interviews with Commission officials, who often refer to 'the European value added of their operations'[5] in the anti-racism field, and from interviews with activists, who feel they are valued as a way of reaching out for an otherwise isolated bureaucracy or for MEPs who often feel less relevant and connected to their constituency than MPs. Consultation with civil society is now a formalised policy area and there is a particular focus on connecting the EU with under-represented constituencies and with local and regional levels of government (Ruzza, 2002).

As a consequence of these institutional needs to 'reach out', a great amount of European resources for the area is spent connecting national and local organisations of member states, and promoting pan-European knowledge in the field, such as through the Raxen initiatives, which include studies and examples of good practice in the field, and other projects connected to the work of the European Monitoring Centre against Racism

(EUMC). This agency was specifically developed to monitor the issue of racism. Recently the mandate of the EUMC has been extended by its conversion into a 'fundamental rights agency', emphasising the connection between racism and human rights.

Thus, specific institutional goals of the entire institutional apparatus of the EU filter transnational norms defining ambits of attention and resource allocation. This filtering process also takes place within individual institutions.

The European Parliament

The European Parliament is traditionally high-minded in terms of principles, possibly because it lacks the powers to set agendas and to monitor the implementation of resolutions, but it also has a high absenteeism rate and not infrequently an accumulation of tasks at national and EU levels that force a strict selection of interests. Consequently, over the years a core of institutional activist MEPs with a specific interest in anti-racism has emerged, an interest that, for some, has lasted several years and has involved participation in a committee that reported on racism in 1986 and in 1991, as well as continuing commitment. They often work on anti-racist issues, both at the national and at the EU levels, where much anti-racist policy work is concentrated in the civil liberties committee and the anti-racist working group. As one MEP noted, the Parliament played a fundamental role in the successful approval of article 13 and successive legislation. Anti-racist parliamentarians have excellent and frequent contacts with the anti-racist organisations in Brussels. MEPs often take the initiative in contacting movements' representatives when they have to be rapporteurs on issues for which they need information. They establish contacts directly, or through their assistants, or often through the Commission's list of contacts.

If, as mentioned, a variable that explains the Parliament's involvement in the area is its desire to acquire institutional relevance, one cannot ignore the impact of cultural factors. In mediating transnational norms of anti-racism, parliamentarians also act on the basis of their personal background, which in the formations of the left is often one of previous involvement in the anti-racism movement.

The Commission

The Commission has been concerned with racism for a long time. This is to be expected, as the Commission has a tradition of identifying under-thematised policy areas in which a European dimension can appear useful and relevant. As Majone (1996) points out, regulatory decisions are often related to societal values, hence policy-makers have a vested interest in the cultural milieu. It is therefore to be expected that this interest grew when the issue became socially more relevant. This is particularly the case for the top tiers of the Commission, which typically act in a political function. The need for legitimacy is, however, as in the case of Parliament, not the only reason for supporting anti-racism. There are also broader generational and ideological factors at play behind the close connection between EU institutions and NGOs. One activist said: 'Activists very often have links that go back to the sixties and the seventies with the people in government. I was able to tell a Commissioner that he was a founder member of one of our organizations. Especially now that there is a social democratic majority in the EU, many ministers were supporters of NGOs.' In addition to these general reasons for involvement there are also specific ones that pertain to the bureaucratic function of operative units in the area.

The main bureaucratic referent for anti-racism is a unit of Directorate-General (DG) Social Affairs, which as a whole deals with the free movement of workers – essentially a legal activity (revision of free movement legislation, action on complaints of infringement against member states, etc.). The unit also deals with the social integration of immigrants, employment programmes of recognised refugees and action against racism. So the latter is only one of the areas of concern. Activists described the last head of unit as very committed – a 'super-converted' – and valued her political sense, her ability to be realistic and effective in her demands, and achieve results.

The unit was created in 1958. It deals with matters, such as free movement of labour, already included in the Treaty of Rome. Integration of immigrants and refugees came later. Anti-racist policy was added in 1986. The relevance of anti-racism work varies according to the tasks at hand, ranging from a handful of people working in the sector to over twenty in periods of special initiatives such as during the 1997 European Year against Racism. Unfortunately, as this head of unit pointed out, mobility is very high in DG Social Affairs and is encouraged by the hierarchy, but she points out that racism is a very special field; if a position is posted, only personally committed people tend to apply. There are therefore in operation dynamics of selection that ensure continued bureaucratic commitment.

The anti-racist work done by units other than DG Social Affairs is not dissimilar in being fairly activist in orientation. The ideological orientation is, as with DG Social Affairs, sustained by a belief in the promotion of Europe, not only for providing legitimacy to EU bodies, but for broader reasons as well. Some activists say that there is in the Commission a fundamental belief that the European model has been an effective social model for many years. It has provided security from wars and affluence, and there is a desire to promote it as a philosophy not just within the EU but outside as well. Hence voluntary organisations such as youth organisations and their activists' concerns are funded in places as distant as Georgia or the Maghreb area. The Commission needs to know about society, and voluntary organisations can provide space for reciprocal knowledge, ranging from activists and volunteers brought to Brussels for consultations and represented in Brussels, to EYF (European Youth Forum) staging Youth in Parliament events (where 500 young people are brought to Brussels for a two- to three-day debate on their living conditions, with the participation of EU bodies' representatives).

The division between an assimilationist and a multiculturalist approach that characterises European anti-racism finds an echo in Brussels. This contradiction hinders the anti-racist community's progress towards identifying shared goals, such as agreement on how best to spend money, where to concentrate efforts and which groups to support. However, according to some activists, the dominant institutional ethos is an assimilationist one, which seems to emerge in interviews with civil servants. For instance, a civil servant stressed that all steps should be taken actively to encourage migrants' access to 'majority' culture, but awareness of migrants' cultural diversity was never expressly mentioned. Much emphasis is placed on, and funds are spent promoting, 'minority' integration. Policy provisions to promote minority cultures and safeguard religious rights are more limited.

The two approaches are not easily combined, as they imply different allocation of resources, but their contrast is even more of a problem for the unity of the movement at large. From their small units in Brussels, institutional actors can espouse a policy of channelling as much in the way of resources as possible to a wide variety of organisations, which might have contrasting approaches. At the same time, in terms of institutional discourse, regulators often prefer to frame anti-racism in terms that are compatible with the broader ethos of the European project. This is based on a neo-liberal ethos within which anti-racism is better conceptualised not as an issue of distributing resources to disadvantaged groups in general or in terms of legislating in order to combat neo-Nazi attacks against migrants. Instead, it will more typically be seen as an issue of right of access to the markets that the EU has been built to enhance and monitor – markets of goods, labour and services. In this perspective racism mainly limits individuals as consumers and workers.

Anti-racism is in fact more congruent with the broader EU ethos when defined with reference to the role of the individual in the labour markets, and in social institutions. In this sense, anti-racism is typically seen in terms of a threat to rights. A brief excerpt from a Commission website encapsulates the way in which anti-racism and more generally the struggle against discrimination is conceptualised in Brussels:

> Employment and occupation are key elements in guaranteeing equal opportunities for all. They contribute strongly to the full participation of citizens in economic, cultural and social life, and to realising their potential. For nearly 50 years, the European Member States have worked towards achieving a high level of employment and social protection, increased standards in living and quality of life, economic and social cohesion and solidarity. They have also endeavoured to create an area of freedom, security and justice. Discrimination can seriously

undermine these achievements, and damage social integration in the labour force and at large.[6]

In other words, discrimination is particularly negative for its impact on economic well-being and social integration. As a value compatible with the overall EU ethos, anti-racism also has a unified function and comes to be defined as a horizontal policy: a policy concern that regulators have to keep in consideration within all the other policy areas and that unifies the Brussels-shared pursuit of an integrated Europe. Thus the transnational norm of anti-racism becomes filtered by a global organisational ethos and comes to be employed as a contributor to the set of interconnected goals that characterise the EU.

Inter-organisational relations

This chapter has so far identified a set of personal and institutional concerns of bureaucratic, political and civil society actors and argued that they are all served by emerging conceptions of anti-racism and its connection to fundamental rights. The interconnection and compatibility between the discourse of different institutional environments needs, however, to be qualified. One has to address the issue of the extent of interconnection between different actors.

It is not generally denied that there is a strict connection between different organisational environments. Their strict involvement in EU decision-making is not accidental. As Peters (1992) has pointed out, the EU has traditionally used strategies of bureaucratisation and fragmentation of negotiations in order to diffuse conflicts and 'technicise' them. This creates an integrated inter-organisational environment in which cohesion is valued and is rooted in constant negotiations and the necessity to agree in the absence of strong majoritarian decision-making rules. Support to principled positions is one of the cohesion-enhancing mechanisms. Principles such as anti-racism, but also environmental sustainability or gender rights, are frequently recruited to its services.

These principles come to be reiterated in informal consultations and sometimes uneasily conjugated with the neo-liberal values of competitiveness, efficiency and technical appropriateness, and have contributed to determining a cohesive decision-making structure. Thus the informal process of coordination among different political and non-political actors takes place from the beginning of the decision-making process, a style of work that has characterised the EU from its inception and was explicitly intended by the Commission. In brief, we can identify a few interacting organisational environments that are unified by their participation in a structured competition where compromise is necessary and in which facilitating factors are bureaucratic procedures, some shared goals and some taken-for-granted norms.

Despite their similarity, the different environments also operate according to distinctive operating procedures, which, for instance, sociological neo-institutionalists have usefully reduced to ideal types (Powell and DiMaggio, 1991). They are bureaucratic environments such as the Commission, political environments such as the Parliament, the sector of business lobbying and public pressure groups and social movements. In bureaucratic environments, transnational norms such as anti-racism are conceived as taken-for-granted. They refer to procedures that need to be followed in a relatively automatic fashion. In activist environments they are the subject of normative commitment and refer to moralised behaviours. In lobbying and some organised civil society environments anti-racism indicates areas where institutional compliance is required to ensure resources or access, and compliance emerges in a mimetic fashion. None the less, despite differences, altogether the resulting organisational environment is generally integrated and supportive of anti-racism, even if individual actors might not identify with it. At the EU level, social movements operate in the absence of the relatively homogeneous structures of the nation state and therefore often face a less oppositional and concerted institutional reaction. The historical form of the social movement that has emerged as a political challenger to the state tends to take a different role in the fragmented EU environment (Marks and McAdam, 1996).

These considerations point to the fact that the relationships among the different organisational environments involved in EU decision-making are not generally based on controversial stances. Instead, the inspiring principle is a willingness to compromise in order to accommodate different interests. Clearly, for negotiation to reach a compromise, interaction is often difficult and protracted and occasionally engenders factious disputes. But in these exchanges a cohesive value orientation is formed, where distinctive values, information-processing mechanisms and goals emerge and bind a community of specialists. In the anti-racism field, technical competence might be somewhat less important than in other fields, but is often supplemented by the stronger value commitment that all the interviews have documented. This institutional commitment, then, also has a personal dimension. For instance, an activist pointed out: 'The institutions with a mandate on racism collaborate closely. In particular, the relevant sections of the Commission, particularly DG Social Affairs and the European Parliament, particularly the Committee on Civil Liberties, collaborate closely. The head of the relevant unit and some staff go to most of the meetings of this committee, and there are frequent personal contacts.' Relations with movement representatives and NGOs are also frequent, and are emphasised within key legal documents such as the first action plan against racism. The importance of dialogue with institutions is also emphasised by the anti-racist movement, as it emerges in in-depth interviews with all actors. They essentially share views on priorities, and just as it is for anti-racism, this is also the case for other areas of concern for social movements (Ruzza, 2006).

A content analysis of policy documents and presentation websites shows that EU institutions and the anti-racist coalition view the main priorities similarly, as: the necessity to concentrate on issues such as improving the implementation of anti-racist legislation in member states, enhancing participation, particularly participation of actors from civil society, emphasising the importance of human rights and related policy principles, and improving knowledge in the field.

This said, important differences also exist between EU institutions and anti-racist movements, which, however, could indicate that anti-racism as a policy effort is not an area captured by vested interests, and in normative terms does not simply reiterate institutional views – organised civil society can play an independent role (Ruzza, 2006). In differing from movement texts, EU texts emphasise the connection between anti-racism and their institutionalised policy concerns. They emphasise the necessity to mainstream anti-racism in all the EU policy areas and the European dimension of the issue, and put less emphasis than anti-racist documents on the role of member states.

The differences between anti-racist groups and EU institutions is none the less mainly a difference of emphasis. The existence of a fairly integrated and proactive anti-racist coalition that crosses different institutional environments is evident. Thus, even when conceiving the EU as a complex and interconnected organisational environment, we can link specific inter-organisational dynamics and general principles of human rights. Anti-racism allows different kinds of actors to interact through a common language. It allows the EU machinery as a whole to project an external image of concern for topical issues that go beyond the often vilified concern for economic prosperity. Article 13 and the subsequent legislation connect the Union to shared social values.

These considerations make activists accepting of EU involvement but also somewhat cynical. Their attitude varies from disenchanted scepticism to belief in the personal commitment of institutional actors. Noting the reiteration in EU bodies of anti-racist concerns, one activist said: 'Regulation of racism is a matter of fashion. Everybody says they are concerned about racism. You had the Council of Europe's campaign, "All different all equal", then the following year was the European Year against Racism. Now you hear much more about it on television and the radio. In the newspapers it has become a fashion. You have to be anti-racist. It is something in the wind.'

Conclusions

In this chapter, the argument has been put forward that the institutionalisation of human rights principles depends on the extent to which emerging global ideas about connected key aspects of social organisation, such as the theme of ethnic discrimination and the fight against racism, are interpreted through the narrative of the extension of rights and then redefined to serve political purposes and justify the involvement of different classes of actors, including social movements and organised civil society. Successful anti-racism policy depends on several variables – one is the political legitimacy that transnational NGOs are able to acquire, which is in turn related to their ability to appear politically responsible defenders of universally supported ideas and therefore able to allay the fears that their presence constitutes a threat to the sovereignty of nation states (Hudson, 2001). This objective has yet to be reached, and recently increasing preoccupations with security have hindered EU-level anti-racism. None the less, with the involvement of anti-racism movements in deliberative forums and the approval of new legis-lation, important steps have been taken in this direction. This chapter exam-ines the various reasons for this partial success, pointing in particular to the need for political legitimacy of the supranational arena.

At the EU level, supporting legitimate universal principles contributes to the legitimacy of the overall European project. In addition, connecting anti-racism to neo-liberal values by relating specific legislation to the detri-mental impact racism has on a well-functioning labour market improves the 'fit' (Keck and Sikkink, 1998: 3) between universal principles and the EU principles that characterise the process of European construction. This further contributes to facilitating the mainstreaming of anti-racism in European-level policies. When successful, human rights related ideas turn into taken-for-granted assumptions whose precise nature and actualisation may remain controversial and subject to advocacy pressure, but that are no longer simply a matter of individual normative choice.

Participation in anti-racism policy is therefore fruitful at least in terms of promoting a democratisation of the EU in terms of the expansion of issue areas and range of actors involved (Dryzek, 1996: 5–6), but there are costs associated to it. These relate to a forced definition of priorities that, while enhancing the 'fit' with EU values and thus ensuring the involvement of institutional actors, to an extent constrains the movements' choices and distorts their objectives. As the debate on the underclass has shown, there has been a growth of policies stressing social obligations above social rights (see Chapter 4), and it is in this context that anti-racism finds a role as an enabling factor in access to labour markets and connected spheres.

However, on balance participation has proven useful, as objectives are still unclear even within the movement, while resources are generally needed for several activities on which all the movements' viewpoints could con-verge. In this respect, as theorists of deliberative democracy argue, deliber-ation has a positive aggregative function for those engaged in it. In this sense, the movement's thematic fragmentation can be helped through its EU-induced necessity to form EU-wide representative networks and to engage in deliberative activities. Finally, another reason for valuing anti-racism advocacy is that due to the impact of globalisation and the hollowing out of the state, control over a growing range of issues has moved to the international arena and is increasingly associated with civil society (Dryzek, 2000: 5). For this reason, it is important for anti-racism to be represented by movements and to face directly other private and public interests.

Notes

1 For a discussion of different approaches within neo-institutionalism, see Peters (2000).
2 For a review of the international relations literature on the role of global ideas and more generally 'knowledge approaches', see Hasenclever *et al.* (1997).
3 There is a debate in the literature on the distinction between social movements and public pressure lobbies. Some authors believe they should be differentiated, others do not. Empirically, and as I will show, in the anti-racist field they are often connected. With reference to the EU-level anti-racist movement, the distinction is not useful and I will refer to mixed formations as 'movement advocacy coalitions' to indicate both their mixed character and the simultaneous engagement in advocacy activities and protest events.
4 The Racial Equality Directive shields against discrimination in employment and training, education, social security, health care, housing and other services, membership and involvement in organisations of workers and employers. The Employment Equality Directive focuses on equal treatment in employment and training irrespective of religion, disability, age or sexual orientation in employment, training and membership and involvement in organisations of workers and employers. It also requires employers to make reasonable accommodation to enable qualified disabled people to participate in training or paid labour.
5 Civil servants in considering all policies are obliged to take into account what has been called 'the European value added'; that is, they have to consider whether policies have a positive impact in furthering the process of European integration.
6 http://europa.eu.int/comm/employment_social/fundamental_rights/index_en.htm

Part III

Meaning, interpretation and rights

Elson's chapter from Part II comes close to the interpretive approaches represented in Part III of this book. Interpretivism is broadly speaking about understanding rights from the inside; from inside choices, sentiments, processes, relationships and cultures. In Chapter 7 the focus is on an integration of social theory and political philosophy, based on the argument that the latter requires a rooting in specific social relations, and, conversely, that social theory would benefit from sustained engagement with moral philosophy. In particular, Stones uses the example of 'duality' as featured in structuration theory and its application in a socio-moral philosophy, to yield an interpretation of moral dilemmas in their social and cultural context. There is no presumption that this choice represents the only or the 'best' example of the integrated approach he advocates, but it is offered as one route into his three chosen examples. The broad intention is to illustrate the development of an 'internal critique' based on empirical exploration of the normative rules, injunctions and sanctions at play in a given situation, against which selected aspects of abstract political philosophy may then be read, with a view to identifying their currency and phenomenological relevance.

Three case studies have been chosen, as a means of examining the issue of individual autonomy and the socially embedded functioning of rights. The cases deal with sexual freedom for gays in Britain (Dworkin, 1978), the Indian tradition of sati (Parekh, 2000) and the choices of Thai sex workers (Aoyama, 2005). In each case, we are presented with a context-sensitive account of the rights at issue, examining the ways in which their operation is inevitably embedded within social relations, institutions and cultural traditions. Attention is paid to expressions of morality other than 'rights', such as religion, communal solidarity or culturally specific conceptions of virtue, and the philosophical underpinnings of a liberal rights tradition are tested against the degree to which they are valued by different people in different contexts. This exercise offers a new perspective on old oppositions, such as universalism and particularism, or liberalism and communitarianism, and potentially frees the liberal approach to rights from its more judgemental tendencies. The aim is to trace the connections between individual narratives, their location in an external structure of relationships and the normative context of values and sanctions within which they operate to yield a commentary on their conditions of action. This, in turn, can aid the understanding and adjudication of conflicting rights claims, either within or between cultures, as elaborated in the case study analyses.

Chapter 8 also adopts an interpretivist position, this time offering an inside perspective on a movement: the case of gay rights, an area of rights that scarcely existed at all as little as 50 years ago. The opening argument of this chapter is that, far from being 'given in nature', rights come out of struggles and have their origins in political and moral 'talk'. This 'talk' is the substance of activist work by the moral crusaders and entrepreneurs who engage in claims and counter-claims, animated by contesting interpretations, rationalisations and definitions of rights. Their movement is aimed at convincing particular audiences of their legitimacy, and overcoming competition and conflict from those with other views. Sexuality is a relatively new terrain for conceptions of rights and Plummer sketches the stages this emergent area of rights has passed through – invisibility, decriminalisation, toleration – on the path to recognition and eventual institutionalisation. These transitions of course raise some of the status issues discussed in Part II, but the emphasis in the present chapter is rather on the interactionist dynamic of rights claims, the gradual shift in perceptions and values, and the way the contested claims of the gay movement have inspired broader notions of sexual citizenship and intimate citizenship. These have now become central areas of concern for many different groups and organisations.

The narrative of the chapter is the emergence of a public homosexual identity, reclaimed from criminalisation, medicalisation and demonisation. The moral debate that ensued, however, was characterised by gay claims to liberty in the realm of personal morality, which ironically threatened to drive them back into invisibility. A full rights agenda had yet to emerge, and a discourse of visibility and pride was central to the development of a Gay Liberation Front. Plummer identifies this as a moment of division between an 'assimilationist' position and a more confrontational stand. It was the tragedy of HIV/AIDS that led to a true institutionalisation, and to the latest galvanisation of the movement. These shifts in meanings, perceptions and identities are the key to a social interaction approach, and Plummer traces further developments: the global advances and attacks on sexual rights, the emergence of broader claims to intimate citizenship and the anti-normalisation embraced by the queer movement. Indeed, the message of the chapter is best summarised as creativity through contestation, or identity through interaction.

Chapter 9 addresses the issue of indigenous rights, beginning with a consideration of Europe's colonial expansion and ideological domination, and moving on to outline the inadequacy of most sociological treatments of these matters. The interpretive core of the argument comes from a consideration of the experience, perspective and culture of the indigenous peoples themselves, and their contestation of the world view of their oppressors. This latter included an assumption of cultural inferiority that was central to the assumed legitimacy of colonial occupations. A variety of devices were used to translate such occupation into a legally defensible position, from agreements between sovereign entities (often violated) to the doctrine of *terra nullius*, which deemed territories inhabited by indigenous people to be open wilderness. In the process, little credence or even attention was given to indigenous law or concepts of rights, and only since the Second World War has there been any serious international debate. Among recent concerns is the very question of how to define indigeneity itself – and the answer seems largely to turn on cultural continuity and distinctiveness.

However, the chapter documents the often appalling conditions under which indigenous people struggle to maintain their beliefs and ways of life, and finds that sociology has traditionally had little purchase on indigenous issues. Constrained by its focus on 'modernity', and often by an implicit evolutionary perspective, classical sociology has treated indigenous culture, if at all, as a residual phenomenon whose study has routinely been left to anthropology. With the awakening of a sociological concern with rights, however, this picture is beginning to change, though Samson and Short note the limitations of a foundational perspective and stress instead political power and interest. They also note that indigenous people are driven to 'claim' their rights within structures and procedures that are culturally alien and part of the very system of rule they seek to challenge. However, the distinct law and traditions of indigenous peoples have no status in either these systems of rule or the liberal philosophies that underpin them, such that cultural 'recognition' within this context is profoundly problematic. Their self-assertion as dispossessed first nations speaks against the pursuit of their rights through the machinery of national citizenship, and increasingly the struggle for recognition and protection of their distinctive cultures and ways of life has come to focus on the international forum of the UN.

7 Rights, social theory and political philosophy

A framework for case study research

Rob Stones

The purpose of this chapter is to outline a research framework that can begin to bring together the insights of both social theory and political philosophy to address rights issues. Their separation is a significant weakness that runs through much of the literature on rights. On the one hand, approaches to rights from the perspective of political philosophy are too often uprooted from any concern with the social, cultural, historical, political and economic specificity of particular cases. Approaches from the perspective of social theory and sociology, on the other hand, have a tendency to adopt the rhetoric of the moral high ground without any effort to engage in the kind of sustained moral argument associated with political philosophy. One of the reasons for this invidious division of labour is the volume and complexity of the relevant literatures in each field and the difficulty of knowing where to start. It is these problems that I address, and I do so by developing some preliminary guidelines for case study research. Such research can explore the field by dividing it into more manageable, bite-sized, portions that are less daunting and less forbidding. The idea would be to develop research strategies into rights issues that are explicitly informed by social theory and by political philosophy, but that radically limit their object of study. The aspect of rights under scrutiny would be limited in having a precise focus – guided by very clear questions or specific problems about the legitimacy of rights claims and/or the feasibility of their implementation.[1] The studies would also be limited in drawing, self-consciously, only on carefully delimited aspects of social theory and political philosophy, thus making realistic demands on the researcher, who will still have to master a testing range of literatures and skills. The intention would be for a series of such piecemeal studies, each produced by a more integrated social theory/ political philosophy approach, not only to offer valuable insights of their own but also to provide the foundations for subsequent cross-study work on rights.

This chapter is organised as follows. First, I note the sense in which it is important to think about rights issues in a holistic or embedded manner, one that roots them in specific sets of social relations and that thinks about particular rights with respect to other cultural and moral principles. I also insist, however, that within this frame one needs, for the kinds of practical reasons mentioned above, to be selective about the sets of concepts one brings to the analysis of particular rights.

Second, I practise what I preach in focusing only on the rights implications of certain very limited aspects of social theory – in this instance those associated with the notion of duality within structuration theory[2] and with what I label 'socio-moral phenomenology' – and on certain limited aspects of normative political philosophy. My focus in the area of political philosophy is on liberalism in general and in particular on the even more delimited notion of the autonomy of the individual within liberalism.[3] As I proceed I provide a basic sense of what is entailed in each of these positions. It is no part of my brief to champion these choices from the lexicon of social theory and political philosophy as the only ones worth bothering with, or as the best for all questions, or even as the best for the questions I directly consider. Instead, my brief is to demonstrate that the research framework I propose entails being selective and pragmatic. The choice of theoretical approach to a given issue will depend partly on one's own, inevitably finite, judgement about what is potentially the most fruitful set of concepts to adopt, and partly on one's own intellectual formation. In the domain of political and moral philosophy, for example, instead of focusing on liberalism it would be quite possible to single out concepts from a communitarian or multicultural view, or from virtue ethics,[4] even in relation to the same case study. The change in the normative focus would lead to a change in empirical focus. No single approach would necessarily exhaust all the significant things to be said about a given case study. A dialogue between different approaches can often be illuminating and I try to give a sense of this in two of the three case studies at the end of this chapter.

Third, and more specifically, the notion of an 'internal critique' is developed. An internal critique is one that respects the socially embedded nature of rights issues and hence sees the need to develop critiques of rights from a vantage point that has a serious grasp of how things look from within those social relations. Here research would begin with the step of trying to establish what the *de facto* popular conception of rights is in relation to a particular issue in a given time and place. Attention would thus be paid to the sociological exploration of empirical specificities, including an exploration of the explicit and tacit normative rules, injunctions and sanctions at play. This would be combined, however, with concerns associated more with political philosophy, embracing aspects of abstract political philosophy thought by the researcher to be relevant to the analysis of the case at hand, but also – and this is a more sociological, empirical, dimension of the role played by political philosophy – a concern to explore the extent to which those aspects are already considered to hold some currency or moral power within the specific set of social relations relevant to the case study.

A researcher pursuing this type of case study strategy would thus:

- Look at the *de facto* system of institutionalised rights and at popular conception of rights, and at any pertinent social divisions within these. (Draw on social theoretical tools to delineate existing social and institutional practices and beliefs regarding rights.)
- Decide on the particular aspects of abstract political philosophy that might be most fruitful to draw upon. (Choose elements of abstract normative philosophy.)
- Explore the extent to which the chosen aspects of abstract moral philosophy have a depth of phenomenological relevance and moral currency in the social relations at hand. The researcher will explore the extent to which the chosen aspects find a 'fit' with deeply held (perhaps latent) moral beliefs and values in the society at hand. This will often involve a radical critique of popular, surface conceptions of rights when those are at odds with the deeper conceptions. The nature of the latter can be clarified through a combination of phenomenologically informed social theory and the chosen elements from moral philosophy. (Critically interrogate the *de facto* social practices and beliefs on the basis of chosen elements from abstract normative philosophy.)

It is integral to the notion of an 'internal critique', which is discussed further below, that a judgement as to whether a particular right is legitimate or illegitimate requires that relevant elements of normative political philosophy are brought into confrontation with the social theoretical delineation and analysis of the *de facto* level of beliefs, practices and institutions.

Finally, I discuss aspects of three case studies in order to draw out some of the challenges involved in adopting the kind of framework suggested. Each case study focuses on the issue of the autonomy of the individual, and each notes the importance of an internal critique that respects the socially embedded nature of rights issues. I hope that in the examination of these limited and selected elements from the three cases the complexity of the issues still remaining serves to illustrate the advantages of a modest, piecemeal approach. The first case focuses on the essay 'Liberty and moralism' from Ronald Dworkin's influential 1978 volume *Taking Rights Seriously*, an essay dealing with the rights of gays in the UK to exercise freedom of choice over issues of sexuality. The second case draws on Bhiku Parekh's discussion in his *Rethinking Multiculturalism* (2000) of the Indian tradition of *sati*, the largely defunct practice of a widow immolating herself on her husband's funeral pyre. The third case is even more exploratory than the first two, in that it expressly sets out to ask more questions than it answers. It involves the experiences and social circumstances of Thai migrant sex workers and draws from a number of sociological sources, but primarily from Kaoru Aoyama's *Becoming Someone Else: Thai Sex Workers from Modernisation to Globalisation* (2005). The fact that the latter case study draws from social theory and sociology, in contrast to the first two, which draw primarily from political philosophy, is revealing, albeit in an unsurprising manner, in that the sociological and empirical detail provided by Aoyama is inevitably much richer and more fine grained than the material provided to support Dworkin and Parekh's arguments. On the other hand, Aoyama's study doesn't set out to have the explicit and sustained focus on moral and rights issues that mark the former accounts. The purpose of introducing the third case is thus in large part to show how the latter focus would reveal new horizons of attention and concern within sociological research.

Socially embedded views of rights

If one is genuinely interested in the real consequences for individuals and social relations of thinking in terms of rights then it clearly follows that one must consider rights issues in terms of how they are embedded within a society and its institutions. This is the case even for those rights often thought to be more universally applicable, at the top of value hierarchies – such as the right to be free from bodily harm or torture – as well as others such as the right to a job, to free health care or to wear certain symbols of religious observance, where there is more often readiness to accept that they may apply only in particular times and places.

Rights are always embedded and always relational. Most serious commentators on rights acknowledge this and note how the exercise of any one distinct right can potentially have implications for the exercise of others. It has always been clear to liberals, for example, that the liberties that can be exercised by an individual must be limited where they conflict with the safety of others. Thus, the need for a degree of order necessary to ensure other people's right to security and freedom from harm has implications for the range of liberties people have a right to. Not only should rights always be seen in relation to each other, they should also be seen in some kind of hierarchy, one that is inevitably related to the socio-political and cultural traditions of the relevant society. They should not be seen either as atomistic, separate from all other considerations, or as somehow uprooted or disembedded from particular social conditions. Rights are always embedded in particular societies, located in specific times and places, with their own historical and institutional legacies and with specific sets of norms and values, themselves more or less homogeneous or pluralistic. We shall see that this doesn't prevent either insiders or outsiders from arguing that a given local conception of rights is inadequate for some reason, but it does mean that to have more than superficial force such an argument must reveal a sensitivity towards, and understanding of, that society and its circumstances.

When we are investigating the role of rights within a society it is important to recognise that societal morality has many other dimensions. Other moral considerations may exist alongside a commitment to rights, more or less equally, or they may exist as an alternative to rights-based thinking. The latter could be true for societies whose morality is based primarily on religious principles, for societies based on cultural systems that emphasise forms of communal solidarity and observance over and above individual rights, or for societies whose moral systems are based on notions of virtuous conduct according to traditional systems of thought. The moral world-view or practical philosophy of a society can be more or less homogeneous and more or less plural and hybrid. Many societies, and liberal societies should be counted among these, combine one or more of the alternative emphases just cited with a concomitant commitment to rights-based morality. The range of rights adhered to, together with the balance of power between them, and between different moral principles, is always part of a negotiated, unsteady and context-dependent balance of moral commitments.

Selected aspects of political philosophy

Moreover, within the liberal tradition itself the very notion of rights can only be made sense of once located within that wider tradition and its philosophical underpinnings. The wider liberal philosophy is one that includes the emphasis on order and security, mentioned above, and also usually a commitment to equality of care and respect and to individual autonomy. The latter notion, of individual autonomy, is one of liberalism's most central concerns and it is the notion I single out for special attention in this chapter. This is partly because a large majority of Western intellectuals and academics value it so highly. The sociological, empirical, side of the bargain I want to strike may reveal that this value is shared by some or many within a given set of social relations, or it may reveal that autonomy is valued only a little or not at all by those people. Such a confrontation between the ideal and the actual can help to prise open some prematurely closed and sealed debates, such as the one between universalism and particularism, and force more grounded debates that take both sides seriously in relation to specific *in situ* predicaments. Autonomy has been central to the liberal tradition from John Stuart Mill, through John Rawls's *A Theory of Justice* (1971) and Dworkin's more legally oriented defence of rights, to the recent influential work of Will Kymlicka and others on minority cultures. It has been so central as it denotes the ability of an individual to choose – notwithstanding the necessary caveats – the way they live their life, to choose their own conception of the good life. An important part of this is that individuals should have the ability and the conditions to revise their ends, their current conception of the good life. It should always be a possibility for them to discover that they have been mistaken about the worth and value of their present practices, and to change them accordingly. It is easy to see how rights are intimately bound up with this commitment to autonomy.

In the web of their tradition liberals also typically strive to protect the individual's right to dissent with respect to any groups they may be a member of, and in this respect they valorise individual rights over the group. In another respect, however, many liberals are concerned to protect the rights of groups against the decisions of the larger society – for example, in the areas of language rights, land rights and federalism, all of which 'are consistent with liberal equality, since they are intended to ensure equality between groups, not to suppress dissent within a group' (Kymlicka, 2004: 132; see also Kymlicka, 1995: Chapter 3). Liberals also place great emphasis on issues of education as part of what Dworkin has called the 'structure of culture' within a community, the external cultural context from which we develop our phenomenological frame and value dispositions. A rich educational and cultural inheritance is one that 'multiplies distinct possibilities or opportunities of value' (Dworkin, 1985: 229; see Kymlicka, 2004: 117). Rights to freedom of association and expression should be understood in this frame, where the ability to form and revise one's conception of how to live one's life depends to a significant extent on the degree to which the social context fosters and facilitates that ability.

Thus, while liberals' commitment to the autonomy of the individual means that they are wary about society or the state interfering with individuals' choices about the kind of life they want to live – that is, with individuals' conceptions of the good life – the wider philosophy reveals, nevertheless, that liberals do have a conception of the social and political conditions necessary for the living of any good life. That is, liberals do have a significant conception of the necessary social and political conditions required for human beings to flourish. It is only in the context of the liberal discourse's unsteady and negotiated combination of commitments to order, equality of care and respect, autonomy, the protection of both individuals and groups, the quality of the cultural structure and a series of overlapping rights that the commitments to any one specific right at a given time and place will make sense.

Selected aspects of social theory

While the notion of autonomy can provide a guiding normative concept for the analysis of specific case studies concerning rights, it has a much more grounded critical presence when it is coupled with limited aspects of social theory. Which aspects are chosen will depend upon the purposes of the task at hand. In situating rights issues in context, large-scale social theoretical studies, such as those on citizenship, can clearly be useful. Writers on citizenship such as T. H. Marshall (1963, 1977), Michael Mann (1987, 1993) and Bryan Turner (1986, 1990) have, between them, provided historically informed accounts of the uneven development of citizenship in a range of societies, and such accounts can be drawn on, often in combination, to situate more specific rights issues in their macro socio-historical context. Thus, for example, it can be very helpful to situate Marshall's historical account of the successive emergence of civil, political and social rights in Britain (Marshall, 1963, 1977) within Mann's account of the rise and character of European liberal states and party democracies (e.g. Mann 1987, 1993: 92–136, 167–213, 766–74), and with respect to the particular configuration of social forces, groups and institutional complexes at play within such societies. These accounts, however, are generally restricted to this macro-level and need to be complemented and extended, and amended where necessary, by more fine-grained forms of analysis that can link insights about the wider social and historical forces to the specific conjuncture. The relevant agents or subjects involved in any particular rights issue need to be identified and situated with respect to relevant networks of social and cultural relations, including relevant normative and coercive influences upon them. They need to be situated both relationally and phenomenologically and I concentrate on this kind of task in what follows.

To this end I focus on the ontological conception of the duality of structure that lies at the heart of structuration theory (Giddens, 1984: 25; Stones, 2005: 4–5, 13–16). This is because the notion of duality, with its concern with how both external social conditions and internal creativity combine within the phenomenological mind and body of the agent, provides a clear basis for locating the ideals of autonomy in actual social and personal conditions. The notion of duality guides one to:

1   Look at the normative and power relations and networks within a conjuncture.
2   Trace how these are experienced, phenomenologically, within the agent. There are two dimensions to this latter aspect. One relates to the relatively enduring values and dispositions that Pierre Bourdieu refers to as habitus (Bourdieu, 1977: 76–87), and the other is the agent's grasp of the immediate circumstances, their perception of the specific conjuncture (Stones, 2005: 87–100).

The notion of autonomy guides one to ask about the implications of these two moments for the agent's freedom. Both the normative conception of autonomy and the ontological conception of duality can thus act as guiding concepts for empirical research. It is ultimately an empirical question whether or not an agent has the internal ability to revise their ends, can gain sufficient critical distance[5] from their conditions of socialisation, habit and routine to be able to 'question, re-examine, and revise (their) beliefs about value' (Kymlicka, 1989: 18). It is also an empirical question as to whether a given agent believes there are likely to be external social costs and sanctions associated with the exercise of autonomy, whether they are correct in their beliefs and whether the costs would be too great for that individual to countenance.[6] These are all empirical questions to which the researcher will be guided by the concepts.

The role of social theory need not be restricted, however, to the process of situating a particular rights issue within its phenomenological, social and historical context. Proponents of some variants of social theory, bordering on political and moral philosophy but without their concern for systematic and deductive reasoning, have spent much time encouraging readers to think deeply about what it means for human beings to flourish and to avoid suffering. This strand of ethical social theory has an affinity with the phenomenological emphasis of structuration theory and with the respect for the individual that, on my reading, motivates it. In fact, it is perhaps best characterised as 'socio-moral phenomenology' and it is evident in a number of otherwise disparate writers. It is there: in Richard Rorty's plea for a 'sentimental education', which improves our ability to appreciate the similarities between ourselves and peoples otherwise very unlike us, 'such little, superficial, similarities as cherishing our parents and our children' (Rorty, 1993: 129), as well as our similarities with respect to pain and humiliation, which novels and ethnographies can move us to understand (Rorty, 1989: 192); in Martha Nussbaum's concern for us to expand our 'recognition and concern' for others, to use narrative art to 'see the lives of others with more than a casual tourist's interest' (Nussbaum, 1997: 88); in Zygmunt Bauman's Levinasian invocation of 'being-for the Other', in which an emotional engagement with the Other that comes before any thought about what should or shouldn't be done 'casts her/him into the universe of under-determination, questioning and openness' (Bauman, 1995: 62). The power of this kind of theory lies in its recognition of the profound levels of engagement that can be secured by the force of narrative, emotion and sympathetic identification. The danger of socio-moral phenomenology on its own is that while its engagement focuses on the concrete, is grounded in real lives, eschewing what it rightly or wrongly sees as the abstract rationalism of much political and moral philosophy, the characters who people its narratives are insufficiently anchored in their social circumstances, including the normative aspects of those circumstances. By tracing the connections between an agent's narratives and phenomenology, on the one hand, and her external social structures and networks on the other, structuration theory can provide much of that anchoring. And by adding to structuration's emphasis on the normative, sanctioning, content of the social context a sustained analysis of the moral legitimacy, or otherwise, of those norms-within-context then political philosophy can potentially provide a powerful commentary on that very context and the power relations that sustain it.

Internal critique and rights

Both the situating perspective of social theory and the more hybridised perspective of human flourishing can be easily and fruitfully articulated with the incisive notion of 'internal social criticism' coined by Mark Cladis in *A Communitarian Defense of Liberalism* (1992), a Durkheimian exploration of contemporary political philosophy. By internal social criticism Cladis means the kind of approach proposed by Durkheim, in which criticism 'seeks to reform society by self-consciously working within its historically fashioned social inheritance, that is, its historically situated ideals, customs, beliefs, institutions, and practices' (Cladis, 1992: 227). Durkheim's socio-logical instincts informed his position on morality. It meant that while he understood that an 'ought' cannot be derived effortlessly for an 'is', without the hard work of detailed argument and dialectical thought, he was ever alert to the pitfalls of voluntarism, of importing the 'should' wholesale from a place elsewhere, without due respect and attention to the here and now. Such an insight can be fruitfully articulated with the tools and insights of structuration theory, as these are clearly designed to help us refine our appreciation of such things as the 'historically fashioned social inheritance' that is necessarily the context for any conflict or disagreement over rights. Grasping this inheritance would, naturally, involve an analysis of the rele-vant society's inherited norms, values, power relations and operative public values.

Durkheim was himself personally committed to a form of moral indi-vidualism but he derived this critically from the conventions of the society in which he lived, from 'internal' social criticism. Relying on internal criticism in a society marked by mechanical solidarity[7] could well, it is true, be unduly conservative, but this is far less likely to be so in societies in which pluralism is a social fact, where there is 'a variety of social spheres and communities with varying degrees of homogeneity pertaining to different values and commitments' (Cladis, 1992: 239). Even though the critic's moral vision will inevitably be shaped, more or less, by the norms and culture of her age, if that age is marked by social, cultural and normative plurality then it is entirely possible for critique and protest to arise within it.

Cladis argues that in such conditions of plurality an internal critique of current practices often emanates from a self-conscious comparison of our deep rooted beliefs and views about social norms with the behaviour that we see is actually fostered and supported by our social institutions and arrangements. Internal critique can also be prompted by discrepancies between our social beliefs. Such discrepancies can be brought to light in the course of practical activity or through the subjection of beliefs to critical analysis. This notion of internal social criticism overlaps with the 'concept of a moral position' elaborated by Dworkin in the essay, examined in the next section, on the conditions under which it is reasonable to restrict another's freedom (Dworkin, 1978: 240–58). It is worth spelling out at this point what I believe this overlap to be, as their combination provides a powerful framework for sociologically informed critique. Dworkin takes a self-consciously liberal position and his concomitant conception of the conditions necessary for human flourishing place a heavy burden of argu-ment on any proposal to restrict the liberty and autonomy of an individual. More than this, his sociological sense of post-war British society suggests that this liberal conception marks society itself. In effect, he believes that the historically situated shared background ideals and beliefs of this society are overwhelmingly liberal (its moral position). Consequently, these socially embedded principles (these deep seated beliefs) can be drawn on in order to engage, from inside the culture, in a critique of any actual or proposed practices or institutions that fail to adhere to their standards (internal critique). Ultimately, much of Dworkin's substantive argument rests on the sociological, empirical claim about the deep rooted beliefs and norms within society, and on the extent to which they are actually shared (which is also the case, for example, for the validity of John Rawls's notion of an 'overlapping consensus'; Rawls, 1993: 134–72). Political philosophy often stops at this point, stops short of an empirical terrain where its pivotal assumptions are often the subject of intense debate and uncertainty in the social sciences. In the past two decades such debate and uncertainty has been evidenced, for example, in radical and variegated disagreements over whether, in the 'highly developed Western societies' taken as a whole, there has been a radical change in values or a limited change of values, a complete loss of values or a proliferation and fragmentation of values (see Inglehart, 1977, 1989; Bellah *et al.*, 1985; Leinberger and Tucker, 1991; Bauman, 1993; Joas, 2000: 1–10). Such empirically based questions – whether at the level of groups of societies or, more manageably, at a more local level – need to be made the subject of investigation and should not be left to the suppositions of political philosophers, no matter how palatable we find what they suppose.

Three case studies in individual autonomy: gay sexual rights, *sati* and migrant sex work

The concept of a moral position and gay sexual rights

In his essay 'Liberty and moralism' Dworkin focuses on a lecture delivered by Lord Devlin to the British Academy in 1958 entitled *The Enforcement of Morals* (1959), and on subsequent rejoinders and replies to critics. Lord Devlin's conclusions are summarised in this statement about the practice of homosexuality:

> We should ask ourselves in the first instance whether, looking at it calmly and dispassionately, we regard it as a vice so abominable that its mere presence is an offence. If that is the genuine feeling of the society in which we live, I do not see how society can be denied the right to eradicate it.
>
> (Devlin, 1959: 17, quoted in Dworkin, 1978: 241–2)

The issue of whether the mere presence of homosexuality is an offence is linked, in turn, to the question of whether it is a threat to the continued existence of valued social customs and institutions, such as marriage, and, more importantly, to the majority's right to follow its moral convictions. Dworkin's response is to argue that, even if it was true that the surface majority view of the time condemned homosexual practices, did indeed think that homosexuality was an abominable vice and was not able to tolerate its presence, Lord Devlin's conclusion is still in error as it is tantamount to equating morality with opinion polling (Dworkin, 1978: 254). He labels such a view the 'anthropological' view of morality, one that takes people's surface views and attitudes at face value as their considered moral standpoint, although the 'opinion polling' view would be fairer, as anthropologists have a tradition of critique every bit as distinguished as those possessed by political philosophy and social theory. In any event, Dworkin insists that this surface conception of morality is an entirely unconvincing one. It is not enough simply to invoke a moral majority. Instead, the credentials of such a putative moral consensus must be tested against what he calls the 'concept of a moral position'. Moral positions must be contrasted and distinguished from many other types of attitudes towards human conduct, qualities or goals, including prejudices against inherited or ascribed characteristics, rationalizations of unjustifiable emotional reactions, manifestations of personal aversion or taste, arbitrary stands and so on. These other types of attitudes need not be accorded the same respect as a moral position as quite simply they offend the basic ground rules of moral reasoning that are 'part of the conventional morality you and I share' (ibid.: 249)[8] and that, in effect, form the background set of understandings within which we carry on our form of life. In the case at hand, the guidance derived from the philosophy of liberalism is that one should not agree to limit the right to sexual choice between consenting adults on, for example, the grounds of prejudice. One should not limit sexual autonomy on these grounds. Dworkin writes that our ground rules of moral conventions stipulate that:

> a man must not be held morally inferior on the basis of some physical, racial or other characteristic he cannot help having. Thus a man whose moral judgements about Jews, or Negroes, or Southerners, or women, or effeminate men are based on his belief that any member of these classes automatically deserves less respect, without any regard to anything else he has done, is said to be prejudiced against that group.
>
> (Dworkin, 1978: 249–50)

Cladis, too, invokes the case of prejudice as something that is susceptible to internal social criticism, for much the same reasons as Dworkin. He argues that just as through introspection people can become aware of deep-seated prejudices, so this is true of social critique. Indeed, social critique, when it is based on a plurality of voices in civil society, is perhaps even more likely to be able to expose prejudices and enhance the self-understanding of both individuals and the culture itself. This is because of its ability to draw attention to prejudices that are 'so much a part of me and seemingly so self-evident that I never imagined alternatives to them' (Cladis, 1992: 236).

Both Dworkin and Cladis also argue that consistency is an important aspect of a moral position. For Dworkin one cannot straightforwardly claim a moral standpoint on a particular rights issue, such as homosexuality, if one's other beliefs and one's actions are inconsistent with this stated belief. Thus, someone could offer as their reason to want to ban homosexual acts the fact that the Bible forbids them, or that homosexual acts make it less likely that a man or woman will marry and raise children. Now, even if these views are sincerely held they will still not be sufficient to convince others that the person holds a moral position if they reject other biblical injunctions that don't suit them, or 'hold that men have a right to remain bachelors if they please or use contraceptives all their lives' (Dworkin, 1978: 251). Given that Cladis sees internal social criticism as a way of protesting against the practices and norms of one's own society on the basis of other values and norms within that society that can be shown somehow to be of greater importance, one can see the significance of exposing discrepancies between beliefs and then striving to establish which of the beliefs best describes the moral identity of that society (Cladis, 1992: 236).

Dworkin concludes that Lord Devlin fails to make his case. Sociologically, Lord Devlin is not able to provide any evidence that homosexual practices present any danger at all to society's existence. Neither is he able to show that the conception of the popular will is a truly moral one, for he does not adequately test the character of the opinion polling, surface, view. It is quite possible that the common opinion is a compound of prejudice, rationalization and personal aversion and, as Dworkin puts it, a critical and fundamental tenet of the actual morality of liberal societies, of the self-conscious principles of liberal democracy, is that the restriction of another's freedom and autonomy cannot be justified on such a basis. Thus, the explication of the concept of a moral position implicit in the culture of a liberal democratic society is one that can be used to test specific proposals, practices, institutions and social arrangements against 'our best norms, standards, and thinking about social justice, ethics and political theory' (Cladis, 1992: 234). In other words, the concept of a moral position informs an internal social critique from within a 'historically fashioned social inheritance', and thus provides at least some of the means by which internal social criticism of a surface majority view is carried out. The protection of the rights of minorities can be justified on this basis. It needs to be said, however, that one could easily imagine an alternative culture with an underlying moral position that did regard homosexuality as an abominable vice. In such cases there may be significant pockets of thought that rejected such a view, or there may be hardly any such pockets. The latter cases would test the empathy of socio-moral phenomenology, but any kind of external critique of that culture would need to engage in a 'being-for-the-other' as much, if not more, in such cases as in others.

In addition to the points made by Dworkin, we can also note that Lord Devlin does not show that gay practices are immoral when measured against the much broader philosophy of deeply held liberal values, principles and models of human flourishing. The practices are not shown to offend any of the standard substantive liberal tests, such as those demanding that practices do not harm self or others, that they do not breach higher norms, undertakings or duties and that they do not restrict the autonomy of others to live their lives in accordance with their own beliefs about what gives value to life (cf. Kymlicka, 1995: 81).

There can be conflicts and disagreements about rights issues within the conventional parameters of Western liberal democratic societies that are more radical than the one discussed by Dworkin. They can be more radical in the following sense. After close analysis it may be agreed that both the opposing, contested, views about a particular practice qualify as 'moral positions' within the framework of the society's operative public values. It is possible that neither involves prejudice, rationalisation, aversion, arbitrariness or inconsistency or poses an unacceptable threat to the shared conception of social order. Both positions can thus be socially embedded and in harmony with many of the norms and ideals of the society but still be at odds with each other. It is for such reasons that Richard Bellamy insists that rights issues are 'essentially contested' and 'lack compossibility', that even within the same political culture there can be incompatible views about what our basic rights are and also the need to choose between rights in conditions of scarcity (Bellamy, 1999: 169). Thus, while proponents of a positive conception of liberty may argue for taxation to support rights to education and welfare that would be met, say, by state-supported schools and a system of social security and health care, libertarians would argue against such rights. They would argue that:

> this would interfere with the right of individuals to do what they wish with their rightfully acquired property. Robert Nozick even goes so far as to argue that such taxation is the moral equivalent of granting property rights in another person and 'is on a par with forced labour', and hence an infringement of our most fundamental civil rights.
>
> (Bellamy, 1999: 168; citing Nozick, 1974)

Even among those who advocate a positive conception of rights there may well be a clash between those who wish to spend scarce resources on education and those who wish to spend them on health care (Bellamy, 1999: 169; also see O'Neill, 2002: 23–39). Behind all these disagreements lie variegated views on the good life, on the optimum conditions required for human beings to flourish. Thus, even within a liberal democratic culture one very quickly comes up against the limits of agreement on basic rights.

There is the need here for close and detailed argument and for the ability to examine the extent to which each side's abstract moral arguments have relevance and currency within the socially situated phenomenological understanding of *in situ* social actors. There is the need for a kind of sociologically informed *phronesis* in which moral judgements are made on the basis of a close engagement with, and understanding of, unfolding contexts of action.[9] There is also, ultimately, the need to be able to articulate the grounds of whatever differences remain.

Sati: a situated conflict between competing rights

As noted, the socially embedded nature of rights will raise different issues in societies with very different historical formations. Each different rights issue within a society will, in turn, require one to address different questions and problems. This indicates the limits but also the strengths of case studies. A closer look at a specific case can help to open up general issues even if it does so in a necessarily partial manner. Bhikhu Parekh, in his rich and reflective landmark study *Rethinking Multiculturalism*, discusses the case of *sati*, the largely defunct practice of a widow immolating herself on her husband's funeral pyre, in order to bring out the importance of the social, cultural and historical context, and the likely empirical consequences, of allowing or forbidding a particular practice (Parekh, 2000: 280–2). The practice had been banned by the British in 1829, with the support of Hindu leaders, and while incidents continued to occur, they were relatively rare. The situation changed in 1987 when Roop Kanwar, an 18-year-old Rajput woman who had been married for eight months, mounted her husband's funeral pyre watched by thousands of enthusiastic supporters. Circumstantial evidence suggested that she was drugged (Parekh, 2000: 280). The incident raised great passions all over India and the size of demonstrations indicated that many Hindus supported the practice. Within a few months of the incident, however, the Indian Parliament not only decided to retain the ban on *sati* but also passed a law forbidding the 'glorification' of the practice. The issue is parallel to the issue of sexual freedom discussed by Dworkin, in that it concerns the scope of the right to liberty and the conditions under which it might be justifiable to restrict another's freedom. It is different in that we will see that a number of competing rights are invoked in the *sati* case, rather than the contest being between the surface preferences of the majority and the rights of the minority, as it was in the previous case. The issues are again similar, however, in that the debate is ultimately about whether the right to commit *sati* is 'a moral position' that can be defended once it is placed alongside other beliefs about rights and the more general ground rules of moral reasoning existing within Indian culture.

Parekh argues that the Indian Parliament was right to sustain the ban on *sati* even if it restricted the woman's right to do what she liked with her life, and denied her the freedom to live by her deeply held religious beliefs and to live according to the Hindu way of life (ibid.: 281). His argument draws on, and respects, liberal notions of autonomy and liberty that he believes to be a part of the Indian culture, and so he chides feminists and secularists who simply dismiss such perspectives by fiat (ibid.). While he takes into account these aspects of the local culture – and such respect for the phenomenological realities of other cultures is a prerequisite for the opening out to others demanded by Bauman and Levinas – he, like Dworkin, goes beyond a surface, 'opinion poll' view of the moral position. His strategy, however, differs. For while he doesn't take the pro-*sati* view at face value, his critique of it does not entail questioning its status as a moral position. Instead, he accepts that moral principles are being invoked but argues that they are too partial given the demands of the case at hand. He thus brings in additional moral considerations that he believes also to be a part of the operative cultural values of Indian society to place alongside the values of the autonomy and liberty of the individual. He doesn't believe that the issue of the formal autonomy of the individual should necessarily trump any other – to invoke internal critique again – relevant societal 'norms, standards, and thinking about social justice, ethics and political theory' (Cladis, 1992: 234). Instead, Parekh draws on notions of community, interdependence and gender inequality, as well as liberty, and then attempts to think through the social situation of the woman-in-focus within the socio-cultural, religious and economic circumstances in which she would exercise formal autonomy. He argues that an:

> individual's life is not exclusively his or hers; others including those closely related to them also have a claim on it, which is why suicide is subject to moral constraints. . . . Since the practice of sati has the limited authority of the tradition behind it, it puts intense pressure on a distraught, confused and socially vulnerable woman to take her life. The fact that her death is of considerable financial benefit to her in-laws provides an additional motive for the pressure. It removes a claimant to the dead man's property and the rest of the family's resources, and enables her in-laws to turn their house into a commercially profitable shrine. The practice also reinforces women's inferiority, devalues human life, generates fear bordering on psychological terror among newly-wedded women and even men, and deprives children of parental love and support.
>
> (Parekh, 2000: 281)

Parekh thus believes not only that the interests of others in the community beside the individual should be taken into account in thinking through issues of self-harm, and that the avoidance of fear and suffering should not be weighed lightly against the goods of autonomy, but also that there are many factors inhabiting an Indian widow's social context that would compromise the translation of her formal autonomy into a meaningful substantive freedom of choice. Parekh's account stands out as a work of political philosophy that is quite remarkably context-sensitive. Notwithstanding this, however, many of the issues he raises would still be susceptible to a good deal more conceptually informed empirical analysis than he provides with respect to particular individuals, such as Roop Kanwar and her significant others, and their networked circumstances of action. Such analysis could, for example, explore more deeply the realities and intensities of the enduring values and dispositions of the habitus of relevant agents, and of their perceived context of choice. This would provide a potentially much richer picture of the character and quality of autonomy in particular circumstances.

Migrant Thai sex workers

In considering the experiences of Thai migrant sex workers I draw on studies whose approach to the empirical is informed more explicitly by social theory and sociology than by normative philosophy. As the result of this is that normative positions, while very evident in some cases, remain relatively unfocused and untheorised, I reverse the emphasis by placing normative questions at the centre of my brief discussion. It thus becomes very apparent just how significantly the conceptual frame shapes the object of study, and more particularly how the introduction of an explicitly normative dimension to this frame qualitatively alters the focus.

Against the backdrop of Parekh's discussion of *sati*, I start by asking a question about teenage girls beyond the age of consent[10] from the poorer northern and north-eastern areas of Thailand who become sex workers in Bangkok, in other Thai provinces or in Tokyo, as was variously the case among Kaoru Aoyama's respondents (Aoyama, 2005). Should these young women be protected by the Thai state or by international human rights law from the pressures put on them by middlemen (and, more often, middle-women), parents, culture and society to leave home to become sex workers? More specifically, should they be protected from their parents if the latter put extreme pressure on them to engage in sex work in order to send money home, and does it make a difference whether this money would be used to pay debt, to buy food and other necessities, to pay for a sibling's education or to build a concrete house to raise the status of the family within the village (Pasuk, 1982: 23–4; Bishop and Robinson, 1998: 105–6; Stones, 2002: 226–30)? To what extent in these circumstances should we respect, for example, the gendered nature of the tradition of *bunkhun* within the Thai culture-structure? *Bunkhun* represents a set of deeply imbued customs whereby daughters in particular feel an obligation to honour the benefits of birth and nurturing their parents have bestowed on them through taking up reciprocal material responsibilities towards their mother and father (Aoyama, 2005: 118–24, 144–8). Where the issue is not one of force, where it is in some sense the girl's decision[11] to engage in sex work, but there is a combination of a limited 'push' from others within the person's social context and that person's own desire to send money home for any of the above reasons, or because of a combination of these reasons and the pull of the city, bright lights, fashion, consumer durables and even a new kind of freedom (Aoyama, 2005: 181–9), then could it ever be legitimate to consider protecting the young women from themselves? Do the specific dangers of the chances of contracting HIV/AIDS or relative differences in working conditions make a difference to our reasoning, and how much empirical evidence about this will we require for our judgement?

These questions clearly raise issues of autonomy and rights. Again the issue is parallel to the previous two case studies in that it concerns the scope of the right to liberty and the conditions under which it might be justifiable to restrict another's freedom. Within the combined frame of political philosophy and social theory it is immediately apparent that any judgement will need to be rooted in the social relations in which the woman is embedded and in her cultural dispositions. If we were talking about a situation of forced trafficking, by definition against the wishes of the young woman, then there is a strong moral justification on the grounds of both liberal autonomy and universal human rights for saying it is wrong and that she should be protected. That is, her freedom should be protected. Even here, however, the sociological dimension would lead one to ask questions about both possibilities and consequences and not just about abstract principles. Who would do the protecting and would this be a likely or feasible proposition in the circumstances? Would the consequences of trying to protect the woman be worse for her and her family than not doing so? There are causal, evaluative and prescriptive dimensions to these questions. If the sex work is not forced but there are some 'push' pressures on the young women, then to what extent can we say that their decision is autonomous?[12] This question acquires even greater force if the relevant push factors appeal to aspects of cultural dispositions (habitus) into which the girl has been socialised since birth and from which she would find it difficult to gain critical distance even if she wanted to.

We are asking questions here about the quality of autonomy in particular times and places. In this case we are also asking whether the possibility of autonomy has already been compromised, years before, by prior socialisation into a cultural structure that is not as rich and diverse as that envisaged by the likes of Mill and Dworkin. And in such a case we also need to ask, if we have liberal values, whether it would in fact be impertinent to suggest that members of that culture question their current idea of the good life. Can a culture not be both homogeneous *and* rich, in ways other than the richness that comes from diversity? If we decided, notwithstanding such concerns, that it wouldn't be impertinent to advocate the liberal view of diversity we would then still need to ask about the likelihood of such encouragement being effective.[13] Against all this it would also be incumbent on any liberal wanting to deny a sex worker the right to choose, or to deny a widow's right to choose the funeral pyre, to spell out very clearly and carefully under which conditions, if any, these people could be agreed to have autonomously chosen such a path.[14]

Finally, to what extent is any notion of autonomy – whether rich or poor in quality – a necessary precondition for any kind of good life worthy of the name? As our questions have been directed by the principle of autonomy, a principle with its intellectual roots in the West, we need to be sensitive to the 'historically situated ideals, customs, beliefs, institutions, and practices' in the northern and north-eastern provinces of Thailand of which we are speaking. To what extent is autonomy something that is valued in these cultures, and to what extent is it justifiably subordinated to values of social duty and obligation to others, particularly parents and elders? If this was the case, at the level of a moral position and not just at the surface level, then would a liberal want to argue for the greater good of autonomy and its attendant rights to freedom of choice, conscience, association, expression, a liberal education and a complex and diverse culture? Such questions about competing moral positions are clearly central to the idea of an internal critique.

Conclusion

I will conclude briefly. I have set out the case for combining social theory and political philosophy in the analysis of rights. I have advocated a case study approach in the first instance, one that is modest, realistic and pragmatic (cf. Stones, 1996: 36–8, 64–83) in drawing on a limited number of elements from the vast literatures of social theory and political philosophy to analyse the chosen case. The cases I have discussed here have explicitly thematised some of the areas in which adopting the joint conceptual frame of political philosophy and social theory is essential if key questions are to be addressed. I believe it would be an entirely positive development if academics and doctoral researchers in sociology and related disciplines were able to begin to employ concepts from political and moral philosophy alongside those from social theory as their guides to research. Likewise, it would be an exciting and potentially fruitful development if political philosophers began to ask more questions about how social theory and sociological research could ground and deepen their own analyses.

Notes

1 For an account of epistemological and methodological issues that provides more background to these points, see Stones (2005: 120–7).
2 The notion of duality was formulated by Giddens in outlining his version of structuration theory. See, for example, Giddens (1984) and Cohen (1989). In Stones (2005), I have attempted to draw together insights from the critiques, counter-critiques and empirical uses of structuration theory by many authors to defend what is invaluable in the concept, while acknowledging the need to refine and develop it.
3 It should be said, however, that the notion of autonomy is always thought within the more general conception of liberalism and is not treated as an independent and free-floating concept. If it was treated in the latter way, then one would clearly be committing the same fallacy committed by a crude checklist version of rights.
4 On communitarianism, see Sandel (1982) and Bell (1993). On multiculturalism, see Gutmann (1992) and Parekh (2000). On virtue ethics, see MacIntyre (1981),

Crisp and Slote (1997) and Flanagan and Jupp (2001). Stout (1990) is an interesting example of an argument for the compatibility of virtue ethics and rights. Mulhall and Swift (1992) and Farrelly (2004) are excellent introductory overviews to the field of contemporary political philosophy.

5 Nicos Mouzelis has carefully and usefully established the need for structuration theory to conceptualise differences in the degree to which agents achieve some critical distance from their perception of the social conditions of action. He establishes the need for a continuum of possibilities ranging from the entirely taken for granted to the critically reflective (Mouzelis, 1991: 28; 2000: 748–9).

6 See Stones (2005: 109–15) on the concept of *irresistible social forces* that can severely limit the range of meaningful choices available to a supposedly autonomous individual.

7 Durkheim (1984) argued that traditional societies are characterised by this kind of solidarity in which few divisions of labour mean that individuals and institutions are relatively undifferentiated and values, symbols and rituals are common to the group, clan or tribe. This is in sharp contrast to the individualism of modern societies.

8 This kind of claim always raises, of course, the question of who is designated by 'you and I' or 'we', and any claim that a particular group shares a set of moral values can in principle be empirically tested, and the results will naturally vary between societal groups and cultures.

9 Structuration theory, with its ability to think systematically about the components of both the conjuncturally specific terrain of action and the agent's enduring dispositions and values, provides the tools with which to anchor phronesis to firmer moorings than the intuitions of an agent's judgement with which it is usually associated. For an analysis of the notion of phronesis as employed by both Aristotle and Gadamer, see Bernstein (1986: 99–104). See also Miller (1991: 225–36).

10 Issues of age of consent and responsibility towards children raise a number of additional complicated factors (see Montgomery, 2001: 80–101). For the sake of clarity in the current argument I therefore just focus on young women above the age of consent. Moreover, for the sake of this argument I focus on young women, although sex workers do of course also include older women, boys, men and transsexuals.

11 The notion of a 'decision' itself is in fact even more complicated than I am suggesting here. In her study, Aoyama (2005: 124–7) carefully disaggregates and problematises the notion.

12 See note 6 above.

13 Lucinda Joy Peach (2001: 167) has questioned whether most women in Buddhist cultures have any understanding of themselves as individuals entitled to rights: 'Thai and Burmese Buddhist women in particular are socialized to be relationally and family oriented selves rather than autonomous, independent individuals.' She argues persuasively for a feminist pragmatist perspective on human rights that pays respect to the role of culture and religion in local cultures, and accepts that a legal rights strategy is unlikely to be effective in empowering women who lack 'rights consciousness' (ibid.: 184). On the other hand, fine-grained sociological analyses of Thai women *in situ*, of the kind carried out by Whittaker (2000) and Aoyama (2005), radically call into question Peach's undifferentiated characterisation of them as lacking an understanding of themselves as autonomous, independent individuals, as lacking 'some sense of themselves as agents of their own lives' (Peach, 2001: 167, 184).

14 This is important even though, as we have seen in Parekh's discussion of *sati*, there are many reasons why the issue of autonomy is not necessarily the last word on this matter.

8   Rights work

Constructing lesbian, gay and sexual rights in late modern times

Ken Plummer

> No international instrument relevant to human rights, prior to 1993, makes any reference to the forbidden 'S' word (other than 'sex' as in biological sexes); that is prior to 1993, sexuality of any sort of manifestation is absent from international human rights discourse.
>
> Rosalind Pollack Petchesky (2000: 82)

Sociologists view rights as inventions. Rights are never 'inalienable', 'given in nature' or 'handed to us by God', though these may well be part of the claims made in order that they can become legitimated and accepted. Instead, they have to be assembled through political (and moral) conflicts and eventually institutionalized into laws, ordinances and declarations. It is a view that is often unpopular among 'rights campaigners' because the suggestion that 'rights are inventions' is somehow seen to weaken them. I do not hold this to be so, and cannot fail to see how all rights in the end come out of power struggles. To show just how rights are constructed may help to rob them of a curious mystique and mythological status, and place them where they firmly belong – in the domain of political and moral talk. This chapter examines some features of the ways in which rights are constructed through an illustrative case study of a very new area of rights – that of 'sexual rights'. Fifty years ago the formal sexual rights of women, lesbians and gays were hardly recognized anywhere in the world (the Netherlands – and France, under the Napoleonic Code – being key exceptions), although there were localized struggles to change this situation. In general, such rights were denied or ignored; and traditionally gays as a group were castigated as ill, immoral or dangerous people deserving of treatment or penal sanction but certainly not 'rights'. But it is a classic tale to make my point: a group with no rights at one point in time can assemble them at a later point.

Rights as symbolic interactions

To be clear about the position I argue from, it may help initially to schematise my general assumptions and argument. Drawing upon both symbolic interactionism and social constructionism,[1] I suggest that:

1 Rights are not given in nature merely waiting to be found.
2 Rights are inventions created by human agents through symbolic interactions. They involve the collective conduct and social meaning of many, and come into being through the interpretive and activist work of social movements and a diverse range of moral crusaders and entrepreneurs: from kings, prophets and philosophers to governments, social movements, writers and NGOs.
3 'Rights work' involves many people in a continuous round of negotiated actions that attempt to interpret, rationalize and define both social identities and related rights. 'Rights work' entails claims makers involved in 'claims' and 'counter-claims', often animated by quasi-arguments and stories.
4 Rights work takes place in rights 'arenas' in public spheres.
5 Sometimes rights work leads to substantive claims made for rights on a broad and abstract level (human rights, such as those laid down in various constitutions and charters); sometimes claims are made for very specific groupings (collective rights such as those of ethnic or indigenous groupings); and sometimes they are made for specific human identities.
6 Rights work moves through certain phases and stages. At one point, it is invisible and hardly articulated; at another it 'finds a voice'; and at a later stage it can become habitualized and institutionalized.
7 All rights claims have histories and these are histories of contestation.
8 Rights claims are animated by schisms and fracturings.
9 The struggles over such rights take place not only in local arenas but also in global ones. They are part of emergent global flows and the search for a global citizenry.
10 Rights claims and counter-claims can become diffused, and often this diffusion takes place on a global level.
11 Although rights can be analysed abstractly, the task for sociologists is to become intimately familiar with the crusaders, their claims and the social processes through which rights emerge. They need to see 'rights' as part of the day-to-day world of lived meaning, and not simply belonging to the theoretical and philosophical or even legal heavens.
12 Ultimately, 'rights work' takes place in morally grounded activities and political practices. It is a struggle over defining what it means to live a good life and to be human.

This is schematic and I do not have space to develop all of this below. Instead, I highlight only a few central issues.

Constructing human rights

A starting concern must lie with those who see human rights as inalienable, given, universal. They were heralded by natural law theories that somehow see such rights as given and inhering naturally in the world. Most religions subscribe to this view – rights (and obligations) may be seen to have been inscribed in Hammurabi's Code, the Bible, the Qur'an, the Vedas. But for the interactionist, such texts do not have inherent meaning. This is clearly witnessed by the debates, schisms, conflicts and different interpretations such authoritative texts have generated throughout history. By contrast, others see rights as constructed: they are built by human beings. Constructionist positions look at the struggles generated around human rights, aware that meanings change over time and across different groups – that such meanings are contested. Constructionists look at the ways in which some people and groups (often social movements) are claims makers and do what might be called 'human rights work'. They clarify laws, write justifications, generate reports and conferences, network in cyberspace, tell stories and generally provide rhetorics for human rights. They provide evidence and arguments, identify key types of people (homosexuals, transgendered and people with AIDS), usually against a moral backdrop that helps to identify 'trouble'. Different claims makers and different moral backgrounds would lead probably to a different sense of just what these rights should be. So while gay activists champion 'gay rights', others would claim this infringes their rights. Likewise, such claims depend upon audiences who will hear and there is inevitable competition(s) between different claims to rights. The world of sexual rights almost inevitably speaks to moral codes: religious, organizational and humanitarian (see Plummer, 1995; Best, 2001; Loseke, 2003, for accounts of the constructionist view in general).

The long view of rights

Micheline Ishay (2004) has produced an account of the history of human rights (although she makes no claim to being an interactionist). Seeing this history as a series of steps both forward and backward, she suggests five major waves: early times, the Enlightenment, socialism and the industrial age, the world wars and international rights, and the global age. In each case, she shows how little positive attention has been given to sexuality. For instance, in much of recorded history, religions have been the seedbeds of rights – they have laid out rule books, codes, commandments, 'ways of living' for societies to observe – and although these are not rights *per se* they often hint at the rights to come. Yet in most of these early codes, same-sex relations are strongly condemned. 'Humanitarian' as they often are in providing a seedbed of values for how to live a good life, they are also harbingers of hate.

What interests me is that only in the last moments of these phases – what is sometimes called late modern times (Giddens, 1991) – do we start to hear a language of rights around sexualities. It is, as international campaigner and academic Rosalind Pollack Petchesky (2000) comments, 'the newest kid on the block'. There are odd hints of such rights in nineteenth-century feminism; hints that grow in a few countries during the twentieth. In the USA, the first major organizations to champion gay rights appear in the late 1950s (the Society for Individual Rights (SIR), along with the Mattachine Society and the Daughters of Bilitis), about the same time as the Homosexual Law Reform Society (HLRS) and Albany Trust (AT) appear in the UK (and go on to campaign for the 1967 Sexual Offences Bill/Act). But such concerns do not become part of the global sexual citizenships debates until the 1990s. We have here a major recent case of the struggle for rights – no one spoke in such terms at the time of the foundation of the great rights documents, such as those of the USA, France and the United Nations (Ishay, 1997). Where were women's rights or gay rights or, more generally, sexual rights to be found in all this?

In part this fits a general model I have been developing elsewhere, suggesting some of the stages through which this process of problem designation moves. In this case we are looking at the ways in which 'rights' appear through 'rights work' (Plummer, 1995: 125).

1   Imagining 'rights'.
2   Articulating/vocalizing: announcing 'rights'.
3   Inventing identities: becoming storytellers about 'rights'.
4   Creating social worlds of 'rights'.
5   Creating a culture of 'public rights'.

Sociologists ask 'how the dimensions are carved out, how the number of people drawn into concern about these discussions is increased, how a common pool of knowledge begins to develop for the arena participants, and how all these sub- processes increase the visibility of the problem' (Wiener, 1981: 14). Rights have long histories stretching back to ancient civilizations and religions, even though the language of rights – 'rights talk' – only really starts to come into its own with the Enlightenment.

Stretching back into the nineteenth century, through pressure group activity and social movement building in a number of countries across the world, 'claims' were slowly made for the right to different kinds of sexual orientations and sexual activities. This chapter examines some of the claims made, some of the stories told and some of the institutions built in order to create new identities, make new laws and eventually establish codes of rights. It also looks at the ways in which some lesbians and gays lay counter-claims (radically rejecting the established, liberal, position), and seek counter-publics, while other groups make more conservative claims to suggest that gay and lesbians should *not* have rights. Rights models remain in contestation. We shall also see how 'sexual citizenship' or 'intimate citizenship' becomes a major discussion of the 1990s and comes to be applied to a wider range of sexualities (such as transgender groups and sadomasochists). Again, at the same time, the notion of 'gay rights' is heavily contested in many countries across the world and is challenged at the United Nations and in many religious organisations. This chapter outlines this contestation and the agenda for the future, and argues that 'rights', once gained, are never permanently settled, and can always be lost again.

Making 'gay rights'

Imagine a time, scarcely less than a hundred years ago, when there was hardly any talk about sexual rights – let alone homosexual or gay rights (the words, after all, had hardly been invented; Plummer, 1981). Throughout most of history such ideas had been more or less unknown, and indeed same-sex relations had usually been taboo through religious and legal sanctions. What we start to see are a series of phases in which such issues become more and more overt: whispered about, spoken about, organized around, campaigned over, and eventually – very recently – turned into full-scale 'rights' claims. This has involved a lot of crusaders both for and against; but bit by bit a gay agenda of rights has evolved that could hardly have been dreamt about two centuries ago. There are now many discussions and listings of such rights (e.g. Nussbaum, 1999).[2] Some of the issues now firmly on the agenda that could not have been raised in the past are:

- the rights of all people to participate worldwide in consensual acts of their choice;
- the acceptance of universal lesbian and gay rights, the inclusion of 'sexual orientation' in charters of human rights and anti-discrimination laws and mandatory training in 'multiculturalism' and 'gay affirmative action' in many workplaces;
- lesbian rights to be recognized as widely as women's rights;
- the importance of 'domestic/registered partnerships' and 'marriage' for lesbian and gays;
- the gay right to adopt and have children, along with self-insemination for lesbians;
- the recognition of gays and lesbians in the military;
- the recognition of 'hate crimes' that target lesbians and gays (and other groups) and the prevention of harassment;
- the recognition of materials speaking positively of ('promoting'?) gays and lesbians in schools and the workplace, as well as the championing of widespread gay and lesbian erotica in art and elsewhere;
- the acceptance of transsexuality and transgender;[3]
- the development of other erotic minorities' rights.

The struggle for gay rights has assumed different emphases such that what was once hardly imaginable as 'on the agenda' has now become reality. Thus, in its earliest days, the gay rights movement had as its focus the ultimate decriminalization of homosexual acts – and perhaps the acceptance (or tolerance) of homosexuality (even if as an illness). These were the ultimate goals of the earliest gay movements. But by the times of Gay Liberation Front (GLF), the claims made were much more strident. There was the claim to legal equality; there was the claim to be accepted on equal grounds with heterosexuals; there was the claim to equal opportunities in school and work; there was the claim to be free from homophobic attack; there was the claim to behave as heterosexuals might in the street – holding hands, even kissing (Gay Is Good, pamphlet, 1970). The emphasis shifted from the decriminalization of specific sexual acts to a wider acceptance of equal rights for gays and lesbians. But as the movement gathered momentum, so the claims became ever more bold and inclusive.

By the mid-1980s, claims were increasingly made that gays and lesbians should have equal rights to what came to be known as 'families of choice' (Weston, 1991). A dual emphasis – on the rights to marriage and the rights to raise children – became more and more prominent.[4] Indeed, in a number of countries where equal rights had been obtained in a number of areas (the laws had been changed, equal opportunities charters had been introduced, governments had incorporated the thinking of many gays and lesbians into governmental policies), it was the only issue that seriously discriminated homosexuality from heterosexuality. And hence in December 1988, the first registered partnership took place in Denmark, followed in quick succession by a number of Scandinavian countries (Sweden, Norway, Iceland, Finland) and then others in Europe, the Netherlands being the first country to legislate for gay and lesbian marriages. Most countries within the European Union have legislated for partnerships. And so have many other countries across the world: from South Africa (also the first country to enshrine gay rights in its charter), Brazil (a country that also tried to make this a universal issue through the United Nations) and Mexico (though not – as is common – without its setbacks). In the United States, the situation is much more fractured, but one thing is clear: it has become a major source of cultural division between the pro- and anti-gay lobbies. It seems to be a major source of 'irreconcilable differences' (Caramagno, 2002).

Does all this change simply mean the discovery of hidden natural rights? Or is it the active work of many people struggling to create a better life for themselves and others. To grasp this would really require a full-scale historical study – something that has yet to be done (although there are now many excellent general histories, e.g. Greenberg, 1988). Still, we can sense, if only schematically, how the changes unfolded.

From around the mid- to late nineteenth century, the idea of 'the homosexual' as a kind of person comes into being – the clinical creature found in the writings of Richard von Krafft Ebing, for instance. Minor campaigns begin that attempt to take the homosexual out of the realm of law and place him within a medical model of understanding and treatment. By the start of the twentieth century, in the works of those like Havelock Ellis and Magnus Hirschfield, we start to see claims being made over the rights of these homosexuals – in the case of Hirschfield (whose work was ultimately destroyed by the Nazis), we see the creation of a centre and an organization designed to campaign for the rights not just of the homosexual but also the transsexual. (On all this, see Lauritsen and Thorsdad, 1974; Weeks, 1990; Oosterhuis, 2000.) In the middle of the twentieth century, we see a proliferation of rather low key, often apologetic (but sometimes communist) organizations who start to put homosexual rights more and more on the political agenda (see D'Emilio, 1983; Dorr Legg, 1994).

In the UK, a history extending from Oscar Wilde to the Wolfenden Report helped to make a public language of homosexuality more and more accessible (Westwood, 1952, 1960). The Wolfenden Report was the result of a government inquiry set up to look into several 'homosexual scandals' in the early 1950s. This commission established a framework for moral discourse in Britain about such matters. For all its flaws, it helped to make homosexuality a public issue and crucial morals crusaders emerged around it – the HLRS and the AT. It argued that there was an area of personal morality that was simply not the law's business. It argued for, and helped to create, a public space controlled by the law and a private space that was not the law's business. Stuart Hall has identified this as 'Wolfenden's double taxonomy: towards stricter penalty and control, towards greater freedom and leniency; together the two elements in a single strategy' (Hall, 1980: 14). Ultimately, Wolfenden's proposals came to be enshrined in the Sexual Offences Act 1967, which effectively decriminalised homosexuality in England and Wales (but later in Scotland, 1980, and Northern Ireland, 1982). What Wolfenden so clearly reinforced was a public/private split – and along with this the culture of the closet. It was far from being a 'rights document', for while homosexual acts between consenting adults were no longer illegal, this was only so in private places between two consenting adults. The division of public and private space was central to this, leaving the stigma of the past still hanging over homosexuality and keeping it a crime in many situations. For most gay men and indeed lesbians (who were not directly touched by the law), this still meant that their lives would be conducted in the closet. Gay cultures have been powerfully shaped by this: the culture of homosexuality was one of passing and hiding (Wolfenden, 1957; Hall, 1980; Plummer, 1981; Jeffery-Poulter, 1991).

The next striking stage in the creation of gay rights was the emergence of the GLF in a number of Western countries in the late 1960s and early 1970s. In many respects a new social movement, it built on a politics of identity to bring out 'gays' as self-identified people demanding rights. With new slogans, lists of demands and rights, badges and marches, it raised public awareness of homosexuality in a way that simply had not happened before. It made 'coming out' a major political process at the forefront of gay politics. 'Gay was good' and it was going visible (Walters, 1980; Weeks, 1990; Power, 1995). These new groups soon divided – either into factions that were more assimilationist, liberal and rights-oriented (seeking equal rights with heterosexuals) or into those who were more radical and challenging (Marotta, 1981) – establishing a split that continues to this day (see below).

Then came a broad phase that was bitter sweet: it was the arrival of HIV/AIDS between 1981 and 1986, and ironically it worked to strengthen the gay movement. For the first time, hitherto 'outcast gays' came to work with the government in shaping policies. They became professionalized. More than this, they had to deal with the linkage between gay rights and health rights – in many ways the latter was much more acceptable than the former, and hence new links over rights talks were established. Perhaps most significantly, since HIV/AIDS was an international issue, it brought gay and health rights on to a world stage. We see the first stages of an internationally recognized gay movement (there were elements before but this firmly established it – the International Lesbian and Gay Association (ILGA) was founded in Coventry in 1979[5]). I do not want to overstate this. AIDS was after all a serious pandemic which brought chronic illness, early death and tragic bereavement for many disproportionately young men. But, in an ironic twist, it also brought a revitalization and professionalism to a slumbering gay movement (Davies *et al.*, 1993; Berridge, 1996).

The globalization and anti-globalization of gay rights regimes

This globalization of gay rights is perhaps the most significant recent development. We have seen the diffusion of sexual rights claims across the world, and the creation of global sexual rights regimes. In part, this has been due to the rise of a global gay movement (Adam *et al.*, 1998), along with an increasing search for 'cosmopolitan democracy' and 'global citizens' (Albrow, 1996). The gay movement has had more success with NGOs such as Amnesty International and Human Rights Watch than with other groups.

However, in practice, as some nations have implemented quite wide-ranging gay rights programmes, others have not. In some cases, this is seen as another attempt by the West to impose its own values and claims (Altman, 1997, 2001; Bell and Binnie, 2000; Binnie, 2004). But in many cases it is seen as much worse than this, as a serious clash of moral values, what has been called 'the clash of sexual civilizations'. Modifying Huntington's (in)famous thesis,

> At this point in history, societies throughout the world (Muslim and Judeo-Christian alike) see democracy as the best form of government. Instead the real fault line between West and Islam, which Huntington's theory completely overlooks, concerns *gender equality* and *sexual*

> *liberalization* . . . the values that separate the two cultures have much
> more to do with Eros than demos.
>
> (Inglehart and Norris, 2003a: 65)

In most 'traditional' societies the issue of gay rights remains abhorrent. Such relationships will be recognized, and indeed are seen in opposition to human rights. In many countries around the world today sexual minorities are outcast: they may be bullied, harassed and mocked, be discriminated against in work and school, suffer unfair arrest and imprisonment, be treated as ill, be rendered the victims of 'hate crimes', fined, flogged, tortured, raped and executed. They may be driven into self-loathing and suicide. More than 70 countries have laws that criminalize homosexual relations. In Iran, Afghanistan, Saudi Arabia and Chechnya, gay sex can lead to the death penalty. From Europe to Africa to the Americas to Asia, case after case of torture, ill treatment, violence and discrimination against lesbians and gay men is documented. In Colombia, 'death squads' routinely target and kill gay men and transvestites as local authorities promote *limpieza social* (social cleansing). The death squads operate without fear of prosecution as the gunmen themselves are often police officers and gays are regarded as 'disposable people'. There are also very many cases of transgender rights activists – 'the ultimate gender outlaws' – being abused across the world. In short, sexual minorities are seen neither to deserve rights nor to be treated in any ways as equals. (See Vanessa Baird, 2001, 2004, for documentation.)

Nor has 'gay rights work' had much success at the level of international governmental organizations (IGOs), though rather more so with the informal level of NGOs. In the world of public cultures of human rights like the United Nations, sexual rights may be seen as the latest and a neglected issue and their claims have been scarcely heard except through the women's movement. Although implicitly they may be read into various charters of rights (the right to happiness and freedom etc. could surely also mean sexual happiness and freedom[6]), and although they have (a much shorter) history built from gay activism with their own gay charters, it is only very recently that they have specifically and directly entered the international public domain. And here it is mainly through the rights work of the women's movement, and especially the work of the transnational women's health movement, which became galvanized in the UN-sponsored women's conferences in Vienna (1993), Cairo (1994) and Beijing (1995), that the situation started to change.[7]

The impact of women's rights

Although traditionally the women's movement's core concern in this field has been with women's reproductive rights, bit by bit they have been able to put together a much more wide-ranging programme that claims sexual rights as human rights like any other essential rights. Women's rights to sexual equality, their right to control fertility or the right to marriage have been mentioned but it is only recently that sexual rights have made any headway. A section of the final Beijing document reads:

> The human rights of women include their rights to have control over and decide freely and responsibly on matters related[?] to their sexuality, including sexual and reproductive health, free of coercion, discrimination and violence. Equal relationships between women and men in matters of sexual relations and reproduction including full respect for the integrity of the person, require mutual respect, consent and shared responsibility for sexual behavior and its consequences.
>
> (Petchesky, 2003: 38)

In these debates many terms can get conflated: sexual rights, gay rights, reproductive rights, intimate rights, human rights and a concern over sexual abuse and violence. They are not the same and each needs to delineate its own domain of duties and responsibilities. In particular, Miller suggests that sexual rights and reproductive rights should not be conflated, as otherwise individuals engaging in non-procreative sex (or non-sexual procreation?) can be disenfranchised. We need to see how these rights connect differently with different issues (Miller, 2000: 96). Miller also wants to be clear about the right to be free from (what can be called a violations approach) and the right to do something (a promotions approach).

Of course, such programmes as these have been open to much attack within the United Nations. Rights are always heavily contested (Smith and Windes, 2000). Indeed, they depend upon contestation in order to take shape and be given life. Thus, the attacks on sexual rights come from many sides: from the Vatican, from Muslim organisations, from the US government and President Bush. And such right-wing and fundamentalist backlashes serve to make the rights claims more visible, while simultaneously managing to impede them. Nevertheless, Rosalind Petchesky (2003: 39) is hopeful about the future, suggesting that 'slowly and incrementally, women's determination . . . to gain some control over their fertility and bodies was starting to make an impact on international human rights'.

Backlash: the global family movement

One interesting 'backlash' alliance between the major monotheistic religions across the world (conservative/fundamentalist versions of Christianity, Islam and Judaism) emerged during the latter decades of the twentieth century to establish what might be called a 'natural family agenda'. A key organization, the Howard Center, puts it well:

> The World Congress of families coalition model represents the final opposition for an effective pro-family model world wide. All coalition

members, usually orthodox religious believers, are asked to set aside their own personal theological and cultural differences and agree on one simple, unifying concept: the natural family is the fundamental unity of society. If coalition members can agree on this concept, then all of their other disagreements may take a back seat.

(Cited in Buss and Herman, 2003: xiv)

This includes such organizations as the Catholic Family and Human Rights Institute, The Howard Center itself, Human Life International, the Family Research Council, Concerned Women for America, the World Family Policy Center and of course the Vatican. The Vatican has not only decreed in various encyclicals, but also has 'permanent observer' status at the United Nations. The 'Holy See' is the official face of the Vatican at the UN. It has led to the World Congress of Families (WCF). It has also produced what Buss and Herman (2003: xxxiii) have called 'Christian right social science'. It has played a key role at a number of international conferences (Cairo, Cairo+5; Beijing, Beijing+5) with all kinds of strange bedfellows (not just Christians with Muslims, but Catholics with Protestants) joining forces globally against the 'global liberal agenda' – and more specifically with feminism, humanism and lesbian and gay rights along with socialism, environmentalism and 'new-age spirituality'. Sexual rights are strongly contested.

Towards intimate citizenship?

One of the most recent developments in the struggles for sexual rights has been the turn to 'citizenship debates'. Citizenship has a long history, and in recent years has become something of a buzz word. What is crucial in all of this is the construction of subjects (or subjectivities) to which rights and obligations may be ascribed. T. H. Marshall's (1950) classic model of citizenship suggested a development model of civil, legal and welfare rights emerging in Westernized societies. But these days it is used more broadly and has come to signify a model of 'social inclusion' or 'full participation', and has been harnessed by feminist and lesbian/gay political agendas seeking to claim their own 'social inclusion' but drawn upon a much wider canvass (Lister, 1997; Richardson, 1998, 2000).

The starting point for discussions of sexual citizenship was David Evans's *Sexual Citizenship*, published in 1993. He is sharply critical of the conventional use of the term. As he puts it, 'The history of citizenship is a history of fundamental formal heterosexist patriarchal principles and practices ostensibly progressively "liberalized" towards and through the rhetoric of "equality" but in practice to effect unequal differentiation' (Evans, 1993: 9). Evans is here making a point close to the idea of civic stratification discussed in Chapter 4, and moves on to introduce his own concept of sexual citizenship, 'which involves partial, private and primarily leisure and life style membership' (ibid.: 64) and which he connects to the market. Most of the book is given over to discussions of specific groups mainly in the UK context, and his major example is of course 'gay rights' and the 'homosexual'. But he goes further and also considers the sexual rights linked to women, bisexuals, transsexuals and children. What is crucial in all of this is the construction of subjects (or subjectivities) to which rights and obligations may be ascribed. Sometimes this can be controversial: in mentioning children – and asking if they are sexual citizens with sexual rights – he heads straight for a minefield of controversies connected to the boundaries of sexualities. But such issues needed surely to be placed on the agenda, along with the more accepted rights of a child.

A few years later, one of the leading UK sex analysts, Jeffrey Weeks, also raised doubts about the ways in which the idea of citizenship had been used in the past. He sees it as a 'major element of sexual politics since the 1970s, largely in the form of campaigns for rights' (Weeks, 1995: 118). But the articulation of the 'sexual citizen' is much more recent and has made much more formal and explicit the idea of sexual rights that much of the gay and lesbian debates had been developing over the past thirty years. He sees a new 'sexual citizen' arriving, and charts how this idea may help to move forward politics connected to the relationships between men and women, families, the denaturalization of the sexual, balancing different communities and their claims and trying to live life with diversity and common humanity. Likewise, Bell and Binnie (2000) look at the place of sexuality in both political and social theory, showing how the sexual is (still, after all these years) routinely minimized, written out, 'trashed'. As they say, in a telling statement, 'we consider all citizenship to be sexual citizenship, as citizenship is inseparable from identity, and sexuality is central to identity'. For them, sexual issues go to the heart of citizenship, and with that the theory of inequalities and the state. Finally, then, by the early twenty-first century, hitherto marginalized discussions of sexual rights start to assume prominence in citizenship theory.

There are a growing number of thinkers who are examining these citizenship rights. Diane Richardson (2000), for instance, drawing on both lesbian politics and women's rights, argues that we live in an age when the politics of citizenship increasingly define 'sexual politics':

> Globally we are witnessing gay and lesbian movements (and sometimes bi/sometimes transgender) which demand 'equal rights' with heterosexuals in relation to age of consent laws, to healthcare, rights associated with social and legal recognition of domestic partnerships including the right to marry, immigration rights, parenting rights, and so on. In a similar vein, there are groups campaigning for 'transsexual rights' including the right to sex change treatment on the National Health Service, the legal right for birth certificate status to be changed, and related to this the right to marry legally. Recently there have been attempts to place 'sexual rights' on the agenda of disability movements,

especially in relation to disabled people's rights to sexual expression. . . .
We can even see some evidence of the language of citizenship being used
in movements or campaigns whose politics are definitely not about seeking formal equality with heterosexuals. An example of this is the
focus on prostitution as a human rights issue by some radical and
revolutionary feminists.

(Ibid.: 9)

Again, she looks at the classic models of citizenship, and trying to see how
they may be applicable to lesbian and gay rights she finds them severely
lacking. She sees that claims to citizenship status generally are not just guilty
of strong male bias, a point made by many feminist writers. The problem
goes further: citizenship also privileges heterosexuality. 'Within discourses
of citizen's rights . . . the normal citizen has largely been constructed as male,
and . . . as heterosexual'. Hence she goes on from this to identify a number
of areas where the rights of sexual – as opposed to heterosexual – citizenship
should be claimed. She names three main areas of sexual citizenships
and rights. The main areas for her are: (a) seeking rights to various forms
of *sexual practice* in personal relationships, including pleasures and self-
determination (e.g. the right not to be raped, as well as the right to have
children); (b) seeking rights through *self-identity definition*, like the option
to name the kind of sexual person one is, alongside the right to self-
realization; (c) seeking rights within social institutions, meaning *public validation of various forms of sexual relationship*, including the right to choose
partners and the right to public recognition (ibid.: 75). Her arguments lead
us to see that just as citizenship is racialized and gendered, so it has been
sexualized.

My own concerns have gone beyond the idea of sexual citizenship. While
this is an important issue, late modern times are witnessing a considerable
array of new personal or intimate dilemmas. Establishing rights and obligations around sexuality are important; but so too are the new decisions that
have to be taken over assisted conception (from surrogate mothering to the
freezing of sperm and embryos), the buying and selling of body parts, the
making of new kinds of families, the new 'transitionings' over gender (as
men become women and women become men), the development of new
relationships over the Internet and the new medical technologies such as
Viagra and 'morning after pills', which could change the ways in which we
conduct our personal lives. Again, these are all globally contested areas.
They lead to debates around what I have called elsewhere intimate citizenship
(Plummer, 2003).

Queering citizenship

A recent development has been a shift from the analysis of 'sexual rights' to
those that emphasize 'queer theory'. This position, which developed in the

late 1980s in the work of Butler, Sedgwick and Warner, challenged the orthodox terminologies of gay, bisexual, lesbian, male and female and advocated a language of deconstruction, destabilization and depolarization (see Plummer, 2005). In this argument there could be no straightforward view of sexual rights, which is seen as a process of the normalization of sexuality. It shuns, for instance, the notion of the 'good and responsible lesbian and gay citizens' who are inside the charmed circle of citizens, with a world of gay and lesbian married couples raising their children. Instead, it looks at a 'a less respectable, dangerous gayness' composed of the sexual outlaw, the sexual fringe, the transgressor. Smyth (1994) makes a particular point about the sexualized lesbian: to see lesbians as highly sexualized, fetishistic, 'fucking' creatures poses a threat to the usually desexualized image of the lesbian citizen. The radical edge of being gay and sexual cannot be simply assimilated into a culture of rights and obligations.

The process being highlighted here has been called 'normalization' (Phelan, 2001). While the normal citizen has been stretched to include the homosexual and the sexual being, it only includes those who fit a certain model – those who want families, conform to gender roles, link love and sex. They want to stress not their differences but their sameness, they want to have and raise children, they want to be inside the armed forces: they share 'family values'. Often they are models of middle-class consumption and individualism. All this has been challenged by the queer movement, which raises orthodox 'sexual rights' as a problem, and starts to speak instead of 'queer rights' as part of a new order entailing a transgression of all categories, a celebration of marginalities and dissidence. For some this may mean the arrival of 'bi-theory' and 'gender bending' as a way of unsettling the certainties of the sexual and gender orders. It has meant, in almost ironic twist, the arrival of gay men who have sex with women, and lesbians who have sado-masochistic sex with men.

A leaflet circulating in 1991 put it bluntly:

> Queer means to fuck with gender. There are straight queers, bi queers, tranny queers, lez queers, SM queers, fisting queers in every single street in this apathetic country of ours. . . . Each time the word 'queer' is used it defines a strategy, an attitude, a reference to other identities and a new self understanding. (And queer can be qualified as 'more queer', 'queer', or 'queerest' as the naming develops into a more complex process of identification.)
>
> (Smyth, 1992: 17, 20)

So 'queer' means theoretically deconstructing and postmodernizing; practically breaking down all categorizations in gender, erotic and intimate lives; and politically following the above through to sustained critiques of the existing sexual/gender rights systems and working to change them.

Conclusion: contested constructions

All these issues are of course strongly and hotly contested, but compared to what could have been argued one hundred years ago, the agenda on sexual and intimate rights is looking strikingly different. Most of the above claims were hardly even thinkable then. What we have witnessed, at the closure of the twentieth century and the opening years of the twenty-first, has been not just the fulfilment of some of the main claims of an earlier lesbian and gay movement, but many of their wilder dreams also becoming a reality in some parts of the world. This is not to disagree with the claims that in all countries there still exist massive and pervasive forms of domination, persecution and discrimination for lesbians and gays and that in many countries throughout the world, no gains at all have been made. But it is to start to recognize that many gains have been made in many places – even though these are very uneven and leave many groups still excluded. A new visible public culture of lesbian rights, gay rights, transgender rights – indeed, intimate citizenship or even queer citizenship – are in the process of being created, even as they are contested.

Notes

1 Symbolic interactionism was a term coined by Herbert Blumer in 1937 (Blumer, 1969) to capture the grounded analysis and intimate familiarity with the creativity of action in social life and the lived processes of everyday life and the languages and meanings that emerge through them. Allied is the constructionist view, which sees social life not as obdurate and fixed but as produced through social life (Berger and Luckmann, 1967). It has been argued by Maines (2001) and Atkinson and Housley (2003) that these positions are really quite widespread within sociology, even if often not acknowledged. They are closely linked to the philosophical traditions of pragmatism identified with Dewey, James and Mead, and more recently Rorty. In any event such positions shape my arguments in this chapter.

2 For example, see Martha Nussbaum's (1999: Chapter 7) discussion. Here she lists: the right to be protected against violence, and in general, the right to equal protection under the law; the right to have consensual adult sexual relations without criminal penalty; the right to non-discrimination in housing, employment and education; the right to military service; the right to marriage and/or its legal benefits; and the right to retain custody of children and/or to adopt.

3 Side by side with this listing is a concern over discriminations, which include sexual offences laws, the use of beatings and tortures in custody, hate crimes, invisibilities, the concern over young gays and lesbians and discriminations against them, employment discrimination, freedom of expression and association, religious leaders supporting discrimination (see Beger, 2004: 107).

4 As ever we must beware of the dangers of essentialising homosexuality and making it look the same across cultures and throughout history. The important work of the late historian John Boswell (1995) – although he was an essentialist – shows that same-sex marriages have existed in the past.

5 In 1993, ILGA was granted 'roster status' as an NGO by the UN Economic and Social Council (but this was later withdrawn, as they could not convince it that they did not condone sex between adults and minors). It now has some 300 ILGA

members groups in more than 80 countries (Felice, 1996: 48). Its key slogan is that 'gay rights are human rights'.

6 Generalist and abstract accounts of sexual rights often draw upon the broad claims of earlier charters. For instance, the charter drawn at the World Congress of Sexology in 1999 often just seems to add the word 'sexual' to rights that have generally been at the forefront of the rights movement. To illustrate, they suggest some eleven rights, such as the right to sexual freedom, which encompasses the possibility for individuals to express their full sexual potential. However, this excludes all forms of sexual coercion, exploitation and abuse at any time and situations in life.

7 The first dealt with gender-based violence, sexual stratification, rape, sexual slavery, harassment and exploitation. The 1994 conference dealt with sexual health and came mainly from health lobbies and HIV prevention. The 1995 conference is more cautious.

9   The sociology of indigenous peoples' rights

Colin Samson and Damien Short

It has become increasingly clear that the vociferous insistence on liberal market capitalism and strong nation states as the solution to all manner of global problems is another expression of Western dominance. These twin globalising forces operate at the expense of both the natural environment and the vitality of small peoples whose ways of life depend on autonomy and cultural continuity. One response to this juggernaut is the appeal to human rights, apparent in the international activism of hitherto separate groups of indigenous peoples. Members of relatively small groups such as the Ogiek, Wirajuri, Mapuche, Nahua, Blackfoot and Innu now pass through the halls of the United Nations and are intimately involved in the negotiation of their rights with states and multinational corporations.

Historians, anthropologists and political theorists have all undertaken research on indigenous peoples and their human and other rights. However, relatively few sociologists have taken an interest in a subject that is now truly global in its ramifications. Starting from the premise that the contemporary consideration of indigenous peoples' rights is bound up with European colonial expansion, we outline some of the features of a sociological under- standing of indigenous rights. We start by considering indigenous–European relationships and the authoritative frameworks within which such relation- ships have been encapsulated. Then we look at the colonial processes of territorial dispossession and forced cultural change, which lie at the heart of contemporary indigenous rights appeals. From there we consider the problematic conceptions of indigenous peoples in sociology and sociological approaches to human rights. Finally, we contrast the social and political critique of rights contained in the writings of various indigenous scholars with the individualistic and statist notions advanced by liberal democratic theorists.

Indigenous peoples and European expansion

During the era of European expansion from the sixteenth to the eighteenth centuries, the rights of 'savages', 'infidels' and 'heathens' were a matter of debate among legal scholars, philosophers, politicians and statesman in the grand courts of Europe. As early as the sixteenth century, the Dominican theologian Francisco de Vitoria was asking the question, 'by what right were the barbarians subject to Spanish rule?' Although Vitoria (1991: 278–92) argued that the right of dominion came from eight possible 'just titles', the occupation of the territories of indigenous peoples in the Americas was no mere formality. Although frequently violated, many of the relations between the European powers themselves were tacitly regulated by various shared agreements on the rights that could be accorded to both European invaders and indigenous peoples. This was especially the case in North America, where the treaty was used as an international instrument, setting out agreements between sovereign entities.

In some areas of colonial expansion, however, no agreements were made because Europeans assumed that they alone were sovereign and that indigenous peoples had no rights whatsoever. This was because their supposed cultural inferiority and non-agricultural mode of subsistence was deemed by influential philosophers such as John Locke and legal scholars such as Emmerich de Vattel to prevent indigenous peoples from exercising any meaningful sovereignty. Under the accompanying doctrine of *terra nullius*, indigenous occupied land was deemed to be an open wilderness. This was the case in a handful of locations, most prominent of which is Australia, where no legal formalities were extended to Aborigines, who were simply dispossessed by settler land grabs, often of a violent nature. In many instances, however, as Jennings (1975) has shown with regard to New England, colonial powers simply used whatever 'principle' was convenient to dispossess the original inhabitants. In practice, indigenous peoples who signed formal agreements fared no better than those who did not, since the terms of treaties were frequently ignored, violated or not enforced.

With time the international rights sketched out by agreement between the various colonial powers gradually came to be treated as matters of domestic state policy.[1] In the long interlude between first contacts and the mid-twentieth century, the international legal basis for the rights of indigenous peoples was conveniently forgotten, and correspondingly little or no consideration was given to the validity of indigenous laws and concepts of rights. Although indigenous peoples' rights vary internationally, such rights have been *granted* within state-centred legal structures operating under simple assertions of sovereignty. Only after the Second World War with various international standards for the treatment of indigenous peoples drawn up by the United Nations, the Organisation of American States and the International Labour Organisation did any serious transnational discussion take place. Over the past decade, the UN Declaration on the Rights of Indigenous Peoples has reinvigorated discussions of rights of indigenous peoples to their lands, laws and ways of life as supranational concerns.

When the UN tackled the issue of indigenous peoples rights in the 1980s, it concentrated on first establishing who they are. The most widely cited definition of indigenous peoples was advanced by Jose Martinez Cobo, the special rapporteur of the subcommission of the Working Group on Indigenous Populations. Cobo defined indigenous peoples as descendants of original inhabitants of regions colonized or invaded by what became a dominant population. Importantly, the definition also emphasized that such peoples had maintained cultural continuity distinct from other groups of state populations and constituted a non-dominant sector of the societies in which they found themselves (Cobo, 1987; Miller, 2003: 63–5; Niezen, 2003: 19). This definition most obviously fits areas of the world such as the Americas and Australasia, where Europeans colonized lands and peoples in the centuries of expansion and left all authority in nation states comprised of settlers and their descendants.

However, even within the Americas considerable differences are apparent in the treatment of indigenous peoples by different colonial powers. For example, as a result of the English emphasis on private property and land ownership, territorial dispossession was carried out with greater despatch in former British colonies than elsewhere (see Seed, 2001). Although the Spanish killed and plundered, their colonialism did not specifically depend as much on ownership *per se*. Indigenous lands in many, although not all, areas of Latin America have been given more formal protections than in the largely Anglo-Saxon United States. While many indigenes simply became absorbed in larger *mestizo* populations, and would technically fall outside Cobo's definition, others have had specific constitutional and jurisdictional rights recognised by the state itself (see Hindley, 1996; Assies, 1998).

Africa and Asia are different again. While they have maintained cultural continuity, African and Asian indigenous peoples are not under the governmental authority of a European diasporic regime. Decolonization on these continents was achieved by simply handing over power to favoured and cooperative ethnic groups or by configuring various ethnic groups into a political elite. In Africa, this became the only route out of colonialism short of armed insurrection (Davidson, 1992: 99–101). In order to ensure political continuity, many colonial powers, Britain in particular, insisted that independence should operate within colonial political structures. Thus, African postcolonial elites proceeded to 'independence' by wielding European instruments of power within European political institutions. This process meant that 'Africa's real nations were superseded by non-nations and their histories, cultures, languages and ways of life were treated as backward and irrelevant' (Hameso, 1997: 9). However, the 'first people' of Africa are considered by the UN to be no less indigenous than those from North America, Australasia and Latin America (Kenrick and Lewis, 2004). These peoples, especially if they are hunter-gatherers, currently face pressures similar to their counterparts elsewhere to give up their lands for agriculture, resource extraction and 'national parks' within a largely European postcolonial order (Woodburn, 2001).

While a peoples' experience of European expansion upon their territories appears to be a major factor in the UN definition of indigenous peoples, much clearly depends on what happened to them over the centuries of European domination. Miller (2003) has drawn attention to the numerous unrecognised indigenes that have been partly absorbed into dominant social groupings or significantly changed through acculturation, intermarriage and violence. Peoples that have been moved off territories and can no longer claim special relationships to land or cultural institutions would also appear to be only partly encompassed in the UN definition. This debate on who exactly is indigenous is likely to continue, especially in view of the United Nations Draft Declaration on the Rights of Indigenous Peoples currently under consideration.

The treatment of indigenous populations

The discussions over indigenous peoples' rights have assumed more urgency in the light of the desperate social, political and economic condition of the vast majority of the world's estimated 250 million indigenous peoples. This has been chronicled at the UN, by independent human rights researchers and most articulately by indigenous peoples themselves. Regardless of whether they are in wealthy states like Canada, the USA and Australia or poor 'Third World' countries in South America and Africa, many of the stories are the same. A recent study highlights 'the extraordinary similarity of experiences of Indigenous Peoples across the Commonwealth – between those in First World Countries and those in Third World countries' (Commonwealth Policy Studies Unit, 2003: 3).

The processes of social transformation from relatively independent and healthy societies to peoples treated as squatters, currently on the verge of cultural and physical extinction, have variously involved military conquest, forced relocation, the spread of disease, land theft and fraud. The effects of these actions were and are often genocidal, with numerous tribal groups dying out completely. Even those that have taken sober and cautious looks at the demographic changes have used the term 'holocaust' to describe indigenous depopulation in North America (Jaffe, 1992: 109; Thornton, 2002: 70).

In many parts of the world, the crises in indigenous societies were deepened by cultural change instigated by assimilation programmes in which children were inducted into European schooling systems, and in many cases, such as the notorious boarding schools in North America (see Assembly of First Nations, 1994; Adams, 1995; Miller, 1996) and Australia (see HREOC, 1997; Manne, 1998; Haebich, 2001), forcibly separated from their families. For example, in Australia at the turn of the twentieth century there was a growing population of mixed-descent children, specifically children born to aboriginal mothers usually with Anglo-Celtic or sometimes Chinese or Pacific Islander fathers. Almost invariably the Australian settlers thought of these mixed-descent children, and of the descendants of these children – whom they labelled, almost zoologically, as 'half-castes' or 'crossbreeds', as 'quadroons' and 'octoroons' – as a growing, fearful social problem (Manne, 1998: 2). In the late 1920s and early 1930s, Australian policy-makers began to develop forced removal and relocation policies based on the science of eugenics that aimed to solve this 'half-caste problem'. The programmes were designed to 'breed out the colour' and subsequently became known as 'the policy of biological assimilation or absorption' (Haebich, 2001: 19). In 1997 the Australian Human Rights and Equal Opportunities Commission published its groundbreaking report *Bringing Them Home*, which documented the full extent of the forced child removal policies, concluding that between one in ten and one in three indigenous children were removed from their families and that this constituted an act of genocide (see HREOC, 1997). The tens of thousands of forcibly removed indigenous children became known as the 'stolen generations'.[2]

In the USA and Canada great inducements were offered for conversion to Christianity, while indigenous religious practices such as shamanism, the potlatch, peyote use, the ghost dance and the sun dance were either suppressed, banned or both during the most intense periods of assimilation (Niezen, 2000: 128–49).[3] In some areas of the USA, the government's Indian Health Service practised forcible sterilization on Native Americans as late as the 1970s (England, 2004). The same occurred in parts of Australia (Robertson, 2002), and there is persuasive evidence that such practices are continuing in Peru (Kleiss, 2004; see also United Nations, 1999). Finally, with indigenous economies wrecked and land confiscated, many indigenous peoples have had little choice but to seek livelihoods through the wage economy, social welfare and, in many areas of the world, crime, prostitution and other high-risk activities within the dominant society. The results of all these processes can readily be seen in the high rates of alcoholism, suicide, solvent abuse and non-traditional drug abuse, as well as physical illnesses, in indigenous communities around the world (see, for example, Bourne, 2003: 34–41; Samson, 2004; Ferreira, 2005).

The experiences of the Innu of the Labrador–Quebec peninsula reflect these patterns very closely. According to numerous reports of European observers, when the Innu were largely independent of external control, they were a healthy and vibrant nomadic hunting people. Near the end of the nineteenth century, ethnologist Lucien Turner (1979: 106) remarked of the Innu at Fort Chimo: 'both sexes attain great age . . . in some cases certainly living over 70 years. Some assert that they were well advanced in years before the white man came in 1827.' Other reports spoke of a hardy, agile, resourceful people. The Finnish geographer Väino Tanner (1947: 663) remarked that 'the birth rate is said to be good and the natural increase in their numbers is satisfactory'. Upon closer observation, Tanner (1947: 599) described the Innu as 'being healthy, families are large, the children fit and jolly . . . never did I see the brand of "fire water" on the face of a Montagnais [southerly Innu]'.

With alcoholism affecting the majority of adults in Innu villages in

Labrador, suicide rates among the highest in the world and a youth gas sniffing epidemic (Samson, 2003: 221–95; Omni Television, 2004), Tanner would not be quite so cheerful were he to visit the Innu today. Crucially, in the intervening time, the Innu have been removed from the land and settled into government villages. Their children have been forced into Euro-Canadian schools run by the Roman Catholic Church, and priests deliberately set out to destroy Innu religious practices. Numerous Innu became victims of paedophile clergy and teachers, and they have faced the additional humiliation of having their land appropriated for industrial mega-projects.

Assimilation policies have been little short of catastrophic across vast swathes of the globe. At present the indigenous peoples of Australia constitute an underclass with the highest incidences of disease and respiratory infections and the lowest life expectancy in the general population (Australian Bureau of Statistics, 2002). According to the Australian Bureau of Statistics (ABS), in 1998–2000 the death rates of indigenous people between the ages of 30 and 64 years were around seven times the rates for the total population in those age groups. Much of the difference between aboriginal and total life expectancy had been attributed to the excessive rates of infant death among indigenous peoples (ibid.). In 1998–2000, the death rate for indigenous infants was around four times the rate in the total population. Suicide is endemic in many aboriginal communities (Tatz, 1999), as is trachoma, an eye disease that has been eradicated in Africa. Indigenous peoples also experience rates of arrest and imprisonment grossly disproportionate to their numbers. In 1987 the Royal Commission into Aboriginal Deaths in Custody found that aboriginal children represented 2.7 per cent of Western Australian young people, but *over half* of the youth in prison were aboriginal (RCIADIC, 1991: 101). The Commission concluded that the root cause of indigenous peoples' structurally entrenched social inequality was the dispossession of their lands and loss of autonomy (RCIADIC, 1991: 256).

The story is much the same in Canada, where aboriginal peoples fair worse on virtually every health measure than the overall population. Although data are difficult to obtain because of the different legal and political statuses of indigenous peoples in Canada, it has been estimated that aboriginal life expectancy is between five and fourteen years shorter, suicide is up to five times higher and both chronic and infectious diseases, as well as social pathologies such as problem drinking, affect aboriginal peoples with much greater frequency than other groups (Canadian Institute of Health Information, 2004: 80–3). Under Canadian government definitions only 56.9 per cent of aboriginal homes were considered adequate shelter, only a little over 40 per cent of these homes had piping to centralized water treatment plants and many of these were required to boil water before drinking (Health Canada, 2003: 65–6).[4] As in Australia, aboriginal people are also overrepresented in jails. Although only 2 per cent of the Canadian population, they account for 17 per cent of custodial admissions. However, in some areas of Canada, such as Saskatchewan, where only 8 per cent of the population, but 76 per cent of prison admissions, are aboriginal, the overrepresentation is massive (Canadian Centre for Justice, 2001: 10). These social pathology statistics for G8 countries are mirrored in much poorer countries. For example, a recent *New York Times* report highlighted the high suicide rates of Colombia's indigenous peoples. In the general population there were only 4.4 suicides per 100,000 people, while in the indigenous communities the rate was as high as 500 (Forero, 2004).

Now that we have given a brief indication of the context for some of the experiences of indigenous peoples that have led to calls for recognition of particular rights, we now examine the conception of indigenous peoples within sociology. This will serve as a general background from which to discuss the various contributions to the sociology of human rights from the standpoint of indigenous peoples' experience.

Founding fathers and indigenous peoples

The creation of social scientific disciplines in the nineteenth century coincided with industrialisation and the consolidation of European colonialism. These deeply entwined processes brought non-European peoples and societies into focus as objects of labour exploitation and academic study. Early sociological theory conceived of non-Europeans principally as illustrations to throw into relief the uniqueness of the *modern* world. This emphasis in sociological research and theorizing on understanding *modern* society, characterised by wage labour, factory production, cities and the movement of capital, meant that there was a need to understand peoples far removed from the cataclysmic changes within civilization itself principally as yardsticks to indicate the pace and character of European progress.

The idea of progress situated indigenous peoples in social configurations that Europeans had already transcended. Karl Marx, Max Weber and Émile Durkheim all evoked linear visions of time in which human society moved gradually and inevitably towards the contours of what they saw in Europe. The indigenous and the tribal were mere vistas into the European and, indeed, the human past. It was to these concerns that the early anthropologists such as Louis Henry Morgan and Edward Tylor, armed with their own evolutionary assumptions, applied themselves. Both equated evolution with progress, and saw European civilization as the pinnacle towards which other cultures were inexorably climbing (Bidney, 1996: 209–10).

Sociologists made very similar assumptions. Marx sketched out a number of historical epochs, all being materially determined by forms of ownership. Hence the earliest stage was the 'tribal', in which patriarchy was prominent, subsistence was achieved through hunting and gathering and only crude divisions of labour were apparent. Property was held in common. As is well known, Marx (1978a: 151–5) then conceives of society as moving through the communal, feudal and capitalist epochs of history. The most recent epoch in Marx's chronology, capitalism, was where Europe found itself at the time. To help to substantiate this evolutionary schema, Marx's colleague Friedrich Engels used Morgan's ethnological study of the Iroquois to demonstrate that American Indians' property and familial relations not only differed from those of Europeans, but represented prior stages in the development of society (see Leacock, 1981).

Since Marx and his followers have been convinced of the linear movements of history from the tribal ('primitive communism') to the feudal, capitalist, socialist and then to communism, the elimination of indigenous distinctiveness and cultural heterogeneity in general was seen as inevitable, even desirable. Marx supported the colonial endeavours of European powers for this reason. Although he commented on the British atrocities in destroying Indian culture and plundering the continent, Marx (1978b) believed that the net effect of the industry, commerce and political unification that the 'advanced peoples' had imposed on India would be regenerating. That is, colonialism would pave the way for a new collective social order. Even in more recent times, Marxists have promoted the globalization of industry and Western technology along with the destruction of tribal bonds in the Third World because these were a means of hastening the overthrow of capitalism (Latouche, 1996: x). At a more conceptual level the positivist and materialist biases of Marxism have been at variance with American Indian land, customs and spirituality (Churchill, 1983).

In Marxist states such as Soviet Russia the push for industrialization led to an aggressive programme of resource extraction in areas of Siberia inhabited by indigenous peoples. The Soviets perceived the indigenous hunters and herders of these regions as culturally backward and inferior to both workers and peasants. Some were driven off the land and had their reindeer confiscated, and eventually some were introduced to industry and agriculture (Slezkine, 1994: 266–71). In the steppe regions of Inner Asia, the Soviet Union pushed through forced sedentarization and collectivized agricultural production among the indigenous mobile pastoralists, causing massive dislocation and hunger. Similar policies in the Chinese regions of Inner Mongolia resulted in widespread famine in the 1960s (Humphrey and Sneath, 1999: 19). More recently in Nicaragua under the Sandinistas (who themselves were threatened by US provocation and intervention), indigenous peoples became enemies of the state. The Miskitu Indians of the Atlantic coast were at war with the Sandinistas, who were engaged in a *mestizo* nation-building project. This ignored Miskitu difference and enforced a kind of *mestizo* state-centred socialism, the promotion of literacy through the Spanish language and other culturally homogenizing programmes. In reaction against this, the Miskitu organized against the Sandinistas and some joined the right-wing Contras (Hale, 1994: 214–16).

In Max Weber's body of sociological writings, we find the same assumption that European ideas, practices and institutions symbolize temporally more recent societal patterns. In *The Protestant Ethic and the Spirit of Capitalism*,

Weber begins by making the observation that only in the West do we find 'rationality'. In 'Western civilization alone cultural phenomena have appeared which have universal significance and value' (Weber, 1976: 13). Weber locates the highest development of rationalism in Western bureaucratic institutions and political authority structures. In general, Weber sees human political authority moving from charismatic domination to bureaucratic leadership. Charisma is seen principally, although not exclusively, as a property of non-Western societies under 'primitive communism', Western societies of the past or Western societies in 'unusual circumstances' or under 'great excitement' (Weber, 1978: 234–6, 247).

If, as Weber suggests, human society moves in this way, then there is little scope for action to preserve the differences and protect the rights of indigenous (and other non-European) peoples. The powerful compulsion of bureaucracies and the rigid rules and regulations that govern the acquisition of wealth anticipate a kind of globalisation of rationality in which all will be behind the bars of the famous 'iron cage'. Like Marx, Weber's (1976: 181) logic strongly implies that global uniformity is inevitable. Puritan asceticism sought to 'remodel the world and work out its ideals in the world'. Such a conclusion generates little enthusiasm for examining indigenous peoples' rights. Why concern ourselves with the rights of peoples whose uniqueness will only disappear as all become imprisoned by rationalism and bureaucracy within nation states?

In contrast to Marx and Weber, Durkheim offers some insights into ways of life that have been displaced by modernity. Durkheim placed much emphasis on the collective nature of human morality, identity and even mental states, and in examining these phenomena he drew on illustrations from both European and non-European societies. However, Durkheim believed that he was witnessing a certain weakening of collective bonds as a result of the rise of individualism, the transition from agrarian to industrial economies and refinements in the division of labour. This was creating anomie, individual pathology and, most dramatically, suicide. In both *Division of Labor in Society* (1964) and *Suicide* (1951), Durkheim portrayed Western society as in a state of flux occasioned by greater refinements of the division of labour, economic growth and the centralization of authority. This naturally displaced many people, who, in this context, lost their social moorings and became anomic. With modernization also came a loss of social regulation, and this multiplied the possibilities of social conflict. With the widespread evidence of the breakdown of indigenous societies in the face of changes relating to 'modernization', Durkheim accurately describes the circumstances in which many indigenous peoples have found themselves. However, because he views change as a politically neutral evolutionary process within societies, Durkheim ignores the purposeful transformations by which colonial powers were able to *impose* modernization in indigenous territories.

Perhaps as a consequence of these kinds of depictions of indigenous peoples in classical sociological theory, discussions of indigenous peoples in sociology have been scarce.[5] In US sociology, for example, American Indians have often been conceived as members of historical communities, rather than as contemporary peoples (Thornton and Grasnick, 1980: 2–3).[6] In US sociology textbooks, American Indians are often depicted as simply one, albeit unfortunate, minority group, caught up within a wider metropolitan culture (see Macionis, 2004: 283–4). Typically, only a few brief pages are devoted to them, and this does not include any discussion of their rights either within the USA or in the international arena. In British texts indigenous peoples are almost never mentioned. Anthony Giddens (2001: 73) is the only sociologist to mention indigenous peoples in a major British textbook, but he does so only with reference to the exploitation of their intellectual property. He includes no discussion of the history of indigenous dispossession and exploitation under colonialism and its legacy, and no discussion of indigenous human rights claims.

Foundationalism, social constructionism and the sociology of human rights

If we turn to rights themselves, we also find that the role of sociology in relation to indigenous peoples is ambivalent. Turner and Rojek (2001: 109) have argued that until relatively recently, sociology largely confined its examination of rights to the realm of citizenship. This was, according to Turner, fuelled by a strong scepticism about 'universalisms' in favour of cultural relativism and social constructionism. Turner (1993, 2001), however, suggests that the concept of citizenship has been closely linked with the modern nation state, and argues that this political form has been the central coordinator of imperialism and globalization. In doing so, it has acted oppressively towards groups such as migrant workers, refugees and indigenous peoples who either cut across states or are simply disadvantageously incorporated within them. While the state has certainly been at the centre of rights claims and has held a virtual monopoly on the conferment of rights, it has become increasingly clear that a full consideration of rights requires us to go beyond mere state citizenship. As globalization has created problems that are not wholly internal to nation states, so the concept of citizenship rights must be extended to engage with that of universal human rights. Turner and Rojek (2001: 119) write: 'The problem with sociology's reluctance to talk about human rights is that human rights have become a powerful institution and play a major role in political mediation of social conflict.' Turner (1993: 502) further argues that the concept of human rights can be understood sociologically by the widespread observation that there is a need to protect vulnerable human beings by establishing rights-promoting institutions.

Yet Turner's analysis goes further than mere explanation. He argues that without some universal moral grounds it is impossible to talk about justice:

'there has to be some foundation of a universalistic character in order for such discussions about justice to take place. Otherwise we are left with a mere talking shop of difference' (Turner and Rojek, 2001: 112). He deploys sociological theory to explore the moral basis of a universalist doctrine of human rights and proposes that a shared experience of bodily vulnerability provides the common ground. As he asserts, 'human frailty is a universal experience of human existence' (ibid.: 110).

Taking issue with Turner's foundationalist approach, Waters (1996) suggests that universal human rights should simply be regarded as a socially constructed phenomena, the product of a certain historical and social context (that is, Western society after the Second World War). Such an approach, he suggests, would view the institutionalization of human rights as little more than the product of a balance of power between political interests. 'Universal' values themselves can become the currency of political manipulation, selectively invoked and enforced, and deployed to reinforce the power of not so vulnerable groups.

Relatively recent developments in Australia may be used to illustrate these ideas. In the Australian context, the domestic institutionalization of international human rights standards as they pertain to indigenous peoples is perhaps best understood with reference to both ideals (a desire to protect the vulnerable) and political interests. In 1992 the High Court of Australia decided in the *Mabo* case that to deny indigenous rights to land would be unjust and contrary to contemporary international human rights standards, especially the principle of racial equality. The court was aware, in Turner and Rojek's (2001: 124) terms, of the 'vulnerability' of dispossessed indigenous people and did not seek to worsen their plight by flouting the international moral code that prohibits racial discrimination. The *Mabo* ruling challenged the theory of *terra nullius*, and further decreed that the notion that indigenous inhabitants of a 'settled' colony had no proprietary interests in land depended on a 'discriminatory denigration of indigenous inhabitants, their social organization and customs' and that such 'an unjust and discriminatory doctrine' could be no longer accepted (Reynolds, 1996: 2). In essence, *Mabo* gave Aborigines rights to ancestral lands not already ceded or fairly compensated.

When the Australian government responded to the landmark case the interests of vulnerable indigenous groups were largely ignored in favour of powerful commercial interests (see Short, 2003a). The net result was legalisation that sought to *limit* indigenous rights behind a veneer of agrarian reform. The mining industry in particular was threatened by the ruling that made some of its existing land titles of questionable validity because no compensation had been paid to resident aboriginal groups at the time of purchase, and this also threatened their hitherto unbridled claims for development of vacant 'Crown land' (Short, 2003a). While the government talked in terms of enshrining and protecting indigenous rights to land, the legislation made sure aboriginal groups could not veto development on their land and defined an extremely restrictive native title claims procedure.

Thus, as Freeman (2002: 85) contends:

> The institutionalisation of human rights may . . . lead, not to their more secure protection but to their protection in a form that is less threatening to the existing system of power. The *sociological* point is not that human rights should never be institutionalised, but, rather, that institutionalisation is a social process, involving power, and that it should be analysed and not assumed to be beneficial.

Freeman's 'sociological point' can be further illustrated by the example of Canada, where the notorious 'extinguishment' clause has become institutionalised within land claims agreements. Recent internal and international criticism, however, has led only to a more restrictive and discriminatory government policy that favours the state and developers. Aboriginal groups that have not signed land treaties with Canada, and therefore according to British precedent and Canadian law have underlying 'aboriginal title' to land, can only have rights appertaining to that title by signing an agreement that extinguishes their title. Canada's reaction to the numerous objections to this has been to omit the word 'extinguishment' in new land claims agreements. However, in return the aboriginal party must now accept that the agreement itself defines the totality of their rights and that they *never* assert their rights granted from any previous treaties or from any violations of aboriginal title that may have occurred in the past. Under this arrangement, the Canadian government is also indemnified against all violations of aboriginal or treaty rights *in perpetuity*. The terms of such agreements limit the exercise of aboriginal rights to such an extent that they have in essence extinguished aboriginal title to traditional territories (see Orkin, 2003; Union of British Columbia Indian Chiefs, 2004).

These examples show that indigenous rights (or their absence) are products of the manoeuvring of states, responding to internal and international pressures, as well as seeking to reconcile these with the demands of constituents (and in the cases of Australia and Canada, with the wishes of dominant settler populations largely unsympathetic to indigenous grievances). The fact that 'rights' are not simply givens, but products of social and political creation and manipulation, is underlined by Wilson's (1997: 3–4) argument that social scientists should be primarily concerned with analysing rights as socially constructed phenomena. He writes: 'the intellectual efforts of those seeking to develop a framework for understanding the social life of rights would be better directed not towards foreclosing their ontological status, but instead by exploring their meaning and use. What is needed are more detailed studies of human rights according to the actions and intentions of social actors, within wider historical constraints of institutionalized power' (ibid.). In short, sociological analysis of rights can go beyond the formal, legalistic and rhetorical dimensions of such rights, where, as Wilson (2001: xvii) points out, they will always be a 'good thing'. Thus, while Turner's idea of human rights as a universalistic means of protecting the vulnerable is important, it offers an insufficiently nuanced understanding of how such rights are invented and subverted, often by the state itself. As our Australian and Canadian examples show, the extension of indigenous rights may be a means of restricting what are already inferior rights. The task of 'claiming' the only means by which indigenous peoples have been able to protect their lands and ways of life is all the more difficult since engagement with a host of culturally alien and often divisive procedures and institutions is necessary.[7]

Indigenous scholarship on the rights of indigenous peoples

Indigenous thinkers have been prominent in adopting broad sociological approaches to the analysis of their rights. For example, Mohawk scholar Taiaiake Alfred has highlighted the continuation of a colonial relationship within liberal 'multicultural' states despite the institutionalisation of indigenous rights to land and other 'recognition' initiatives. Alfred (1999: 58) suggests that 'rights' granted to aboriginal peoples by states should be viewed as *part of* colonialism and not a remedy for its effects, since such 'rights' are invariably created, controlled and limited by states themselves. Furthermore, because many of the rights granted are simply those taken away by colonists and states, Alfred (ibid.) questions how meaningful indigenous rights are:

> given Canada's shameful history, defining Aboriginal rights in terms of, for example, a right to fish for food and traditional purposes is better than nothing. But to what extent does that state-regulated 'right' to food-fish represent justice for people who have been fishing on their rivers and seas since time began?

He adds that to 'frame the struggle to achieve justice in terms of indigenous "claims" against the state is implicitly to accept the fiction of state sovereignty. . . . Arguing for rights within that framework only reinforces the state's anti-historic claim to sovereignty by contract' (ibid.).

A sociological imagination is evident in the work of many indigenous scholars, who seek to explain historical and contemporary indigenous/settler relations by demonstrating how the contemporary nation state operates according to the same colonial political agenda as former colonial powers. Writers such as Kevin Gilbert, Ward Churchill and Taiaiake Alfred, to name but a few, have shifted attention towards explanations that emphasise both the historical context and the negative impact of imposed colonial legal, political and cultural structures. For example, Alfred (1999: 48) invokes a Foucauldian understanding of state power, which highlights its repressive capacity:

A critique of state power that sees oppression as an inevitable function of the state, even when constrained by a constitutionally defined social-political contract, should have special resonance for indigenous people, since their nations were never party to any contract and yet have been forced to operate within a framework that presupposes the legitimacy of state sovereignty over them.

While he is also interested in the imposition of settler state sovereignty, the works of aboriginal writer Kevin Gilbert (1977: 3, 238) tend to focus more on the destructive force of colonial history and the impact of the state's emphasis on 'material progress' in Australia:

> For two hundred years we have been subjected to death, abuse and denial of dignity and basic human rights by the white usurpers of our land. Today we are the products of the ravages of white settlement. . . . As Aborigines began to sicken physically and psychologically, they were hit by the full blight of the alien way of thinking. They were hit by the intolerance and uncomprehending barbarism of a people intent on progress in material terms, a people who never credited that there could be cathedrals of the spirit as well as of stone.

Indigenous scholars have deepened the analysis of rights by critically analysing law itself. While reviewing state/indigenous legal relations, many have been at pains to show not only that the law is the political instrument of their colonizers, but that it is a highly fluid set of practices, used almost exclusively as an instrument of domination. Thus, elements of federal Indian law such as treaties, many of which were instituted in order to protect American Indian peoples' rights, have nearly all been broken. Thus there is little correspondence between what the law says in relation to indigenous peoples and what it does. This applies to both the USA and Canada (Deloria, 1985; Morris, 1992; Churchill, 1999; Orkin, 2003).

While alien laws were imposed, indigenous economies were being destroyed by colonization and settlement. The industrially driven material prosperity created by European usurpation of indigenous territories in Australia and North America provided indigenous peoples only with the dubious benefits of culturally destructive individualized wage labour and welfare dependency. This aspect of the indigenous/settler state relationship has been the focus of sociological analysis in the works of many indigenous scholars, such as Vizenor (1984), Deloria (1985), Gilbert (1994) and Mudrooroo (1995), as well as the subject of a great deal of Native American creative art and literature. Australian aboriginal writer Mudrooroo (1995: 87) concludes: 'colonial expansion is a process which continues until its power is total, by a combination of coercion and assimilation. An integral part of this colonisation is welfare, which only perpetuates the subjugation of the indigenous people . . . and leads to assimilation.' Despite the destructive effects of colonialism, many indigenous writers also emphasize the incredible resilience of indigenous cultural forms and commitments to community. This is evident in indigenous cultural revitalization (Nagel, 1996), articulated in the profusion of Native American literature (see Weaver, 1997) and evident in the autobiographies of many Native Americans (see Momaday, 1976; Vizenor and Lee, 1999). This cultural continuity and claim to various realms of autonomy is clearly vital to the current movement of indigenous peoples to claim rights.

Liberal scholarship and the rights of indigenous peoples

The extension and exercise of indigenous peoples' rights runs up against not only powerful states and corporations, but large sections of the academic and public policy communities specializing in the analysis of human and other rights. In mainstream circles, liberalism has become the dominant philosophical orientation within which the rights of indigenous peoples have been conceptualised. The contemporary expression of this in both politics and academia has roots in the splicing together of nineteenth-century utilitarianism, a doctrine that places primacy on private property, permanent representative democracy and individual rights, with classical economics, a body of thought that reified and naturalized the self-regulating market economy.

In many ways, these ideas were instrumental in both European colonial expansion and the founding of settler societies in North America (Rogin, 1987: 135). Building on earlier writings by Hobbes and Locke, philosophers in the widely Benthamite tradition presumed an egoistic human nature. Based on this a priori assumption, they advanced a prescription that law and society ought to be based on Bentham's famous felicific calculus, the principle of 'the greatest happiness for the greatest number'. If laws were predicated on this principle, there would eventually be a natural identity of interests in society (see Halévy, 1955). With this as a guiding framework, indigenous peoples' rights have primarily been defined as a form of minority interest, subject to the higher moral weight of Bentham's 'greatest number'.

Following on from these origins, conventional liberal-democratic theory deals with all social groups that have become 'minorities' as sets of 'outvoted individuals' (Freeman, 1995: 25). As such, they are only guaranteed individual rights, which provide them with the opportunity to become members of the majority on occasions when their interests coincide. Thus, under conventional liberal thinking, indigenous peoples, as a 'minority', would simply be conferred the same rights as other individual citizens of the settler state. In recent times, however, some prominent liberal rights theorists have sought to broaden liberal theory in this regard, arguing that minorities should be protected *collectively* via what they term 'group rights', since an individual is likely to suffer if their way of life or ethnic group is neglected, disparaged, discriminated against or misrecognized by wider society (see Freeman, 1995: 25; Kymlicka, 1995; Taylor, 1995: 236). As Taylor (1995) observes, social recognition is central to an *individual's* identity and well-being and misrecognition can seriously damage both. Kymlicka (1995) has argued that individuals are often discriminated against by the wider society not merely as individuals but as *members of a cultural group*. Consequently, the well-being of *individual* group members may require that their cultural practices be protected *from* the wider society, as other groups may be hostile to such practices. Thus, despite the collective nature of such measures, the foundational justification is intrinsically individualistic.

It is easy to understand why some writers believe that the spectre of colonialism lurks inside liberalism. Indeed, there is a forceful argument, put forward by many indigenous writers and postcolonial theorists, such as Bhikhu Parekh, which asserts that modern liberalism is founded on an assertion of cultural superiority, because Western value systems are afforded normative priority. As Parekh (1998) observes, liberal notions of justice and fairness are understood via the assertion of universalized values, such as individualism, in contrast to the supposedly backward, primitive societies that were 'enlightened' by colonialism. Consistent with the cultural evolutionism that has been a pervasive feature of Western social scientific thought for several centuries, indigenous and other non-European societies were simply regarded as prior versions of Europe. In liberal theory, their distinct laws and traditions have no status whatsoever. Signifying the underlying belief that non-Western values are inferior, Kymlicka (1995: 153) argues that cultural protection should only be available to indigenous nations 'if, and in so far as, they are themselves governed by liberal principles'.

In liberal theory, indigenous peoples become recipients of rights conferred by policy-makers acting in accordance with universalized Western values. Therefore, even those liberal writers who might be considered champions of minorities, like Taylor and Kymlicka, skip over the 'first step in questioning the sovereignty of the authoritative traditions and institutions they serve to legitimate' (Tully, 1995: 53; Samson, 1999). Such writers, while recognizing the importance of culture to indigenous peoples, talk in terms of participation *within* liberal institutions, and their solutions to collective disadvantage are framed in a liberal discourse of rights that is ultimately the product of force. Kymlicka, for example, concedes that indigenous peoples' special relationship to land is significant enough to justify recognition via the notion of 'group rights' and 'differentiated citizenship', but he exposes the colonial underpinnings of such liberalism by denying indigenous peoples full political autonomy. By presuming the legitimacy of the settler state's jurisdiction over indigenous nations, such an approach presupposes exactly what is in question (see Tully, 2000: 55).

Indigenous peoples at the national and international level strongly resist classification as 'minorities'. They emphasize their uniqueness both culturally and via the issue of 'consent', which is perhaps the most distinctive aspect of indigenous/settler state relations. While voluntary immigrant minorities have chosen to become citizens of European diaspora nations such as those in the former British Empire, many indigenous peoples have never willingly ceded their lands or political autonomy. Indigenous peoples hold distinct moral claims as *dispossessed first nations*, whose 'forebears will usually have been massacred or enslaved by settlers, or at the very least cheated out of their land, to which they will often retain a . . . spiritual attachment' (Robertson, 1999: 183).

It is here that the liberal politics of 'recognition' fail to accord indigenous peoples the equality espoused. The distinct moral claims of indigenous peoples as peoples are frequently trivialised by liberal 'recognition' theorists (see Kymlicka, 1991, 1995, 2000; Kukathus, 1992; Taylor, 1995) when they combine discussion of indigenous peoples with minorities and largely focus on internal citizenship-based 'solutions' to 'indigenous problems'. Coincidentally, this is exactly the stance of many states with regard to indigenous peoples' rights.

Citizenship is often associated with nation building and state legitimacy and as such is an unhelpful concept for those 'citizens' who question the legitimacy of an imposed nation state. As Tully (2000: 39) points out, and numerous indigenous scholars have articulated this at some length, providing 'recognition' to indigenous peoples through the granting of citizenship rights is simply an element of internal colonialism. Human rights, however, are extra-governmental and have traditionally been used to counteract the repressive capacity of states (Turner, 1993). This is one of the reasons why many indigenous peoples have accepted the United Nations Draft Declaration on the Rights of Indigenous Peoples as an articulation of their rights, as opposed to merely relying on the citizenship rights granted by states.[8] For indigenous peoples, recognition of the collective right to self-determination, as proposed in articles 3 and 6 of the Draft Declaration, will offer a greater degree of cultural protection than is attainable through pure individualism. If adopted, this would contradict liberal positions, and, in being consistent with the greater tendency among indigenous peoples to define themselves by reference to the group and the environment, would permit a greater range of cultural expression needed for the long-term survival of indigenous peoples as distinct communities.

Conclusion

As the example of liberalism demonstrates, the dominant modes of analyses of indigenous peoples rights do not question the legitimacy of the state itself and assertions of sovereignty over indigenous peoples and their lands. Such a critique would be fundamental to a critical sociological formulation of indigenous peoples' rights, and accords with many of the writings of indigenous scholars. A major area in which sociology can contribute to an understanding of the broader issues surrounding the rights of indigenous peoples is in its analysis of the role of the state, the histories by which states came to create and assume authority over indigenous peoples and the current social and political conflicts over the conceptualization of rights themselves.

As former President of the UN Human Rights Commission and of Ireland, Mary Robinson (2004) recently remarked, the expertise and research of sociologists can play a vital role in making states responsible and challenging market fundamentalism. Human and other rights are fast becoming the tools for making states accountable for the ethical treatment of all populations. With pressing issues related to indigenous health, welfare and cultural survival, a critical public sociology could actually operate as Mary Robinson suggested. As long as it refuses to collaborate in the political fiction that indigenous rights are solely state citizenship rights and recognizes indigenous struggles to maintain cultural continuity, sociology could help to challenge the current patterns of state and market dominance and question the fatalistic notions that cultural distinctiveness is a thing of the past.

Notes

1 For more extended commentaries on conceptions of rights as they were played out between Europeans and indigenous peoples, see the extensive discussions in Deloria (1985), Williams (1990), Tully (1995), Pagden (1995) and Keal (2003).
2 The 'stolen generations' were the focus of the 2002 Oscar-nominated film *Rabbit Proof Fence*.
3 As Wunder (1994: 33) has noted, such policies were direct violations of the freedom of religion guaranteed by the Bill of Rights in the US Constitution.
4 With widespread substandard housing for aboriginal peoples in Canada, lawsuits are now being brought against the federal government for violating the Constitution, which clearly spells out the government's responsibilities for aboriginal housing (Janzen, 2004).
5 This is not to say that classical sociological theory could not be valuable for understanding particular social processes affecting indigenous peoples. Marxist understandings of the expansion of capitalism could be used in interpreting resource extraction policies on indigenous lands. Weber's ideas of bureaucracy could also be important in looking at state imposed land claims policies.
6 In a recent empirical study of the phenomenon of military toxic waste dumping close to Indian reservations in the USA, Hooks and Smith (2004) note the limited sociological literature on Native Americans and environmental injustice. Environmental sociology, they argue, focuses on class and race dynamics in urban areas, with capitalism, rather than the state, as the main causal force. Some sociologists have, of course, written about American Indians in more depth. Exemplars include Thornton (1987), Cornell (1988) and Nagel (1996).
7 Morgan (2004) has documented this predicament in the international arena. In the Canadian national context studies by Brody (1981), Samson (2001, 2003) and Nadasdy (2003) show how aboriginal peoples must configure themselves into

culturally alien political forms and engage in processes that undermine group solidarity in order to claim rights. This predicament is particularly acute for northern hunting peoples, whose very survival has depended on consensus, communitarianism and the avoidance of open conflict.

8 For an overview and discussion of these rights, see Pritchard (1998).

Part IV

The clash of rights

The final part of this book deals less with a specific approach than a common problem: the clash of rights. The three chapters look respectively at the rights of prisoners, the rights of mental health patients and the phenomenon of hate speech; all cases in which civil rights and freedoms have been contested. Chapter 10 considers the justifications that have been given for denying the civil rights of offenders by imprisonment. Philosophical justifications range from utilitarian arguments based on the claimed reduction of future crime, to the categorical imperative of retribution. Sociological purchase on such arguments includes the Marxist view of penal systems as the protection of class interest, Durkheimian views of punishment as the assertion of shared values and a Weberian perspective informed by the oppressive nature of authority, the iron cage of rationality and bureaucracy that will imprison us all. Analysis of the micro-management exerted by all systems of authority has been most fully explored by Foucault, with particular attention to marginal groups such as prisoners, the 'mad' and homosexuals. Conversely, postmodern theory inspired by Levinas offers an approach to rights based on unconditional responsibility towards the 'other': a radical justice of alterity. The feminist critique of false universals can also be viewed in this light, as can proposals for a feminist jurisprudence that challenges claims to gender neutral legal thought.

The main problem for sociological approaches to liberal penal policy, as sketched out in Chapter 10, is that a focus on individual rights and responsibilties ignores the social conditions producing criminality and is challenged by the justice of alterity. This position condemns the demonisation of offenders and embraces unconditional responsibility towards them, thus highlighting the importance of human rights as a system of protection for those beyond empathy. In contrast to these sentiments, the chapter highlights the continuing legacy of 'civil death' for prisoners, and the fact that prisons themselves have operated as 'lawless agencies', with prisoners subject to the exclusive control of the authorities. The chapter then documents some challenges to this arrangement, including the 1975 ruling that deemed prisoners to fall under the purview of the European Convention on Human Rights, and the eventual acknowledgement that prison authorities must act within legally defined powers. The impact on prisoners is argued to be slight thus far, and their protections against damage or ill-treatment remain weak, rendering them a classic case of vulnerability that requires protection but evokes little sympathy: candidates for the 'justice of alterity'. A movement is now under way to ensure that the conditions of imprisonment conform to human rights standards.

Chapter 11 considers the related case of human rights issues raised in the treatment of mental disorder, reviewing the traditional denial of rights to this group, their gradual but incomplete acquisition and the question of how far denial of rights can itself induce mental disorder. The chapter draws on the work of Foucault to chart changing characterisations of 'madness' from the language of lunacy to the language of illness, the latter being accompanied by an expansion of recognised conditions such that mental disorder today cannot be equated with eighteenth-century ideas of madness as 'unreason'. The chapter then considers Marshall's model of citizenship as community membership, noting his acknowledgement that full equality had not been achieved, his (often ignored) recognition of the role of struggle in the accretion of rights and the role of social class in mediating their realisation (or otherwise). This then provides the context for a consideration of the traditional denial of liberty to those deemed mad, the 'civil death' referred to in Chapter 10, though here a majority of those detained had committed no offence.

Despite the gradual change in the nature of treatment from forcible restraint to moral management the denial of rights continued, though with an accompanying tension between restraint and therapy. The mid-nineteenth century saw the introduction of clear procedures for admission to an institution that was a first step in clarifying the rights of those who might be subject to detention, though the principle concern was to protect the rights of the sane rather than assert the rights of the 'mad'. Certification was, of course, hugely stigmatising and the introduction of voluntary admission in the twentieth century was thus a step forward. However, the chapter goes on to document a number of perverse effects of the reduction of institutionalised treatment for mental disorder, including 'trans-institutionalisation', whereby the patients rotate through different forms of residential care or detention. Alternatively, where provision for alternative care and treatment is inadequate we find the patient facing a series of practical difficulties, often rooted in class inequality. Thus, the chapter argues, a vicious circle may be established whereby the lack of rights to adequate provision exacerbates the original problem.

Chapter 12 addresses a fundamental liberal dilemma of how to weigh freedom of expression against freedom from discrimination. This can also be construed as another instance of universalism versus particularism; how far should the universal freedom of expression be constrained in favour of the protection of vulnerable minorities? The chapter starts by documenting New Labour's specific concern with racially aggravated offences –

influenced to some degree by legislation and debate in the USA – and details a gradual expansion of British law in this field, from race to religion, and also to sexuality and disability. Through this account we see the dilemmas surrounding such legislation: from the supporting arguments that crimes motivated by hate cause damage to the victim beyond the crime itself, that this additionally infects a wider community with fear and trauma, and constitutes an assault on the dominant values of society; to the opposing view that legislating against 'hate' crime is totalitarian, punishes thought and bad values and treats equal crimes unequally. The chapter shows how sociological evidence can be brought to bear in evaluating these positions.

Holocaust denial is then addressed as a special case of 'hate speech', which has not yet been outlawed in Britain, though there is such legislation in a number of other European countries – part of a movement against the trivialisation of crimes against humanity. Some of the hesitation in Britain has been related to the problem of offering singular protection to a particular group in the context of an ethnically and religiously diverse society. The issue of freedom of expression arises again in this debate, and to date, incitement to racial hatred has been addressed only in the context of public order. Again the chapter considers the problems of appropriate evidence, but also outlines the difficulties of addressing holocaust denial under this legislation, and provides a background to current plans for a new offence of incitement to religious hatred. Proposed legislation in this area is considered to be especially relevant to Muslim groups, who fall outside of laws framed in terms of racial hatred, and are potentially vulnerable to discrimination via anti-terrorist measures. The fear of eroding freedom of expression has arisen again in this context, and the symbolic force of legislation is a key factor in attempts to strike a balance between fundamental freedoms and acceptable norms of personal conduct.

10 Punishment, rights and justice

Eamonn Carrabine

The punishment of offenders raises profound questions over human rights, civil liberties and social justice, as punishment will always involve the loss of some basic rights and in the case of the death penalty extinguishes the most fundamental: the right to life. A key issue that immediately arises is what gives any social institution the moral right to inflict deliberate suffering on wrong doers? There are a number of common and competing justifications, which have come to revolve around the central problem of reconciling punishment as state coercion alongside a valuing of individual autonomy. The oldest known justification is a system of vengeance whereby revenge is considered a social duty in societies governed by shame (Cantarella, 2001: 476), while the earliest documented response to checking the vindictive passions is also to be found in the classical Greek pantheon where the Erinyes (or Furies in later Roman mythology) dispensed justice. However, this desire for revenge did not go uncontested in the ancient world, as the emergence of Stoicism and Christianity attacked the very legitimacy of the vindictive passions themselves on the basis that such emotions were both irrational and wicked (Murphy, 2000: 132).

Modern philosophical thinking insists that punishment is justified, 'as it protects the freedom of individual citizens to go about their lives safe from the threat of crime' (Duff and Garland, 1994: 3), while individual rights are advocated as essential defences against the abuse of power by the state. As we see below this conceptualization underpins approaches to prisoners' rights, and one of the aims of this chapter is to highlight how the different sociological traditions expose the limits of liberal individualism in the penal field. Critical criminologists have long been influenced by the sociological scepticism towards rights and have argued that the struggle for civil liberties simply results in 'a reformism which strengthens the existing system', while maintaining that the 'actual administration of criminal justice . . . bears very little resemblance to its imaginary conception in law' (Carlen, 1980: 20). However, for some the radical commitment to debunking the pretensions of equality before the law ought to be now within 'a positive rights discourse and agenda which recognises the determining contexts of social injustice' (Scraton, 2002: 36). It is this agenda that this chapter supports by pointing to the importance of structural inequalities and the recognition of social differences in what follows.

Moral philosophy and sceptical sociology

Liberal justifications of punishment

All legal systems presuppose some notion of 'rights' as belonging to citizens in, at the very least, the negative sense of entitling them to behave in ways that are not specifically prohibited. While the classical natural law tradition, which was established in the earliest written legal codes of ancient Babylon, Greek city states and imperial Rome, did grant positive powers to particular classes of citizen, the greater concern was to identify 'the duties owed by citizens to God, the state, or society' (Feldman, 2002: 21). Certainly, by the Middle Ages the doctrine of the 'Divine Right of Kings' had become a highly developed justification of feudal power based on the 'laws of nature': rules that were ordained by God and sustained the absolutist sovereignty of monarchies across Europe. The first appearance of 'rights' in their modern usage emerged in England during the 'Glorious Revolution' and were declared in the 1688 Bill of Rights. The Bill was philosophically grounded in the writings of Thomas Hobbes, whose *Leviathan* was published in 1651 and was produced in the aftermath of civil war, and John Locke, whose *Two Treatises of Civil Government* two years later defended the achievements of the 'Glorious Revolution' and who was the first political thinker to suggest that government should be by popular consent. Hobbes regarded it an absolute duty of subjects to obey the sovereign, while Locke insisted the duty was conditional on the ruler protecting 'natural liberty' and respecting 'natural rights'. Not only did Locke's ideas introduce the central tenets of modern liberalism, they were also enthusiastically taken up by European philosophers in the burgeoning Enlightenment.

By the middle of the eighteenth century, Jean-Jacques Rousseau's proclamation that 'Man is born free, and everywhere he is in chains' controversially reversed the conventional Christian view that humans are intrinsically corrupt and in need of religious salvation, while also suggesting the universal right to liberty. Yet it took the French and American revolutions to give legal force to the political theory that declared 'all men are created equal' (except, of course, slaves, women, indigenous populations, children, etc.), while the Terror that subsequently engulfed France at the end of the eighteenth century revealed that populist governments can disregard human freedom as easily as absolutist monarchies. As revolutionaries replaced aristocrats on the guillotine in the years after the French Declaration of the Rights of Man and Citizen, the executions provided 'a practical refutation of its claim that "rights" were natural, let alone inalienable and sacred' (Robertson, 2000: 5). It was Jeremy Bentham who mounted an influential liberal attack on natural rights and the conservative disposition of natural law that upheld unjust legal systems, which became a pivotal force driving social reform in the nineteenth century. Moreover, his utilitarian form of moral reasoning has provided one of the two major liberal justifications for state punishment.

Utilitarian philosophy establishes what is good to do on the grounds of social usefulness and it judges actions by their consequences. It stipulates that 'the good' is human happiness, not some abstract metaphysical property, like the idea of 'natural rights', which Bentham famously dismissed as 'nonsense on stilts' or an empirically unknowable object, as in the will of God. Bentham's objective was to establish the law on a rational basis, which for him meant the facts of pleasure and pain rather than the vague fictions of natural rights. In this context, the utilitarian justification of punishment is that the wrong experienced by the offender is outweighed by the compensating good effects of overall human well-being. By pointing to a future or greater 'good' the focus is on the instrumental 'ends' of punishment. On this basis it is argued that future crime can be reduced by a number of strategies, such as deterring potential offenders, reforming actual criminals or keeping actual or potential offenders out of circulation (Carrabine *et al.*, 2004: 233–5). For Bentham the only rights were legal rights: 'legitimate, enforceable rights come not from nature but from laws duly passed by the supreme authority of the state' (Feldman, 2002: 25) and justified by arguments of social utility. Utilitarianism thereby inspired a 'positive rights' tradition grounded in the legal positivism that continues to be influential in human rights and other areas of the law.

The second major liberal philosophical justification of punishment is the retributive, which insists that wrongdoers should be punished because they deserve it, regardless of any future beneficial consequences. It is a principle that dates from antiquity and is enshrined in the phrase 'an eye for an eye'. This principle of equivalence was developed by the Enlightenment philosopher Immanuel Kant into a highly influential critique of utilitarian justifications of punishment, which use offenders as means rather than fully recognising their humanity so that the innocent can be deliberately punished if it is for the general good. Kant introduced a crucial distinction between what it would be *good* to do on the grounds of utility and what we have a *right* to do (Murphy, 1994: 49). Missing this important distinction between desire and duty reveals the illiberal consequences that can flow from utilitarian reasoning, as there will be times when the individual is sacrificed for the general welfare of the many, with torture being perhaps the most controversial example (Morgan, 2000). In Kantian terms, justice is an issue of doing right rather than what would be good to do.

The duty to punish was, as he defined it, a 'categorical imperative' that restored the moral equilibrium – a view that led him to declare that even on the dissolution of society 'the last murderer remaining in prison must first be executed' (cited in Walker, 1991: 77). This grim view flows from his insistence that it is a necessary condition of any moral principle that it is strictly and universally applied. The doctrine is fundamental, as it grounds individual rights and advocates equal freedom. On this reckoning crime deserves punishing as the criminal takes an unfair advantage over others and the purpose of punishment is not only to restore the balance, but is the *right* of the criminal; the offender as a rational being has willed a system of punishment to ensure that no one benefits from wrongdoing (Murphy, 1994).

This abstract understanding of right, as might be expected, has been condemned by utilitarians as nothing more than useless vengeance that appeals to primitive vindictive passions. Others insist there is no meaningful sense in which offenders have willed their own punishment, except in abstract liberal theory. In practice, utilitarian and retributive principles are combined in uneasy hybrids. For instance, it has been recognized that the utilitarian substantive aim of reducing crime is a fitting general justification for a system of punishment, but that the pursuit of crime prevention must be subjected to specific constraints of procedural justice that prevent deliberately punishing the innocent and excessively punishing the guilty (Duff, 1996: 3). The problem, however, with pragmatically combining the virtues of each is that the underlying assumptions guiding utilitarian and retributive thought remain unchallenged, and it is these challenges I now outline.

Classic sociological critiques

Although there are fundamental differences between these justifications, they do share some significant common understandings. In particular, they share the values attached to the individualism that lies at the heart of liberalism as both a moral philosophy and political theory. These values have been challenged by Marxists and communitarians, while the assumption of sameness has been questioned by feminist and postmodernist critics, who have pointed out that what appear to be abstract and universal principles are Western fabrications and in reality merely partial. The scepticism of sociologists towards rights can be traced to Marx's 1844 essay 'On the Jewish question', which wondered what bearing the French Declaration could have on the discrimination experienced by Jews. His formidable critique is that the 'rights of man' are simply the rights of 'egoistic man', divorced from community, motivated only by whim and self-interest. Subsequent Marxists have regarded human rights as ideological constructs that seek to universalize capitalist values, like freedom of enterprise at the expense of social responsibility, while concealing the structured inequalities of class-divided societies, though for a more optimistic scenario see Chapter 1.

Consequently, many sociological critiques demonstrate how the existing economic, cultural and political inequalities of societies render the equal rights talk of liberal discourse as pure rhetoric incapable of being realized in substantive practice. Marxists have tended to consider punishment in relation to economic structures to reveal the class interests served by penal practices. In particular, some have stressed the relationships between the form that punishments take and the economic requirements of particular modes of production (Rusche and Kirchheimer, 1968), while others have emphasized the role of punishment in ideological class struggles so that all forms of 'bourgeois legalism' must be rejected (Pashukanis, 1978). However, E. P. Thompson (1977: 266) argued from a humanistic Marxist position that the 'the rule of law' is an 'unqualified good', which was read as an important rebuke of Marxism for abandoning civil liberty issues – viewing them as mere legal reformism and not the proper object of socialist politics (Taylor, 1980).

While Marxists demonstrate how punishing offenders reinforces the positions of the powerful, Durkheim's sociology challenges this class-divided view by examining the forces producing social solidarity. Durkheim recognizes that punishment is not a particularly effective way of controlling crime – in fact he insists this is a modern fantasy – but its significance lies in publicly declaring that a wrong has been committed and that it is right to feel outraged by this violation of the social order. For Durkheim, punishment is fundamentally a moral process that reaffirms the shared values and collective sentiments as crime damages the basic values that hold societies together. He emphasizes the expressive qualities and communicative aspects of punishment. Although we might wonder how widely shared collective values are, there is an important sense in which he shows how punishment is both 'necessary and destined to a degree of futility' (Garland, 1990: 80).

It has also been argued that a communitarian justification of punishment can overcome the problems of liberal individualism by making the symbolic dimensions of punishment fundamental (Duff, 2001; Lacey, 2003). In particular, the liberal tendency to abstract individuals from their social contexts is rejected in the communitarian critique of rights, as not only do the needs of the community overshadow those of the individual but, they argue, our identities are created in the socially embedded relations in which we live our lives. It is important to distinguish this epistemological critique of liberalism from the 'Third Way' political communitarianism that rose to prominence in the 1990s, which maintains that rights entail responsibilities to justify welfare state reforms that continue to criminalize the poor (Kennedy, 2004: 230). Nevertheless, the danger is clear. The communitarian critique finds it difficult, if not impossible, to protect unpopular minorities and individuals from the menacing authoritarian drift of contemporary political culture and the intolerant collective sentiments that have been persistently aroused against strangers, outsiders and pariah groups.

Of the founding figures of sociology, Max Weber concerned himself the least with punishment, but it is clear that many of his arguments and themes have informed a number of influential studies. His bleak view that the 'iron cage' of rationality and bureaucracy will ultimately imprison us all is expanded in Michel Foucault's (1977) *Discipline and Punish*. A key inspiration was Nietzsche, who insisted that all interpretation is selective and partial, while all forms of reason are particular expressions of the will to power. This is not to suggest, as some critics do, that any of these thinkers advocates a naive relativism incapable of distinguishing between interpretations of the world. Nietzsche (1996: 22) certainly felt that the tuneless mediocre nihilism of modern life had to be overcome and was never slow to condemn the 'slave revolt in morals' bequeathed by Christianity and given secular expression in liberalism and socialism, which resentfully define the weak as 'good' and the strong 'evil' to negate his cherished aristocratic values.

This enduring theme of highlighting the relativity of knowledge to the interests of those concerned is developed by Foucault, who dissects every body of knowledge for traces of the will to power it epitomizes. Likewise, Weber understood modern society as an endless violent struggle for domination in which different social classes and status groups compete with each other for a monopoly of resources. The 'law' and 'rights' have become crucial elements in these conflicts and are ultimately clashes of value that are irreconcilable. In response, Weber presented value-freedom as the way of dealing with the collapse of ideals that tell us how we ought to live (captured in the nihilist slogan 'God is dead'). His famous 1918 lecture 'Science as a vocation' explains that science informs us of what is possible, not what is desirable. As Turner (1993: 493) argues, the troubling implication of these arguments is that 'in the absence of a moral framework like natural law, might is right'. This sceptical interpretation of rights and the demise of normative foundations have left a legacy of suspicion that continues in postmodern critiques of both liberalism and Marxism.

Postmodern and feminist critiques

Jacques Derrida (1990) and Zygmunt Bauman (1993) have each contributed distinctive postmodern arguments by reclaiming the ethical dimension of justice repressed in liberal preoccupations with distributive fairness, egalitarian sameness and formal procedures. Both draw on Emmanuel Levinas's (1969) ethics of unconditional responsibility towards the Other. Liberal ethics are based on recognising the essential similarity between the self and others, and it is precisely this understanding of shared intersubjectivity and reciprocity that postmodern thinkers contest by emphasizing the singular, particular and local. The appeal of Levinas lies in his insistence that there can be no shared agreement as there is always something about the Other that escapes comprehension and it is this ethical opening to alterity that must be acknowledged. This moral responsibility towards difference goes much further than the contingency of liberal tolerance, which is dependent on the disposition of the superior tolerator and can be granted or abandoned, since the Other is placed in relations of inferiority. For Derrida (2003: 127), tolerance involves a 'condescending condescension', and he advances the notion of unconditional hospitality to deconstruct the apparent neutrality of tolerance. In Levinas there is a radical reversal of modern ethics by giving priority to the negative Other, 'which was once unquestionably assigned to the self' (Bauman, 1993: 85).

Critics of liberalism have long pointed out how exclusion is integral to constructing pre-rational children, irrational women, uncivilized black and Oriental others who, defined by their lack of identification with Western citizenship, become targets for repression. Under liberalism the 'discursive logic dictates that for rights to have meaning, to be cognitively as well as politically recognised, there must be groups without rights' (Hudson, 2003: 181), and we will see below how prisoners have long been denied rights according to this logic. The fact that slavery accompanied the Enlightenment, modernity produced the Holocaust and mass incarceration is now a defining feature of social policy in the USA exposes the gaps between the law and justice. For Derrida (1990), the contradiction can never be resolved and justice will always remain tantalizingly out of reach, but he insists that a radical justice of alterity is the only source of moral orientation by which existing laws can be brought to account.

In recent years there have been attempts to reconcile the postmodern justice of alterity with Jürgen Habermas's defence of Kantian liberalism (Honneth, 1995; Critchley, 1999). Before we discuss the difficulties involved in this project, it is worth emphasizing that Habermas (1984, 1987a) seeks to reaffirm the liberal ideals of rights and equality by proposing the communicative ethics of ideal speech situations where the better argument wins, thereby consensually settling disputes under equal and democratic conditions to build a discourse ethics of justice. Discourse ethics provides a procedure along the lines of Kant's categorical imperative for adjudicating between competing positions. Habermas (1987b) is highly critical of postmodernists for abandoning the Enlightenment project and surrendering to an irrational conservatism. The implications of his discourse ethics for criminal justice have been developed by Peter Bal (1996), who insists that Habermas's two moral principles of justice and solidarity should be at the heart of criminal justice, with human rights as the practical discourse, so that due process and mutual respect should be central to criminal justice systems. However, the gap (or rather gulf) between Habermas and postmodernists should be clear. In Habermas the goal of discourse ethics is consensus and fixing meaning through universal concepts, which, postmodernists argue, vanquishes those who lose out to or challenge the better argument.

Consequently, Axel Honneth's (1995) valiant attempt to combine Habermas and Derrida is one of bridging universalism with the postmodern 'ethics of care'. He recognizes that this ethics of care cannot be incorporated under the Habermasian notion of solidarity and proposes that the 'other of justice', based on Levinas's ethics of alterity, protects the fragile vulnerability of human relations.[1] The supreme irony in this appeal to alterity, as Simon Critchley (1998: 268) has amusingly pointed out, is that Levinas's ethics are based on his desire to put Judaic wisdom into the language of philosophy, and raises the prospect that the Bible is one of the founding postmodern texts. Other critics have been less kind and have held that all Levinas succeeds in doing is transforming ethics into 'a category of pious discourse' (Badiou, 2002: 23). Although this point might stand for Levinas, Derrida's (2001: 28) later writings are concerned with deconstructing forgiveness in 'Abrahamic language', which brings together 'Judaism, the Christianities and the Islams', and traces its impact on Western political discourse. He defines conditional forgiveness (calculable punishment or reconciliation processes) as that which predominates in the realm of law and politics, while unconditional forgiveness (forgiving the unforgivable) poses an enigma that cannot be reconciled as it belongs to the realm of the incalculable, the immeasurable and perhaps inconceivable. It is a 'madness of the impossible', yet without the idea of unconditional forgiveness there would be no forgiveness at all (Derrida, 2001: 39). Derrida is not as much pious here as pushing at the limits to unravel the implications of such absolute giving (see also Derrida, 1996).

The issue of alterity also arises in the history of women's struggle for rights, and feminists have exposed how abstract universal norms are in fact partial male constructs. For instance, Simone de Beauvoir (1949) explained how women are oppressed by being a secondary Other to man's primary Self, whose existence is determined by being unlike men. The patriarchal subordination of the feminine is discussed further by Luce Irigaray (1985), who argues that the polis, from Plato's ideal republic to Hegel's universal sphere, is founded on exclusion through which women are forced to resemble men and reject their specificity in order to participate in civic life. Consequently, she is critical of liberal feminists who have called for the power imbalances between women and men to be reversed by struggling for equality, as ultimately it involves accepting the existing terms of debate and forces women to become like men. The difficulties in the liberal feminist position were similarly revealed in the struggles over equality in criminal justice practice, as the best that can be achieved is the right to be treated like men (MacKinnon, 1987). Thus, Carol Smart (1989: 139) argued that the early feminist struggle over equal rights had become problematic, as the language and institutions built to protect rights are based on male ways of understanding the world.

Consequently, a number of proposals for a 'feminist jurisprudence' (Daly, 1989; Carlen, 1990; Naffine, 1990) have been made on two main premises. The first is that legal categories that are supposedly gender-neutral reflect male dominance (MacKinnon, 1987); the second is that there is a kind of reasoning, characteristic to women, that is excluded from criminal justice decision-making. While feminists continue to emphasize the need to bring women's experiences into legal theorizing through advocating 'woman-wise penology' (Carlen, 1990), there is widespread dispute over whether there is a universal 'female voice'. The tensions between 'different voice' (Gilligan, 1982) and 'male dominance' (MacKinnon, 1987) perspectives have structured much debate. One influential approach was Francis

Heidensohn's (1986) use of the care/justice dichotomy in the criminal justice system. She defines the logic of justice in terms of the *Portia* principle (rational, judicial and masculine), and the ethics of care as the *Persephone* principle (relational, informal and feminine).[2] Her conclusion was that both approaches have been used at various times in ways not always beneficial.[3]

The concept of feminist moral reasoning proved to be controversial as it sought to replace one distorted unitary view of the world, the male, with another unitary female view (Walklate, 2001), while the term care has been criticized by disability activists and postmodernists for its oppressive and 'carceral' undertones (Hughes *et al.*, 2005: 263). Recent feminist work has attempted to move beyond essentialist readings of difference in ways that anticipate and parallel developments in postmodern thinking (Cornell, 1992, 1995). Nancy Fraser (1995, 1997) has struck an important and influential note of caution against the indiscriminate celebration of difference at the expense of economic injustice. Although she distinguishes between cultural recognition and material disadvantage, her own preferred strategy is one of a 'deep restructuring' in both the relations of economic production and 'the relations of recognition' that would be mutually supportive and capable of responding appropriately to varieties of difference (Fraser, 1995: 86–91).

So far I have outlined a number of classical and contemporary sociological positions and objections to liberal understandings of rights. Many of these arguments have been quite abstract and before I turn to a more concrete set of issues surrounding prisoners rights it is important to pause here and reflect on what lessons can be learnt. One of the key problems in liberal penal philosophy is that the focus on individual rights and responsibilities ignores the social conditions producing criminality. Derrida's rethinking of justice, for instance, forces a revision of responsibility based on Kantian free-willing individual autonomy. Not only does the conventional view of responsibility provide an impoverished understanding of the differing social contexts of human action, but it cannot radically respond to or make 'one responsible for the other "in oneself" ' (Borradori, 2003: 168). A justice of alterity reveals not only how the social construction of offenders often involves creating 'evil monsters' beyond compassion and understanding, but that we have an unconditional ethical responsibility towards difference and that this comes before reciprocity. In fact, as argued below, the importance of human rights is that they can protect those who are 'beyond our empathy and beyond our recognition as fellow-citizens of good standing' (Hudson, 2003: 222).

Moreover, the socialist tradition has criticized liberal conceptualizations of legal and moral responsibility at the level of the individual by revealing how this obscures 'the recognition of collective agents such as corporations as criminally responsible for harms which result from their activities or failures of action' (Benton, 1993: 129). Stanley Cohen (1988: 120, emphasis in original) has explained how radical criminologists in the 1970s attacked state definitions of crime by showing how social systems are themselves criminal, but it was 'not always too clear whether we are being asked to condemn these evils *instead of* conventionally defined crimes or *in addition* to these crimes'. Although 'exposé criminology' was derided for these contradictions, the very secrecy of the criminal justice and penal systems 'offer[s] good reason to expect a radical criminology *continuously* to expose the fraudulent claims (to distributive justice) of a law whose administration is over-determined by exploitative social relations' (Carlen, 1980: 22, emphasis in original). It is precisely to these matters that this chapter now turns, by examining some of the concrete issues that surround prisoners and rights.

Prisoners and rights

Beyond the law

The modern prison was born in the late eighteenth century and since then it has been justified according to the liberal positions discussed earlier in this chapter, such as the utilitarian aims of deterrence, incapacitation and rehabilitation or the retributive principles of just desert, hard labour and less eligibility. Each of these often conflicting goals has come to dominance at some point over the past 200 years and they have been combined in uneasy compromises ever since. The paradox is that throughout Europe up to the eighteenth century trials were usually held in secret, with the accused often unaware of the specific details of the case against them, while torture was routinely used to extract confessions. As Foucault (1977) emphasized, this intense secrecy stood in stark contrast to the sheer visibility of punishment as a public spectacle. Although the legal rights of the accused (rights to a fair trial, innocent until proven guilty, due process constraints and so forth) have since become regarded as essential defences against arbitrary and oppressive practices, the convicted are still tainted by the feudal doctrine of 'civil death', which was based on the assumption that the proven criminal was an 'outlaw' without any legal rights (Tappan, 1954: 99).

Many critics have argued that prisons have remained 'lawless agencies' (Greenberg and Stender, 1972) and that in 'Britain . . . the law for most purposes tends to stop at the prison gates, leaving the prisoner to the almost exclusive control of the prison authorities' (Zellick, 1974: 331). The continuing irony is that while there is a complex web of rules and regulations surrounding a prisoner's daily life, the institution itself possesses enormous discretion, with the rule of law practically non-existent. The authorities enjoy considerable power over the confined, as not only are the rules themselves extensive and vague but prisoners are often unaware of their specific content. Indeed, they are frequently denied access to the mass of standing orders, circular instructions and service standards that supplement the statutory rules. The formal rules do not, in any case, provide a code of legally enforceable rights for prisoners and the courts have generally been reluctant to intervene in prison life even when prisoners have had solid grounds for challenging decisions.

Such factors reveal the continuing legacy of 'civil death' and compound the arbitrary character of prison regimes, as legal authority offers no defence against the highly discretionary power of the custodians. Lord Denning's (1972) ruling in *Becker* v. *Home Office* that the Prison Act did not give 'any colour of right' to a prisoner confirmed the longstanding judicial view that prison managers should be left to manage and that prisoners are unreliable troublemakers. Hence he commented that if 'the courts were to entertain actions by disgruntled prisoners, the governor's life would be made intolerable', as the 'discipline of the prison would be undermined' (cited in Schone, 2001: 72). However, the past 30 years have seen important developments in prison law and the emergence of some judicial recognition of prisoners' rights.

Prisoners' rights jurisprudence

The gradual and uneven development of judicial intervention began in Strasbourg when the European Court of Human Rights (ECtHR) decided in favour of Sidney Golder, who had wrongfully been accused of taking part in a riot at Parkhurst prison and had been unable to obtain redress in the English courts.[4] In *Golder* v. *UK* (1975) the ECtHR established that a number of Golder's rights had been violated under articles 6 (fair trial) and 8 (privacy of correspondence) of the European Convention on Human Rights (ECHR). This was a clear indication that the ECtHR regarded imprisonment as within the scope of the convention and the court has continued to uphold the rights of prisoners to have access to the courts and legal advice, and to sustain communication with the outside world (Livingstone, 2000: 317). The judgement was symbolically powerful and influenced subsequent domestic judicial activity.

The seminal case of *St Germain* in the Court of Appeal (1979) marked the first break with the traditional 'hands off' doctrine practised by domestic courts and dealt with the cavalier disciplinary proceedings held after a riot at Hull prison in 1976. Over the next decade the domestic courts busied themselves with developing procedural guidelines to ensure fair hearings at disciplinary proceedings (Livingstone *et al.*, 2003: 555). In consequence much judicial activism, influenced by European human rights jurisprudence, has concentrated on rights of access to legal advice and to the courts. The landmark case of *Raymond* v. *Honey* (1982) held that the prison authority's interception of a prisoner's correspondence with a solicitor was a violation of his 'constitutional rights' and thereby a contempt of court. The case contained Lord Wilberforce's defining statement on the legal status of the convicted, which is that a prisoner 'retains all civil rights which are not taken away expressly or by necessary implication' (cited in Richardson, 1985: 26).

Although there are some fundamental difficulties with this understanding of retained rights, it is important to recall that the common law position had long been that convicted prisoners had lost *all* their civil rights and that prisons themselves were impervious to the rule of law.

Several cases in the 1980s revealed a continuing judicial reluctance to intervene in either the discretionary exercise of prison administrative decisions or the disciplinary powers of governors. It was not until the successful case of *Leech* v. *Deputy Governor of Parkhurst Prison* (1988) that it was established that the courts could judicially review prison governors' disciplinary awards. This important precedent was set only after appeal to the House of Lords and the battle was won against 'a prevailing culture of pragmatism and sovereignty' (Lazarus, 2004: 209). The current boundaries of prisoners' rights jurisprudence were subsequently clarified in *Hague* v. *Deputy Governor of Parkhurst Prison* (1992). The case finally established that jurisdiction extended to administrative decisions and that the prison authorities must act within their legally defined powers. However, the House of Lords did not 'give any real endorsement to a notion of prisoners having any rights which they might assert against the authorities, or rights which might shape or constrain the exercise of official power' (Livingstone *et al.*, 2003: 553).

The judgement in *Hague* marks a turning point, with the courts having since proven reluctant to intervene in managerial issues but more than willing to act on challenging the discretionary powers of the Home Secretary over life sentences. During the 1990s a series of cases (*Doody, Pierson, Thompson* and *Venables*) combined to set procedural limits on the executive's authority to alter sentence duration so that 'a pattern of judicial bifurcation between the protection of prisoners' personal liberty and the forestalling of administrative rights' had become entrenched (Lazarus, 2004: 220). The judicial lack of concern with the discretionary powers of administrative policies was likewise revealed in a number of recent cases (*Hargreaves, Hepworth* and *Duggan*), which indicated that the legitimate expectations of prisoners will not receive much support in the courts – to the extent that some argue that the end of the 1990s saw a judicial retreat from positive legal rights activism and that the introduction of the Human Rights Act 1998 will have a limited impact on prison litigation (Schone, 2001). The Act came into force in 2000 and, while it does offer the judiciary an enhanced supervisory role, the decisions to date indicate a continuing deference to prison policy and administration, with the ECtHR remaining the more progressive on issues of prisoners rights (Livingstone *et al.*, 2003: 563).

The limits of judicial intervention

It is important to put this judicial activism into sociological perspective. Although many of these cases have been hard won, their actual impact on prisoners' lives has been very selective, and this highlights the difficulties of relying on the legal establishment to defend and define rights. The successes have been restricted to residual individual liberties such as correspondence with lawyers, access to courts, disciplinary hearings and release procedures – all matters that the judiciary are confident in dealing with. In contrast, the courts have not intervened in controversial administrative issues, such as transfers, segregation and living conditions that have a debilitating effect on prisoners. The fact that the courts have had such a negligible impact on most areas of prison life is partly explained by the longstanding scepticism towards natural rights in English political life, while the continuing deference to parliamentary sovereignty ensures that 'the statutory regime governing prisons in England is concerned, not with the definition of the prisoners' legal status or the creation of legally enforceable rights, but with clarifying lines of political control and accountability' (Lazarus, 2004: 251).

Although the highly active domestic penal reform movement has won some important victories here, including a critical Prisons Inspectorate and Prisons Ombudsman that monitor regimes and complaints, the campaign for prisoners' rights suffers not simply from a lack of popular interest. More importantly, it is damaged by the deeper dynamics of penal forces that intersect with the cynical exploitation of public anxieties surrounding crime by successive governments since the late 1970s. It is in the political context of 'authoritarian populism' (Hall, 1979) that the current modest conception of the prisoner's legal status has developed, which is that a prisoner 'retains all civil rights which are not taken away expressly or by necessary implication' (in *Raymond* v. *Honey*, 1 All ER 756, 1982: 759). However, Richardson (1985: 27) has argued that this understanding of retained rights is problematic 'due to the considerable uncertainty created by both the elusive legal concept of civil rights and the breadth of the phrase "by necessary implication" '. Instead, she proposes that prisoners ought to be entitled to 'special rights' against the authorities because of the specific forms of vulnerability and dependence that the confined routinely encounter. Her position is one that is sociologically richer than the legal conception of rights used in judicial activism, as she recognizes that 'any concept of prisoners' rights which is restricted to a residue of the rights generally possessed by non-prisoners against the state, most of which are best classified as "civil and political", and ignores the prisoners' claims to additional and often "social and economic" rights, would be seriously deficient' (Richardson, 1995: 181). Yet as should now be clear there has not been any judicial recognition of prisoners having any entitlements that protect them against ill-treatment and the long-term damages inflicted by the institution.

Of course, prisoners do not attract much public sympathy, nor is there any political capital to be gained in the cause of prisoners' rights. But it is precisely because of their marginalization and vulnerability that the confined need protection. As the Chief Inspector of Prisons, Anne Owers, has explained:

It is particularly the marginalised who need the protection of human rights: by definition, they may not be able to look for that protection to the democratic process, or the common consensus. And most of those in our prisons were on the margins long before they reached prison (look at the high levels of school exclusion, illiteracy, mental disorder, substance and other abuse); and may be even more so afterwards (with difficulty in securing jobs, homes, continued treatment, and even more fractured and community ties). Prisons exclude literally: but they hold those who already were and will be excluded in practice.

(Owers, 2003: 1–2)

It is significant that she goes on to document, among other things, the human rights abuses that routinely occur to children in English prisons (such as strip-searching, segregation and intimidation), while highlighting the systemic failures that lead to deaths in custody and recognising 'that much of what I am describing would not found a successful human rights challenge in the courts' (Owers, 2003: 4).

The implicit argument is that human rights are not simply legal entitlements but are moral obligations that ought to condition social relations in and beyond prison walls. In important respects, this returns us to the sociological critiques of liberal thinking that this chapter has introduced – namely that the assumption of sameness before the law masks the determining contexts of already existing economic inequalities, social injustice and political marginalization. Clearly the law and justice are not the same, but bridging the gulf that separates them is the space that human rights can occupy so that the universalism of due process is combined with mutual respect and an ethics of responsibility. As Hudson (2001: 145) describes it, the 'formal elements of the law involve applying legal rules consistently, and therefore if carried out fulfil the requirements of justice as fairness; substantive justice involves making the right decisions, providing the right remedy, for the particular case, and thus corresponds with the principle of justice as alterity'. The crucial point is that although these are complementary principles they often conflict, as when repressive crime control policies carried out in the name of a substantive good curtail due process conventions. This is borne out in the current detention of asylum seekers, where 'legal rights are overridden by populist policies based on security and control' (Malloch and Stanley, 2005: 66). Bal's (1996) argument that human rights can provide the moral substance for criminal justice practice is a significant one, as it states not only that offenders should be protected from instrumental policies but that the conditions of imprisonment themselves must be subjected to human rights principles. It is to such conditions that the chapter now turns.

Continuing controversies

The current penal problems can be regarded as simply too many offenders in too few prison places, which give rise to overcrowding, understaffing and decrepit conditions. The striking increase in Britain's prison population, which rose from 42,000 in 1991 to 74,023 in 2003, is due to the courts sending more people to prison and sending them there for longer. For instance, the proportion of adults convicted in the crown courts who were sent to prison increased from 45 per cent in 1992 to 64 per cent in 2001 (Kennedy, 2004: 281–2). Although the country lies some way behind the global leaders in imprisonment – Russia, the USA, China and South Africa – this should not detract from the fact that England and Wales consistently uses imprisonment to a greater extent than practically every country in Western Europe (Carrabine *et al.*, 2004: 290). The expanding prison system was initially fuelled by the infamous insistence of the then Conservative Home Secretary, Michael Howard, in 1993 that 'prison works' and the introduction of a range of austere policies that subjected prisoners to grim regimes. The Labour government has continued to rely on expanding the prison system, but by 'making prisons work', in the words of the new Home Secretary Jack Straw in 1998, through rescuing rehabilitative programmes.

As the prison population has spiralled so has the problem of overcrowding, especially in local prisons. It has been estimated that by June 2003, 85 out of 138 prisons were overcrowded, as were 9 of the 13 new prisons built since 1993 (NACRO, 2003: 6). The problems generated by overcrowding have to be located in the material context of dilapidated physical conditions in which many prisoners are contained, combined with poor sanitation, scarcely edible food, decaying cramped cells, clothing shortages and brief, inadequate family visits.[5] Compounding this deprivation are the severely restricted and oppressive regimes that are imposed in the absence of space, facilities and resources to provide prisoners with a range of training, work and educational opportunities. Hence, conditions of almost total 'lock-down' prevail.

Over the past decade the number of women in prison has trebled. Although women make up only 6 per cent of the prison population, 20 per cent of prison suicides from January to August 2004 were women, with nearly half of all self-harm incidents involving women (Scraton and Moore, 2004: 35–6). Half of all women in prison are on prescribed medication such as anti-depressants or anti-psychotics, with two-thirds having children under the age of 16, which has been estimated at 24,000 children (Kennedy, 2004: 285). The government's own *Strategy for Women Offenders*, published in 2000, recognizes that the 'current system does impact differently on women and men' (cited in Scraton and Moore, 2004: 36), which echoes longstanding feminist criticisms, discussed above, that treating women the same as men only compounds inequality. For instance, Carlen (1998: 10) has argued that women's imprisonment 'incorporates and amplifies all the anti-social modes of control that oppress women outside the prison', and that the rationales for reducing the imprisonment of women have been subverted and are now used to lock up more women through processes of 'carceral clawback' (Carlen, 2002).

The controversies surrounding deaths in custody raise fundamental questions over the state's responsibility to protect prisoner's lives and prevent death. The Strasbourg court has consistently held that the state's article 2 positive obligation of the ECHR to protect life extends to prisoners. In *Keenan* v. *United Kingdom* (2001) the ECtHR held that this obligation included a duty to prevent suicides when authorities were aware of a 'real and immediate risk'. This positive obligation was further clarified in *Edwards* v. *United Kingdom* (2002), where the court held that the authorities had failed to appreciate the vulnerability of Christopher Edwards, who was murdered by his cell-mate at Chelmsford prison, as both prisoners suffered from mental illness (Scott, 2004: 20). The Prison Service is still under scrutiny following the murder of an Asian teenager, Zahid Mubarek, at Feltham Young Offenders Institution in 2000, who was put in a cell with a known racist who had openly fantasized about committing a racist murder.

It has also been argued that the brutal deaths of ethnic minorities while in prison custody is similar to the deaths of African/Caribbeans in police custody, as there is 'a tendency for prison staff to overreact to disruptive behaviour by African/Caribbean prisoners, whereby the stereotype of "Big, Black and Dangerous" seems to predominate in determining their response' (Bowling and Phillips, 2002: 208). This view is confirmed in the BBC documentary *Death on Camera* (2004), which broadcast CCTV footage of the death in police custody of Christopher Alder, who had been left to die on the floor of a Hull police station in 1998. The fact that black people are six times more likely to be imprisoned than whites, even if it is their first offence, combined with the substantial evidence of racial discrimination in the police, courts and prisons, confirms that there is systematic injustice in the criminal justice system.

The United Nations Committee on the Rights of the Child (2002) has formally raised a range of concerns over youth justice policy and practice in England and Wales, not least since the country imprisons twice as many children as the rest of Western Europe combined. Critics of Labour's youth justice policy are especially concerned with the government's continuing reliance on custodial sentences for young offenders, with campaigners arguing 'that the Government's "obsession" with teenagers on street corners had contributed to the sharp rise in the number of young people in prison'. In particular, there has been 'a ninefold rise in the number of children under 15 being sentenced to custody' (Bright, 2003: 9). It has been estimated that 40 per cent of young people in prison have been in local authority care, while a staggering 90 per cent have mental health or substance abuse problems. Nearly a quarter have literacy and numeracy skills below those of an average seven-year-old and a significant proportion have suffered physical and sexual abuse (Kennedy, 2004: 292). This punitive direction in youth justice is as inhumane in its violation of rights as it is ineffective in preventing crime.

Conclusion

This is by no means an exhaustive discussion of the current controversies in prisons, yet what it does illustrate is that 'democratic states with strong legal institutions and rights traditions can and do abuse the human rights of their citizens' and that they 'can do so with perfect legality' (Ignatieff, 2000: 37–8). Human rights are social inventions. They are not intrinsic to individuals but are attached, created and removed by external forces. As Arendt (1973) has shown, human rights depend on strong political arrangement to enforce and protect them. Her account of how the Nazis dehumanized Jews highlights how fragile are appeals to common humanity in defending the vulnerable and marginalized. The importance of human rights legislation is that it mandates 'an obligation to respect human agency' (Ignatieff, 2000: 39). What this brief discussion of prison conditions has shown is that the combination of structural disadvantages and demonizing media representations masks the grim realities of many prisoners' lives. It is these social injustices that demand recognition and their human rights that need defending. Of course, this is not to deny that crimes need to be censured, but the material covered in this chapter should be seen as advancing a fuller acknowledgement of social wrongs and a fuller protection of the human rights of all.

Notes

1 There are certain affinities here with Turner's (1993: 506) appeal to 'collective sympathy' as a means of generating moral intersubjectivity through Durkheimian compassion rather than Kantian duty.
2 Portia is the female character in Shakespeare's *Merchant of Venice* who tricks the money-lender Shylock out of his pound of flesh, while Persephone was a goddess in Greek mythology who spent part of each year with her husband Hades in the underworld and then returned to the upper world for part of the year with her mother. The myth is seen as explaining the changing seasons and fertility cycles, with the world grieving her absence in winter and blossoming on her return in spring. This solution is seen as exemplifying the virtues of relational justice, as it is acceptable to all involved, rather than distinguishing between right and wrong.
3 Sentencing is often used as an example to illustrate how the two elements are combined, as there is a formal element that involves dealing with offenders in a procedurally consistent fashion to ensure fairness and a substantive element of doing what is the most appropriate in the particular case. Not only can this result in an individualized and paternalistic form of justice for female offenders (Edwards, 1984), but the balance between the two shifts over time and has in recent years moved in a logic of justice direction over the ethic of care (Hudson, 1993).
4 Since 1966 individuals have been able to take their cases to the European Court of Human Rights in Strasbourg (Schone, 2001: 73) and in Britain the Human Rights Act now provides domestic remedy (as of 2000).
5 The domestic courts and Strasbourg institutions have been reluctant to intervene in these routine conditions of neglect. The ECtHR has taken the view that article 3 of the convention, which prohibits torture, inhuman or degrading treatment or punishment, was not intended to find the inevitable deprivations of imprisonment as human rights violations. For instance, in *Reed* v. *United Kingdom* (1983)

'spending three weeks in a cockroach-infested cell was held not to be enough', but in a more recent case, *Tekin* v. *Turkey* (1998), the court found a breach of article 3 'where the applicant was held for four days in a police cell in freezing conditions and with little food and water'; but the fact that the prisoner also received regular beatings means that 'the decision leaves it unclear whether the neglect or physical mistreatment alone might amount to inhuman or degrading treatment' (Livingstone, 2000: 314–15). In contrast, the European Committee for the Prevention of Torture and Inhuman or Degrading Treatment or Punishment (CPT) has used the terms 'inhuman' and 'degrading' to describe custodial living conditions, but has taken a cumulative view so that 'the combination of overcrowding, lack of integral sanitation, almost unalleviated cellular confinement and/or lack of outdoor exercise have on several occasions been judged to amount to inhuman and degrading treatment' (Morgan, 2001: 728). However, the CPT has no judicial function. The distinction is that the ECtHR aims at ' "conflict solution" on the legal level, the CPT's activities aim at "conflict avoidance" on the practical level . . . to strengthen the "cordon sanitaire" that separates acceptable and unacceptable treatment or behaviour' (Evans and Morgan, 1999: 6). The more important point is that international human rights standards lay a floor (i.e. the minimum an individual should expect) rather than set a ceiling (i.e. aspiration) of obligations (Scraton and Moore, 2004: 22).

11 Mental disorder and human rights

Joan Busfield

In this chapter I draw on sociological ideas, as well as those of other theorists, to explore human rights issues in relation to mental disorder – a term that is more or less interchangeable with that of mental illness, though it has fewer medical connotations. I consider two main areas. First, the frequent tendency to deny human rights, particularly liberty, to individuals identified as having a serious mental disorder that involves residential care. Those with severe mental disorders have not, of course, been the only group to be denied human rights, even in societies where human rights have become quite well established, but they are a significant group, and the denial of human rights to this particular group reveals some of the assumptions that underpin the acquisition of such rights. Second, I move on to consider the acquisition of human rights by those with severe mental disorders. How and to what extent are these rights acquired? What factors underpin the shift from a situation of the denial of human rights to the acquisition of at least some rights? In seeking to examine these issues, I do not cover either criminal insanity or learning difficulties, since these would require specialist discussion, well beyond the scope of this chapter. I want to start by considering some theoretical ideas about both mental disorder and human rights.

Theoretical underpinnings

Theorising mental disorder

Before we can consider human rights in relation to mental disorder, we first need to have some understanding of the term 'mental disorder'. Theoretical thinking about the concept of mental disorder is extensive and diverse. However, for the purposes of this chapter I want to draw on two sets of ideas in examining the concept. The first set of ideas is provided by Michel Foucault's conceptualisation of 'madness', a narrower term than that of mental disorder, which is to be found in his influential book *Madness and Civilisation* (1967). In this study Foucault seeks to document the changes in the way societies understood and responded to madness in the seventeenth and eighteenth centuries, a period he terms the Classical Age. He argues that madness is best viewed as a form of 'unreason' and that in Western societies from the Middle Ages onwards reason and madness have stood in an opposi-tional but closely intertwined relationship: 'the Reason–Madness nexus constitutes for Western culture one of the dimensions of its originality' (ibid.: xiii). Irrationality and unreason are at the heart of our notions of madness. This is highlighted very effectively by Michael MacDonald's important study of madness and anxiety in seventeenth-century Britain, *Mystical Bedlam* (1981). MacDonald examined the case notes of an early seventeenth-century astrological physician, Richard Napier, who was con-sulted about a diverse range of problems that we would now call psycho-logical. Like Foucault, MacDonald sees reason as at the heart of judgements of insanity – 'Madness stripped men of their reason, the essential accoutre-ment of humankind' (ibid.: 130) – and, drawing on Napier's case notes, he documents its symptoms. Complaints that would be considered indicative of madness, or mania (to use the medical term of the time), were characterised by 'terrible energy and mental incoherence' and were evidenced in popular eyes by 'frantic behaviour, excess talk, odd laughter' by destructive actions, particularly actions that seemed inexplicable, such as attacks on family mem-bers or personal property or self-violence. Attacking what was highly valued by most people was a sign of madness, since it seemed incomprehensible – lacking in reason.

Foucault's focus on irrationality as the defining characteristic of madness has been highly influential and is grounded, as MacDonald's study made clear, in lay understandings – as when we nowadays talk of someone being 'out of their mind'.[1] In present day classifications the term 'madness' corres-ponds most closely to the category of psychosis, often defined loosely by psychiatrists as involving a 'loss of contact with reality', or in legal contexts as being of 'unsound mind'.[2] Such conceptualisations can clearly help to legitimate a denial of rights to those deemed mad, since reason is central to our notions of humanity and assumptions about the capacity for reason underpin many human rights. They also help to account for the stigma attendant on madness. Mad people are frequently stigmatised, marginalised, subject to discrimination and treated as 'other'.

A second set of ideas is, however, highly pertinent to the developments in understandings of mental disorder in the nineteenth and twentieth centuries. These are the ideas surrounding the notion of 'medicalisation' – a term first used in the early 1970s (see Zola, 1972; Illich, 1975) and also found in Foucault's later work. In the case of madness, this involved its transform-ation in both professional and lay understandings into mental illness, a far wider category than madness.[3] As MacDonald's study shows, people not only brought problems indicative of madness to Richard Napier, they also brought less severe problems that suggested they were 'troubled in mind', 'melancholic' or 'mopish' (a more plebeian version of melancholia).[4] Of these only melancholia embodied a medical categorisation that, along with mania, had already entered lay discourse. However, during subsequent centuries the involvement of doctors in the treatment of madness, and of a far broader range of mental troubles, increased enormously – troubles where the issue of irrationality is less obviously at stake and the social response is likely to differ.[5]

Foucault examined changing ideas about madness during the seventeenth and eighteenth centuries, ending with the 'birth of the asylum'. In the nineteenth century the number and size of asylums, often publicly funded, began to expand in many European countries and the USA, and as the century progressed most became increasingly custodial, serving as 'warehouses' for the unwanted, often, though not exclusively, those from the lower classes (Donnelly, 1983). It was in this context that the medical specialty that we now know as psychiatry developed and there were growing efforts to medicalise the care and treatment of insanity. These changes helped to displace the language of lunacy and madness and replace it with the medical language of mental illness.[6] They also helped to expand the range of mental health problems defined as mental illnesses and incorporated into official psychiatric classifications.[7] In the seventeenth and eighteenth centuries the key contrast in medical formulations had been between mania and melancholia. During the nineteenth century classifications became more numerous and diverse, and in the twentieth century not only were there moves to greater standardisation, but a range of new disorders of emotion and behaviour were also introduced – affective disorders, such as depression, the neuroses and behaviour or personality disorders (Busfield, 2002).

In his study *Creating Mental Illness* (2002), Alan Horwitz examines the expansion of the category of mental illness in the past three decades, and links this particularly to decisions by the influential American Psychiatric Association to define mental illness in later editions of the *Diagnostic and Statistical Manual of Mental Disorders* in terms of 'overt symptoms regardless of the cause or context of these symptoms' (Horwitz, 2002: 89).[8] One can, however, also emphasise the importance of new treatments to this expansion, especially the increasingly widespread use of psychotropic drugs from the 1950s onwards (see, for instance, Healey, 1997), as well as the development of welfare regimes in which more resources have been devoted to health care (including mental health). Horwitz argues, as other authors have done, that some of the mental illnesses listed in psychiatric classifications should be regarded not as illnesses at all but as normal psychological reactions to difficult situations – hence the need to focus on causes and contexts in making judgements about the presence or absence of disorder, not just on symptoms. He argues that where 'symptoms' are normal psychological reactions to difficult situations they cannot be regarded as forms of irrationality (what he terms internal psychological dysfunctions).[9] Such points are important to any consideration of mental disorder and human rights, since we need to recognise that the use of the term mental disorder has changed markedly over time and this has consequences for the rights of those identified as having such a disorder. Eighteenth-century madness cannot be equated with twenty-first-century mental illness or mental disorder, although as Napier's study shows, the 'symptoms' of many of the new disorders may have been regarded as problematic in earlier centuries and as requiring some form of help.

Theorising rights

I now turn to consider sociological theorising about human rights. Probably the best-known discussion is to be found in T. H. Marshall's influential essay 'Citizenship and social class' (1963), based on a lecture given in 1949.[10] In this essay Marshall does two things. First, he provides a categorisation of the rights of citizenship – that is, being a member of a community – into civil, political and social rights; second, he offers an account of the factors underpinning the acquisition of citizenship rights and their relation to social class. Both the categorisation and his theoretical analysis are useful when considering the linkages between mental disorder and human rights. Marshall defines civil rights as the set of rights relating to individual freedom embedded in the law: 'liberty of the person, freedom of speech, thought and faith, the right to own property and to conclude valid contracts, and the right to justice' (ibid.: 74). These rights include the right to work and are, he contends, the rights necessary for capitalism, a system that requires people to engage as individuals in the market. At the institutional level, these rights are supported by the civil courts. They tend, he argues, to be achieved earliest, suggesting that they were formally achieved as universal rights in Britain in the eighteenth century; the same was true in the USA, where they were incorporated into the 1776 Declaration of Independence, and in France, where they were the basis of the 1789 Declaration of the Rights of Man.

Political rights refer to 'the right to participate in the exercise of political power, as a member of a body invested with political authority or as an elector of the members of such a body' (ibid.: 74). The institutions here are the national and local governing bodies. In Britain political rights were secured for many members of the population in the nineteenth century after considerable political struggle, although universal suffrage was not fully achieved until the twentieth century. Again, the speed and timing of their introduction varied across Europe and the USA. However, unlike civil rights, political rights are, Marshall contends, a threat to capitalism, since they include not only the right to vote (and so potentially the power to get rid of governments) but also the right to collective bargaining through trade unions.

Social rights are the third type of right identified by Marshall and include 'the right to a modicum of economic welfare and security and the right to share to the full in the social heritage and to live the life of a civilized being according to the standards prevailing in society' (ibid.). The corresponding institutions are the educational system and welfare services, such as health services, and social security benefits covering unemployment, retirement and sickness. Marshall contends that social rights, like political rights, are a threat to capitalism because of the way they modify market arrangements (an example is unemployment benefit, which may affect an individual's willingness to work as well as rates of pay), and again they have only been achieved (to the extent that they have) after considerable political struggle.

Social rights were not included in the eighteenth-century codification of rights such as the US Declaration of Independence or the French Declaration of the Rights of Man, and were largely secured in the twentieth century. Article 25 (1) of the 1948 United Nations Universal Declaration of Human Rights asserts:

> Everyone has the right to a standard of living adequate for the health and well-being of himself and of his family, including food, clothing, housing and medical care and necessary social services, and the right to security in the event of unemployment, sickness, disability, widowhood, old age or other lack of livelihood in circumstances beyond his control.

Such rights were more fully elaborated in the 1966 UN International Covenant on Economic, Social and Cultural Rights (which paralleled a similar covenant on civil and political rights the same year). Article 12 of this covenant asserts 'the rights of everyone to the enjoyment of the highest attainable standard of physical and mental health' and set out the steps to be taken to realise this right, including 'the creation of conditions which would assure to all medical service and medical attention in the event of sickness'. The right is not a right to be healthy but a right to services that help to maintain health and treat sickness (United Nations, 2005: para. 32). However, it needs to be noted that the UN Declaration and the UN Covenants did not have legal status and had to await incorporation into national laws, a process that has occurred very unevenly.

Marshall suggests that citizenship, with its focus on rights, is a system that provides a basic equality of status for those who hold it, but that this equality is qualified. On the one hand, the principle of equality before the law may be difficult to achieve in practice, and there may be barriers to securing access to this equality. On the other hand, and related to this, the inequalities of social class can continue; indeed, the rights associated with citizenship may help to legitimate the inequalities of social class. For instance, the educational system can reinforce the stratification involved in occupational structures. Moreover, citizenship rights may make other social inequalities less visible.

Marshall's work is arguably more complex that his critics have allowed. It is tempting to see his framework as assuming a linear, evolutionary development of rights. However, I would contend that, notwithstanding the claims of others (see, for instance, Mann, 1987), he does recognise the possibility of major conflicts over rights in which there can be a reversal of rights (welfare rights provides a clear example where rights may be gained but later lost). Moreover, although his examples are from Britain, in my view his categorisation of rights and his consideration of the tensions between citizenship and capitalism can be applied to other societies. Subsequent authors have developed his analysis in a number of different ways. For instance, as Morris outlines in Chapter 4 of this volume, Lockwood (1996), like Marshall, explores the relationship between citizenship and social inequality in capitalist welfare state democracies. He portrays the contrast between the status of citizenship and the stratification dependent on moral and material resources as two axes with binary positions: the presence or absence of rights, on the one hand, and the possession of moral or material resources, on the other. This generates four types of 'civic stratification'. The first two are 'civic gain' and 'civic deficit'; in both instances citizenship rights have been achieved but moral and material resources are present in one case and absent in the other. The second two are 'civic expansion' and 'civic exclusion'; in both citizenship rights are absent, but in one moral and material resources are present, in the other they are absent. Amending this model, Morris suggests inclusion should be paired with exclusion, and introduces a third axis into the model, involving an opposition between civic expansion and civic contraction to refer to the 'shifting character of a regime of rights'. What is important in the work of all three authors is consideration of the interplay of the rights of citizenship with social stratification.

We can, however, also draw on the ideas of other authors to look at the development of rights. Esping-Andersen's (1990) model of welfare regimes is of particular relevance to the acquisition of social rights, and in the case of marginal groups may have implications for civil and political rights, since welfare regimes may, for instance, have an impact on the use of confinement. Looking at modern welfare regimes, he identifies three types of regime: liberal, corporatist and social democratic. In liberal welfare regimes such as the USA, welfare is largely dependent on the ability to pay and there is only residual public welfare provision. In corporatist welfare regimes such as Germany, welfare rights, which are usually beyond minimal levels, largely attach to employment and not the ability to pay. In social democratic regimes – for instance, Sweden in the 1960s and 1970s – welfare benefits are universal and beyond minimal levels. Esping-Andersen also provides an analysis of how different welfare regimes develop, an analysis that focuses on the class dynamics within particular countries, including the nature of class mobilisation, as well as the legacy of regime institutionalisation.

Drawing on these theoretical foundations I now explore human rights and mental disorder.

The denial of rights to those with severe mental disorder

In some historical periods and in some societies mad people have been imbued with religious significance and have been regarded as having special powers. However, the denial of liberty to persons deemed mad – that is, persons whom we would now consider as having a severe, usually psychotic, mental disorder – has a long history, and in many Western societies predates Enlightenment thinking and the acquisition of civil rights, such as the right to liberty. Those considered dangerous might be chained or locked away in jail in the interests of the safety of the local population. Foucault argues that in France the general confinement of the mad alongside the poor, criminals and the morally depraved increased in the seventeenth century, to be followed at the end of the eighteenth by the development of new asylums. In Britain as early as the seventeenth century some private madhouses were set up, a practice associated with the entrepreneurial endeavour of nascent capitalism. The madhouses catered for more affluent individuals or for lunatics sent there under poor law provisions. They were followed in the eighteenth century by charitable asylums for the respectable poor, and then in the nineteenth century by publicly funded asylums primarily for pauper lunatics, as the idea of institutional solutions to a range of social issues and problems took hold – workhouses, hospitals, prisons and penitentiaries (Busfield, 1986). And there were similar developments in many other Western countries, albeit often at a different pace.

There seems little doubt that at least up to the nineteenth century confinement was frequently associated with harsh and often brutal treatment – a treatment that in the case of the insane was associated with a view that the insane were more like animals than humans in their wildness and ferocity:

> Madness borrowed its face from the mask of the beast. Those chained to the cell walls were no longer men whose minds had wandered, but beasts preyed upon by a natural frenzy: as if madness, at its extreme point, freed from that moral unreason in which its most attenuated forms are enclosed, managed to rejoin, by a paroxysm of strength, the immediate violence of animality. This model of animality prevailed in the asylums, and gave them their cage-like aspect, their look of the menagerie.
>
> (Foucault, 1967: 72)

As animals, the wildness and ferocity of the mad had to be tamed. Confinement and physical restraint, which deprived mad people of their liberty, were clearly justifiable given this conception, but so too was the use of fear in dealing with those confined: 'Fear, being a passion that diminishes excitement, may therefore be opposed to the excess of it; and particularly to the angry and irascible excitement of maniacs.'[11] The only legal remedy against the confinement of a mad person was a writ of *habeas corpus*, which might be taken out by a member of the family seeking to secure the release of a person confined, an expensive procedure that was only sometimes successful.

The end of the eighteenth century is usually regarded as a turning point in Western conceptions and treatment of madness. In both Britain and France, a new philosophy of the 'moral management' of the insane was developed by writers such as Samuel Tuke and Philippe Pinel, in which the focus was less on physical restraint and more on 'psychological' control. The new philosophy emphasised the role of the institution as a place where the individual could escape the pressures of everyday life – hence the term asylum – where harshness and coercion were to be replaced by moral authority and where order and regularity were to encourage the capacity for self-restraint. The use of fear still had a place in the management of patients but 'it was not to be excited, beyond that degree which naturally arises from the necessary regulations of the family' (Tuke, 1813: 141). The implications are clear: mad persons might lack rationality but they were humans rather than animals and were capable of exercising some control.

> Insane persons generally possess a degree of control over their wayward propensities. Their intellectual, active and moral powers, are usually rather perverted than obliterated; and it happens, not unfrequently, that one faculty only is affected. The disorder is sometimes more partial, and can usually only be detected by erroneous views, on one particular subject. On all others the mind appears to retain its wonted correctness.
>
> (Ibid.: 133–4)

While there is evidence that such a conception of insanity was not entirely new (a more humane view of those with melancholia, often individuals from the upper classes, had existed prior to this), important changes in conceptions of madness did occur during this period and did so at precisely the same time that an emphasis on the liberty of the subject was developing and civil rights were being acquired by most of the population. However, the changes in conceptions of madness did not free mad people from the possibility of confinement and the attendant loss of rights – civic exclusion in Lockwood's terms. In law, for instance, lunatics had in effect the status of children and contracts they made were not enforceable. This denial of rights occurred even though the majority had not committed any criminal offence that might justify their detention. Confinement of mad people and the attendant loss of rights were justified in terms of their irrationality (albeit often partial) and the potential power of the asylum to correct it. The aim, though frequently over-optimistic, was to restore the person to rationality so that they could return to the community and share the same rights that others were acquiring.[12] Indeed, the confinement of mad people increased across Europe in the nineteenth century, in part because of a new therapeutic optimism, itself encouraged by the increasing claims by medical men of their power to cure insanity (which would reduce the burden of dependency), but also because, once established, the asylums rapidly filled up with those persons (often only a relatively small proportion of those admitted) whose problems were long term and could not easily be remedied. None the less, while it did not secure the rights of those detained during the nineteenth century, the changed conception of madness did start to lay the foundations for the subsequent acquisition of rights by those deemed mad or disordered in mind, which I consider in the next section.

One important area of change during the nineteenth and twentieth centuries was the formulation of clearer legal procedures for admitting someone to an institution because of the loss of liberty that resulted and the public's fears of arbitrary incarceration.[13] These procedures required certificates to be signed if a person were to be admitted to an asylum – a medical certificate becoming necessary in most cases. In France, for instance, the 1838 Lunacy Act, widely regarded as a piece of pioneering legislation that became a model for many other countries, required a petition by a relative or friend and a medical certificate for admission in non-emergency cases. Admission in emergency cases, where there was a threat to public order or the safety of others, required a signature from a prefect, followed by a clinical assessment within 24 hours of admission and then again within 14 days, with a report to the prefect on each occasion.

Certification procedures provided some regulation of admission to the asylum, even though they did not prevent the admission of some individuals who were not severely disturbed. The procedures were, however, largely designed to protect the civil rights of those who were not mad – to prevent wrongful detention. They did not ensure any rights to inmates: those admitted continued largely to be denied their civil rights, especially if they ended up as long-stay patients, and they were also excluded from the emerging political rights being secured by key groups in the population. Moreover, for all the therapeutic optimism that had facilitated the development of asylums, certification served as a reminder of the legal compulsion underpinning asylum use and became highly stigmatising, since it required clear evidence of insanity. Indeed, there was an ongoing tension between custodial models of the asylum symbolised by certification and compulsory detention, and therapeutic models symbolised by the presence of medical men. This tension has continued to the present, since the legal powers to detain on grounds of severe mental disorder (along frequently with the perceived dangers to the public) remain.[14] However, the use of these powers is now more regulated and restricted and the rights of those so detained have generally increased. In the section that follows I look at the acquisition of rights by those confined on grounds of severe mental disorder.

The acquisition of rights by those with severe mental disorder

Two key developments in mental health services occurred during the twentieth century at a different pace and timing in different countries, both of which had implications for the rights of those with severe mental disorders. The first development involved policies to permit voluntary admission of patients into asylums. The second involved the introduction of policies of community care and a move away from the asylum altogether.

The idea of allowing individuals to be admitted into asylums or private madhouses without the complex processes of certification was often underpinned in many Western countries by the desire to medicalise asylums and to make them more like hospitals. Certification procedures had, as we have seen, been formalised in an effort to ensure that the associated loss of liberty on admission should only be applied when it was fully justified. But this meant that mental problems usually had to be severe and well-established before any person would be admitted. Asylums had become places of last resort. Yet this was entirely contrary to medical philosophies that emphasised the importance of trying to treat an illness as early as possible. The Report of the British 1924–6 Royal Commission on Lunacy and Mental Disorder made the point like this:

> An anomaly which has much struck us is that except in the case of registered hospitals and licensed houses the doors of our institutions for the treatment of the mentally afflicted are closed to all but certified cases. In order that a patient may qualify for the benefit of treatment in any of the mental hospitals maintained with public money . . . he must first be certified. But the pre-requisite of certification is that the patient's disease shall be so definite and well-established that he can be declared by a medical practitioner to be actually of unsound mind and in a condition justifying compulsory detention. In the case of every other institution for the treatment of disease the aim is to get in touch with the patient at the earliest possible stage of his attack and by care and treatment to ward it off or at least to mitigate its effects. Not so in the case of insanity.
>
> (Royal Commission on Lunacy and Mental Disorder, 1926: 18–19)

Voluntary admission would circumvent this problem, though its introduction in the public asylums, which by then dominated asylum care, was contingent on the willingness of government to accept and implement more expansionist welfare philosophies and move away from viewing public provision as a matter of last resort. It was formally introduced in Britain in 1930 (along with changes in language in which asylums were renamed mental hospitals), a year after the Poor Law system was formally abolished. However, as the extract from the commission's report indicates, there had been some use of voluntary admission for private but not pauper patients before this date. In the USA a number of states had begun to pass laws to permit voluntary admission towards the end of the nineteenth century (Massachusetts was the first) and by 1924 twenty-eight states allowed voluntary admission (Lunbeck, 1994: 83). In France voluntary admission was first formally permitted in 1945.

Voluntary admission was not intended to replace compulsory admission. It was recognised that there would continue to be cases where compulsory powers were required because of the severity of the disorder, including issues around dangerousness. But where patients were willing to be admitted compulsory powers need not be deployed and the use of voluntary admission spread rapidly in Britain, and became even more extensive when the 1959 Mental Health Act said willingness should be assumed unless the individual was clearly and explicitly unwilling to be admitted (prior to this voluntary admission was only to be used where a person actively consented to admission).

The implications of voluntary admission for the rights of those admitted are harder to assess. On the one hand, all such patients formally had the right to discharge themselves, but against this it has to be noted that psychiatrists could, if they thought discharge was undesirable, institute a procedure for compulsory detention, and such a strategy would often be successful. Consequently the threat of compulsory detention sometimes gave patients little choice but to agree to admission and, once admitted, not to discharge themselves except on medical advice. Moreover, those admitted on a voluntary basis often in practice faced the same loss of rights as those admitted compulsorily (initially their rights to refuse treatment were not clearly specified and they could not vote). Yet against this it has to be said that the introduction of voluntary admission not only reflected a change in the perception of madness (now increasingly termed mental illness) but also helped to change perceptions. In part this was because voluntary admission, which was intended to facilitate the admission of those early in their illness, encouraged the admission of those with less severe problems – persons whose rights were harder to deny. The presence of such individuals almost certainly helped to encourage greater awareness of the conditions experienced by mental hospital inmates as well as of patients' rights, especially of those admitted on a voluntary basis. It is interesting, for instance, that following the Second World War there was growing interest in documenting the dehumanising qualities of asylum life, most obviously reflected in Erving Goffman's classic essays in the 1950s collected together as *Asylums* (1961), but also in a range of studies on the mental hospital and the problems of institutionalisation (Stanton and Schwartz, 1954; Barton, 1959).

In the post-war period there was also growing recognition of human rights issues and the 1948 UN Declaration of Human Rights, was followed in 1950 by the Council of Europe's European Convention on Human Rights and Fundamental Freedoms, which was subsequently incorporated into the national laws of many European countries. While there is no specific reference in the convention to health or health services there is a clause on discrimination. Article 14 asserts that:

> The enjoyment of the rights and freedoms set forth in this convention shall be secured without discrimination on any grounds such as sex,

race, colour, language, political or other opinion, national or social origin, association with a national minority, property, birth or other status.

This clause provides a potential basis for claims by those with mental disorder or other marginal groups whose rights are denied. Certainly during this period there were increasing efforts in a number of countries to strengthen the rights of those detained on a compulsory basis, and mental health pressure groups were also set up.[15] In Britain the 1959 Mental Health Act gave patients the right to contest their admission by seeking to be discharged through the framework of mental health review tribunals, and the 1983 Mental Health Act further strengthened patients' rights *vis-à-vis* 'exceptional' treatments such as ECT and psychosurgery. In the USA the laws governing compulsory detention varied between states, but many states began to strengthen patients' rights. In addition to the impact of studies such as *Asylums* on awareness of conditions in mental hospitals, the focus on civil rights in the USA and Europe in the 1960s undoubtedly increased consciousness of issues surrounding the rights of mental hospital patients. For instance, the American psychiatrist and libertarian Thomas Szasz, in his book *Law, Liberty and Psychiatry* (1963), argued that compulsory detention of those with mental illness was a form of imprisonment and an attack on human rights.[16] Increasingly, too, a range of authors and activists emphasised the importance of listening to patients and new campaign groups were formed, some exclusively for patients, calling for improvements in the care and support of those with mental illness.

The second change of key importance was the policy of community care, which began to be introduced at varying speed and intensity across Europe and the USA from the mid-1950s. Narrowly defined, this was a policy of providing facilities outside the hospital – small residential and rehabilitation units – for those with more severe problems who were previously long-term inmates in mental hospitals or might otherwise have ended up as long-term inmates. More broadly it was a policy of providing mental health facilities away from the old mental hospitals, not only for long-stay patients, but also services such as outpatient clinics, drop-in centres, and acute and emergency services (whether in units attached to general hospitals or in community mental health centres – the US model) for those with less severe or acute problems. Consequently, the policy of community care became associated with plans to close down the old mental hospitals altogether, relocating former inmates into smaller units or trying, where possible, to help individuals with mental health problems to manage in their existing environments. In the USA the mental hospital population reduced very rapidly (from a 1955 peak of 559,000 state hospital inpatients to 137,180 in 1980 (Brown, 1985: 5)), new community mental health centres were opened and state mental hospitals began to be closed. In Italy the policy changes were even more sudden, with legislation passed in 1978 to close down all mental hospitals. In Britain after a slow decline in inpatients from the mid-1950s, a growing number of mental hospitals were closed from the 1980s onwards.

A number of factors underpinned the development of community care, including changing welfare regimes, the undermining of the pro-institutional ideologies on which the asylum system had been founded, as well as belief in the value of new drug treatments to control symptoms. However, instead of the deinstitutionalisation envisaged by community care policies there has frequently been a process of 'trans-institutionalisation', with those who might formerly have stayed in mental hospitals ending up in nursing homes, old people's homes, secure units for patients considered dangerous and even prisons. Significantly, much of this residential provision, where it exists, is now increasingly owned and administered by the private sector rather than the state. In the case of old people's homes and nursing homes, legal powers of detention may not be involved, but admission may be constrained by the lack of alternative provision and residents may be subject to treatment regimes that are in practice difficult to contest. In the case of secure units or prisons, compulsory detention is involved and the individual's rights are curtailed, not only the right to liberty but also frequently the right to vote. Not surprisingly, as the number of psychiatric beds has declined the proportion detained on a compulsory basis has increased and frequently there has been a shift to a higher proportion of male inmates.[17] Moreover, even where a patient is not compulsorily detained they may be subject to compulsory treatment in the community. This is currently possible, for instance, in some US states and in Australia and is under discussion in Britain.

There is also evidence that mental hospitals have been closed down without adequate provision of alternative services, with the consequence that those with severe mental health problems have faced neglect and some have ended up on the streets (Dear and Wolch, 1987; Knowles, 2000). This raises the wider issue of the extent to which those with mental health problems have adequate access to care and support in dealing with their problems. This, of course, is a matter of the social rights of those with such problems, not their civil or political rights. There is considerable evidence that such rights have been neglected and that there have often been inadequate services (mental health services are frequently the Cinderella services within welfare provision). One aspect of this neglect is the heavy reliance on psychiatric drugs to deal with mental health problems and the absence of much in the way of alternatives – for instance, psychotherapy or various forms of social support. This absence is an especial problem given that many psychiatric problems have their underlying causes in the conditions and circumstances people face in their everyday lives.

In this context it is important to note that mental health problems are not evenly distributed across the population but vary according to social class, ethnicity and gender. Numerous studies have shown, for instance, a clear link between social class (measured in various ways) and mental ill-health in a wide range of societies (see, for instance, Hollingshead and Redlich, 1958; Robins and Regier, 1991; Meltzer *et al.*, 1995), and it is interesting that the links with social class even apply to forms of cognitive brain impairment such as Alzheimer's disease (Evans *et al.*, 2003). Studies also show that these associations are typically the product of psycho-social processes, including the uneven distribution of long-term difficulties, adverse situations and personal circumstances (see, for instance, the classic study by Brown and Harris, 1978) – a point recognised in the reference in UN article 25 (1) to the right to a standard of living adequate for health and well-being.[18]

We also need to note that the infringement of other human rights, such as the right not to be 'subject to torture or to cruel, inhuman or degrading treatment or punishment' (UN Declaration: article 5), is usually highly traumatic for the individual and can generate severe psychological problems. Although not specifically mentioned in article 5, sexual violence and abuse, such as rape, is one form of infringement of an individual's rights that needs to be included in any listing of inhuman and degrading treatment. There is now, for instance, a wide range of evidence of the adverse impact of child sexual abuse, which may be long term (Browne and Finkelhor, 1986; Beitchman *et al.*, 1992). Significantly, the impact of extreme events on psychological health is recognised through older illness categories such as shellshock, as well as newer ones such as post-traumatic stress disorder (PTSD), although the range of mental disorders generated by traumas like these is far wider.[19]

Such issues return us to Marshall's and Lockwood's interest in the intersection of citizenship and social stratification. On the one hand, individuals with severe mental disorder may face a loss of rights, especially if they need residential treatment. On the other hand, their disorder may itself be partly generated or sustained by the denial of moral and material resources for adequate conditions of living or by inhuman and degrading treatment, as well as lack of adequate and appropriate mental health services. In that respect those with severe mental health problems can face a dual disadvantage: adverse circumstances may underpin their mental disorder and then, as a result of their disorder, they may be denied specific human rights.

Conclusion

Individuals with severe mental health problems have long faced poor treatment, have often been confined on the grounds of public protection and have usually been excluded from the human rights that most other groups have gradually acquired. Irrationality and unreason, which have been at the heart of lay and professional judgements of madness and severe mental disorder, have been seen as denying full humanity to the individual and have legitimated the denial of well-established rights. Instead, those with severe mental disorders have frequently been stigmatised, marginalised and treated as social outcasts and subject to discrimination.

To some extent the wider acquisition of human rights in Western societies has over time helped to improve the rights of those with severe disorders.

Their powers to contest detention and to challenge extreme forms of treatment have been enhanced, and some have been allowed the right to vote. Overall, however, services for those with mental health problems have often been neglected and their social rights downplayed. Moreover, severe mental health problems may themselves result from the infringement of human rights. While human rights are supposedly universal rights, in practice this is often not the case, and those with severe mental disorder all too frequently face exclusion from many human rights prior to, and during, their disorder.

Notes

1 R. D. Laing (1967) sought to argue that although the behaviour of individuals might be judged irrational, in fact it was intelligible if the situation was carefully examined from the point of the individual concerned.

2 Discussing the concept of psychosis, the DSM-IV comments 'Finally, the term has been defined conceptually as a loss of ego boundaries or a gross impairment in reality testing' (American Psychiatric Association, 1994: 273).

3 The term mental disease is an older one; it is linked with the earliest involvement of doctors and can be traced back to ancient Greece.

4 While the term mopish is now more or less archaic we do still use the verb to mope and talk of people 'moping' and 'moping around'.

5 It is possible to argue, however, that some irrationality is still involved (see Busfield, 1996: 69–75).

6 In Britain the formal change was made in the 1930 Mental Treatment Act.

7 Lay understandings already incorporated a wide range of 'psychological' problems, such as being 'troubled in mind', which was clearly differentiated from madness.

8 Along with the International Classification of Diseases' section on mental disorders, this is a very widely used official psychiatric classification.

9 The problem with this argument is that 'normal' reactions can still be dysfunctional.

10 It is interesting that this lecture followed the year after the 1948 publication of the UN Universal Declaration of Human Rights.

11 William Cullen, *First Lines in the Practice of Physic*, 4th edn, 1784 (Hunter and MacAlpine, 1963: 473–8).

12 In fact many of those admitted were discharged relatively quickly.

13 Daniel Defoe, writing in 1728, attacked private madhouses because of the dangers of wrongful detention (Hunter and MacAlpine, 1963: 266–7).

14 Dangerousness is not a criterion for compulsory detention in all European countries (European Commission, 2002)

15 In Britain the National Association for Mental Health (later MIND) was formed in 1946 (Crossley, 1998).

16 He later used the phrase 'a crime against humanity' (Szasz, 1970).

17 This is partly linked to issues around dangerousness, which more typically involve men, but also because of the use of such units for those with severe problems with alcohol or drugs.

18 Biological factors play a part in the causal mechanisms linking psycho-social stress and mental disorder, and part of the dispute about biological and psycho-social explanations of mental disorder is about what counts as an adequate causal account.

19 The presence of PTSD in current psychiatric classifications is significant, given the explicit desire to eschew aetiological assumptions in these classifications.

12 Free to speak, free to hate?

Paul Iganski

Legal instruments against manifestations of racism in the form of 'hate speech' and 'hate crime' confront a dilemma in striking a balance between the potentially conflicting right to freedom of expression (and by implication the thought and opinion behind expression) and the right to freedom from discrimination and victimisation on the basis of 'racial', ethnic or religious identity. The UK Labour Government elected in 1997 after 18 years of Conservative Party rule began to institute a radical legislative agenda against racist hate. After nearly a decade in power it is instructive to evaluate how the balance between these rights has been negotiated by the Labour Government. Although it is not quite the time yet for an 'end of term' report, such a review serves to illuminate the ways in which rights are brought into conflict when legal instruments are used against racist hate and other forms of bigotry. Furthermore, when examined through the sociological lens of expressive theories of punishment, the Labour Government's approach to criminalising racist hate provides an instructive case study of how a state can aim to promote a collective moral consciousness through the denunciation of racist hate through the criminal law, within the constraints of a dominant normative value of the right of citizens to freedom of expression.

In 1997, the new Labour Government was elected with a manifesto commitment to review legislative provisions against racist violence. It put its commitment into action in the 1998 Crime and Disorder Act, which established provisions for racially aggravated offences to enable more severe punishment of offences that are racially motivated, as well as offences in which there is manifest racial hostility. The provisions were shaped by policy learning on so-called hate crime laws in the USA, where most states (and the District of Columbia) have established statutes that punish offenders more severely when their crimes are motivated by prejudice against the race, religion, sexual orientation, gender, disability, age or political affiliation of their victims, although not all of these 'categories' are covered by legislation in all states.

So called 'hate speech' plays a significant role in the conceptualisation of hate crime under the British provisions, as words that the offender uses while committing the offence – racial abuse or racist epithets, for example –

or uses immediately before or after the offence is committed, provide a prime indicator of manifest racial hostility. This raises fundamental questions of social justice, as evidence used to secure a conviction for a racially aggravated offence, things that the offender says before, after or while committing the offence, are not likely to be intrinsically unlawful. The prosecution of racially aggravated offences would therefore at first sight appear to constitute restrictions on freedom of expression and thought, which are not a priori proscribed. There are few circumstances where racist speech is proscribed in Britain and they are only where the speech arguably takes the form of an act, as in instances of incitement to racial hatred (1986 Public Order Act), chanting at a football match (1991 Football Offences Act) and the use of threatening, abusive or insulting words that threaten, provoke or generate a fear of violence (1996 Public Order Act, sections 4 and 5).

The impetus for legislation to establish racially aggravated offences in Britain came in part from the consistent rise in the number of racist incidents reported to the police across the 1990s, and Home Office commissioned British Crime Survey evidence revealing a far great number of racist incidents than captured by police records (Aye Maung and Mirrlees-Black, 1994; Percy, 1998; see also Virdee, 1997). (An apparent escalation of racist attacks across a number of European countries in the late 1980s and early 1990s (Commission of the European Communities, 1993) similarly provided the impetus for policy exhortation for the European Union.) Abhorrence against violence and other incidents motivated by racism appeared to provide a broad consensual support for legislation in Britain, as evidenced in particular by the reaction to the racist murder of Stephen Lawrence in South London in 1993. However, courts had not been fully using the powers available to them in disposing of offences involving racial aggravation. Penalty enhancement for racial aggravation was enabled by the 1991 Criminal Justice Act (sections 3(3) and 7(1)) and an explicit lead was provided in 1995 by the then Lord Chief Justice in *R v. Ribbans, Duggan and Ridley* ((1995) 16 Cr App R(S) 698) for 'a proven racial element to be taken into account as an aggravating factor when sentencing'. However, a study by the Crown Prosecution Service for 1997–98 observed that in only 22 per cent of cases studied where racial motivation was a factor were sentences enhanced by the courts (Press Release 146/98, 20 October). Such inconsistencies in the treatment of convicted offenders generated suspicions that the courts were institutionally insensitive to racist incidents. In this vein, the Association of Directors of Social Services in their response to the consultation paper preparing the way for the provisions for racially aggravated offences in the 1998 Crime and Disorder Act argued:

It is necessary for the Criminal Justice System to repudiate charges that it produces discrimination in the way it delivers its service to ethnic groups. Inconsistencies in applying the Ribbons judgement have done nothing to aid this course, and the proposed legislation does give a clear statement of intent in how seriously racially motivated offences will be treated in future.

Similarly, the Association of Chief Officers of Probation argued:

> The fact that racial crime is being taken so seriously may assist in rebuilding confidence in the criminal justice system on the part of members of ethnic minority communities. However, the extent to which that is achieved will also depend heavily on how those involved in the criminal justice system implement and respond to the spirit and intention of the legislation, and are seen to take it seriously.
>
> (Iganski, 1999: 391)

In the wake of concern about Islamophobic incidents in Britain following the terrorist attack on the World Trade Center and the Pentagon in September 2001, Britain's hate crime provisions were extended under the 2001 Anti-Terrorism, Crime and Security Act to cover religiously aggravated offences. These provisions addressed a loophole in British law, as Muslims are not recognised as a 'racial' group – as defined by the 1976 Race Relations Act – and hence hate crimes committed against them without manifest racial motivation or hostility were beyond the remit of provisions against racially aggravated offences. The new religiously aggravated offences crept in without opposition under cover of the controversy over government plans – subsequently suspended until a recent resurrection – to establish provisions against incitement to religious hatred. In an exemplar of 'domain expansion' (Jenness and Grattet, 2001: 98) the provisions against racially and religiously aggravated offences were extended even further under the 2003 Criminal Justice Act (section 146), to enable penalty enhancement in offences where at the time of committing the offence, or immediately before or after it, the offender demonstrates hostility based on the sexual orientation (or presumed sexual orientation) of the victim, or a disability (or presumed disability) of the victim. Again, words spoken by the offender provide a prime indicator of manifest hostility.

A review of provisions against incitement to religious hatred and possible legislation against Holocaust denial were also on the policy agenda of the incoming Labour Government in 1997, although they were not stated in the Labour Party's election manifesto. These provisions involve potentially more tenuous connections between 'hate speech' and 'hate crime' than the provisions for racially aggravated offences and they have not attracted the same degree of consensus. They throw into much greater relief the conflict between rights to freedom of expression and rights to freedom from victimisation on the basis of racial, ethnic and religious identity when legislating against bigotry, as evidenced by the considerable controversy generated by government plans to outlaw incitement to religious hatred. The controversies and conflict over rights involved in each of these measures are unfolded in more detail below.

The hate crime law debate

Opposition to hate crime laws in the USA has been longstanding and persistent, and it is instructive to consider the debate. Two major objections are raised by critics. First, with an eye to the fundamental human right to freedom of expression (as enshrined in the First Amendment to the US Constitution, for instance), opponents argue that the additional punishment meted out by the courts for hate crimes, constitutes the punishment of ideas (Gey, 1997), 'bad character' (Hurd, 2001), 'improper thinking' and 'extra punishment for values, thoughts, and opinions which the government deems abhorrent' (Jacobs and Potter, 1997: 10). Bigoted speech, and the thought behind it, provides the main indicator of motivation behind hate crimes. Therein lies the problem. Without a predicate – or underlying – offence, hate speech is generally protected in the USA. By implication, the thoughts that the speech manifests are protected too. One recent critic, Tammy Bruce, argues that hate crime laws involve 'the actual criminalization of the most private, personal, and subjective part of our lives – what we think', and she consequently suggests that the laws amount to 'totalitarianism in its purest form' (Bruce, 2001: 45–6). A similar allegation has been levelled by one of the few public critics of hate crime laws in Britain, columnist Melanie Phillips, who argued that they are an 'Orwellian response to prejudice' (Phillips, 2002).

The second major objection raised by opponents of hate crime laws in the USA concerns the equitable treatment of crime victims by the criminal justice system. Critics suggest that the laws establish a hierarchy of victims in otherwise identical crimes. Columnist Jeff Jacoby has argued that 'In a society dedicated to the ideal of "equal justice under law" – the words are engraved over the entrance to the Supreme Court in Washington, DC – it is unjust and indecent for the statute books to enshrine a double standard that makes some victims more equal than others' (Jacoby, 2002: 116). On a personal note, Tammy Bruce again forcefully argues that 'As a gay woman, I refuse to be part of a system that tells me that I count more than any other woman who gets raped or murdered' (Bruce, 2001: 39). In view of such objections, it is a paradox that the argument of equity for crime victims has also been used in support of extending hate crime laws. Prior to the provisions of the 2003 Criminal Justice Act enabling penalty enhancement in cases where the offender demonstrates hostility on the basis of the sexual orientation of the victim, human rights activist Peter Tatchell argued that 'the British government proclaims equality for all, but legislates greater equality for a few. . . . Instead of cracking down on all prejudice inspired attacks, the official British government policy on hate crimes seems to be that some victims should be granted privileged legal protection and that all other victims should be ignored' (Tatchell, 2002: 54, 55).

The debate about the justification of hate crime laws rarely deviates from the liberal foundation upon which the arguments have been built, as even advocates of the laws ardently defend the right to freedom of speech by arguing that expression, the thought behind the crimes, or motivation, are not being punished (see Iganski, 2001). Instead, supporters argue that the laws impose greater punishment for the greater harms they believe are inflicted by hate crimes (cf. Weinstein, 1992; Lawrence, 1999; Levin, 1999). From this viewpoint, the thought behind the crime, as perhaps manifest in the words that are spoken while committing the act, is only relevant to determine whether the particular act committed is a type of act – a hate-motivated crime – that inflicts greater harms than the type of act – the same conduct, but otherwise motivated – that causes lesser harms.

Problematically, however, there is arguably little authoritative evidence about the nature of the alleged harms inflicted by hate crimes over and above the underlying crimes, and arguably what actually hurts is the thought behind the crime. This is evident if the alleged harms inflicted by hate crime offenders are critically unpacked. To take physical injuries as a result of crime, for instance, some advocates of hate crime laws have suggested that hate crimes are more likely to involve 'excessive violence' (Levin, 1999: 15), cause injury and lead to hospitalisation than criminal assaults in general (Levin and McDevitt, 1995; Levin, 1999: 15). The empirical evidence to support these claims is weak, however, and intuitively the claims are less than convincing. It would be remarkable if every violent crime of a particular type – say grievous bodily harm – resulted in greater injury when motivated by 'hate' than when otherwise motivated. Even if the majority of hate crimes inflict more serious injuries it would surely be unjust to punish more severely an individual perpetrator of a hate crime that did not result in greater injury because on average hate crimes inflict more injuries. Those hate crimes that do inflict greater physical injury deserve more severe penalties, but such crimes do not justify the establishment of a category of punishment beyond the particular circumstances of any particular criminal incident. Logically, crimes that do inflict greater physical harms will be prosecuted at the appropriate level. The same considerations apply to emotional injuries. Arguably, to justify more severe punishment of hate crimes on the basis of emotional harm it would need to be demonstrated that they normally inflict greater emotional injury on the victims than identical but otherwise motivated crimes. While there has been some research on the psychological and emotional impact of hate crimes that indicates the effects upon victims, overall the findings are equivocal on the question of whether or not hate crimes always hurt more at the emotional level. For instance, Herek *et al.* (1999) compared a purposive sample of lesbians and gay men who had been victims of bias crimes ($n = 69$) with a sample ($n = 100$) who had been victimised on grounds other than their sexual orientation. They observed that the hate crime victims recorded statistically significant higher scores on measures of depression, traumatic stress and anger. However, while their data reveal that on average victims of hate crimes suffer more emotional harms, the evident variation in the scores indicates that not all victims experience harm to the same extent, and potentially that some victims of hate crimes suffer less emotional harm than some victims of similar but otherwise motivated crimes.

In turning to another type of harm, hate crimes arguably send out a terroristic message to members of the victim's group in the immediate neighbourhood and beyond. In the words of one commentator, 'violence constitutes a threat of more violence to minority group members' (Weinstein, 1992: 8). The terroristic harms generated by hate crimes arguably spread beyond the individual to the initial victim's 'group' or community in the wider neighbourhood community. They are also likely to spread to others in the 'group' who know the victim and hear of their experience, and who may live beyond the initial victim's neighbourhood. Other persons who share the victim's characteristics – and come to hear of the victim's plight – may potentially be affected by a hate crime. Research carried out in Britain in the mid-1990s demonstrated the wider behavioural impact in question. The Fourth National Survey of Ethnic Minorities (Modood *et al.*, 1997) revealed that nearly one-quarter of black and Asian respondents worried about being 'racially harassed', and 14 per cent of the respondents reported having taken measures to avoid potential harassment. Measures ranged from avoiding going out at night – the most commonly reported behavioural response – to changes in leisure activity (Virdee, 1997: 284–5). A larger proportion of respondents 'reported being worried about racial harassment than had experienced it in the last year'. A conclusion drawn was that this 'suggests that the impact of having suffered some form of racial harassment at any time in the past, or having heard about an incident of racial harassment even though it may be unrelated to the respondent themselves, can still have an influence in creating an atmosphere of fear and anxiety' (Virdee, 1997: 284–5). However, again, justification of the punishment of hate crimes as a separate class of crimes needs to be supported by evidence that the terroristic impact of a hate crime usually goes above and beyond the impact of the underlying – but otherwise motivated – crime. Unfortunately, the research design of the Fourth National Survey did not permit such a comparison as questions on crime victimisation solely focused on racially motivated crime.

It might be thought that the contest between the opposing sides in the hate crime debate might be resolved by empirically determining whether hate crimes do actually hurt more than the same underlying, but otherwise motivated, crimes. Yet there is a fundamental flaw in this contest, as Kahan (2001) has argued. Opponents of hate crime laws who propose that the laws are illegitimate because they take the offender's values into account in determining punishment (and thereby amount to 'thought crimes'), when the criminal law generally does not, face the problem that the criminal law does commonly use an offender's motivating values to determine the seriousness of the offence and the appropriate punishment. Alternatively, proponents of punishing hate crimes on the basis that they inflict greater harms – not because of the thought behind them – face the problem that the greater harms inflicted involve, in many instances, an aversion to the offender's values. As one commentator has argued, the motivation of the hate crime offender 'violates the equality principle, one of the most deeply held tenets in our legal system and our culture' (Lawrence, 1994: 365). But more severe punishment of hate crimes – compared with parallel crimes – on the grounds that they offend societal values can amount to nothing else than punishing the bad values of the offender. While this is conceding the argument of opponents of hate crime laws, their position is weakened by the common criminal law use of offenders' motivating values to determine the seriousness of an offence and the appropriate punishment (Steiker, 1999; Kahan, 2001). The fact that self-defence, for instance, is seen as a mitigating factor in terms of culpability for a crime even though the consequences of the crime might be identical to the same offence committed out of malice, indicates that 'good' – or normatively desirable – values are rewarded, and 'bad' values punished. As Kahan (2001: 193) argues: 'Conceptually and practically speaking it is impossible to draw a distinction between the harms that violent criminals inflict and the values that motivate them to act. Hate crime laws do punish offenders for their aberrant values in this sense. But so do the rest of the provisions that make up the criminal law. It's impossible to imagine things otherwise.' Offenders' values are not inviolable, then, when it comes to the application of the criminal law, although in the case of 'hate crimes' aberrant values are only punished when they accompany an otherwise criminal act. The association between speech and action is weakened in the case of racist hate speech, however, and hence attempts to criminalise such speech have attracted greater controversy than hate crime provisions.

Hate speech and the incitement of hatred

Denial of the historical facts of the Holocaust might be regarded as a specific case of hate speech where the words used inflict a unique injury.[1] Towards the end of the 1990s a confluence of events occurred that arguably made the British government more receptive than at any time in the past to criminalising Holocaust denial. The libel case lost by David Irving in the High Court in London brought the problem of Holocaust denial into the public consciousness with a potency that it had never had before. Professor Deborah Lipstadt, Director of Judaic Studies at Emory University, Atlanta, was sued by Irving for alleging in her book *Denial of the Holocaust* that 'Irving is one of the most dangerous spokespersons for Holocaust denial' (Lipstadt, 1994: 181). Lipstadt was not alone in her view. In an early day motion in the British Parliament's House of Commons in 1989 Irving was described as a 'Nazi propagandist and long-time Hitler apologist'.[2] The libel trial brought into the public consciousness the political agenda behind Holocaust denial. Trial judge Charles Gray, for instance, concluded that Irving 'is antisemitic and racist and . . . associates with right wing extremists who promote neo-Nazism' High Court Judgement 11 April 2000, para. 13.167. As matters stood, the absence of a Holocaust denial law in Britain set the country against the trend of its European neighbours, such as Austria, Belgium, France, Germany, Spain and Switzerland, which have all outlawed Holocaust denial. And at the supranational level in Europe, in 1995, while the last Conservative government held office in Britain, the European Parliament's Kahn Commission proposed that all member states should establish specific offences of Holocaust denial and the trivialisation of other crimes against humanity. The pressure from Europe met an incoming Labour government that was far more receptive than previous governments to the idea of outlawing Holocaust denial. While the Labour Party was in opposition it passed a motion at its annual conference in 1996 calling for a Labour government to 'make it a criminal offence to publish, broadcast, distribute or display any material for the purpose of denying the Holocaust' (Bristow, 2000). One year later, Labour Member of Parliament Mike Gapes introduced his Holocaust Denial Bill to the House of Commons. Despite some cross-party support it was allotted insufficient parliamentary time under the presiding Conservative government and failed. The incoming Labour government stalled in its enthusiasm to establish a specific Holocaust denial law to consult with representatives of Britain's Jewish communities (Travis, 1999).

Significantly, the Institute for Jewish Policy Research (IJPR) (a leading 'think tank' on Jewish affairs in Britain) made its recommendations about punishing Holocaust denial in June 2000 in a report presented to the then Home Secretary Jack Straw (IJPR, 2000). The report was written by a panel of legal experts chaired by high-profile lawyer Anthony Julius, who served as counsel for the defence in the Irving–Lipstadt trial. The report was based on some 18 months of research, written and oral inquiries and testimony from historians and Holocaust survivors. The conclusion: a Holocaust denial law in Britain would be 'inadvisable'. Instead, the panel recommended that consideration be given to amending the provisions against incitement to racial hatred. Alternatively, it recommended enacting a new law that would cover Holocaust denial under hate speech provisions more broadly. This was not the first time that recommendations had been made to amend Britain's provisions against incitement to racial hatred to enable prosecution of Holocaust denial. Similar recommendations were made in a report published by the Board of Deputies of British Jews, the representative body of Anglo-Jewry, in 1992 (Board of Deputies of British Jews, 1992).

The case for incorporating Holocaust denial into incitement to racial hatred provisions lies in the political context in which Holocaust denial operates. It is commonly argued that enactment of a specific Holocaust denial law would inevitably stimulate a welter of competing political claims.

To support such a view one need look no further in Britain than the media's reaction to the Home Secretary's announcement in January 2000 declaring a National Holocaust Memorial Day. Why, the pundits wanted to know, should the integrity of the memory of the Holocaust be protected when other acts of genocide and historical tragedies are forgotten and even distorted? What about the slaughter of Armenian Christians by Ottoman Turks in 1915? Or the crimes of the African slave trade? One correspondent to the *Guardian* posited that 'Jewish victimhood' was used to justify 'Israeli aggression and oppression', thereby warranting as well a public commemoration of the exile of the Palestinian people. And this was only potentially the tip of the iceberg. If denial or distortion of the facts of these tragedies is not outlawed, the argument goes, supporters of a Holocaust denial law would need to defend the selective use of law for some historical tragedies but not others. Lawrence Douglas (1988: 71) has made this point more emphatically: 'Why would the *state* provide the facticity of the Holocaust a degree of legal insulation not offered other facts? By proscribing Holocaust denial in specific, doesn't the liberal state abandon its putative neutrality in order to protect the sensitivities of a particular group within a heterogeneous community?' The IJPR also recognised this dilemma. As stated in its report:

> In Britain, where Jews comprise but one of a large number of diverse minority groups, the existence of a Holocaust-denial law might likewise be expected to provoke calls for it to be extended to cover other instances of denial. If such calls were heeded, it is difficult to imagine where and on what basis the limits of the law would eventually be set. If, conversely, the law continued to restrict itself to Holocaust denial, British Jews would face the accusation that they were demanding and receiving special treatment.
>
> (IJPR, 2000: 24)

Perhaps the strongest argument of all against Holocaust denial legislation is the conflict it creates between its intent on the one side to curb the assault on historical truth and the emotional damage it does to survivors and their families, and on the other side, claims by deniers to rights to freedom of expression. Holocaust deniers regularly exploit free speech by portraying themselves as its first victims. Irving pursued a similar angle when he sought to argue his case on the back of claims to freedom of expression. The IJPR law panel recognised this fundamental dilemma in its key objection to Holocaust denial law. Instead it proposed the outlawing of Holocaust denial by the back door by amending Britain's incitement to racial hatred – or 'hate speech' – provisions. Such a course of action, though, would have marked a significant departure from past legislative tradition, and was not subsequently adopted by the Labour government. It is most useful to review that tradition, as it informs analysis of the most recent conflict over rights involved in the government plans to establish legal provisions against incitement to religious hatred.

Hate speech has been largely protected in Britain unless it is associated with public disorder or an underlying crime, as in the case of racially aggravated offences as discussed above. Existing provisions against hate speech – or 'incitement to racial hatred' as it is called by law – make it an offence for a person to publish or distribute written matter, or use words in any public place or public meeting, provided they are threatening, abusive or insulting. Additional preconditions for prosecution are an *intent* to stir up racial hatred or, alternatively, the *likelihood* for hatred to be stirred up having regard to all the circumstances.[3]

Historically, prosecutors have found the incitement prerequisites difficult to prove. As a result, in an effort to find stronger means to combat Holocaust denial, the IJPR panel, while adhering to its arguments against special legislation to combat it, sought their 'third way'. They proposed removing the 'threatening, abusive and insulting' prerequisite as a condition for prosecution – words the IJPR jurists saw as inhibiting the process of bringing Holocaust deniers to judgement. This proposal, if it had been accepted, however, would have had radical consequences. The words 'threatening, abusive or insulting' are there for good reason. They reflect a concern, reiterated by government each time the incitement provisions have been reviewed, to protect freedom of expression unless disorder is threatened. This was made clear in parliamentary discussion of the failed Holocaust Denial Bill introduced by Mike Gapes MP in 1997. The then Home Office Minister responsible for race relations, Timothy Kirkhope, observed that 'Parliament concluded that the freedom to express minority views should be preserved – however repugnant those views may be – except when public order and safety are threatened.'[4]

There is a long historical precedent in Britain for the protection of freedom of expression, unless there is a threat of disorder. Legislative provisions specifically against incitement to racial hatred were first established by Section 6 of the Race Relations Act 1965. The primary justification provided by the government sponsor of the provisions for restrictions on speech was the threat allegedly posed to public order by the speech in question (Wolffe, 1987: 345). The provisions of the Act were not unprecedented. It had long been possible to invoke the criminal law against persons who incite racial hatred, but only if it was likely to lead to violence or a breach of the peace. Before the 1965 Race Relations Act there had been prosecutions for seditious libels that involved incitement to racial hatred. Cases that succeeded involved actual violence, or the likelihood of violence. The Public Order Act 1936 was also used against incitement to racial hatred. The connection to violence is clear. The Act was introduced to deal with public disorder associated with clashes in London's East End at the time between supporters of the British Union of Fascists and their opponents (Lester and Bindman, 1972: 350; Supperstone, 1981: 5).

When the 1965 Race Relations Act was reviewed, the then Labour government was emphatic about its support of the principle of freedom of expression, the only exception being where public order was threatened. The White Paper preparing the way for new race relations legislation stated the government's view that it was 'not justifiable in a democratic society to interfere with freedom of expression except where it is necessary to do so for the prevention of disorder or for the protection of other basic freedoms'.[5] The resultant 1976 Race Relations Act removed the provisions against incitement to racial hatred from the remit of race relations legislation altogether and incorporated them into public order law. When that law was in turn later reviewed in 1985 the then Conservative government stated its own support for the principle of freedom of expression. It believed that 'the reasonable exercise of freedom of expression should be protected, however unpleasant the views expressed'.[6]

Under the incitement provisions currently in force and established by the 1986 Public Order Act there have been no prosecutions specifically for the production or distribution of Holocaust denial material, or any other Holocaust denial activity. It is instructive to consider exactly why this has been the case. It helps to understand the potential ramifications of classifying Holocaust denial as incitement – which the JPR jurists wished to do.

Chiefly, those words, 'threatening, abusive or insulting', which have prevented the prosecution of Holocaust denial, have arguably been regarded by prosecutors as 'representing a descending order of violence' (Williams, 1970: 108). The word 'insulting' is perhaps at the minimal end of the continuum of violence represented by these three words. But its situation in public order legislation arguably infers that insulting words – as well as words that are threatening and abusive – must intrinsically be liable to provoke a physical reaction or severe hostility among a reasonable audience, irrespective of the context in which they are used. By understanding this it is arguably possible to comprehend the last Conservative government's attitude towards Holocaust denial. In parliamentary discussion of the 1997 Holocaust Denial Bill it was observed that in the view of the Crown Prosecution Service 'it is possible to prove that such literature is offensive and untruthful, but it is not possible to prove that it is insulting'.[7] The vast majority of people would surely regard Holocaust denial as an insult. But it cannot be so classified legally.

Holocaust denial remains outside the scope of legal recourse because it is not usually characterised by aggressive or profane expression. It is commonly couched in reasonable language and frequently presented in an academic style. For instance, David Irving, in his introduction to the Leuchter Report, a leading contribution to Holocaust denial literature, alleges that 'Too many hundreds of millions of honest, intelligent people have been duped by . . . the propaganda story that the Germans were using "gas chambers" to kill millions of Jews and other "undesirables" '.[8] But it would be a severe distortion to allege that Irving's words, and some of the foremost works of Holocaust denial, such as *The Hoax of the Twentieth Century* or *Did Six Million Really Die?*, would provoke a violent response, even among those hurt and offended by the material.

However, while words have to be 'threatening, abusive or insulting' to warrant prosecution as incitement to racial hatred, the Board of Deputies of British Jews – in their deliberations on Holocaust denial law – argued that Britain's incitement provisions do not require an *immediate* breach of the peace. In their view 'over a period of time racist words or conduct can "beget violence" although they may not present a clear and immediate threat of violence and disorder' and 'such conduct will ultimately of itself create a climate of public opinion or influence public attitudes or behaviour in a way which threatens tranquility and order within society' (Board of Deputies of British Jews, 1992: 29–30). Although it is not stated in the same way, it can safely be inferred that the same assumption lay behind the IJPR's recommendation for the 'threatening, abusive or insulting' precondition to be removed. Their assumption may have been correct. But once conceded as grounds for prosecution it would set a dangerous precedent. Many public utterances expressed as part of mainstream political discourse arguably contribute to a climate of racist violence and hatred by having a cumulative effect over time. Such utterances may even conceivably provoke racist violence among those who are predisposed to such behaviour. But clearly a line has to be drawn to protect rights to freedom of expression and a tangible connection between violence and the words that provoke it argu-ably provide such a line. Given this context, the most recent controversy over government plans to establish a new offence of incitement to religious hatred – modelled on the law against incitement to racial hatred – can be put into perspective.

Although the provisions will apply to all religions, they have commonly been regarded as offering special protection to Muslims,[9] and indeed repre-sentative bodies of Muslim communities in Britain such as the Muslim Council of Britain and the Muslim Public Affairs Committee have supported the measures. At the most basic level the provisions close a loophole in British law, as Muslims are not recognised as a 'racial' group – as defined by the 1976 Race Relations Act – and hence incitement targeted against them has fallen outside the scope of the legislation against incitement to racial hatred. In its memorandum to the House of Commons Home Affairs Committee (Session 2004–5, House of Commons Paper No. 165, Memo-randum 27) the Muslim Public Affairs Committee UK argued that legislation is needed

> to provide Muslims with equal protection to other minority groups who are already protected under the Race Relations Act – including protec-tion from incitement to hatred. (Extending this protection to Muslims would be consistent with the inclusion of Jews as a group protected

under the Race Relations Act who, like Muslims, are a group with diverse geographical origins but sharing a common religious heritage).

And in their memorandum to the Home Affairs Committee (Session 2004–5, House of Commons Paper No. 165, Memorandum 26) the Muslim Council of Britain expressed their concern with the

> lack of protection that is afforded to the Muslim community per se. The lack of legislation protecting followers of multi-ethnic faiths such as Islam and the failure to outlaw incitement to religious hatred exposes one of the most vulnerable and marginalized minorities in the UK to further harm and contributes to the ensemble of factors that lead many to conclude that Muslims are discriminated and victimized by the current spate of anti-terror measures. Our democracy is deficient for its want of protection for a minority actively discriminated against and mainstream legislation is clearly its proper place . . . it is important that all minorities are equally protected, not least the one that is most disaffected.

Some commentators suggested that plans to introduce the measures were part of the Labour government's electoral strategy to harness the support of Muslim communities in some key parliamentary constituencies. Comedian Rowan Atkinson, for instance, a prominent critic of the measures, argued in a speech to the House of Lords[10] in January 2005 that:

> I don't doubt the sincerity of those who are seeking this legislation but I do question the government's enthusiasm for it so close to a General Election, an enthusiasm that must be rooted in their belief that this measure could help their cause in some marginal constituencies with large religious populations, many of whom are critical of the government's prosecution of the war in Iraq. It seems a shame we have to be robbed permanently of one of the pillars of freedom of expression because it's needed temporarily to shore up a wobbling edifice elsewhere.

Atkinson's concerns that the legislation would trounce rights to freedom of expression were typical of those opposed to the new law:

> I question also the ease with which the existing race hatred legislation is going to be extended simply by the scoring out of the word 'racial' and the insertion of 'racial or religious hatred' as if race and religion are very similar ideas and we can just bundle them together in one big lump. When it seems clear to me and to most people that race and religion are fundamentally different concepts, requiring completely different treatment under the law. To criticise people for their race is manifestly irrational but to criticise their religion, that is a right. That is a freedom. The freedom to criticise ideas – any ideas – even if they are sincerely held

beliefs – is one of the fundamental freedoms of society and a law which attempts to say you can criticise or ridicule ideas as long as they are not religious ideas is a very peculiar law indeed. It promotes the idea that there should be a right not to be offended, when in my view, the right to offend is far more important than any right not to be offended, simply because one represents openness, the other represents oppression.

Concerns that criticism and ridicule of a religion will fall foul of the new provisions against incitement to religious hatred were fuelled by some advocates of the new law, who were indeed expecting it to provide blanket protection against those who are offensive or rude about Islam.[11] However, such expectations, and also the concerns about the law eroding rights to freedom of expression, are unfounded once the application of the provisions against incitement to racial hatred are appreciated, as discussed above. The new provisions against incitement to religious hatred will be subject to similar constraints and applied to only the most egregious expressions that threaten public order.

The expressive value of criminalising hate

When examining the legislative programme of the post-1997 Labour governments on legislation against hate crime and hate speech, it is apparent that a careful and consistent balance has been struck between the rights that racist hate bring into conflict: the right to freedom of expression for the perpetrators (and the thoughts behind such expression) and the right of individuals to freedom from discrimination and victimisation on the basis of their 'racial', ethnic or religious identity. Rights to freedom of expression have only been curtailed where there is a direct association with criminal action – as in the case of provisions against racially and religiously aggravated offences – or where there is a close association between words uttered and a threat to public order – as in the case of incitement to racial and religious hatred. Examining Labour's legislative programme through a sociological lens arguably reveals that by establishing such a careful balance in the conflict over rights the legislation has reinforced and promoted dominant norms about a fundamental freedom – the right to freedom of expression – and also norms about personal conduct in civil society as the law expresses social opprobrium against the perpetrators of racist hate and the acts they commit. In the case of the latter, expectations about the symbolic force of legislation have been evident in commentary on the legislation against hate crime and hate speech. At the beginning of Labour's legislative programme, in responding to the Home Office's consultation exercise on the provisions against racially aggravated offences, the Association of Chief Police Officers declared that:

> The legislative changes will do much to reinforce the seriousness with which the vast majority of members of our society view crime and

conduct motivated by racial hatred. It will send out important messages to perpetrators and victims alike, that racist violence and harassment will not be tolerated and that positive action will be taken where this is exhibited.

(Iganski, 1999: 389)

Such a sentiment has been expressed repeatedly in commentary and debates on Labour's legislative programme against racist hate.

Notes

1 The prevalence and characteristics of Holocaust denial in Western Europe and the USA have been well documented (see Seidel, 1986; Lipstadt, 1994; Shermer and Grobman, 2000). Before the defeat of the Third Reich, denials of atrocities committed were heard well before the genocide had reached its full conclusion. Some Nazi sympathisers outside Germany dismissed claims of atrocities as 'mostly Jew invention' (Aronsfeld, 1979). In the years immediately following the Second World War, in the early 1950s, neo-Nazis in Germany claimed that 'the fairy tale of the six million' had been invented by the Allies to divert attention away from the atrocities they had committed. The view was also propagated that the atrocities against Jews were carried out secretly by fanatics – in one variant of this claim, under special orders from Himmler – 'behind the back of the German people, German soldiers, even behind the back of the National Socialists and the hundreds of thousands of SS men fighting on all fronts' (Aronsfeld, 1979). Hitler, it was claimed, was unaware of their activities. Doubts were cast on the number of Jews murdered. It was even claimed that Zionists – who had allegedly infiltrated the German authorities – were involved in orchestrating the genocide. Variants of all these claims persist within Holocaust denial material today. In the late 1960s and in the 1970s a number of publications were distributed that have since become seminal works of Holocaust denial. Today, a number of them can be read on the Internet by following links from the websites of extreme right groups. The material published during this period is characterised by a pseudo-scholarly guise in their presentation and referencing of sources. But they are also characterised by distortion and falsification of the sources used. In his publication *Die Auschwitz Luge* (1973), Thies Christophersen claimed that Auschwitz was just a gigantic armanents factory. Richard Harwood, in his publication *Did Six Million Really Die?*, claimed that the 'myth' 'that no less than six million Jews were exterminated' was designed to 'arouse sympathy' for the state of Israel and to extract financial reparation from Germany. Harwood drew extensively from an earlier booklet, *The Myth of the Six Million*, published anonymously in the United States in 1969. The pseudo-scholarly guise of Holocaust deniers is epitomised by the Institute for Historical Review – established in the United States in the late 1970s – and its journal, the *Journal of Historical Review*, which have provided the core of the more contemporary Holocaust denial movement (Stern, 1995). The 'Institute' believes that dissemination of its material is protected under the First Amendment to the United States Constitution, and by article 19 of the International Covenant on Civil and Political Rights.

2 Early day motion no. 99, 'David Irving and Holocaust denial', House of Commons, 20 June 1989, Session 1988–9.

3 In outlawing 'incitement to racial hatred' in the UK the Public Order Act 1986 makes it an offence for a person to publish or distribute 'written matter which is threatening, abusive or insulting' or use 'in any public place or at any public

meeting words which are threatening, abusive or insulting' with an intent to stir up racial hatred or, alternatively, 'in a case where having regard to all the circumstances, hatred is likely to be stirred up against any racial group in Great Britain by the matter or the words in question' (Public Order Act 1986, Part III, Section 18).

4 UK House of Commons 1997, Standing Committee C, Holocaust Denial Bill, col. 22.

5 UK 1975, Cmnd 6234, *Racial Discrimination*, para. 125.

6 UK Home Office, Scottish Office 1985, Cmnd 9510, *Review of Public Order Law*, London: HMSO.

7 UK House of Commons 1997, Standing Committee C, Holocaust Denial Bill, cols 8–9.

8 David Irving, Introduction to the Leuchter Report (www.fpp.co.uk/Auschwitz/Leuchter/ReportIntro.html), accessed 5 December 2005. The full section from which this quote has been drawn reads: 'Nobody likes to be swindled, still less where considerable sums of money are involved. (Since 1949 the State of Israel has received over 90 billion Deutschmarks in voluntary reparations from West Germany, essentially in atonement for the "gas chambers of Auschwitz".) And this myth will not die easily: Too many hundreds of millions of honest, intelligent people have been duped by the well-financed and brilliantly successful post-war publicity campaign which followed on from the original ingenious plan of the British Psychological Warfare Executive (PWE) in 1942 to spread to the propaganda story that the Germans were using "gas chambers" to kill millions of Jews and other "undesirables". As late as August 1943 the head of the PWE minuted the Cabinet secretly that despite the stories they were putting out, there was not the slightest evidence that such contraptions existed, and he continued with a warning that stories from Jewish sources in this connection were particularly suspect.'

9 Mick Hume in the online magazine *Spiked* 19 July 2005 argued: 'every government minister or official spokesman has emphasised their commitment to defend "tolerance" – which, in the Newspeak of New Labour, means that they will not tolerate anything that they deem to be intolerant of Islam or Muslims.'

10 Rowan Atkinson speaks to the Lords, 25 January 2005 (www.secularism.org.uk/31964.html), accessed 5 December 2005.

11 In evidence to the House of Commons Home Affairs Committee, Session 2004–5, the Director of Public Prosecutions stated: 'I think the main issue around that is managing expectations. . . . One of the dangers around incitement to religious hatred is that communities – and indeed representatives of the Muslim communities have said this to me – believe somehow this is going to protect them from people being offensive or rude about Islam. It is not going to do that. You are perfectly free to be offensive or rude about any religion, there is no law against it. The danger is that if people think it is going to protect them from that and it does not feel very let down by us, by the police, by the Government and by everybody else, and we get accused of being racist or incompetent, or a combination of the two, when in fact we are just applying the law. So it is very important that people understand what that offence will achieve: it will stop the grossest sort of conduct, but it is not going to stop people being rude about Islam.' See also the memorandum submitted by the National Secular Society (House of Commons Home Affairs Committee, Session 2004–5, House of Commons Paper No. 165, Memorandum 29).

A foundation for rights or theories of practice?

Lydia Morris

We opened this collection with a reference to Turner's argument that sociology as a discipline has maintained a sceptical distance from the issue of rights because of the absence of any clear ontological grounding. Though a number of the chapters in this volume have found his suggestion of human frailty and social precariousness to be an interesting vehicle for thinking about rights, and especially universal human rights, it has also proved useful to side-step the question of theoretical foundations and ask instead what sociology as a discipline can more readily bring to this topic. In fact, a tendency in much of the relevant literature has been to press the case of particularities not readily embraced by existing conceptions of the universal, while some of the chapters in this volume have seen the functioning of rights as a possible basis for inequality (both intended and unintended). Other chapters have referred to a postmodern critique of the cultural and political ideals of modernity, challenging the certainty of its truth claims, its idea of progress and its Western ethnocentricity (see Chapters 1, 9 and 10). Nevertheless, the appeal of some form of universalism has been difficult to resist, as we see in the growing interest and support for the notion of universal human rights, which seems to offer a possible basis for cohesion in the face of fragmentation, diversity and loss of collective value frames. Thus Zerilli (2004) speaks of the 'homecoming narrative' of the 'new universal', and Benhabib (1992) has argued that one legacy of modernity worth rehabilitating is moral and political universalism, based on equal respect for all persons. She, like Donnelly (2003), argues that the project of modernity itself – through war, environmental destruction, economic exploitation – accounts for the very need to embrace such an ideal (cf. Chapter 1).

The appeal of human rights lies in its potential as a set of principles grounded in common humanity that is both apolitical and universally applicable. As we have seen, however, such a position has in the past been open to the political charge that it is neither neutral nor universal but disguised particularism, based on a Western, masculine world view and the assumptions of liberal individualism (see Chapters 1, 5 and 9). The ideal of universal human rights has also been subject to the philosophical charge that it is not clearly grounded in a universal ontology and hence can provide no convincing account of its origins or justification for its claims. This leaves sociology as a discipline caught between a search for foundations through the abstractions of moral philosophy and political theory, or an acceptance of the tautology of legal positivism, in which rights are simply the entitlements recognised in law (Dworkin, 1978). Neither option sits easily within the traditional terrain of sociology and this raises the question of whether the discipline has anything at all to offer in this field.

The search for foundations

We have seen how Turner (1993) has attempted to solve the problem of foundations through the sociology of the body, and this approach certainly has its strengths, not least in identifying a common feature of humanity that is applicable across cultures. A particular appeal of Turner's position is that it offers not just an ontological foundation for claims to rights, but also a plausible account of why they generate support, by evoking human sympathy. There is, however, a question about the precise status of his argument, and this has been outlined by Waters (1996), who sets out two possibilities. The argument seems to present either a basis for claims to rights, in which case some explanation of which claims succeed and which do not would seem necessary; or a theory of the origins of existing rights, in which case an empirical account of their emergence would also be required. In fact, Turner (1997) rejects both positions, stating that his intention is instead to provide a normative basis for the evaluation of human rights abuse.

This position does not in itself escape uncertainty, and at the very least requires some definition of frailty, for as Turner concedes, disabilities of various kinds have in the past been the basis for exclusion from the moral/political community (see Chapter 11). Where the boundary of inclusion/exclusion will be drawn is by no means self-evident, and as Wilson (1997: 6) has argued, we cannot even suppose that all cultures have a conception of the 'human', or base their own legal systems on a notion of the individual, autonomous subject. In fact, any attempt to ground the universal in a foundational ontology will become particular once the substance of that ontology requires specification. Turner's solution also seems to offer an oddly passive foundation for claims to rights, and in this it strikes a contrast with Donnelly's (2003) argument that human rights find their philosophical justification in the moral agency that is distinctive to human existence. While Turner might wish to argue that his theory embraces this point, for without the body there can be no agency, Donnelly's emphasis on active responsible personhood and the realisation of human potential offers a view of human rights as constitutive rather than regulative, and a fuller and more plausible vision of what it is that human rights are intended to protect or promote.

Social and political theory has meanwhile begun to shy away from the question of definition and foundations, and Habermas's theory of communicative ethics has inspired a more discursive approach to universal rights, as in Benhabib's (1992) interactive universalism and Lister's (2003) notion of differentiated universalism. The emphasis here is on process and procedure, giving everyone an equal voice and embracing the obligation to listen and to seek mutual understanding. This also chimes well with Donnelly's emphasis on moral agency, though the impediments to achieving such an outcome have also received attention (Chambers, 1996; Norval, 2004). A more radical position is taken by Laclau (1996), through his conception of the universal as an empty signifier, a constantly contested space. Since the demands of the particular can only be made in terms of principles that are universally shared, this means the universal must be constantly negotiated and renegotiated. Once given substance, it will always be particular and its content historically contingent, an open series of demands, in the face of which 'philosophy comes to an end and the realm of politics begins' (ibid.: 123).

We might also argue that where philosophy ends, sociology begins, and some of the chapters in this volume have demonstrated the way in which the content of the universal, and the categories to which it applies, have been negotiated over time (see Chapters 8 and 11). That would certainly be the argument of the social constructionist position advocated by Waters (1996), which sees the content of rights as historical configurations of interest with their related value commitments. Thus, 'human rights is an institution that is specific to cultural and historical context just like any other . . . its very universality is itself a human construction' (ibid.: 593). Is it the case, then, that sociology must necessarily, as Turner claims, absent itself from moral debate? Waters's interest in part lies in the relationship between claims and norms; or between rights 'talk' as a means of unlocking social closure, and the eventual institutionalisation of some claims. This latter stage is in part explained by the advantages offered in terms of consolidating political support (cf. Giddens, 1985; Mann, 1987), but is often arrived at through the construction of a moral case and the gradual accretion of public recognition and support (see Chapters 5, 6 and 8).

It is easy to see why Wilson (1997: 14) has argued that we should set philosophical deliberation to the side, 'and proceed with our contingent and historical investigations'. The moral issues at play do not stand apart from the fray but, as Waters argues, are deeply implicated in the construction and endorsement of human rights. Claims-making may involve a claim for recognition, resources and even power, but will also contain a moral claim that must convince in terms of the 'universalisation of human interest', albeit in the context of existing social institutions and the machinery of power. The question for sociology is not so much how we evaluate the moral worth of the claim, but what are the means whereby a claim moves from the initial engagement with a rights issue, through the process of garnering support, to formal recognition and finally institutionalisation. It may be the claim to belong to the relevant moral community, as Turner might put it, that is at issue, as much as the substance of the right *per se*, and historical accounts show surprising shifts in the boundaries of belonging (see Chapters 8 and 11).

The practice of rights

In keeping with this view, Donnelly (2003) sees human rights as emergent and processual, rather than firmly grounded in philosophical foundations. Such foundations can be firm, he argues, only because we have agreed to treat them as such, citing the fact that societies have denied 'the moral centrality, even the existence, of our common humanity' (ibid.: 19). Thus, 'foundational arguments reflect contingent and contentious agreements to cut off certain kinds of questions' (ibid.: 20). He goes on to argue that foundational positions provide us with (only) the reassurance of internal consistency, rather than external validation. The picture is therefore one of emergent consensus through argument and persuasion, rather than of clear incontrovertible foundations, a conclusion that echoes Durkheim's view of social facts as things, with rights not inherent in persons but bestowed on them by society. This therefore places considerable significance on the study of the social arrangements surrounding rights, the way in which they function in relation to social structures and institutions, the way that rights are accrued in particular areas by particular social groups and the contexts in which they are implemented and given meaning.

This point was touched on in the introduction, with reference to Lukes's (1991) observation that, although there is some difficulty in establishing a firm foundation for human rights, there is clear evidence of broad agreement in the way the idea is applied in practice. Donnelly (2003) too makes the point that there is remarkable international normative consensus, and expands on the nature of human rights as rights 'of the highest order'. However, he also notes that the objects of many rights can be claimed as 'ordinary' legal rights in most national systems, and that human rights claims often seek to establish lower-level rights. Indeed, the conventional rights of citizenship, as, for example, outlined by Marshall, are an instance of the delivery of civil, political and social rights at national level, though Marshall's work and the rights themselves predate the two principle treaties associated with the Universal Declaration. The holders of rights will typically use the lowest level of entitlement available, unless denied, in which case there may be an appeal to a higher order of rights. As we have seen, Dworkin (1978) makes a related distinction between 'background' rights and 'institutional' rights, and between principles and policy.

This book, however, has been about the practice of rights rather more than the theory of foundations, and we should not overlook Lukes's point that not all human rights are fully recognised in practice and that few are absolute. Our title refers to 'rights' rather than 'human rights', in recognition of these issues, and one point of interest raised in Chapter 4 has been the way in which access to rights can constitute a form of stratification, with even established human rights containing their own hierarchy of absolute, limited and qualified rights. Does this mean that – despite claims to the contrary – the present work remains trapped in a position of legal positivism, whereby rights are defined purely and simply by the letter of the law? There are a number of ways in which the contents of this volume depart from such a view, so Chapter 6, for example, shows how the recognition of certain norms in transnational law (e.g. European Union anti-discrimination law) does not easily translate into coherent policy and practice. Other chapters have focused on the struggle that some groups have waged in order to establish their claims or elevate them to the level of recognised 'human rights' (see Chapters 5 and 8).

The possibility of movement is a central issue for rights theorists (e.g. Dworkin, 1978; Donnelly, 2003) and inevitably renders a static positivistic view of rights inadequate. Donnelly sees the practice of rights as involving three types of social interaction: the assertion of the right, active respect by the duty holder and objective enjoyment of the right. If we think about the *establishment* of a right, then this series could be adapted and augmented to yield the following sequence: the assertion of a claim, the accumulation of moral credibility and support, recognition of the claim and finally its institutionalisation. In this sense, social action is at the root of human rights; as Donnelly (2003: 16) puts it, 'a moral posit rather than a fact of nature', which carries with it an accompanying social project 'to make real the world that they envision' (ibid.: 21; cf. Chapters 6 and 8). Dworkin (1978) is also interested in the question of movement and recognises that we think in terms of the law changing and evolving, such that some of the standards to which judges and lawyers appeal cannot be captured in terms of basic rules or a fundamental test.

We have already noted that a key issue for Dworkin is the application of law in the light of 'background principles', and the quest for absolute foundations may therefore be at the cost of exploring process and negotiation, and the huge significance that attaches to interpretation of the law. There are hints of this position in Derrida's (1992) distinction between justice and the law. Both arguments open up channels for the representation of particularist meaning according to specific circumstances or with reference to specific social groups. For Wilson (1997), the opposition of universalism and relativism is too polarising: while universalism makes comparison possible, relativism grants precedence to immediate context and encourages sensitivity to diversity, and both are of value. As an anthropologist, he places particular emphasis on the way that rights are used: 'how rights-based normative discourses are produced, translated and materialised in a variety of contexts' (ibid.: 13). The substantive interpretation that people give to the language of rights then becomes central, and this can also play an important part in a sociological treatment of rights, stressing dynamism, practice and meaning. But we have also seen how contextual issues apply in another sense, and that is in relation to the broader social structures that provide the framework for social life, be they economic, political, institutional, cultural, familial, etc.

Classical themes

Sociology has something to offer on each of these analytical levels, as we discover from the material reviewed in the introduction, and from the structuring of the chapters that followed. In what remains of this conclusion, I first identify the key themes and issues that emerged from the introduction and the way in which they have been engaged or advanced by the various chapters, before briefly reviewing the four different parts, or approaches, into which the contributions to the volume have been grouped. As we saw, a consideration of classical works yielded several contrasting but not necessarily mutually exclusive perspectives on the issue of rights, from which a number of substantive themes emerge. My focus now is less on these perspectives *per se*, but more on their scope for application to the study of rights, especially as taken up in the various contributions to this volume.

We have seen that Durkheim was principally interested in the bases of social cohesion, especially under conditions of fragmentation and anomie. Although an adherent of moral individualism, he also stressed the role of beliefs in providing a foundation both for identity and for a communal bond between members of society. He offered a view of rights as social facts, in the gift of society but representing a recognition and sanctification of human potential. This potential he thought best realised through the freedoms and protections of liberalism, but in the context of a communion with others. Chapter 1 takes up these issues to argue that no fully human life is possible without some connection with the life of society and the meaning that this provides, and here we have a view of the individual situated within a system of beliefs and values that gives meaning to their social relations and interactions. For Benton, a reasonable expectation of a system of rights is that it should acknowledge and enable this interconnectedness. Similar ideas are explored in Chapter 7, through a view of rights as rooted in society, its values and institutions, while ideas about the meaning of commonality and the way in which it might structure our thinking about rights are also present in Chapters 2 and 3, which respectively consider pensions rights and the right to care as being variously embedded in the pattern of both familial and societal responsibilities across the generations.

The introduction shows how Weber, like Durkheim, was interested in the disenchantment of modern life, which he argued to result from an unremitting drive towards rationality. This process was, in part, built on the efficient administration of state and society through the elaboration of law and bureaucracy, yielding a set of rationally objective rules and procedures for governing and regulating individuals. For Weber, this is the context in which a regime of rights must operate, and he gives us a key to understanding how such a system may also be bound up with the struggle for power and resources, shaped by techniques of social closure. These struggles are manifest in what Lockwood (1996) terms a system of civic stratification, illustrated in Chapter 4 through a discussion of welfare, immigration and asylum, while Chapter 5 shows how women's claim to full human rights was built explicitly on a claim to equal status, which was also in part a claim for resources. This approach is also apparent, though less central, in the account of the struggle for gay rights in Chapter 8 and the discussion of indigenous rights in Chapter 9, both of which document struggles for status and recognition. Chapter 6 discusses the importance of advocacy coalitions in the pursuit of rights, but shows how this may also involve a collision or compromise over strategy and competition over resources.

In Marx's work we have a view of rights as functioning in service to the economic system and the ruling powers of capitalism, and a critique of any conception of rights based on self-sufficient and egoistic individuals, whose social existence is premised on personal autonomy and the right to property, without regard for other social bonds. However, Chapter 1 offers an account of Marx's position that differs from some of his critics, noting in particular that civil and political rights could be the basis for actions that challenge the status quo, in the name of human emancipation. The argument opens up further debate about the possible future of rights once such liberation has been achieved, and this Benton believes must be rooted in social belonging, embodiment and environmental integrity. Such a 'systems' based approach to rights is also present in different ways in Chapter 2, which considers pension rights in the context not only of intergenerational justice, but also the tension between public and private schemes, and the different questions of responsibility and liability each raises. Chapter 3 adopts a related approach in considering the culturally variable patterns of exchange, reciprocity and obligation that underpin different systems of care.

I include in this section on classical themes the work of T. H. Marshall (1950), as the first sociologist to place the issue of rights at the centre of analysis. His essay on citizenship and social class is informed by some of the ideas discussed above, and indeed places the tension between citizenship and capitalism at its core. The work is also a recognition of the significance of status in modern capitalist society, and considers rights as a possible source of social cohesion and integration, while also being a potential source of inequality. A number of chapters in this collection take Marshall's work as a starting point for their own discussion. Chapter 4 sees in Marshall a development of the Weberian tradition through a status based approach to rights, which considers both formal standing and informal prestige factors in the struggle for recognition and resources. Chapter 8 also considers the way in which a Marshallian model of citizenship has underpinned some of the claims of the gay and lesbian movement, while Chapter 11 uses Marshall's analysis to consider the linkages between mental disorder and human rights, making the point that his argument is more complex than critics have recognised, especially his recognition of rights as a terrain of struggle.

Particularism versus universalism

Struggle and movement have been at the centre of much critical comment on Marshall, and this is the area from which the more recent work on the dynamic nature of rights has emerged. The most trenchant criticisms hinge on the universalist/particularist opposition and stem from an argument that the rights guaranteed by citizenship, and even more so by universal human rights, elevate a particularist model of social life to the level of the universal. This argument has been adopted in relation to the exclusion of a variety of specific groups from entitlement to the full range of rights, and each in its turn has fuelled a related social movement for establishing a claim to the rights at issue. Many of these critiques are expressed as critiques of Marshallian citizenship, and while some may envisage universal human rights as a solution, often the same criticisms will also have a salience at that level.

For example, the feminist critique of Marshall (e.g. Phillips, 1992; Lister, 1997) notes his neglect of the gendered assumptions structuring citizenship. As a status of the public sphere, citizenship is argued to ignore the public/private divisions that inform the concept of rights, and that systematically disadvantage women. Feminism has therefore entailed a claim to sameness (that is, to be treated as equal to men) and a claim to be different (that is, to have their particularity recognised and accommodated). These arguments, and some of their attendant difficulties, are addressed in Chapter 5, which documents the struggle of the women's movement for full recognition on the international stage, demonstrating the way in which dilemmas generated at the level of citizenship may be writ large at the level of human rights. The feminist movement itself, however, has generated its own particularities, as Elson makes clear, and has led to the charge that the concerns of black and 'Third World' women have been submerged in the agendas of 'First World' feminism. Arguments such as these have fuelled the deconstructive strand of feminism (Nash, 2002), which seeks to challenge all classification and categorisation that tends to essentialism.

We noted in the introduction that the feminist critique of 'false universals' is closely associated with an interest in the embodiment of rights, which emphasises the lived experience of difference, and hence applies not only to gender difference but to sexuality, race, ethnicity, disability and age. Each of these sources of difference can lead to demands that are perhaps best seen in terms of claims for particularist inclusions, or Lister's differentiated universalism, which seeks an incorporation of these varied perspectives in the granting and delivery of rights. Chapter 8 provides an example by means of a narrative of the gay rights movement, revealing the sameness/difference dilemma in another guise. Part of the movement may seek the right to be the same as the heterosexual population: to marry, found families and claim the recognition and entitlements that accompany this. Others seek the right to be different: to establish a way of living that does not approximate to the recognised patterns of conventional intimate life, a claim that is closely associated with 'queer theory'. In Chapter 6 we see how the sameness/difference dilemma arises again in the context of anti-racism, and in Chapter 12 we find a discussion of the clash between a universal right to free expression and particular needs for protection.

Some particularist positions have criticised the neglect of cultural rights in Marshallian notions of citizenship, and also at the level of universal human rights more generally. Their arguments are rooted in a communitarian critique of liberalism, apparent in Chapter 1, and also informing the arguments of Chapter 7. The former, as we have seen, challenges the construction of rights around a model of the isolated and autonomous individual, conceived as unencumbered and unsupported by intimate social relations. The latter attempts an interpretation of moral dilemmas in their social and cultural context, to illustrate the socially embedded nature of rights and consider the alternative expressions of morality within which they may operate. Chapter 9 considers the case of indigenous rights, to illustrate the ethnocentric assumptions of universalist frameworks of rights that deny the legitimacy of indigenous systems and offer compensation in the context of a citizenship and sovereignty they do not recognise.

An associated criticism of Marshallian citizenship challenges the taken-for-granted status of the nation state in his conception of rights; his failure to deal with national boundary drawing and the position of non-citizens. Chapter 4 considers this issue, weighing the arguments that see citizenship as a form of social closure against the view that national citizenship has been superseded by universal personhood. The chapter seeks a path between the two positions by using the notion of civic stratification to illustrate the way in which rights can be a means of constructing inequalities. The debate is, however, indicative of a more general tendency to look to the development of transnational institutions for the assertion and protection of rights, as discussed in Chapters 5 and 6. In particular, there has been a tendency to expand Marshallian conceptions of national citizenship to embrace the universal (e.g. Parry, 1991; Soysal, 1994; Meyer *et al.*, 1997), though this position is also open to criticism, by virtue of the limited purchase of many human rights guarantees, and the danger of continuing the evolutionary mind-set for which Marshall has been (somewhat unfairly) criticised.

There is one other treatment of particularism considered in this volume and noted in the introduction, which has classically drawn on Foucauldian discourse analysis of the construction and management of marginal groups such as prisoners, the mad and homosexuals. Foucault's work provides a conception of disciplinary discourse and regimes of power that might appear as the converse of rights, but that can often function through their administration and implementation (Woodiwiss, 2005). He also emphasises the force of subjugated knowledges, awakened by the application of disciplinary discourses to challenge the power and authority they embody. This work is drawn on by Chapter 11, which discusses the tradition of denying rights to those held in detention for mental disorder, before documenting the process that led to a change in this tradition, in part through changed conceptions of 'madness'. Chapter 10 similarly considers the denial of prisoners' rights, but moves on to engage with a 'justice of alterity', which asserts the rights of those for whom there is no empathy, and to document the slow but significant recognition of prisoners' claims to human rights.

In many cases, the particularist positions reported in this volume seem to stake a claim for recognition in terms of equal status and worth, but not necessarily in terms of the conventions of established rights. We are thus faced with the question of how to respond to scepticism about claims to universalism, and whether proliferation of diversity and increasing fragmentation is the inevitable outcome. As we noted above, the implementation of rights and adjudication of claims will almost always involve an element of interpretation, and a central issue here is the use of 'rights talk': the way in which a particularist claim is expressed, perhaps in a manner translatable into universalist guarantees, albeit in revised form. These claims often provide the momentum that fuels changes in the law and in conceptions of rights, as referred to in earlier discussion. We have already noted another element of interpretation that could be brought into play in the assertion and understanding of rights: that of the broader context of structures, values and relationships in which people live their lives. A truly enabling system of rights would build these considerations into its design and implementation, and sociological analysis can help to provide the background understanding that might make this possible.

Sociological approaches to the study of rights

In identifying the sociological contribution to an understanding of rights, we need to distinguish between the substantive issues addressed and the available analytical approaches that could in theory apply to any or all. The previous sections considered the themes and issues emerging from existing literature, but we can go a little further in attempting to identify and clarify distinctive approaches to the sociological study of rights. I have therefore separated a review of the substantive issues (as detailed above) from a brief review of approaches, distinguishing the latter by the four rough headings into which the contributions to this volume have been sorted. These are: political economy; status, norms and institutions; meaning and interpretation; and finally the clash of rights. It should be obvious from the discussion of the contributions so far that very few are confined to one approach only and the division into categories of this kind is in some sense artificial. However, for the purpose of clarifying quite what it is that sociology as a discipline brings to the study and understanding of rights, I hope it proves a worthwhile exercise.

The first grouping of chapters, under the political economy heading, have in common a holistic approach to social relations and institutions, which places them in the context of wider economic and political arrangements. Rights are then viewed as one aspect of these arrangements, a feature of the model of social relations that underpins a given political and economic regime. So, for example, rights will be shaped by conceptions of the appropriate means for the distribution of resources in society, which is in turn a feature of the principles shaping the dominant economic system. The chapters in this grouping thus draw upon a Marxist analysis of the social relations of capitalism, and on Durkheimian conceptions of social cohesion. Both analyses provide the context for the critique in Chapter 1 of the liberal tradition of rights, and the argument for an approach to rights that replaces liberal individualism with an acknowledgement of the multiple harms that threaten individuals and their environments, of the unequal command of resources affecting access to rights and of the personal and community bonds that make life meaningful. Chapter 2 similarly addresses the question of community bonds through the nature and degree of cross-generational responsibility for the elderly. The range of possible options is placed in the context of political decisions about taxation, investment, profit and the location of responsibility, be it individual, familial or societal. Chapter 3 extends these considerations to the question of the right to care, which is placed in comparative context as part of a web of culturally variable relationships, such that the right to and need for care is revealed as a socio-historical construction. We then see how the varied systems of provisioning that emerge generate their own correlative rights, which are not necessarily formally enshrined.

The second grouping of chapters, under the heading of status, norms and institutions, is concerned with the establishment and functioning of rights in their institutional setting. It shows, for example, how status can operate in two ways with respect to the establishment and implementation of normative standards – through the formal statuses that determine entitlement to rights, and through the informal prestige factors that shape access to rights, resources and recognition. The perspective is clearly influenced by Weberian conceptions of the status order, and the Marshallian model of citizenship, both of which figure in Lockwood's (1996) notion of civic stratification. Chapter 4 applies these ideas both to an analysis of the underclass debate, especially in relation to the British welfare system, in which informal deficit is particularly apparent, and to a consideration of immigration and asylum, in which formal status differences are a major factor enabling systems of 'managed migration'. Chapter 5 argues that the assertion 'women's rights are human rights' is a claim to equal status, and shows how even within the UN this has entailed a struggle for recognition and resources. The treatment of the Convention for the Elimination of Discrimination against Women as a secondary convention is one mark of the civic deficit confronting women, which is in turn tied to their association with the private sphere and the lesser status this attracts. Chapter 6, on EU anti-discrimination law, discusses the factors that helped to establish EU anti-discrimination law, particularly the role of advocacy coalitions and the achievement of 'fit' with other EU priorities. Though the norms represented by this law can still be mediated by different national interests, and agreement on strategy and resources will require a degree of compromise, the very assertion of this supranational principle is itself deemed significant.

The third grouping of chapters, under the heading of meaning, interpretation and rights, stresses the role of meaning in relation to both the practice of rights and claims-making, and is the approach best placed to provide an understanding of a variety of particularities in relation to rights. Meaning may function in the sense of the values and assumptions that inform and structure social relations, the discourses lying behind the classification and treatment of specific social groups, or in the sense of distinctive cultural traditions, beliefs and institutions. This part contains examples of each. Chapter 7 explores the normative rules and sanctions at play in three different case studies with different rights at issue – the sexual freedom of gay men in Britain, the Indian tradition of sati and the choices of Thai sex workers – to reveal the embedded nature of 'rights'. Through these cases, the assumptions of the liberal rights tradition are tested against the extent to which they are valued in different contexts and relevant to the individual agents concerned. Chapter 8 looks at the constructions that have been placed on homosexuals in the past, and the shifts in meaning, perceptions and identities that lie behind their claims to rights and recognition in contemporary society. Chapter 9 looks at meaning in the context of indigenous belief systems and their contestation of the world view of the colonising powers. Denial of the validity of these 'meanings' has meant that indigenous peoples are driven to claim their rights through an engagement with a system of rules that are culturally alien and that in fact deny established rights in the context of their own beliefs.

Finally, the last grouping provides less an approach than a common problem, that of the clash of rights, and for two of the chapters this is explored in the context of what has been termed 'alterity': the construction of particular groups for whom the denial of rights has been deemed acceptable. Such a denial raises questions of on what terms and under which authority it could be permissible, while the third case, on combating hate crimes, considers how to weigh the freedoms forfeited against the harms inflicted. Chapter 10 takes the case of prisoners' rights, or, rather, their restrictions. Among other points explored by the chapter is the limitation of an individualised approach to rights, which fails to address the social roots of criminality and thus disguises the degree of collective responsibility a society might owe its criminal population. Similar issues arise in Chapter 11, which discusses the treatment of mental disorder. As well as charting the historical construction of 'madness', the chapter shows how rights issues are implicated both in the withholding of civil and political rights in early treatments and, more recently, through instances of inadequate provision, which can prompt a recurrence or worsening of the original condition. Chapter 12 discusses both racially aggravated crime and a variety of forms of hate speech, highlighting the potential symbolic role of the law in (ideally) protecting freedoms and asserting appropriate values. The associated dilemmas extend beyond the universalist/particularist opposition weighing free speech against the need for protection, and raise difficult questions about equal treatment before the law, and the possibility of identifying 'extra harms' imposed by the sentiment underpinning a crime.

Though the question of a clear theoretical foundation for rights may remain unanswered, each of these approaches or orientations helps to advance contemporary understanding and analysis of rights. The four parts of the book respectively address context and structure, operation and implementation, meaning and experience and, finally, conflict and alterity. Together the contributions to this volume draw attention to different aspects of the social construction of rights, from the political and economic system, through the institutionalisation of prestige and resources, to the dynamic claims for recognition, and the question of when rights can be legitimately denied. It is the multifaceted nature of rights: as tools of governance, as expressions of moral responsibility, as elements in a status ranking, as components of belief systems, as elements of an economic system and as claims in a political engagement that makes the terrain so intellectually fascinating and challenging, especially from the standpoint of sociology. I hope something of this has been conveyed by the work contained in our collection.

Bibliography

Adam, B., Duyvendak, J. W. and Krouwel, A. (eds) (1998) *The Global Emergence of Gay and Lesbian Politics*. Phildelphia: Temple University Press.

Adams, D. W. (1995) *Education for Extinction: American Indians and the Boarding School Experience, 1875–1928*. Lawrence: University Press of Kansas.

Adelmann, L. and Moorshead, P. (1995) Bad laws make hard cases: hate crime laws and the Supreme Court's opinion in Wisconsin v. Mitchell. *Gonzaga Law Review*, 30: 1–27.

Albrow, M. (1996) *The Global Age*. Cambridge: Polity Press.

Alfred, T. (1999) *Peace, Power, Righteousness: An Indigenous Manifesto*. Don Mills, Ontario: Oxford University Press.

Alink, F., Boin, A. *et al.* (2001) Institutional crises and reforms in policy sectors: the case of asylum policy in Europe. *Journal of European Public Policy*, 8: 286–306.

Altman, D. (1997) Global gays/global gaze. *Gay and Lesbian Quarterly*, 3: 417–36.

Altman, D. (2001) *Global Sex*. Chicago: University of Chicago Press.

American Psychiatric Association (1994) *Diagnostic and Statistical Manual of Mental Disorders*, 4th edn. Washington, DC: American Psychiatric Association.

Anaya, S. J. (1996) *Indigenous Peoples in International Law*. New York: Oxford University Press.

Anthias, F. and Yuval-Davis, N. (1992) *Racialised Boundaries*. London: Routledge.

Aoyama, K. (2005) Becoming someone else: Thai sex workers from modernization to globalization. PhD thesis, University of Essex.

Arendt, H. (1973) *The Origins of Totalitarianism*. New York: Harcourt and Brace.

Ariès, P. (1979) *Centuries of Childhood*. Harmondsworth: Penguin Books.

Aronsfeld, C. C. (1979) *After the Murders – the Lies. Denials of the Holocaust*. London: Institute for Jewish Affairs.

Assembly of First Nations (1994) *Breaking the Silence: An Interpretive Study of Residential School Impact and Healing as Illustrated by the Stories of First Nation Individuals*. Ottawa: Assembly of First Nations.

Assies, W. (1998) Indigenous peoples and reform of the state in Latin America. In W. Assies, G. van der Haar and A. Hoekema (eds), *The Challenge of Diversity: Indigenous Peoples and Reform of the State in Latin America*. Amsterdam: Thela Thesis.

Atkinson, P. and Housley, W. (2003) *Interactionism: An Essay in Sociological Amnesia*. London: Sage.

Australian Bureau of Statistics (2002) *Australian Social Trends 2002. Health – Mortality and Morbidity: Mortality of Aboriginal and Torres Strait Islander Peoples.* Canberra: AGPS.

Aye Maung, C. and Mirrlees-Black, C. (1994) *Racially Motivated Crime: A British Crime Survey Analysis.* London: Home Office.

Badiou, A. (2002) *Ethics: An Essay on the Understanding of Evil.* London: Verso.

Baird, V. (2001) *No Nonsense Guide to Sexual Diversity.* London: New Internationalist.

Baird, V. (2004) *Sex, Love and Homophobia.* London: Amnesty International.

Baker, D. and Wiesbrot, M. (2000) *Social Security.* Chicago: University of Chicago Press.

Bal, P. (1996) Discourse ethics and human rights in criminal procedure. In M. Deflem (ed.), *Habermas, Modernity and the Law.* London: Sage.

Bane, M. J. (1988) Politics and policies of the feminization of poverty. In M. Weir, A. S. Orloff and T. Skocpol (eds), *The Politics of Social Policy in the United States.* Princeton, NJ: Princeton University Press.

Barbalet, J. M. (1988) *Citizenship.* Milton Keynes: Open University Press.

Barry, B. (1989) *A Treatise on Social Justice. Volume 1, Theories of Justice.* Oxford: Oxford University Press.

Barton, R. (1959) *Institutional Neurosis.* Bristol: John Wright.

Bauman, Z. (1993) *Postmodern Ethics.* Cambridge: Polity Press.

Bauman, Z. (1995) *Life in Fragments: Towards a Postmodern Morality.* Oxford: Blackwell.

Baxi, U. (2002) *The Future of Human Rights.* New Delhi: Oxford University Press.

Bechhofer, F. (1996) Comment on Lockwood. *British Journal of Sociology*, 47: 551–5.

Beck, U. (1992) *Risk Society: Towards a New Modernity.* London: Sage.

Beck, U. and Beck-Gernsheim, E. (2002) *Individualisation: Institutionalized Individualism and Its Social and Political Consequences.* London: Sage.

Beger, Nico J. (2004) *Tensions in the Struggle for Sexual Minority Rights in Europe: Que(e)rying Political Practices.* Manchester: Manchester University Press.

Beiner, R. (ed.) (1995) *Theorising Citizenship.* Albany: State University of New York Press.

Beitchman, J. H., Zucker, K. J., Hood, J. E., Dacosta, G. A., Ackman, D. and Cassavia, E. (1992) A review of the long-term effects of child sexual abuse. *Child Abuse and Neglect*, 16: 101–18.

Bell, D. (1993) *Communitarianism and Its Critics.* Oxford: Oxford University Press.

Bell, D. and Binnie, J. (2000) *The Sexual Citizen: Queer Politics and Beyond.* Cambridge: Polity Press.

Bellah, R., Madsen, R., Sullivan, W. M., Swidler, A. and Tipton, S. (1985) *Habits of the Heart: Individualism and Commitment in American Life.* Berkeley: University of California Press.

Bellamy, R. (1999) *Liberalism and Pluralism: Towards a Politics of Compromise.* London: Routledge.

Benhabib, S. (1992) *Situating the Self.* London: Routledge.

Benton, T. (1993) *Natural Relations: Ecology, Animal Rights and Social Justice.* London: Verso.

Ben-Tovim, G. (1997) Why 'positive action' is 'politically correct'. In T. Modood and

P. Werbner (eds), *The Politics of Multiculturalism in the New Europe: Racism, Identity and Community*. London: Zed Books.

Berger, P. and Luckmann, T. L. (1967) *The Social Construction of Reality*. Harmondsworth: Allen Lane.

Bernstein, R. J. (1986) *Philosophical Profiles: Essays in a Pragmatic Mode*. Cambridge: Polity Press.

Berridge, V. (1996) *AIDS in the UK: The Making of Policy 1981–1994*. Oxford: Oxford University Press.

Best, J. (1990) *Threatened Children: Rhetoric and Concern about Child Victims*. Chicago: University of Chicago Press.

Best, J. (2001) *How Claims Spread: Cross National Diffusion of Social Problems*. New York: de Gruyter.

Bhabha, J. (1996) Embodied rights. *Public Culture*, 9: 3–32.

Bhabha, J. and Shutter, S. (1994) *Women's Movement*. Stoke-on-Trent: Trentham Books.

Bidney, D. (1996) *Theoretical Anthropology*, 2nd edn. New Brunswick, NJ: Transaction Books.

Binnie, J. (2004) *The Globalization of Sex*. London: Sage.

Bishop, R. and Robinson, L. (1998) *Night Market: Sexual Cultures and the Thai Economic Miracle*. London: Routledge.

Blackburn, R. (2002) *Banking on Death or Investing in Life: The History and Future of Pensions*. London: Verso.

Blackburn, R. (2003) Eurodenial. *New Left Review*, 18.

Blackburn, R. (2004a) The pension crisis and how to tackle it. *Challenge: The Magazine of Economic Affairs*, July/August: 95–111.

Blackburn, R. (2004b) How to rescue a failing pension regime: the British case. *New Political Economy*, December: 559–81.

Blair, T. (2000) Values and the power of community. Presentation to the Global Ethics Foundation, Tübingen University, 30 June.

Bloch, A. and Schuster, L. (2002) Asylum and welfare: contemporary debates. *Critical Social Policy*, 22: 392–414.

Blumer, H. (1969) *Symbolic Interactionism: Perspective and Method*. Englewood Cliffs, NJ: Prentice Hall.

Board of Deputies of British Jews (1992) *Group Defamation. Report of a Working Party of the Law, Parliamentary and General Purposes Committee*. London: Board of Deputies of British Jews.

Bobbio, N. (1995) *The Age of Rights*. Cambridge: Polity Press.

Boje, T. and Leira, A. (2000) *Gender, Welfare State and Market: Towards a New Division of Labour*. London: Routledge.

Bolderson, H. and Roberts, S. (1995) New restrictions on benefits for migrants. *Benefits*, January: 11–15.

Boli, J. and Thomas, G. M. (eds) (1999) *Constructing World Culture: International Nongovernmental Organizations since 1875*. Stanford, CA: Stanford University Press.

Bonnett, A. (2000) *Anti-Racism*. London: Routledge.

Borradori, G. (2003) Deconstructing terrorism – Derrida. In G. Borradori (ed.), *Philosophy in a Time of Terror*. Chicago: University of Chicago Press.

Boswell, J. (1995) *The Marriage of Likeness: Same-Sex Unions in Pre-Modern Europe*. London: Fontana.

Bottomore, T. (1992) Citizenship and social class forty years on. In T. H. Marshall and T. Bottomore, *Citizenship and Social Class*. London: Pluto Press.

Bourdieu, P. (1977) *Outline of a Theory of Practice* (trans. R. Nice). Cambridge: Cambridge University Press.

Bourne, R. (2003) *Invisible Lives: Indigenous Peoples in the Commonwealth*. London: Commonwealth Policy Studies Unit.

Bower, B. (1993) *A Place at the Table*. New York: Poseidon Press.

Bowling, B. and Phillips, C. (2002) *Racism, Crime and Justice*. Harlow: Longman.

Boyer, R. (1997) The variety and unequal performance of really existing markets: farewell to Doctor Pangloss. In J. R. Hollingsworth and R. Boyer (eds), *Contemporary Capitalism. The Embeddedness of Institutions*. Cambridge: Cambridge University Press.

Bright, M. (2003) Youth hit hardest by wave of new laws. *Observer*, 13 April: 9.

Bristow, J. (2000) Who's afraid of Holocaust denial? *LM Archives*, 19 June (www.informinc.co.uk/LM/LM97/LM97_Denial.htm).

Bristow, J. and Wilson, A. R. (eds) (1993) *Activating Theory: Lesbians, Gay, Bisexual Politics*. London: Lawrence and Wishhart.

Brody, H. (1981) *Maps and Dreams*. New York: Pantheon.

Brown, G. and Harris, T. (1978) *Social Origins of Depression*. London: Tavistock.

Brown, P. (1985) *The Transfer of Care: Psychiatric Deinstitutionalization and Its Aftermath*. London: Routledge & Kegan Paul.

Browne, A. and Finkelhor, D. (1986) Impact of child sexual abuse: a review of research. *Psychological Bulletin*, 99: 66–77.

Brubaker, W. R. (1989) *Immigration and the Politics of Citizenship in Europe and America*. Lanham, MD: University Press of America.

Bruce, T. (2001) *The New Thought Police*. New York: Three Rivers Press.

Bunch, C. (1990) Women's rights as human rights: toward a re-vision of human rights. *Human Rights Quarterly*, 12: 486–98.

Burchell, G., Gordon, C. and Miller, P. (eds) (1991) *The Foucault Effect: Studies in Governmentality*. London: Harvester Wheatsheaf.

Burger, A. and Dekker, P. (2001) *The Nonprofit Sector in the Netherlands*. Working Document 70. The Hague: Social and Cultural Planning Office.

Busfield, J. (1986) *Managing Madness: Changing Ideas and Practice*. London: Unwin Hyman.

Busfield, J. (1996) *Men, Women and Madness: Understanding Gender and Mental Disorder*. London: Macmillan.

Busfield, J. (2002) The archaeology of psychiatric disorder. In G. Bendelow, M. Carpenter, C. Vautier and S. William (eds), *Gender, Health and Healing*. London: Routledge.

Buss, D. and Herman, D. (2003) *Globalizing Family Values: The Christian Right in International Politics*. Minneapolis: University of Minnesota Press.

Butler, J. (1990) *Gender Trouble: Feminism and the Subversion of Identity*. New York: Routledge.

Canadian Centre for Justice (2001) *Aboriginal Peoples in Canada*. Statistics Profile Series. Ottawa: Statistics Canada.

Canadian Institute for Health Information (2004) *Improving the Health of Canadians*. Ottawa: Canadian Institute for Health Information.

Cantarella, E. (2001) Private revenge and public justice: the settlement of disputes in Homer's *Iliad*. *Punishment and Society*, 3: 473–83.

Caramagno, T. C. (2002) *Irreconcilable Differences: Intellectual Statements in the Gay Rights Debate*. London: Greenwood.

Carlen, P. (1980) Radical criminology, penal politics and the rule of law. In P. Carlen and M. Collison (eds), *Radical Issues in Criminology*. Oxford: Martin Robertson.

Carlen, P. (1990) *Alternatives to Women's Imprisonment*. Buckingham: Open University Press.

Carlen, P. (1998) *Sledgehammer: Women's Imprisonment at the Millennium*. London: Macmillan.

Carlen, P. (2002) Carceral clawback: the case of women's imprisonment in Canada. *Punishment and Society*, 4: 115–21.

Carrabine, E., Iganski, P., Lee, M., Plummer, K. and South, N. (2004) *Criminology: A Sociological Introduction*. London: Routledge.

Chambers, S. (1996) *Reasonable Democracy: Jürgen Habermas and the Politics of Discourse*. Ithaca, NY: Cornell University Press.

Charlesworth, H. (1995) Human rights as men's rights. In J. Peters and A. Wolper (eds), *Women's Rights, Human Rights: International Feminist Perspectives*. New York: Routledge.

Cheal, D. (1988) *The Gift Economy*. London: Routledge.

Checkel, J. (1999) Norms, institutions and national identity in contemporary Europe. *International Studies Quarterly*, March: 83–114.

Christophersen, T. (1973) *Die Auschwitz-Luge*. Mohrkirch: KritikVerlag.

Churchill, W. (1983) Introduction: journeying towards a debate. In W. Churchill (ed.), *Marxism and Native Americans*. Boston: South End Press.

Churchill, W. (1999) The tragedy and the travesty: the subversion of indigenous sovereignty in North America. In T. Johnson (ed.), *Contemporary Native American Political Issues*. Walnut Creek, CA: Alta Mira Press.

Cladis, M. S. (1992) *A Communitarian Defence of Liberalism: Emile Durkheim and Contemporary Social Theory*. Stanford, CA: Stanford University Press.

Cobo, J. M. (1987) *Study of the Problem of Discrimination against Indigenous Populations, Volume 5*. UN doc. E/CN.4/Sub. 2/1986–7/Add. 4.

Cohen, I. (1989) *Structuration Theory: Anthony Giddens and the Constitution of Social Life*. London: Macmillan.

Cohen, S. (1988) *Against Criminology*. New Brunswick, NJ: Transaction Books.

Commission of the European Communities (1993) *Legal Instruments to Combat Racism and Xenophobia*. Luxembourg: Office for Official Publications of the European Communities.

Commonwealth Policy Studies Unit (2003) *Recognising and Protecting Indigenous Peoples' Rights in the Commonwealth*. Memorandum to the Commonwealth Heads of Government attending the Commonwealth Heads of Government Meeting (CHOGM) Abuja, Nigeria, 1–7 December. London: Commonwealth Policy Studies Unit.

Cook, R. J. (1993) Women's international human rights law: the way forward. *Human Rights Quarterly*, 15: 230–61.

Cornell, D. (1992) *The Philosophy of the Limit*. New York: Routledge.

Cornell, D. (1995) What is ethical feminism? In S. Benhabib, J. Butler, D. Cornell and N. Fraser, *Feminist Contentions*. London: Routledge.

Cornell, S. (1988) *The Return of the Native: American Indian Political Resurgence*. New York: Oxford University Press.

Crisp, R. and Slote, M. (eds) (1997) *Virtue Ethics*. Oxford: Oxford University Press.

Critchley, S. (1999) *The Ethics of Deconstruction: Derrida and Levinas*, 2nd edn. Edinburgh: Edinburgh University Press.

Crossley, N. (1998) Transforming the mental health field: the early history of the National Association for Mental Health. *Sociology of Health and Illness*, 20: 458–88.

Cruz, A. (1995) *Shifting Responsibility*. Stoke-on-Trent: Trentham Books.

D'Emilio, J. (1983) *Sexual Politics, Sexual Communities*. Chicago: University of Chicago Press.

Daly, K. (1989) Criminal justice ideologies and practices in different voices: some feminist questions about justice. *International Journal of the Sociology of Law*, 17: 1–18.

Daly, M. (2002) Care as a good for social policy. *Journal of Social Policy*, 31: 251–70.

Daly, M. (2003) Governance and social policy. *Journal of Social Policy*, 32: 113–28.

Daly, M. and Lewis, J. (1999) Introduction: conceptualising social care in the context of welfare state restructuring. In J. Lewis (ed.), *Gender, Social Care and Welfare State Restructuring in Europe*. Aldershot: Ashgate.

Daly, M. and Lewis, J. (2000) The concept of social care and the analysis of contemporary society. *British Journal of Sociology*, 51: 281–99.

Davidson, B. (1992), *The Black Man's Burden: Africa and the Curse of the Nation State*. New York: Times Books.

Davies, P., Hickson, F., Weatherburn, P. and Hunt, A. (1993) *Sex, Gay Men and AIDS*. London: Falmer Press.

de Beauvoir, S. (1949) *Le Deuxième Sexe*. Paris: Gallimard.

Dean, H. (1998) Popular paradigms and welfare values. *Critical Social Policy*, 18: 131–56.

Dear, M. and Wolch, J. (1987) *Landscapes of Despair*. Princeton, NJ: Princeton University Press.

Deloria, V. (1985) *Behind the Trail of Broken Treaties: An Indian Declaration of Independence*. Austin: University of Texas Press.

Dent, J. A. (1998) *Research Paper on the Social and Economic Rights of Non-Nationals in Europe*. London: ECRE.

Department of Social Security (1998) *New Ambitions for Our Country: A New Contract for Welfare*, Cm 3805. London: HMSO.

Derrida, J. (1990) Force of law: the 'mystical foundations of authority'. *Cardozo Law Review*, 11: 919–1045.

Derrida, J. (1992) Force of law: the mystical foundations of authority. In D. Cornell, M. Rosenfeld and D. G. Carlson (eds), *Deconstruction and the Possibility of Justice*. London: Routledge.

Derrida, J. (1996) *The Gift of Death*. Chicago: University of Chicago Press.

Derrida, J. (2001) *On Cosmopolitanism and Forgiveness*. London: Routledge.

Derrida, J. (2003) Autoimmunity: real and symbolic suicides. In G. Borradori (ed.), *Philosophy in a Time of Terror*. Chicago: University of Chicago Press.

Devlin (1959) *The Enforcement of Morals: The Second Maccabean Lecture to the British Academy*. London: Oxford University Press.

Dickens, R. (2001) Is welfare to work sustainable? *Benefits*, 34: 88–91.

DiMaggio, P. and Powell, W. (1991) The iron cage revisited: institutional isomorphism and collective rationality. In P. DiMaggio and W. Powell (eds), *The New Institutionalism in Organizational Analysis*. Chicago: University of Chicago Press.

Directorate General of Economic and Financial Affairs (2002) *European Commission, Economic Paper 170*, May. Brussels: EU.

Donnelly, J. (2003) *Universal Human Rights in Theory and Practice*. Ithaca, NY: Cornell University Press.

Donnelly, M. (1983) *Managing the Mind*. London: Tavistock.

Dorr Legg, W. (ed.) (1994) *Homophile Studies in Theory and Practice*. San Francisco: One Inc GLB Publications.

Douglas, L. (1988) Policing the past: Holocaust denial and the law. In R. C. Post (ed.), *Censorship and Silencing: Practices of Cultural Regulation*. Los Angeles: The Getty Research Institute for the History of Art and the Humanities.

Dryzek, J. (1996) *Democracy in Capitalist Times: Ideals, Limits, and Struggles*. Oxford: Oxford University Press.

Dryzek, J. (2000) *Deliberative Democracy and Beyond: Liberals, Critics, Contestations*. Oxford: Oxford University Press.

Duff, R. (1996) Penal communications: recent work in the philosophy of punishment. *Crime and Justice: A Review of Research*, 20: 1–97.

Duff, R. (2001) *Punishment, Communication, and Community*. Oxford: Oxford University Press.

Duff, R. and Garland, D. (1994) Introduction: thinking about punishment. In R. Duff and D. Garland (eds), *A Reader on Punishment*. Oxford: Oxford University Press.

Durkheim, E. (1933) *The Division of Labor in Society* (trans. W. D. Hall). New York: Free Press (first published 1893).

Durkheim, E. (1938) *The Rules of Sociological Method*. New York: Free Press (first published 1895).

Durkheim, E. (1951) *Suicide: A Study in Sociology* (trans. J. Spaulding and G. Simpson). Glencoe, IL: Free Press (first published 1897).

Durkheim, E. (1961) *The Elementary Forms of Religious Life*. London: Allen and Unwin (first published 1912).

Durkheim, E. (1964) *The Division of Labor in Society* (trans. G. Simpson). Glencoe, IL: Free Press.

Durkheim, E. (1974) The determination of moral facts. In *Sociology and Philosophy*. New York: Free Press (first published in 1906).

Durkheim, E. (1975) Individualism and the intellectuals. In W. S. F. Pickering (ed.), *Durkheim on Religion*. London: Routledge and Kegan Paul (first published 1898).

Dworkin, R. (1978) *Taking Rights Seriously*. Cambridge, MA: Harvard University Press.

Dworkin, R. (1985) *A Matter of Principle*. Cambridge, MA: Harvard University Press.

Edwards, S. (1984) *Women on Trial*. Manchester: Manchester University Press.

Ehrenreich, B. and Hochschild, A. R. (eds) (2003) *Global Woman: Nannies, Maids and Sex Workers in the New Economy*. London: Granta.

Ellison, N. (1997) Towards a new social politics: citizenship and reflexivity in late modernity. *Sociology*, 31: 697–717.

Elson, D. (2002) Gender justice, human rights and neo-liberal economics. In M. Molyneuz and S. Razavi (eds), *Gender Justice, Development and Rights*. Oxford: Oxford University Press.

Elson, D. and Gideon, J. (2004) Organising for women's economic and social rights: how useful is the International Covenant on Economic, Social and Cultural Rights? *Journal of Interdisciplinary Gender Studies*, 8: 133–52.

England, C. (2004) A look at the Indian Health Service policy of sterilization, 1972–1976 (www.diskshovel.com/IHSSterPol.html).

Esping-Andersen, G. (1990) *The Three Worlds of Welfare Capitalism.* Cambridge: Polity Press.

Esping-Andersen, G. (1999) *Social Foundations of Postindustrial Economies.* Oxford: Oxford University Press.

Etzioni, A. (2000) *The Third Way to a Good Society.* London: Demos.

European Commission, Health and Consumer Protection Directorate-General (2002) *Compulsory Admission and Involuntary Treatment of Mentally Ill Patients: Legislation and Practice in EU-Member States.* Brussels: European Commission.

European Parliament (2000) Charter of Fundamental Rights of the European Union. *Official Journal of the European Communities.*

Evans, D. (1993) *Sexual Citizenship.* London: Routledge.

Evans, M. and Morgan, R. (1999) The CPT: an introduction. In R. Morgan and M. Evans, *Protecting Prisoners: The Standards of the European Committee for the Prevention of Torture in Context.* Oxford: Oxford University Press.

Evans, O., Singleton, N., Meltzer, H., Stewart, R. and Prince, M. (2003) *The Mental Health of Older People.* London: The Stationery Office.

Ewijk, H. van, Hens, H. and Lammersen, G. (2002) *Mapping of Care Services and the Care Workforce. Consolidated Report.* WP3 of Care Work in Europe Current Understandings and Future Directions (www.ioe.ac.uk./tcru/carework.htm).

Farrelly, C. (2004) *An Introduction to Contemporary Political Theory.* London: Sage.

Feldman, D. (2002) *Civil Liberties and Human Rights in England and Wales,* 2nd edn. Oxford: Oxford University Press.

Felice, W. F. (1996) *Taking Suffering Seriously: The Importance of Collective Human Rights.* Albany: State University of New York Press.

Ferguson, J. (1990) *The Anti-Politics Machine.* Cambridge: Cambridge University Press.

Ferreira, M. (ed.) (2005) *Indigenous Peoples and Diabetes.* Durham, NC: Carolina Academic Press.

Field, F. (1989) *Losing Out.* Oxford: Basil Blackwell.

Finch, J. and Groves, D. (1983) *Labour and Love: Women, Work and Caring.* London: Routledge and Kegan Paul.

Fink, J. (ed.) (2004) *Care: Personal Lives and Social Policy.* Bristol: Policy Press.

Finnemore, M. and Sikkink, K. (1998) International norm dynamics and political change. *International Organization,* 52: 887–917.

Flanagan, K. and Jupp, P. C. (2001) *Virtue Ethics and Sociology: Issues of Modernity and Religion.* London: Palgrave Macmillan.

Fligstein, N. (2001) *The Architecture of Markets. An Economic Sociology of Twenty-First Century Capitalist Societies.* Princeton, NJ: Princeton University Press.

Flynn, D. (2004) *Tough as Old Boots: Asylum, Immigration and the Paradox of New Labour Policy.* JCWI Discussion Paper. London: JCWI.

Ford, G. (1992) *Fascist Europe: The Rise of Racism and Xenophobia.* London: Pluto Press.

Forero, J. (2004) In a land torn by violence, too many troubling deaths. *New York Times,* 23 November.

Foucault, M. (1967) *Madness and Civilisation. A History of Insanity in the Age of Reason*. London: Tavistock Publications.

Foucault, M. (1977) *Discipline and Punish: The Birth of the Prison*. Harmondsworth: Penguin.

Fraser, A. (1999) Becoming human: the origins and development of women's human rights. *Human Rights Quarterly*, 21: 853–906.

Fraser, N. (1995) From redistribution to recognition? Dilemmas of justice in a 'post-socialist' age. *New Left Review*, 212: 68–93.

Fraser, N. (1997) *Justice Interruptus: Critical Reflections on the Post-Socialist Condition*. New York: Routledge.

Fraser, N. (2003) Social justice in the age of identity politics. In N. Fraser and A. Honneth (eds), *Redistribution or Recognition?* London: Verso.

Freeden, M. (1996) *Ideologies and Political Theory: A Conceptual Approach*. Oxford: Clarendon Press.

Freeman, G. P. (1986) Migration and the political economy of the welfare state. *Annals of the American Academy of Political and Social Science*, 485 (May): 51–63.

Freeman, G. P. (1995) Modes of immigration politics in liberal democratic states. *International Migration Review*, 29: 881–902.

Freeman, M. (1995) Are there collective human rights? *Political Studies*, 43: 25.

Freeman, M. (2002) *Human Rights: An Interdisciplinary Approach, Key Concepts*. Cambridge: Polity Press.

Friedman, E. (1995) Women's human rights: the emergence of a movement. In J. Peters and A. Wolper (eds), *Women's Rights, Human Rights: International Feminist Perspectives*. New York: Routledge.

Fultz, E. (2004) Pension privatisation in Poland and Hungary. In G. Hughes and J. Stewart (eds), *Pension Reform in Europe*. Cheltenham: Edward Elgar.

Garland, D. (1990) *Punishment and Modern Society: A Study in Social Theory*. Oxford: Oxford University Press.

Gerth, H. H. and Wright Mills, C. (eds) (1948) *From Max Weber: Essays in Sociology*. London: Routledge and Kegan Paul.

Gey, S. G. (1997) What if Wisconsin v. Mitchell had involved Martin Luther King Jnr? The constitutional flaws of hate crime enhancement statutes. *George Washington Law Review*, 65: 1014–70.

Giddens, A. (1984) *The Constitution of Society*. Cambridge: Polity Press.

Giddens, A. (1985) *The Nation State and Violence*. Cambridge: Polity Press.

Giddens, A. (1990) *The Consequences of Modernity*. Cambridge: Polity Press.

Giddens, A. (1991) *Modernity and Self Identity*. Cambridge: Polity.

Giddens, A. (1994) *Beyond Left and Right*. Cambridge: Polity Press.

Giddens, A. (1998) *The Third Way*. Cambridge: Polity Press.

Giddens, A. (2001) *Sociology*, 4th edn. Cambridge: Polity Press.

Gilbert, K. (1977) *Living Black: Blacks Talk to Kevin Gilbert*. Ringwood, Victoria: Allen Lane.

Gilbert, K. (1994) *Because a White Man'll Never Do It*, 4th edn. Sydney: Angus and Robertson.

Gilbert, N. (2004) *The Transformation of the Welfare State: The Silent Surrender of Public Responsibility*. Oxford: Oxford University Press.

Gilligan, C. (1982) *In a Different Voice*. Cambridge, MA: Harvard University Press.

Gilroy, P. (1990) The end of anti-racism. In W. Ball and J. Solomos (eds), *Race and Local Politics*. London: Macmillan.

Glennerster, H. (2003) *Understanding the Finance of Welfare*. Bristol: Policy Press.

Glucksmann, M. (2000) *Cottons and Casuals: The Gendered Organisation of Labour in Time and Space*. Durham: Sociology Press.

Goffman, E. (1961) *Asylums: Essays on the Social Situation of Mental Patients and Other Inmates*. Harmondsworth: Penguin.

Graham, H. (1991) The concept of caring in feminist research: the case of domestic service. *Sociology*, 25(1): 61–78.

Green, D. G. (1999) *An End to Welfare Rights*. London: Institute of Economic Affairs.

Greenberg, D. (1988) *The Construction of Homosexuality*. Chicago: University of Chicago Press.

Greenberg, D. and Stender, F. (1972) The prison as a lawless agency. *Buffalo Law Review*, 21: 799–839.

Guardian (2000) Ministers agree voucher review. *Guardian*, 28 September.

Guardian (2003) Judges saving asylum seekers from starvation. *Guardian*, 4 November.

Guardian (2004) Woolf leads judges' attack on ministers. *Guardian*, 14 March.

Guardian (2005) Plans to overhaul incapacity benefit. *Guardian*, 27 January.

Guardian Weekly (2004) Extra 1000 places planned for asylum detention. *Guardian Weekly*, 24 September.

Guiraudon, V. (1998) Citizenship rights for non-citizens: France, Germany and the Netherlands. In C. Joppke (ed.), *Challenge to the Nation State*. Oxford: Oxford University Press.

Gullette, M. M. (2003) *Aged by Culture*. Chicago: University of Chicago Press.

Gupta, A. and Ferguson, J. (1997) Culture, power, place: ethnography at the end of an era. In A. Gupta and J. Ferguson (eds), *Culture, Power, Place: Explorations in Critical Anthropology*. Durham, NC: Duke University Press.

Gutierrez, M. and Palomo, N. (2000) A woman's eye view of autonomy. In A. Mayor (ed.), *Indigenous Autonomy in Mexico*. Copenhagen: International Work Group for Indigenous Affairs.

Gutmann, A. (1992) *Multiculturalism and the Politics of Recognition*. Princeton, NJ: Princeton University Press.

Habermas, J. (1984) *The Theory of Communicative Action, Volume 1*. Cambridge: Polity Press.

Habermas, J. (1987a) *The Theory of Communicative Action, Volume 2*. Cambridge: Polity Press.

Habermas, J. (1987b) *The Philosophical Discourse of Modernity*. Cambridge: Polity Press.

Hacker, J. (2002) *The Divided Welfare State: The Battle over Public and Private Social Benefits in the United States*. Cambridge: Cambridge University Press.

Haebich, A. (2001) *Broken Circles: Fragmenting Indigenous Families 1800–2000*. Fremantle: Fremantle Arts Centre Press.

Hale, C. (1994) *Resistance and Contradiction: Miskitu Indians and the Nicaraguan State, 1894–1987*. Stanford, CA: Stanford University Press.

Hale, S. (2004) Community by contract? Paper presented at the Political Studies Association conference.

Halévy, E. (1955) *The Growth of Philosophical Radicalism* (trans. M. Morris). Boston: Beacon Press.

Hall, S. (1979) The great moving right show. *Marxism Today*, January: 14–20.

Hall, S. (1980) Reformism and the legislation of consent. In National Deviancy Conference (eds), *Permissiveness and Control: The Fate of the Sixties Legislation.* London: Macmillan.

Hameso, S. (1997) *Ethnicity and Nationalism in Africa.* Commack, NY: Nova Science Publishers.

Harrington Meyer, M. (ed.) (2000) *Care Work: Gender, Class and the Welfare State.* New York: Routledge.

Hasenclever, A., Mayer, P. and Rittberger, V. (1997) *Theories of International Regimes.* Cambridge: Cambridge University Press.

Healey, D. (1997) *The Anti-Depressant Era.* Cambridge, MA: Harvard University Press.

Health Canada (2003) *Statistical Profile on the Health of First Nations in Canada.* Ottawa: Health Canada.

Heidensohn, F. (1986) Models of justice: Portia or Persephone? Some thoughts on equality, fairness and gender in the field of criminal justice. *International Journal of the Sociology of Law*, 14: 287–98.

Heise, L. (1989) International dimensions of violence against women. *Response*, 12(1).

Herek, G. M., Gillis, J. R. and Cogan, J. C. (1999) Psychological sequelae of hate-crime victimization among lesbian, gay, and bisexual adults. *Journal of Consulting and Clinical Psychology*, 67: 945–51.

Heritage, J. (1984) *Garfinkel and Ethnomethodology.* Cambridge: Polity Press.

Hernandez Castillo, R. (1997) Between hope and adversity: the struggle of organized women in Chiapas since the Zapatista rebellion. *Journal of Latin American Anthropology*, 3: 102–20.

Hills, J. (2001) What rights? Whose responsibilities? In A. Park, J. Curtice, K. Thomson, L. Jarvis and C. Bromley (eds), *British Social Attitudes: The 18th Report.* London: Sage.

Hindley, J. (1996) Towards a pluricultural nation: the limits of indigenismo and article 4. In R. Aitken *et al.* (eds), *Dismantling the Mexican State.* Basingstoke: Macmillan.

Hobhouse, L. T. (1922) *The Elements of Social Justice.* London: George Allen and Unwin.

Holden, K. (2001) Family, caring and unpaid work. In I. Zweiniger-Bargielowska (ed.), *Women in Twentieth Century Britain.* Harlow: Longman.

Holden, K. (2004) Personal costs and personal pleasures: care and the unmarried woman in interwar England. In J. Fink (ed.), *Care: Personal Lives and Social Policy.* Bristol: Policy Press.

Hollifield, J. F. (1992) *Immigrants Markets and States.* Cambridge, MA: Harvard University Press.

Hollingshead, A. B. and Redlich, F. C. (1958) *Social Class and Mental Illness.* New York: John Wiley.

Home Office (2000) *Statistics on Race and the Criminal Justice System, 2000.* London: Home Office Research, Development and Statistics Directorate.

Honneth, A. (1995) The other of justice: Habermas and the ethical challenge of postmodernism. In S. White (ed.), *The Cambridge Companion to Habermas.* Cambridge: Cambridge University Press.

Hooks, G. and Smith, C. (2004) The treadmill of destruction: national sacrifice areas and Native Americans. *American Sociological Review*, 69(4): 558–75.

Horwitz, A. V. (2002) *Creating Mental Illness*. Chicago: University of Chicago Press.

HREOC (1997) *Bringing Them Home: Report of the National Inquiry into the Separation of Aboriginal and Torres Strait Islander Children from Their Families*. Canberra: AGPS.

Hudson, A. (2001) NGOs' transnational advocacy networks: from 'legitimacy' to 'political responsibility'? *Global Networks*, 1: 331–52.

Hudson, B. (1993) *Penal Policy and Social Justice*. Basingstoke: Macmillan.

Hudson, B. (2001) Punishment, rights and difference: defending justice in the risk society. In K. Stenson and R. Sullivan (eds), *Crime, Risk and Justice: The Politics of Crime Control in Liberal Democracies*. Cullompton: Willan.

Hudson, B. (2003) *Justice in the Risk Society*. London: Sage.

Hughes, B., McKie, L., Hopkins, D. and Watson, N. (2005) Love's labour lost? Feminism, the disabled people's movement and an ethic of care. *Sociology*, 39: 259–75.

Hughes, G. and Sinfield, A. (2004) Financing pensions by stealth. In G. Hughes and J. Stewart (eds), *Reforming Pensions in Europe*. Cheltenham: Edward Elgar.

Humphrey, C. and Sneath, D. (1999) *The End of Nomadism? Society, State and the Environment in Inner Asia*. Durham, NC: Duke University Press.

Hunter, R. and MacAlpine, I. (eds) (1963) *Three Hundred Years of Psychiatry, 1535–1860*. Hartsdale, NY: Carlisle.

Hurd, H. (2001) Why liberals should hate 'hate crime legislation'. *Law and Philosophy*, 20: 215–32.

Ibhawoh, B. (1999) Between culture and constitution: evaluating the cultural legitimacy of human rights in the African state. Paper presented to the Conference on Reconstructing Human Rights: A Critical Project for the 21st Century?, University of Sussex.

Iganski, P. (1999) Why make hate a crime? *Critical Social Policy*, 19: 385–94.

Iganski, P. (2001) Hate crimes hurt more. *American Behavioral Scientist*, 4: 626–38.

Ignatieff, M. (2000) *The Rights Revolution*. Toronto: House of Anansi Press.

Illich, I. (1975) *The Limits to Medicine*. Harmondsworth: Penguin.

Inglehart, R. (1977) *The Silent Revolution: Changing Values and Political Styles among Western Publics*. Princeton, NJ: Princeton University Press.

Inglehart, R. (1989) *Cultural Change*. Princeton, NJ: Princeton University Press.

Inglehart, R. and Norris, P. (2003) *Rising Tide: Gender Equality and Cultural Change around the World*. Cambridge: Cambridge University Press.

Institute for Jewish Policy Research (2000) *Combating Holocaust Denial through Law in the United Kingdom*. London: Institute for Jewish Policy Research.

Irigaray, L. (1985) *Speculum of the Other Woman*. Ithaca, NY: Cornell University Press.

Irwin, S. (1996) Age related distributive justice and claims on resources. *British Journal of Sociology*, 47: 69–82.

Ishay, M. (ed.) (1997) *The Human Rights Reader*. New York: Routledge.

Ishay, M. (2004) *The History of Human Rights*. Berkeley: University of California Press.

Jacobs, J. B. and Potter, K. A. (1997) Hate crimes: a critical perspective. *Crime and Justice*, 22: 1–50.

Jacobs, J. B. and Potter, K. A. (1998) *Hate Crimes: Criminal Law and Identity Politics*. New York: Oxford University Press.

Jacoby, J. (2002) Punish crime, not thought crime. In P. Iganski (ed.), *The Hate Debate. Should Hate Be Punished as a Crime?* London: Profile.

Jaffe, A. J. (1992) *The First Immigrants from Asia: A Population History of North American Indians*. New York: Plenum.

Janzen, L. (2004) Better housing a right, says First Nation. *Winnipeg Free Press*, 16 December: A5.

Jeffery-Poulter, S. (1991) *Peers, Queers and Commons: The Struggle for Gay Law Reform from 1950 to the Present*. London: Routledge.

Jenness, V. and Grattet, R. (2001) *Making Hate a Crime*. New York: Russell Sage Foundation.

Jennings, F. (1975) *The Invasion of America: Indians, Colonialism and the Cant of Conquest*. New York: W. W. Norton.

Joas, H. (2000) *The Genesis of Values*. Chicago: University of Chicago Press.

Joint Council for the Welfare of Immigrants (1987) *Out of Sight*. London: JCWI.

Jones, G. S. (2004) *The End of Poverty*. London: Profile.

Jordan, B., James, S., Kay, H. and Redley, M. (1992) *Trapped in Poverty*. London: Routledge.

Kahan, D. M. (2001) Two liberal fallacies in the hate crimes debate. *Law and Philosophy*, 20: 175–93.

Kaufman, N. and Lindquist, S. (1995) Critiquing gender-neutral treaty language: the Convention on the Elimination of All Discrimination against Women. In J. Peters and A. Wolper (eds), *Women's Rights, Human Rights: International Feminist Perspectives*. New York: Routledge.

Keal, P. (2003) *European Conquest and the Rights of Indigenous Peoples: The Moral Backwardness of International Society*. Cambridge: Cambridge University Press.

Keck, M. E. and Sikkink, K. (1998) *Activism Beyond Borders*. Ithaca, NY: Cornell University Press.

Kennedy, H. (2004) *Just Law*. London: Chatto & Windus.

Kenrick, J. and Lewis, J. (2004) Indigenous peoples' rights and the politics of the term 'indigenous'. *Anthropology Today*, 20(2): 4–9.

Kleiss, K. (2004) Peru's government forced sterilization on 300,000 women. *Edmonton Journal*, 12 November.

Klug, F. (2003) *Values for a Godless Age*. Harmondsworth: Penguin Books.

Knijn, T. (2000) Marketization and the struggling logics of (home) care in the Netherlands. In M. Harrington Meyer (ed.), *Care Work: Gender, Class and the Welfare State*. New York: Routledge.

Knijn, T. and Kremer, M. (1997) Gender and the caring dimension of welfare states: toward inclusive citizenship. *Social Politics: International Studies in Gender State and Society*, 4: 328–61.

Knijn, T., Jonsson, I. and Klammer, U. (2003) Care packaging: minding the children and/or work. In U. Gerhardt and T. Knijn (eds), *Working and Mothering: Social Practices and Social Policies*. Frankfurt am Main: Beck Verlag.

Knowles, C. (2000) *Bedlam on the Streets*. London: Routledge.

Kotlikoff, L. and Burns, S. (2005) *The Coming Generational Storm*. Cambridge, MA: MIT Press.

Kukathas, C. (1992) Are there any cultural rights? *Political Theory*, 20(1): 105–39.

Kymlicka, W. (1989) *Liberalism, Community and Culture*. Oxford: Clarendon Press.

Kymlicka, W. (1995) *Multicultural Citizenship: A Liberal Theory of Minority Rights*. Oxford: Clarendon Press.

266   *Bibliography*

Kymlicka, W. (2000) American multiculturalism and the 'nations within'. In D. Ivison, P. Patton and W. Sanders (eds), *Political Theory and the Rights of Indigenous Peoples*. Cambridge: Cambridge University Press.

Kymlicka, W. (2004) Dworkin on freedom and culture. In J. Burley (ed.), *Dworkin and His Critics*. Oxford: Blackwell.

Lacey, N. (2003) Penal theory and penal practice: a communitarian approach. In S. McConville (ed.), *The Use of Punishment*. Cullompton: Willan.

Laclau, E. (1996) *Emancipation(s)*. London: Verso.

Laing, R. D. (1967) *The Politics of Experience and the Bird of Paradise*. Harmondsworth: Penguin.

Lam, M. (2000) *At the Edge of the State: Indigenous Peoples and Self-Determination*. New York: Transnational.

Lan, P.-C. (2003) Among women: Filipina domestics and their Taiwanese employers across generations. In B. Ehrenreich and A. R. Hochschild (eds), *Global Woman: Nannies, Maids and Sex Workers in the New Economy*. London: Granta.

Landsberg-Lewis, I. (ed.) (1998) *Bringing Equality Home: Implementing the Convention on the Elimination of All Forms of Discrimination against Women*. New York: United Nations Development Fund for Women.

Laslett, P. (1989) *A Fresh Map of Life: The Emergence of the Third Age*. London: Weidenfeld and Nicholson.

Laslett, P. (1996) *The New Map of Life*, 2nd edn. Basingstoke: Macmillan.

Latouche, S. (1996) *The Westernization of the World: The Significance, Scope and Limits of the Drive towards Global Uniformity* (trans. R. Morris). Cambridge: Polity Press.

Lauritsen, J. and Thorstad, D. (1974) *The Early Homosexual Rights Movement (1864–1935)*. New York: Times Change Press.

Lawrence, F. M. (1994) The punishment of hate: towards a normative theory of bias-motivated crimes. *Michigan Law Review*, 93: 320–81.

Lawrence, F. M. (1999) *Punishing Hate*. Cambridge, MA: Harvard University Press.

Lazarus, L. (2004) *Contrasting Prisoners' Rights: A Comparative Examination of Germany and England*. Oxford: Oxford University Press.

Lazreg, M. (1990) Feminism and difference: the perils of writing as a woman on women in Algeria. In M. Hirsch and E. Fox Keller (eds), *Conflicts in Feminism*. London: Routledge.

Leacock, E. B. (1981) Introduction to L. H. Morgan, *Ancient Society*, Parts I, II, III, IV. In E. B. Leacock (ed.), *Myths of Male Dominance: Collected Articles on Women Cross-Culturally*. New York: Monthly Review Press.

Lee, Y. J., Parish, W. L. and Willis, R. J. (1994) Sons, daughters and intergenerational support in Taiwan. *American Journal of Sociology*, 99(4): 1010–41.

Lehmann, J. (1994) *Durkheim and Women*. Lincoln: University of Nebraska Press.

Leinberger, P. and Tucker, B. (1991) *The New Individualists: The Generation after the Organization Man*. New York: HarperCollins.

Leira, A. and Saraceno, C. (2002) Care, actors, relationships and contexts. In B. Hobson, J. Lewis and B. Siim (eds), *Contested Concepts in Gender and Social Politics*. Cheltenham: Edward Elgar.

Lester, A. and Bindman, G. (1972) *Race and Law*. London: Longman.

Levin, B. (1999) Hate crimes. Worse by definition. *Journal of Contemporary Criminal Justice*, 15: 6–21.

Levin, J. and McDevitt, J. (1995) Landmark study reveals hate crimes vary significantly by offender motivation. *Klanwatch Intelligence Report* (Southern Poverty Law Center), August.

Levinas, E. (1969) *Totality and Infinity: An Essay on Exteriority.* Pittsburgh: Duquesne University Press.

Levinas, E. (1987) Language and proximity. In *Collected Philosophical Papers* (trans. A. Lingis). The Hague: Martinus Nijhoff.

Levinas, E. (1993) *Outside the Subject.* Stanford, CA: Stanford University Press.

Lewis, J. (1992) Gender and the development of welfare regimes. *Journal of European Social Policy*, 2: 159–73.

Lewis, J. (ed.) (1999) *Gender, Social Care and Welfare State Restructuring in Europe.* Aldershot: Ashgate.

Lewis, J. (2001) The decline of the male breadwinner model: implications for work and care. *Social Politics*, 8: 152–69.

Lillard, L. A. and Willis, R. J. (1997) Motives for intergenerational transfers: evidence from Malaysia. *Demography*, 34(1): 115–34.

Lin, C. J. (1999) *Filipina Domestic Workers in Taiwan: Structural Constraints and Personal Resistance.* Taipei: Taiwan Grassroots Women's Center.

Lin, C. J. (2003) Transforming patriarchal kinship relations: four generations of 'modern women' in Taiwan, 1900–99. Unpublished PhD thesis, University of Essex.

Lipstadt, D. (1994) *Denying the Holocaust: The Growing Assault on Truth and Memory.* Harmondsworth: Penguin.

Lister, R. (1997) *Citizenship: Feminist Perspectives.* London: Macmillan.

Lister, R. (2000) To Rio via the Third Way: New Labour's 'welfare' reform agenda. *Renewal*, 8: 9–20.

Lister, R. (2003) *Citizenship: Feminist Perspectives*, 2nd edn. London: Palgrave.

Livingstone, S. (2000) Prisoners' rights in the context of the European Convention on Human Rights. *Punishment and Society*, 2: 309–24.

Livingstone, S., Owen, T. and MacDonald, A. (2003) *Prison Law*, 3rd edn. Oxford: Oxford University Press.

Lockwood, D. (1996) Civic integration and class formation. *British Journal of Sociology*, 47: 531–50.

Loffreda, B. (2000) *Losing Matt Shepard: Life and Politics in the Aftermath of Anti-Gay Murder.* New York: Columbia University Press.

Loseke, D. (2003) *Thinking about Social Problems: An Introduction to Constructionist Perspectives*, 2nd edn. New York: Aldine de Gruyter.

Lukes, S. (1973) *Emile Durkheim: His Life and Work.* Harmondsworth: Penguin.

Lukes, S. (1985) *Marxism and Morality.* Oxford: Oxford University Press.

Lukes, S. (1991) *Moral Conflict and Politics.* Oxford: Clarendon Press.

Lunbeck, E. (1994) *The Psychiatric Persuasion.* Princeton, NJ: Princeton University Press.

Lyon, D. (2005) The organisation of care work in Europe: gender and migrant labour in the new economy. Paper presented at the 13th annual conference of the *Indiana Journal of Global Legal Studies*, Globalization and the New Politics of Labor, Indiana University School of Law, Bloomington.

McConville, S. (ed.) (2003) *The Use of Punishment.* Cullompton: Willan.

MacDonald, M. (1981) *Mystical Bedlam: Madness, Anxiety and Healing in Seventeenth Century England.* Cambridge: Cambridge University Press.

McDowell, L. (2003) *Redundant Masculinities*. Blackwell: Oxford.

MacIntyre, A. (1981) *After Virtue*. London: Duckworth.

Macionis, J. (2004) *Society: The Basics*. Upper Saddle River, NJ: Prentice Hall.

MacKinnon, C. (1987) *Feminism Unmodified: Discourses on Life and Law*. Cambridge, MA: Harvard University Press.

Maines, D. (2001) *The Faultline of Consciousness: A View of Interactionism in Sociology*. New York: Alison de Gruyter.

Majone, G. (ed.) (1996) *Regulating Europe*. London: Routledge.

Malloch, M. and Stanley, E. (2005) The detention of asylum seekers in the UK: representing risk, managing the dangerous. *Punishment and Society*, 7: 53–71.

Mann, M. (1986) *The Sources of Social Power. Volume 1, A History of Power from the Beginning to AD 1760*. Cambridge: Cambridge University Press.

Mann, M. (1987) Ruling class strategies and citizenship. *Sociology*, 21: 339–54.

Mann, M. (1993) *The Sources of Social Power. Volume 2, The Rise of Classes and Nation-States 1760–1914*. Cambridge: Cambridge University Press.

Manne, R. (1998) Stolen generations. In P. Craven (ed.), *Best Australian Essays*. Melbourne: Black Inc Books.

Manne, R. (2001) In denial: the stolen generations and the right. *Australian Quarterly Essay*, 27: 1.

March, J. G. and Olson, J. P. (1989) *Rediscovering Institutions: The Organizational Basis of Politics*. New York: Free Press.

Marks, G. and McAdam, D. (1996) Social movements and the changing structure of political opportunity in the European Union. In G. Marks, F. W. Scharpf, P. C. Schmitter and W. Streeck (eds), *Governance in the European Union*. London: Sage.

Marotta, T. (1981) *The Politics of Homosexuality*. Boston: Houghton Mifflin.

Marshall, T. H. (1950) *Citizenship and Social Class and Other Essays*. Cambridge: Cambridge University Press.

Marshall, T. H. (1963) Citizenship and social class. In *Sociology at the Crossroads and Other Essays*. London: Heinemann.

Marshall, T. H. (1977) *Class, Citizenship and Social Development*. Chicago: Chicago University Press.

Marshall, T. H. and Bottomore, T. (1992) *Citizenship and Social Class*. London: Pluto Press.

Marx, K. (1975) On the Jewish question. In *Karl Marx and Frederick Engels: Collected Works, Volume 3*. New York: International Publishers.

Marx, K. (1978a) The German ideology, Part 1. In R. Tucker (ed.), *The Marx–Engels Reader*. New York: W. W. Norton.

Marx, K. (1978b) On imperialism in India. In R. Tucker (ed.), *The Marx–Engels Reader*. New York: W. W. Norton.

Math, A. (2004) The impact of pension reforms on older people's incomes. In G. Hughes and J. Stewart (eds), *Reforming Pensions in Europe*. Cheltenham: Edward Elgar

Mead, L. M. (1986) *Beyond Entitlement*. New York: Free Press.

Medhurst, A. and Munt, S. R. (eds) (1997) *Lesbian and Gay Studies: A Critical Introduction*. London: Cassell.

Meidner, R. (1978) *Employee Investment Funds*. London: Allen and Unwin.

Meltzer, H., Gill, B., Petticrew, M. and Hinds, K. (1995) *The Prevalence of Psychiatric Morbidity amongst Adults Living in Private Households*. London: Office of Population Censuses and Surveys.

Menon, N. (1995) The impossibility of 'justice': female foeticide and feminist discourse on abortion. *Contributions to Indian Sociology*, 29: 369–92.

Meyer, J. (1980) The world polity and the authority of the nation state. In A. Bergesen (ed.), *Studies of the Modern World System*. New York: Academic Press.

Meyer, J., Boli, J., Thomas, G. M., and Ramirez, F. O. (1997) World society and the nation state. *American Journal of Sociology*, 103: 144–81.

Mill, J. S. (1982) *On Liberty* (ed. G. Himmelfarb). Harmondsworth: Penguin.

Miller, A. M. (2000) Sexual but not reproductive: exploring the junctions and disjunction of sexual and reproductive rights. *Health and Human Rights*, 4: 68–109.

Miller, B. G. (2003) *Invisible Indigenes: The Politics of Nonrecognition*. Lincoln: University of Nebraska Press.

Miller, J. R. (1996) *Shingwauk's Vision: A History of Native Residential Schools*. Toronto: University of Toronto Press.

Miller, R. B. (1991) *Casuistry and Modern Ethics: A Poetics of Practical Reasoning*. Chicago: Chicago University Press.

Modood, T., Berthoud, R., Lakey, J., Nazroo, J., Smith, P., Virdee, S. and Beishon, S. (eds) (1997) *Ethnic Minorities in Britain. Diversity and Disadvantage*. London: Policy Studies Institute.

Mohanty, C. (1991) Under Western eyes: feminist scholarship and colonial discourses. In C. Mohanty, A. Russo and L. Torres (eds), *Third World Women and the Politics of Feminism*. Bloomington: Indiana University Press.

Molyneux, M. and Razavi, S. (2002) Introduction. In M. Molyneux and S. Razavi (eds), *Gender Justice, Development and Rights*. Oxford: Oxford University Press.

Momaday, N. S. (1976) *The Names: A Memoir*. Tucson: University of Arizona Press.

Montgomery, H. (2001) Imposing rights? A case study of child prostitution in Thailand. In J. K. Cowan, M.-B. Dembour and R. Wilson (eds), *Culture and Rights: Anthropological Perspectives*. Cambridge: Cambridge University Press.

Morgan, R. (2000) The utilitarian justification of torture: denial, desert and disinformation. *Punishment and Society*, 2: 181–96.

Morgan, R. (2001) The European Committee for the Prevention of Torture and Inhuman or Degrading Treatment or Punishment. In D. van Zyl Smit and F. Dünkel (eds), *Imprisonment Today and Tomorrow: International Perspectives on Prisoners' Right and Prison Conditions*. Hague: Kluwer.

Morgan, R. (2004) Advancing indigenous rights at the United Nations: strategic framing and its impact on the normative development of international law. *Social and Legal Studies*, 13(4): 481–500.

Morris, G. (1992) International law and politics: toward a right to self-determination for indigenous peoples. In M. A. Jaimes (ed.), *The State of Native America: Genocide, Colonization and Resistance*. Boston: South End Press.

Morris, L. D. (1994) *Dangerous Classes*. London: Routledge.

Morris, L. D. (1996) Researching living standards. *Journal of Social Policy*, 25: 459–83.

Morris, L. D. (1998) Governing at a distance: rights and controls in British immigration. *International Migration Review*, 32: 949–73.

Morris, L. D. (2002a) *Managing Migration: Civic Stratification and Migrants' Rights*. London: Routledge.

Morris, L. D. (2002b) The shifting contours of rights: Britain's asylum and immigration regime. *Journal of Ethnic and Migration Studies*, 28: 409–25.

Morrison, D. (2004) New Labour, citizenship and the discourse of the Third Way. In S. Hale, W. Leggett and L. Martell (eds), *The Third Way and Beyond*. Manchester: Manchester University Press.

Mouzelis, N. (1991) *Back to Sociological Theory: The Construction of Social Orders*. London: Macmillan.

Mouzelis, N. (1995) *Sociological Theory: What Went Wrong? Diagnosis and Remedies*. London: Routledge.

Mouzelis, N. (2000) The subjectivist–objectivist divide: against transcendence. *Sociology*, 34: 741–62.

Mudrooroo (1995) *Us Mob, History, Culture, Struggle: An Introduction to Indigenous Australia*. Sydney: Angus and Robertson.

Mulhall, S. and Swift, A. (1992) *Liberals and Communitarians*. Oxford: Blackwell.

Murphy, J. G. (1994) Marxism and retribution. In R. Duff and D. Garland (eds), *A Reader on Punishment*. Oxford: Oxford University Press.

Murphy, J. G. (2000) Two cheers for vindictiveness. *Punishment and Society*, 2: 131–43.

Murray, C. (1984) *Losing Ground*. New York: Basic Books.

Murray, C. (1990) *The Emerging British Underclass*. Choice in Welfare Series No. 2. London: Health and Welfare Unit, Institute of Economic Affairs.

NACRO (2003) Overcrowded jails aren't working. *Safer Society Magazine*, Autumn: 6–7.

Nadasdy, P. (2003) *Hunters and Bureaucrats: Power, Knowledge and Aboriginal–State Relations in the Southwest Yukon*. Vancouver: University of British Columbia Press.

Naffine, N. (1990) *Law and the Sexes*. London: Allen and Unwin.

Nagel, J. (1996) *American Indian Ethnic Renewal: Red Power and the Resurgence of Identity and Culture*. New York: Oxford University Press.

Narayan, U. (1997) *Dislocating Cultures: Identities, Traditions and Third World Feminism*. London: Routledge.

Nash, K. (2002) Human rights for women: an argument for 'deconstructive equality'. *Economy and Society*, 31: 414–33.

National Association of Citizens Advice Bureaux (1996) *Failing the Test*. London: NACAB.

National Association of Citizens Advice Bureaux (2000) *A Person Before the Law*. London: NACAB.

Nelson, R. R. (2002) On the complexities and limits of market organisation. In S. M. Metcalfe and A. Warde (eds), *Market Relations and the Competitive Process*. Manchester: Manchester University Press.

Nietzsche, F. (1996) *On the Genealogy of Morals*. Oxford: Oxford University Press (originally published 1887).

Niezen, R. (2000) *Spirit Wars: Native North American Religions in the Age of Nation Building*. Berkeley: University of California Press.

Norval, A. (2004) Democratic decisions and the question of universality: rethinking recent approaches. In S. Critchley and O. Marchart (eds), *Laclau: A Critical Reader*. London: Routledge.

Nozick, R. (1974) *Anarchy, State and Utopia*. Oxford: Blackwell.

Nussbaum, M. (1997) *Cultivating Humanity: A Classical Defense of Reform in Liberal Education*. Cambridge, MA: Harvard University Press.

Nussbaum, M. (1999) *Sex and Social Justice*. Oxford: Oxford University Press.

Nussbaum, M. (2000) *Women and Human Development: The Capabilities Approach*. Cambridge: Cambridge University Press.

O'Brian, R., Goetz, A. *et al.* (2000) *Contesting Global Governance*. Cambridge: Cambridge University Press.

Observer (2000) Nowhere left to run to. *Observer*, 31 December: 17.

O'Connor, J. (1993) Gender, class and citizenship in the comparative analysis of welfare state regimes: theoretical and methodological issues. *British Journal of Sociology*, 44: 501–18.

O'Connor, J., Orloff, A. and Shaver, S. (1999) *States, Markets, Families: Gender, Liberalism and Social Policy in Australia, Canada, Great Britain and the US*. Cambridge: Cambridge University Press.

Omni Television (2004) *The Mushuau Innu: Surviving Canada*, documentary film directed by Ed Martin.

O'Neill, O. (2002) *A Question of Trust: The BBC Reith Lectures 2002*. Cambridge: Cambridge University Press.

Oosterhuis, H. (2000) *Stepchildren of Nature: Krafft-Ebing, Psychiatry, and the Making of Sexual Identity*. Chicago: University of Chicago Press.

Orkin, A. (2003) When the law breaks down: aboriginal peoples in Canada and governmental defiance of the rule of law. *Osgoode Hall Law Journal*, 41(2/3): 445–62.

Orloff, A. (1993) Gender and the social rights of citizenship: the comparative analysis of gender relations and welfare states. *American Sociological Review*, 58: 303–28.

Orloff, A. (1996) Gender in the welfare state. *Annual Review of Sociology*, 22: 51–78.

Ostner, I. (1999) The politics of care policies in Germany. In J. Lewis (ed.), *Gender, Social Care and Welfare State Restructuring in Europe*. Aldershot: Ashgate.

Owers, A. (2003) BIHR Human Rights Lecture: Prison inspection and the protection of human rights (www.homeoffice.gov.uk/docs2/bihrlecture.html), accessed 19 September 2004. Reprinted in *European Human Rights Law Review*, 2 (2004).

Pagden, A. (1995) *Lords of All the World: Ideologies of Empire in Spain, Britain and France c.1500–c.1800*. New Haven, CT: Yale University Press.

Pahl, R. (2000) *On Friendship*. Cambridge: Polity Press.

Pahl, R. and Spencer, L. (2004) Personal communities: not simply families of fate or choice. *Current Sociology*, 52: 99–221.

Parekh, B. (1998) Superior people: the narrowness of liberalism from Mill to Rawls. *Times Literary Supplement*, 25 February: 11–13.

Parekh, B. (2000) *Rethinking Multiculturalism: Cultural Diversity and Political Theory*. London: Palgrave Macmillan

Parkin, F. (1992) *Durkheim*. Oxford: Oxford University Press.

Parkin, F. (2002) *Weber*. London: Routledge.

Parry, G. (1991) Conclusion: paths to citizenship. In U. Vogel and M. Moran (eds), *The Frontiers of Citizenship*. Basingstoke: Macmillan.

Pashukanis, E. (1978) *Law and Marxism: A General Theory*. London: Ink Links (originally published 1924).

Pasuk Phongpaichit (1982) *From Peasant Girls to Bangkok Masseuses*. Geneva: International Labour Organization.

Patterson, O. (1991) *Freedom: Freedom in the Making of Western Culture*. New York: Basic Books.

Peach, L. J. (2001) Are women human? The promise and perils of 'women's rights as human rights'. In L. S. Bell, A. J. Nathan and I. Peleg (eds), *Negotiating Culture and Human Rights*. New York: Columbia University Press.

Pensions Commission (2004) *Pensions: Challenges and Choices, the First Report of the Pensions Commission*. London: TSO.

Percy, A. (1998) Ethnicity and victimization: findings from the 1996 British Crime Survey. *Home Office Statistical Bulletin*, 6/98. London: Home Office.

Petchesky, R. P. (2000) Sexual rights: inventing a concept, mapping an international practice. In Richard Parker *et al.* (eds), *Framing the Sexual Subject: The Politics of Gender, Sexuality and Power*. Berkeley: University of California Press.

Petchesky, R. P. (2003) *Global Prescriptions: Gendering Health and Human Rights*. London: Zed Books.

Peters, B. G. (1992) Bureaucratic politics and the institutions of the European Community. In A. Sbragia (ed.), *Euro-Politics*. Washington, DC: The Brookings Institution.

Peters, B. G. (2000) *Institutional Theory in Political Science: The 'New Institutionalism' in Political Science*. London: Continuum International.

Peterson, V. S. and Parisi, L. (1998) Are women human? It's not an academic question. In T. Evans (ed.), *Human Rights Fifty Years On, A Re-appraisal*. Manchester: Manchester University Press.

Phelan, S. (2001) *Sexual Strangers: Gays, Lesbians and Dilemmas of Citizenship*. Philadelphia: Temple University Press.

Phillips, A. (1992) Universalist pretentions in political thought. In M. Barrett and A. Phillips (eds), *Destabilising Theory*. Cambridge: Polity Press.

Phillips, M. (2002) Hate crime: the Orwellian response to prejudice. In P. Iganski (ed.), *The Hate Debate. Should Hate Be Punished as a Crime?* London: Profile.

Pickering, W. S. F. (ed.) (1975) *Durkheim on Religion*. London: Routledge and Kegan Paul.

Pickering, W. S. F. and Watts Miller, W. (1993) *Individualism and Human Rights in the Durkheimian Tradition*. Occasional Papers No. 1. Oxford: British Centre for Durkheimian Studies.

Pierson, P. (1997) *Dismantling the Welfare State? Reagan, Thatcher and the Politics of Retrenchment*. Cambridge: Cambridge University Press.

Plender, R. (1999) *Basic Documents on International Migration Law*. The Hague: Kluwer Law International.

Plummer, K. (ed.) (1981) *The Making of the Modern Homosexual*. London: Hutchinson.

Plummer, K. (1995) *Telling Sexual Stories: Power, Change and Social Worlds*. London: Routledge.

Plummer, K. (1999) The lesbian and gay movement in the UK 1965–1995: schisms, solidarities and social worlds. In A. Barry, J. W. Duyvendak and A. Krouwel (eds), *Gay and Lesbian Movements since the 1960s*. Philadelphia: Temple University Press.

Plummer, K. (2003) *Intimate Citizenship: Private Decisions and Public Dialogues*. Seattle: University of Washington Press.

Plummer, K. (2005) Critical humanism and queer theory. In Y. Lincoln and N. Denzin (eds), *Handbook of Qualitative Research*, 3rd edn. Thousand Oaks, CA: Sage.

Pontusson, J. (1994) Sweden: the people's home in danger. In P. Anderson and P. Camiller (eds), *Mapping the Left in Western Europe*. London: Verso.

Povinelli, E. A. (1998) The state of shame: Australian multiculturalism and the crisis of indigenous citizenship. *Critical Inquiry*, 24: 575–610.

Povinelli, E. A. (2002) *The Cunning of Recognition: Indigenous Alterities and the Making of Australian Multiculturalism*. Durham, NC: Duke University Press.

Powell, W. P. and DiMaggio, P. (eds) (1991) *The New Institutionalism in Organizational Analysis*. Chicago: Chicago University Press.

Power, L. (1995) *No Bath but Plenty of Bubbles*. London: Cassell.

Prins, N. (2004) *Other People's Money: The Corporate Mugging of America*. New York: The New Press.

Pritchard, S. (1998) *Indigenous Peoples the United Nations and Human Rights*. Sydney: Federation Press.

Putnam, R. D. (2000) *Bowling Alone*. New York: Simon and Schuster.

Rao, A. (1995) The politics of gender and culture in international human rights discourse. In J. Peters and A. Wolper (eds), *Women's Rights, Human Rights: International Feminist Perspectives*. New York: Routledge.

Rawls, J. (1971) *A Theory of Justice*. Cambridge, MA: Harvard University Press.

Rawls, J. (1993) *Political Liberalism*. New York: Columbia University Press.

RCIADIC (1991) *National Report*. Canberra: Royal Commission on Aboriginal Deaths in Custody.

Red–Green Study Group (1992) *What on Earth Is to Be Done?* Manchester: RGSG.

Rex, J. (1986) *Race and Ethnicity*. Milton Keynes: Open University Press.

Reynolds, H. (1996) *Aboriginal Sovereignty: Three Nations, One Australia*. Sydney: Allen and Unwin.

Rheinstein, M. (ed.) (1954) *Max Weber on Law in Economy and Society*. Cambridge, MA: Harvard University Press.

Richardson, D. (1998) Sexuality and citizenship. *Sociology*, 32: 83–100.

Richardson, D. (2000) Claiming citizenship? Sexuality, citizenship and lesbian feminist theory. *Sexualities*, 3: 255–72.

Richardson, D. (2002) *Theorising Heterosexuality*. London: Sage.

Richardson, G. (1985) The case for prisoners' rights. In M. Maguire, J. Vagg and R. Morgan (eds), *Accountability and Prisons: Opening Up a Closed World*. London: Tavistock.

Richardson, G. (1995) Prisoners and the law: beyond rights. In C. McCrudden and G. Chambers (eds) (1994), *Individual Rights and the Law in Britain*. Oxford: Clarendon.

Risse, T., Ropp, S. *et al.* (eds) (1999) *The Power of Human Rights*. Cambridge: Cambridge University Press.

Risse Kappen, T. (1994) Ideas do not float freely: transnational coalitions, domestic structures, and the end of the Cold War. *International Organization*, 48: 185–214.

Risse Kappen, T. (1995) *Bringing Transnational Relations Back In: Non-State Actors, Domestic Structures and International Institutions*. Cambridge: Cambridge University Press.

Roberston, R. (1992) *Globalization: Social Theory and Global Culture*. London: Sage.

Robertson, G. (1999) *Crimes Against Humanity: The Struggle for Global Justice*. London: Allen Lane.

Robertson, G. (2002) The great socialist shame: left-wing thinkers backed policies that tore aborigine girls from their mothers. *New Statesman*, 11 November.

Robins, L. N. and Regier, D. A. (eds) (1991) *Psychiatric Disorders in America*. New York: Free Press.

Robinson, F. (1998) The limits of a rights-based approach to international ethics. In T. Evans (ed.), *Human Rights Fifty Years On, A Re-appraisal*. Manchester: Manchester University Press.

Robinson, M. (2004) Public sociologies and human rights: finding common ground. Paper presented at the American Sociological Association conference, San Francisco, 14 August.

Rogin, M. P. (1987) *Ronald Reagan, The Movie and Other Episodes in Political Demonology*. Berkeley: University of California Press.

Rorty, R. (1989) *Contingency, Irony and Solidarity*. Cambridge: Cambridge University Press.

Rorty, R. (1993) Human rights, rationality and sentimentality. In S. Shute and S. Hurley (eds) *On Human Rights: The Oxford Amnesty Lectures 1993*. New York: Basic Books.

Royal Commission on Lunacy and Mental Disorder (1926) *Report*. London: HMSO.

Rusche, G. and Kirchheimer, O. (1968) *Punishment and Social Structure*. New York: Russell and Russell (originally published 1939).

Ruzza, C. (2002) 'Frame bridging' and the new politics of persuasion, advocacy and influence. In A. Warleigh and J. Fairbrass (eds), *Influence and Interests in the European Union: The New Politics of Persuasion and Advocacy*. London: Europa Press.

Ruzza, C. (2004) *Europe and Civil Society: Movement Coalitions and European Governance*. Manchester: Manchester University Press.

Ruzza, C. (2006) European institutions and the policy discourse of organised civil society. In S. Smismans (ed.), *Civil Society and Legitimate European Governance*. London: Elgar.

Sainsbury, D. (ed.) (1999) *Gender and Welfare State Regimes*. Oxford: Oxford University Press.

Samson, C. (1999) The dispossession of the Innu and the colonial magic of Canadian liberalism. *Citizenship Studies*, 3(1): 5–26.

Samson, C. (2001) Sameness as a requirement for the recognition of the rights of the Innu of Canada: the colonial context. In J. Cowan, M.-B. Dembour and R. Wilson (eds), *Culture and Rights: Anthropological Perspectives*. Cambridge: Cambridge University Press.

Samson, C. (2003) *A Way of Life that Does Not Exist: Canada and the Extinguishment of the Innu*. London: Verso Press.

Samson, C. (2004) The dis-ease over Native North American drinking: experiences of the Innu of Northern Labrador. In R. Coomber and N. South (eds), *Drug Use and Cultural Contexts: Beyond the West*. London: Free Association Books.

Samuelson, P. (1958) An exact consumption-loan model of interest with or without the social contrivance of money. *Journal of Political Economy*, December.

Sandel, M. (1982) *Liberalism and the Limits of Justice*. Cambridge: Cambridge University Press.

Sassen, S. (1996) *Losing Control*. New York: Colombia University Press.

Sassen, S. (1998) *Globalisation and Its Discontents*. New York: The New Press.

Schone, J. (2001) The short life and painful death of prisoners' rights. *Howard Journal of Criminal Justice*, 40: 70–82.

Scott, D. (2004) The politics of prisoners' rights: the potential and limitations of legal discourses. Paper presented to the European Deviance Group conference, Bristol, September.

Scott, J. W. (1988) *Gender and the Politics of History*. New York: Columbia University Press.

Scraton, P. (2002) Defining 'power' and challenging 'knowledge': critical analysis as resistance in the UK. In K. Carrington and R. Hogg (eds), *Critical Criminology: Issues, Debates, Challenges*. Cullompton: Willan.

Scraton, P. and Moore, L. (2004) *The Hurt Inside: The Imprisonment of Women and Girls in Northern Ireland*. Belfast: Northern Ireland Human Rights Commission.

Sedgwick, E. K. (1990) *Epistemology of the Closet*. London: Harvester Wheatsheaf.

Seed, P. (2001) *American Pentimento: The Invention of Indians and the Pursuit of Riches*. Minneapolis: University of Minnesota Press.

Seidel, G. (1986) *The Holocaust Denial. Antisemitism, Racism and the New Right*. Leeds: Beyond the Pale Collective.

Sen, A. (1999) *Commodities and Capabilities*. Oxford: Oxford University Press.

Sen, A. (2005) Mary, Mary, quite contrary. *Feminist Economics*, 11: 1–9.

Sevenhuijsen, S. (1998) *Citizenship and the Ethics of Care*. London: Routledge.

Shermer, M. and Grobman, A. (2000) *Denying History*. Berkeley: University of California Press.

Short, D. (2003a) Australian 'aboriginal' reconciliation: the latest phase in the colonial project. *Citizenship Studies*, 7(3): 291–392.

Short, D. (2003b) Reconciliation, assimilation and the indigenous peoples of Australia. *International Political Science Review*, 24(4): 491–513.

Sierra, M. (2002) *The Challenge to Diversity in Mexico: Human Rights, Gender and Ethnicity*. Working Paper No. 49. Halle: Max Planck Institute for Social Anthropology.

Slezkine, Y. (1994) *Arctic Mirrors: Russia and the Small Peoples of the North*. Ithaca, NY: Cornell University Press.

Smart, C. (1989) *Feminism and the Power of Law*. London: Routledge.

Smith, A. (1891) *An Inquiry into the Nature and Causes of the Wealth of Nations*. London: T. Nelson and Sons.

Smith, A. (1995) *Nations and Nationalism in a Global Era*. Cambridge: Polity Press.

Smith, A. M. (1992) Resisting the erasure of lesbian sexuality: a challenge for queer activism. In K. Plummer (ed.), *Modern Homosexualities*. London: Routledge.

Smith, A. M. (1994) *New Right Discourse on Race and Sexuality: Britain, 1968–1990*. Cambridge: Cambridge University Press.

Smith, J., Chatfield, C. and Pagnucco, R. (eds) (1997) *Transnational Social Movements and Global Politics: Solidarity Beyond the State*. Syracuse, NY: Syracuse University Press.

Smith, R. R. and Windes, R. R. (2000) *Progay/Antigay: The Rhetorical War over Sexuality*. London: Sage.

Smyth, C. (1992) *Lesbians Talk Queer Notions*. London: Scarlett Press.

Soysal, Y. (1994) *Limits of Citizenship*. Chicago: University of Chicago Press.

Stamatopoulou, E. (1995) Women's rights and the United Nations. In J. Peters and A. Wolper (eds), *Women's Rights, Human Rights: International Feminist Perspectives*. New York: Routledge.

Stanton, A. and Schwartz, M. (1954) *The Mental Hospital*. New York: Basic Books.

Stark, A. and Regner, A. (2002) *In Whose Hands? Work, Gender, Ageing and Care in Three EU Countries*. Linkopings: Linkopings Universitet, Tema genus report No. 2.

Steiker, C. S. (1999) Punishing hateful motives: old wine in a new bottle calls for prohibition. *Michigan Law Review*, 97: 1863–70.

Steiner, H. J. and Alston, P. (1996) *International Human Rights in Context.* Oxford: Clarendon Press.

Stephen, L. (2003) The gendered dynamics of agrarian counter-reform and indigenous rights in southern Mexico. Paper presented at a conference at the Institute of Latin American Studies, University of London.

Stern, K. (1995) Denial of the Holocaust: an anti-Semitic political assault. In J. R. Chanes (ed.), *Antisemitism in America Today.* New York: Birch Lane Press.

Stivens, M. (2000) Introduction: gender politics and the reimagining of human rights in the Asia-Pacific. In A.-M. Hilsdon, M. Macintyre, V. Mackie and M. Stivens, *Human Rights and Gender Politics: Asia-Pacific Perspectives.* London: Routledge.

Stones, R. (1996) *Sociological Reasoning: Towards a Post-Modern Sociology.* London: Macmillan.

Stones, R. (2002) Social theory, documentary film and distant others: simplicity and subversion in *The Good Woman of Bangkok. European Journal of Cultural Studies,* 5: 217–37.

Stones, R. (2005) *Structuration Theory.* London: Palgrave Macmillan.

Stout, J. (1990) *Ethics after Babel: The Languages of Morals and Their Discontents.* Cambridge: James Clark & Co.

Strauss, L. (1953) *Natural Right and History.* Chicago: University of Chicago Press.

Supperstone, M. (1981) *Brownlie's Law of Public Order and National Security,* 2nd edn. London: Butterworths.

Szasz, T. S. (1963) *Law, Liberty and Psychiatry.* New York: Macmillan.

Szasz, T. S. (1970) Involuntary mental hospitalisation: a crime against humanity. In *Ideology and Insanity.* New York: Doubleday.

Tanner, V. (1947) *Outlines of the Geography, Life and Customs of Newfoundland-Labrador (The Eastern Part of the Labrador Peninsula),* two volumes. Cambridge: Cambridge University Press.

Tappan, P. (1954) The legal rights of prisoners. *The Annals,* 293: 99–111.

Tatchell, P. (2002) Some people are more equal than others. In P. Iganski (ed.), *The Hate Debate: Should Hate Be Punished as a Crime?* London: Profile.

Tatz, C. (1999) Aboriginal suicide is different: aboriginal youth suicide in New South Wales, the Australian Capital Territory and New Zealand: towards a model of explanation and alleviation. *Criminology Research Council Report* (www.aic.gov.au/crc/reports/tatz; accessed December 2005).

Taylor, C. (1979) *Hegel and Modern Society.* Cambridge: Cambridge University Press.

Taylor, C. (1994) *Multiculturalism.* Princeton, NJ: Princeton University Press.

Taylor, C. (1995) *Philosophical Arguments.* Cambridge, MA: Harvard University Press.

Taylor, L. (1980) Bringing power to particular account: Peter Rajah and the Hull Board of Visitors. In P. Carlen and M. Collison (eds), *Radical Issues in Criminology.* Oxford: Martin Robertson.

Therborn, G. (2004) *Between Sex and Power: Family in the World, 1900–2000.* London: Routledge.

Thomas, C. (1993) De-constructing concepts of care. *Sociology,* 27: 649–69.

Thompson, E. P. (1977) *Whigs and Hunters: The Origin of the Black Act.* Harmondsworth: Penguin.

Thornton, R. (1987) *American Indian Holocaust and Survival: A Population History since 1492.* Norman: University of Oklahoma Press.

Thornton, R. (2002) Health, disease and demography. In P. Deloria and N. Salisbury (eds), *A Companion to American Indian History*. Oxford: Blackwell.

Thornton, R. and Grasnick, M. (1980) *Sociology of American Indians: A Critical Bibliography*. Bloomington: Indiana University Press.

Titmuss, R. M. (1970) *The Gift Relationship: From Human Blood to Social Blood*. London: Allen and Unwin.

Travis, A. (1999) Delay on Holocaust denial law. *Guardian*, 19 October.

Tronto, J. (1993) *Moral Boundaries. A Political Argument for an Ethic of Care*. London: Routledge.

Tuke, S. (1813) *A Description of the Retreat*. York: W. Alexander.

Tully, J. (1995) *Strange Multiplicity: Constitutionalism in the Age of Diversity*. Cambridge: Cambridge University Press.

Tully, J. (2000) The struggles of indigenous peoples for and of freedom. In D. Ivison, P. Patton and W. Sanders (eds), *Political Theory and the Rights of Indigenous Peoples*. Cambridge: Cambridge University Press.

Turner, B. S. (1986) *Citizenship and Capitalism: The Debate over Reformism*. London: Allen and Unwin.

Turner, B. S. (1988) *Status*. Milton Keynes: Open University Press.

Turner, B. S. (1989) Ageing, status politics and sociological theory. *British Journal of Sociology*, 40: 588–60.

Turner, B. S. (1990) Outline of a theory of citizenship. *Sociology*, 24: 189–214.

Turner, B. S. (1993) Outline of a theory of human rights. *Sociology*, 27: 485–512.

Turner, B. S. (1997) A neo-Hobbesian theory of human rights: a reply to Malcolm Waters. *Sociology*, 31(1): 565–71.

Turner, B. S. and Rojek, C. (2001) *Society and Culture: Principles of Scarcity and Solidarity*. London: Sage.

Turner, L. (1979) *Ethnology of the Ungava District and Hudson Bay Territory: Indians and Eskimos in the Quebec-Labrador Peninsula*. Quebec City: Presses Comeditex (first published 1889).

UN (1999) *Report of the Working Group on Indigenous Populations*. Seventeenth Session, Geneva, 26–30 July, Chairperson-Rapporteur E.-I. A. Daes. Geneva: United Nations.

UN Committee on the Rights of the Child (2002) *Concluding Observations on the Committee on the Rights of the Child: United Kingdom of Great Britain and Northern Ireland*. Geneva: United Nations.

UN Economic and Social Council (2005) *Economic, Social and Cultural Rights: Report of the Special Rapporteur on the Right of Everyone to the Enjoyment of the Highest Attainable Standard of Physical and Mental Health*. New York: United Nations.

UN Population Division (2000) *World Population Prospects: The 1998 Revision. Volume III, Analytic Report*. New York: United Nations.

UN Population Division (2001) *Replacement Migration: Is It a Solution to Declining and Ageing Populations?* New York: United Nations.

Ungerson, C. (ed.) (1990) *Gender and Caring: Work and Welfare in Britain and Scandinavia*. London: Harvester Wheatsheaf.

Union of British Columbia Indian Chiefs (2004) Certainty: Canada's struggle to extinguish aboriginal title (www.ubcic.bc.ca/certainty.htm).

US Department of Justice, Bureau of Justice Assistance (1997) *A Policymaker's*

Guide to Hate Crimes. Washington, DC: US Department of Justice, Bureau of Justice Assistance.

Useem, M. (1996) *Investor Capitalism*. Princeton, NJ: Princeton University Press.

Van Reenan, J. (2001) No more skivvy schemes? In D. Card and R. Freeman (eds), *Seeking a Premier League Economy*. Chicago: University of Chicago Press.

Vanstone, J. W. (1974) *Athapaskan Adventures. Hunters and Fishermen of the Subarctic Forests*. Chicago: Aldine Publishing Company.

Virdee, V. (1997) Racial harassment. In T. Modood, R. Berthoud, J. Lakey, J. Nazroo, P. Smith, S. Virdee and S. Beishon (eds), *Ethnic Minorities in Britain. Diversity and Disadvantage*. London: Policy Studies Institute.

Vitoria, F. de (1991) *Political Writings*. Cambridge: Cambridge University Press.

Vizenor, G. (1984) *The People Named the Chippewa: Narrative Histories*. Minneapolis: University of Minnesota Press.

Vizenor, G. and Lee, A. R. (1999) *Postindian Conversations*. Lincoln: University of Nebraska Press.

Vogel, U. (1997) Emancipatory politics between universalism and difference: gender perspectives on European citizenship. In P. Lehning and A. Weale (eds), *Citizenship, Democracy and Justice in the New Europe*. London: Routledge.

Waerness, K. (1984) Caring as women's work in the welfare state. In H. Holter (ed.), *Patriarchy in a Welfare Society*. Oslo: Universitetsforlaget.

Walby, S. (2002) Feminism in a global era. *Economy and Society*, 31: 533–57.

Walker, N. (1991) *Why Punish?* Oxford: Oxford University Press.

Walklate, S. (2001) *Gender, Crime and Criminal Justice*. Cullompton: Willan.

Walters, A. (ed.) (1980) *Come Together: The Years of Gay Liberation (1970–1973)*. London: GMP.

Waters, M. (1996) Human rights and the universalization of interests. *Sociology*, 30: 593–600.

Weaver, J. (1997) *That the People Might Live: Native American Literature and Native American Community*. New York: Oxford University Press.

Webber, F. (2004) Asylum – from deterrence to destitution. *Race and Class*, 45: 77–85.

Weber, K. E. M. (1948) Class, status and party. In H. H. Gerth and C. W. Mills (eds), *Essays in Sociology*. London: Routledge and Kegan Paul.

Weber, K. E. M. (1949) *The Methodology of the Social Sciences*. New York: Free Press.

Weber, K. E. M. (1976) *The Protestant Ethic and the Spirit of Capitalism* (trans. T. Parsons). New York: Charles Scribner's Sons.

Weber, K. E. M. (1978) The nature of charismatic domination. In W. G. Runciman (ed.), *Weber: Selections in Translation* (trans. E. Matthews). Cambridge: Cambridge University Press.

Weeks, J. (1990) *Coming Out: Homosexual Politics in Britain from the Nineteenth Century to the Present*, 2nd edn. London: Quartet Books.

Weeks, J. (1995) *Invented Moralities*. Cambridge: Polity Press.

Weeks, J. (1998) The sexual citizen. *Theory, Culture and Society*, 15: 35–52.

Weinstein, J. (1992) First Amendment challenges to hate crime legislation: where's the speech? *Criminal Justice Ethics*, 11: 6–20.

Weston, K. (1991) *Families We Choose*. New York: Columbia University Press.

Westwood, G. (1952) *Society and the Homosexual*. London: Gollancz.

Westwood, G. (1960) *A Minority: A Report on the Life of the Male Homosexual in Britain*. London: Longman.

White, S. (2000) Review article: Social rights and the social contract – political theory and the new welfare politics. *British Journal of Political Science*, 30: 507–32.

Whittaker, A. (2000) *Intimate Knowledge: Women and Their Health in North-East Thailand*. Sydney: Allen and Unwin.

Wiener, C. (1981) *The Politics of Alcoholism*. New Brunswick, NJ: Rutgers.

Willetts, P. (ed.) (1982) *Pressure Groups in the Global System: The Transnational Relations of Issue-Oriented Non-Governmental Organizations*. London: Frances Pinter.

Williams, D. G. T. (1970) Protest and public order. *Cambridge Law Journal*, 108: 96–121.

Williams, F. (2001) In and beyond New Labour: towards a new political ethics of care. *Critical Social Policy*, 21: 467–93.

Williams, F. (2004) *Rethinking Families*. London: Calouste Gulbenkian Foundation.

Williams, R. A. (1990) *The American Indian in Western Legal Thought: The Discourses of Conquest*. New York: Oxford University Press.

Wilson, A. R. (ed.) (1995) *A Simple Matter of Justice: Theorising Lesbian and Gay Politics*. London: Cassell.

Wilson, R. A. (ed.) (1987) *Human Rights Culture and Context*. London: Pluto Press.

Wilson, R. A. (2001) *The Politics of Truth and Reconciliation in South Africa: Legitimising the Post Apartheid State*. Cambridge: Cambridge University Press.

Wolfe, A. (1992) Democracy versus sociology: boundaries and their consequences. In M. Lamont and M. Fournier (eds), *Cultivating Differences*. Chicago: University of Chicago Press.

Wolfenden, Lord (1957) *Report of the Departmental Committee on Homosexual Offences and Prostitution*. London: HMSO, Cmnd 247.

Wolffe, W. J. (1987) Values in conflict: incitement to racial hatred and the Public Order Act 1986. *Public Law*, 85: 345.

Wood, E. M. (2003) *The Empire of Capital*. London: Verso.

Woodburn, J. (2001) The political status of hunter-gatherers in present-day and future Africa. In A. Bernard and J. Kenrick (eds), *Africa's Indigenous Peoples: 'First Peoples' or 'Marginalized Minorities?'* Edinburgh: Centre for African Studies, University of Edinburgh.

Woodhouse, D. (1998) The judiciary in the 1990s. *Policy and Politics*, 26: 458–70.

Woodiwiss, A. (2005) *Human Rights*. London: Routledge.

Wunder, J. (1994) *'Retained by the People': A History of American Indians and the Bill of Rights*. New York: Oxford University Press.

Zellick, G. (1974) Prisoners' rights in England. *University of Toronto Law Review*, 24: 334–9.

Zerilli, L. (2004) This universal which is not one. In S. Critchley and O. Marchart (eds), *Laclau: A Critical Reader*. London: Routledge.

Zola, I. K. (1972) Medicine as an institution of social control. *Sociological Review*, 20: 487–504.

Zwingel, S. (forthcoming) From intergovernmental negotiations to (sub)national change: a transnational perspective on the impact of the CEDAW Convention. *International Journal of Feminist Politics*.

Index